Literature, Travel
and Colonial Writing
in the English Renaissance

Literature, Travel, and Colonial Writing in the English Renaissance
1545–1625

ANDREW HADFIELD

Ex Libris

MHM

Mitchell M. Harris

OXFORD
UNIVERSITY PRESS

OXFORD
UNIVERSITY PRESS

Great Clarendon Street, Oxford OX2 6DP

Oxford New York

Athens Auckland Bangkok Bogotá Buenos Aires Calcutta
Cape Town Chennai Dar es Salaam Delhi Florence Hong Kong Istanbul
Karachi Kuala Lumpur Madrid Melbourne Mexico City Mumbai
Nairobi Paris São Paolo Singapore Taipei Tokyo Toronto Warsaw
and associated companies in
Berlin Ibadan

Oxford is a registered trade mark of Oxford University Press

Published in the United States
by Oxford University Press Inc., New York

© Andrew Hadfield 1998

The moral rights of the author have been asserted

First published 1998

First published in paperback 2007

All rights reserved. No part of this publication may be reproduced,
stored in a retrieval system, or transmitted, in any form or by any means,
without the prior permission in writing of Oxford University Press.
Within the UK, exceptions are allowed in respect of any fair dealing for the
purpose of research or private study, or criticism or review, as permitted
under the Copyright, Designs and Patents Act 1988, or in the case of
reprographic reproduction in accordance with the terms of the licences
issued by the Copyright Licensing Agency. Enquiries concerning
reproduction outside these terms and in other countries should be
sent to the Rights Department, Oxford University Press,
at the address above

British Library Cataloguing in Publication Data
Data available

Library of Congress Cataloging in Publication Data

Hadfield, Andrew.
Literature, travel, and colonial writing in the English
Renaissance, 1545–1625/Andrew Hadfield.
Includes bibliographical references (p.).
1. English literature—Early modern, 1500–1700—History and
criticism. 2. Travel in literature. 3. English literature—Great
Britain—Colonies—History and criticism. 4. British—Travel—
Foreign countries—History—16th century. 5. British—Travel—
Foreign countries—History—17th century. 6. Travelers' writings,
English—History and criticism. 7. Politics and literature—Great
Britain—History. 8. Imperialism in literature. 9. Colonies in
literature. 10. Renaissance—England. I. Title.
PR428.T73H33 1998 820.9'32171241'9031—dc21 98–34187

ISBN 978-0-19-818480-5 (Hbk.) 978-0-19-923365-6 (Pbk.)

1 3 5 7 9 10 8 6 4 2

Typeset by Laserwords Private Limited, Chennai, India
Printed in Great Britain
on acid-free paper by
Biddles Ltd., Guildford and King's Lynn

FOR ALISON

Preface

This book and its two predecessors, *Literature, Politics and National Identity: Reformation to Renaissance* (1994) and *Spenser's Irish Experience: Wilde Fruit and Salvage Soyl* (1997), form a loosely conceived trilogy analysing the interrelationship between literary, cultural and political representation in early modern England. The first dealt with English conceptions of England and Englishness in sixteenth-century literature; the second, with English representations of Ireland, simultaneously England's first overseas colony and a sovereign territory of the English monarch. I have now turned my attention to the ways in which travel and colonial writing were used to reflect on, change and, sometimes, redefine perceptions of English identity and English politics, a process which was often deliberate and conscious, sometimes dictated by circumstances. Overall, I hope the three books make some contribution to an understanding of the ways in which English writers tried to make sense of their complex and often contradictory notions of identity.

This book was written while I held a Leverhulme Research Fellowship for the academic year 1996–7. I am extremely grateful to the Leverhulme Trust for awarding me the funds to release me from my teaching and administrative duties for that year, and for providing additional funds for research expenses. I am also grateful to my colleagues in the Department of English, University of Wales, Aberystwyth, for making light of the additional burdens I placed upon them, especially those who work in the Medieval and Renaissance team, Michael Smith, Diane Watt, and Claire Jowitt. Much of the research has been carried out in the National Library of Wales, Aberystwyth, and I am grateful to the staff for making my time there so pleasant and profitable.

Many scholars have given their time generously to aid me with my project. For supporting my application for a fellowship,

I would like to thank Paul Hammond, Lyn Pykett, and Robert Welch; for reading chapters and sections of the work, I would like to thank Michael Brennan, Mark Thornton Burnett, Tom Healy, Claire Jowitt, John McVeagh, Willy Maley, Robert Maslen and Michael Smith; for help with some Spanish translations, I would like to thank Robert Stone; for help with some sixteenth-century legal questions, I would like to thank Richard Ireland. Some of the material contained in the book has been presented in papers at the IFK Institute, Vienna, the University of Strathclyde, the University of Manchester, the MLA Conference at Toronto, the University of Wales, Aberystwyth, Hampton Court, Herefordshire, the NACBS Conference at the Asilomar Conference Center, Pacific Grove, California; I would like to thank Klaus Reichert, Willy Maley, Tony Crowley, Susan Wofford, Linda Gregerson, Claire Jowitt, David Daniell, and David Baker, for inviting me to speak at these venues, and the audiences at each for their often helpful and penetrating questions. I am also grateful to the institutions who have funded my visits: the IFK Institute, Vienna, the British Academy, the University of Wales, Aberystwyth, and the Van Kampen Foundation. The production of the book has been helped enormously by the working relationship I have had with Jason Freeman at Oxford University Press. His useful advice, patience, good humour, and ability to listen to my endless monologues without nodding off have all been much appreciated.

Various sections of this work have appeared in print before in earlier guises; I would like to thank the editor of *Parergon* for permission to reprint a revised version of my article, 'Two Representations of Venice in Late Tudor and Early Stuart England'; the editors of *Connotations* for permission to reprint a revised version of my article, 'Peter Martyr, Richard Eden and the New World: Reading, Experience, and Translation'; the editor of *Reformation* for permission to reprint sections from my article, 'Late Elizabethan Protestantism, Colonialism, and the Fear of the Apocalypse'; Cambridge University Press for permission to reprint a part of my essay, 'From English to British Literature: John Lyly's *Euphues* and Edmund Spenser's *The Faerie Queene*', in Brendan Bradshaw and Peter Roberts (eds.), *British Consciousness and Identity* (Cambridge:

Cambridge University Press, 1998); The Macmillan Press for permission to reprint a part of my essay, ' "Hitherto she ne're could fancy him": Shakespeare's British Plays and the Exclusion of Ireland', in Mark Thornton Burnett and Ramona Wray (eds.), *Shakespeare and Ireland: History, Politics, Culture* (Basingstoke: Macmillan, 1997).

My greatest debt, as ever, has been to my family, Alison, Lucy, Patrick, and Maud Hadfield, who have ensured that my self-obsession has had to be limited at times. I would also like to acknowledge the support I have received from my parents, David and Hilary Hadfield, and that of David and Mary Yarnold, which has been so important to me over the years.

A. H.

Contents

List of Illustrations

Figs. 1, 2, 3, 4, 7, 8, 10, 11 are reproduced with kind permission from the British Library; Figs. 5, 6, 9, 12 are reproduced with kind permission of the British Museum; Fig. 13 is reproduced with kind permission from the National Library of Wales, Aberystwyth

Abbreviations

CSPD	*Calendar of State Papers, Domestic Series*
CI	*Critical Inquiry*
DNB	*Dictionary of National Biography*
ELH	*English Literary History*
ELR	*English Literary Renaissance*
ES	*English Studies*
HJ	*The Historical Journal*
HLQ	*Huntington Library Quarterly*
IHS	*Irish Historical Studies*
JEH	*Journal of Ecclesiastical History*
JHI	*Journal of the History of Ideas*
L. & H.	*Literature and History*
MLQ	*Modern Language Quarterly*
MP	*Modern Philology*
MRTS	Medieval and Renaissance Texts and Studies
N. & Q.	*Notes and Queries*
NACBS	*North American Conference on British Studies*
OED	*Oxford English Dictionary*
P. & P.	*Past and Present*
PHR	*Pacific Historical Review*
PLL	*Papers in Language and Literature*
PMLA	*Publications of the Modern Language Society of America*
PQ	*Philological Quarterly*
RD	*Renaissance Drama*
RES	*Review of English Studies*
RQ	*Renaissance Quarterly*
RS	*Renaissance Studies*
SEL	*Studies in English Literature, 1500–1900*
Sh. Q.	*Shakespeare Quarterly*
Sh. Sur.	*Shakespeare Survey*
SP	*Studies in Philology*
STC	A. W. Pollard and G. R. Redgrave (eds.), *A Short Title Catalogue of Books Printed in England, Scotland, and Ireland, and of English Books Printed Abroad,* 1475–1640 (2nd edn., 3 vols., London, 1976–91). Vols. I (1986), II (1976) and III (1991) ed. by Pollard and

Redgrave, revised and enlarged by W. A. Jackson,
F. S. Ferguson, Katherine F. Panzer, and Philip R. Rider.

TCBS   *Transactions of the Cambridge Bibliographical Society*
TRHS   *Transactions of the Royal Historical Society*
WMQ   *William and Mary Quarterly*
YES   *Yearbook of English Studies*

Changing Places in English Renaissance Literature

WHAT IS the purpose of writing about other lands or recounting one's experiences of foreign travel? The obvious answer is that such representations increase our knowledge of other cultures, providing information which in some ways may prove useful, challenging, or, at worst diverting. Of course, undertaking the enterprise involves a series of reflections on one's own identity and culture which will inevitably transform the writer concerned—and quite possibly the reader—and will call into question received assumptions, inducing a sense of wonder at the magnificence of the other, or reaffirming deeply felt differences with a vengeance.

Travel writing is now a named and accepted category of writing in the English-speaking world, ubiquitous, popular, unavoidable, and, most importantly perhaps, unremarkable. This book is a study of the significance and purpose of 'travel writing' in the second half of the sixteenth century and the first quarter of the seventeenth, an era when the use of print as a medium for the dissemination of information was uncertain and fluid, and certain generic distinctions which we take for granted today—including that of 'travel writing'—were by no means clear or distinct. My purpose is not to provide a balanced historical assessment of early modern travel writing, or to attempt to cover every aspect of a series of representative texts which depicted foreign peoples and locations. Rather, I wish to explore one particularly crucial purpose of such works; namely, the ways in which they reflected on contemporary problems within the English—sometimes, the British—body politic.[1] Sometimes such reflection was quite conspicuous and

---

[1] The distinction is an important but not easily defined one for the purpose of this study. James's attempts to unite the kingdoms of Britain failed to sway the—English—parliament even though he styled himself 'king of Britain'. Ireland was

involved the allegorical representation of a foreign setting, a deliberate means of reflecting on domestic affairs while avoiding explicit, potentially dangerous comment. Elsewhere writers' aims were less clear cut, and the very act of representing a foreign location inaugurated anthropological speculation or the study of comparative government. This second type of self-reflection was more prevalent when English—or British—identity was called into question, most obviously the case when colonization of foreign lands was involved, as I argue in Chapter 2.[2]

Travel and colonial writing were undoubtedly political genres in a double sense. First, as I have suggested, they often possessed a political content. Second, they were frequently caught up in the turbulent political history within which they were produced. To give two examples, both analysed at greater length below: William Thomas's *The Historie of Italie* (1549) advertised itself as a work which would provide a host of examples which would enable the new regime of Edward VI to govern more effectively. Thomas's commitment to a democratically oriented Protestant creed led to his involvement in Wyatt's rebellion, and he was executed in 1554, a factor which may have increased the suspicion with which travel to Italy and imitation of Italianate manners and social mores were regarded in government circles. Similarly, Richard Eden's translation of Peter Martyr's *De Orbe Novo Decades* (1555) was the first of many sixteenth-century works which saw the need for an English empire to counteract the success of the Spanish, but was also alive to the sectarian reality of contemporary Europe,

---

granted the status of an independent kingdom ruled over by the king of England in the Irish parliament of 1541; Wales was 'united' with England in 1536. Hence most of the writers examined in this book make no clear and obvious distinction between England and Britain, sometimes including Wales, Scotland and Ireland as 'domestic' lands; at others writing of them as if they were foreign (most frequently in the case of Ireland). For further discussion, see Brendan Bradshaw and Peter Roberts (eds.), *British Consciousness and Identity* (Cambridge: Cambridge University Press, 1998); Hugh Kearney, 'The Making of an English Empire', in Hugh Kearney (ed.), *The British Isles: A History of Four Nations* (Cambridge: Cambridge University Press, 1989), ch. 7.

    [2] For a recent exploration, see Denise Albanese, 'Making it New: Humanism, Colonialism, and the Gendered Body in Early Modern Culture', in Valerie Traub, M. Lindsay Kaplan, and Dympna Callaghan (eds.), *Feminist Readings of Early Modern Culture* (Cambridge: Cambridge University Press, 1996), 16–43.

demonstrating that colonial and national histories did not occur, and were not regarded, in isolation. Eden's translation set the pattern for the dual function of the colonial text; on the one hand, such works sought to represent a reality to a curious public; on the other, they exhorted citizens to support colonial enterprises, with either manpower or money.

Given this involvement in political controversies, it is hardly surprising that travel and colonial writings were often viewed with suspicion by the upper echelons of society, nor that the messages of such texts were often—but by no means exclusively—critical of the status quo and could be read subversively. An obvious parallel which can be made is with historical works which chose to represent controversial events in English history, most notoriously the deposition of Richard II.[3] Annabel Patterson has recently argued that Holinshed's *Chronicles* (1577, 1587), far from being the unwieldy morass of undigested chronicle material which they are commonly characterized as being, were a concerted attempt by a united group of scholars to argue a liberal case for the importance of the principle of 'indifference' in both writing and state affairs, as a means of protecting the individual from unwelcome state interference.[4] As a result, the *Chronicles* were mutilated by censorship.[5] Some of the texts analysed in this study have agendas which are not dissimilar to the project which Patterson finds in Holinshed's collective enterprise, especially those which focus on the constitution of the republic of Venice.[6] Others provide hints and criticisms which are less well-developed. But it is important to recognize that the field was one of lively debate, and participants obviously recognized the potential of arguing

---

[3] See *The First and Second Parts of John Hayward's The Life and Raigne of King Henrie IIII*, ed. John J. Manning (London: Royal Historical Society, 1991; Camden Fourth Ser. 42); Howard Erskine-Hill, *Poetry and the Realm of Politics: Shakespeare to Dryden* (Oxford: Clarendon Press, 1996), 40–3, *passim*; Annabel Patterson, *Censorship and Interpretation: The Conditions of Writing and Reading in Early Modern England* (Madison: University of Wisconsin Press, 1984).

[4] Annabel Patterson, *Reading Holinshed's Chronicles* (Chicago: Chicago University Press, 1994).

[5] Patterson, *Reading Holinshed's Chronicles*, ch. 11. See also Cyndia Susan Clegg, *Press Censorship in Elizabethan England* (Cambridge: Cambridge University Press, 1997), ch. 7.

[6] For an overview, see Erskine-Hill, *Poetry and the Realm of Politics*, pt. 2.

the toss over the nature and purpose of representing foreign countries. Roger Ascham's famous attack on Italianate romances and the vogue for travel to Italy in *The Schoolmaster* (1570), King James VI of Scotland's defence of hereditary kingship against enthusiasts for the Venetian constitution (1598), and Sir Thomas Palmer's defence of the useful nature of travel as a means of training citizens to serve the state loyally, are all reactions to more aggressive appropriations of material in common circulation. Perhaps the most interesting literary example is Thomas Nashe's *The Unfortunate Traveller* (1594), a cynical attack on the purpose of travel and travel writing, and a work which appears to place him on the opposite side in this debate to that of his erstwhile ally, John Lyly, who had been employed by the state, like Nashe, to write propaganda against the Marprelate pamphlets in the early 1580s. Lyly's two prose romances centred around the figure of the Athenian Euphues are, in contrast, observations on the condition of England through the use of an outsider's eye, as well as bitter reflections on the constraints placed upon the serious discussion of politics in Elizabeth's reign.

Although travel was carefully controlled and restricted so that a licence had to be granted to any would-be European traveller, and, as I have already pointed out, the radical conclusions which some travellers drew from their experiences were vigorously opposed by other writers, travel writing was rarely directly censored.[7] One reason for this, as my first chapter will argue, is that in fact very little travel writing as such was produced until the start of the seventeenth century. The first significant works by travel writers—Fynes Moryson, Thomas Coryat, William Lithgow—betray signs of anxiety and confusion concerning their exact purpose and generic identity. *Coryat's Crudities* was privately published and contained a plethora of prefatory material which denigrated the author, representing him as a comical and inconsequential figure. Moryson's *Itinerary* has never been published in full and, significantly, it omitted a great deal of the more overtly political

---

[7] On the first point see Clare Howard, *English Travellers of the Renaissance* (London: John Lane, 1914), ch. 6. See also Sir Thomas Palmer, *An essay of the meanes how to make our travailes more profitable* (London, 1606), fo. 11.

analysis which Moryson had written, much of which still remains in manuscript. Another reason, I would suggest, is that a clear understanding of the limits to which the form could be pushed were accepted by both writers and officials who may have taken an interest in preventing any such material reaching a wider public, a sign that early modern censorship was not always as draconian as is sometimes suggested by modern commentators, and also an indication of the vigorous political debates which did take place under various non-political guises.[8] Equally, it is important to note that just because texts were not actually censored does not mean that writers did not operate under the fear of censorship, or even more hostile attention from the authorities. There is enough evidence of the censorship of numerous forms of literature to suggest that it is by no means implausible to assume that writers of travel and colonial literature probably operated under the assumption that if they overstepped certain marks then they would have to face unpleasant consequences, or that they had no need to disguise what they wanted to say. My suggestion is that a mutually accepted game of cat-and-mouse developed, a nervously agreed forum for debate, where readings were often uncertain and messages expressed in a manner which would always allow the sender to provide an alternative explanation, or deny a troublesome allegorical meaning.

Markku Peltonen has recently argued in an important and substantial work that classical republicanism was not a political doctrine which emerged *ex nihilo* in England in the 1650s, but was, in fact, an important part of English political life from the early sixteenth century.[9] Peltonen's definition of 'republicanism' is wide enough for him to include not simply the desire for 'a constitution without a king', but also the theory of the 'mixed constitution' which sought to balance the influence of the monarch with that of the elected councils of state (most

---

[8] See Clegg, *Press Censorship in Elizabethan England*; Richard Dutton, *Mastering the Revels: The Regulation and Censorship of English Renaissance Drama* (London: Macmillan, 1991). A more negative picture is provided in Janet Clare, *'Art Made Tongue-Tied by Authority': Elizabethan and Jacobean Dramatic Censorship* (Manchester: Manchester University Press, 1990).

[9] Markku Peltonen, *Classical Humanism and Republicanism in English Political Thought, 1570–1640* (Cambridge: Cambridge University Press, 1995). See also David Norbrook, *Poetry and Politics in the English Renaissance* (London: Routledge, 1984), chs. 8–10.

notably parliaments) and the more democratic inclusion of the
people in general. Even more generally, republicanism could be
used simply to refer to the aim of establishing 'a good and just
constitution'.[10] While Peltonen's study provides substantial
evidence for these varieties of republicanism in contemporary
political treatises, my study of travel and colonial writing
suggests that such a range of opinion was even more widespread than Peltonen concludes, and that some of the most
vociferous expressions of republican sentiment were contained
in representations of other countries and cultures.

It is important to recognize, when attempting to reconstruct
the history of sixteenth-century political debate, that one
cannot easily separate contemporary political works from
fictional material. Jennifer Loach, in her study of Tudor parliaments, has argued that 'although Elizabeth did not summon
parliament as frequently as her predecessors had done in the
1530s, 1540s, and 1550s, there is no reason to believe that her
subjects were disquieted by their monarch's choice'.[11] Perhaps
not, if one examines parliamentary records; but feelings that a
more effective forum for public debate was badly needed
abound in many literary works written in the second half of
Elizabeth's reign.[12] The interrelationship between fictional and
non-fictional writing is especially significant when one is dealing with colonial texts, because it cannot be assumed that the
fiction is a reflection of a reality, textual or otherwise, and that
it comes after the fact. The most important English book of
travel writing of the late Middle Ages was *The Travels of Sir
John Mandeville*, a work which clearly owed as much to
medieval romances as it did to factual observation, and which
inspired Columbus's decision to try to circumnavigate the globe
by sailing west to find Cathay.[13] The first book to mention the

---

[10] Peltonen, *Classical Humanism and Republicanism*, 2.

[11] Jennifer Loach, *Parliament under the Tudors* (Oxford: Clarendon Press,
1991), 5.

[12] For a more general overview of political discontent in the 1590s, see John
Guy (ed.), *The Reign of Elizabeth I: Court and Culture in the Last Decade*
(Cambridge: Cambridge University Press, 1995).

[13] *The Travels of Sir John Mandeville*, trans. C. W. R. D. Moseley
(Harmondsworth: Penguin, 1983), 31–2. A work which argues that Mandeville's
travels were real is Giles Milton, *The Riddle and the Knight: In Search of Sir John
Mandeville* (Bridgend: Allison & Busby, 1996).

New World was Sebastian Brandt's *Das Narrenschiff*, translated into English by Alexander Barclay as *The Ship of Fools* in 1509.[14] The first book to have a major impact on English readers in relating the discovery of the New World was Thomas More's *Utopia* (1516), a work which overshadows much subsequent literature dealing with overseas travel, colonial expansion, and contact with non-European peoples.[15] The fiction comes first. Indeed, so well-known had *Utopia* become in Elizabethan times, and so central a part of late Tudor humanist culture, that Sir Thomas Smith, in his own influential analysis of England, *De Republica Anglorum* (1565, published 1583), sees fit to remind the reader that the commonwealth he describes is real, 'not in that sort as *Plato* made his common wealth, or *Zenophon* his kingdome of Persia, nor as *Syr Thomas More* his *Utopia* being feigned common wealths, such as never was nor never shall be, vaine imaginations, phantasies of Philosophers to occupie the time and to exercise their wittes'.[16] Smith's vehement denial that his work is not 'feigned' indicates the acceptance of a close relationship between political analysis and fiction in sixteenth-century English intellectual life.

The most important aspect of *Utopia*'s vast subsequent influence, for my purposes, lies in the manner in which More consciously sought to relate European political problems to the ways in which other cultures were represented. As J. H. Hexter pointed out long ago, More almost certainly added the first book to the description of the 'feigned common wealth' in an attempt to make the purpose of his work clearer to the reader.[17]

---

[14] John Parker, *Books to Build an Empire: A Bibliographical History of English Overseas Interests to 1620* (Amsterdam: New Israel, 1965), 18.

[15] For two widely different accounts of the book's subsequent influence, see A. L. Morton, *The English Utopia* (London: Lawrence and Wishart, 1952); Jeffrey Knapp, *An Empire Nowhere: England, America, and Literature from* Utopia *to* The Tempest (Berkeley: University of California Press, 1992). Donna B. Hamilton argues that Miranda and Ferdinand's game of chess in *The Tempest*, Act V, is a recollection of the game the Utopians play which is 'not unlike chess'; *Virgil and* The Tempest: *The Politics of Imitation* (Columbus, Oh.: Ohio State University Press, 1990), 103–4.

[16] Sir Thomas Smith, *De Republica Anglorum: A Discourse on the Commonwealth of England*, ed. L. Alston (Shannon: Irish Academic Press, 1972, rpt. of 1906), 142.

[17] J. H. Hexter, *More's Utopia: The Biography of an Idea* (New Haven: Yale University Press, 1952), pt. 1.

More casts the fictional traveller, Raphael Hythloday, as a voyager with Amerigo Vespucci, who decided to remain in the New World when the others returned to Portugal, 'being more anxious for travel than about the grave'.[18] Such detail authenticates and locates Raphael's experience in the newly discovered Americas. However, the rest of the first book, which precedes the description of Utopia, concentrates on burning issues in contemporary European politics, cast through an extensive dialogue between More himself, Raphael, the Cardinal, and a lawyer. Our experience of Utopia is undoubtedly qualified by and mediated through their discussion. Before the participants even get to the Aristotelian question of political formations and their relative merits, they have to decide whether giving advice to rulers is worthwhile anyway. In this particular debate, the fictional More and Raphael articulate diametrically opposed views. More advocates the usefulness of counselling the monarch; Raphael has a much more gloomy outlook. Raphael represents himself as a free spirit, living exactly as he pleases (p. 57) and claims that his experiences have taught him that 'there is no room for philosophy with rulers' (p. 99). He suggests that his knowledge is, in effect, useless to change the course of events, and rejects More's suggestion that he should apply his 'talent and industry to the public interest':

I have no such ability as you [More] ascribe to me and, if I had ever so much, still, in disturbing my own peace and quiet, I should not promote the public interest. In the first place almost all monarchs prefer to occupy themselves in the pursuits of war—with which I neither have nor desire any acquaintance—rather than in the honourable activities of peace . . .
  In the second place, among royal councillors everyone is actually so wise as to have no need of profiting by another's counsel, or everyone seems so wise in his own eyes as not to condescend to profit by it, save that they agree with the most absurd saying of, and play the parasite to, the chief royal favorites whose friendliness they strive to win by flattery. (p. 57)

[18] Sir Thomas More, *Utopia*, ed. Edward Surtz, S.J. and J. H. Hexter (New Haven: Yale University Press, 1965). All subsequent references to this edition in parentheses in the text.

More has little time for such self-fulfilling logic. After Raphael has, at the Cardinal's request, made a number of radical and contentious suggestions concerning the reform of English penal laws, More exhorts Raphael to make his wisdom available to those who have the power to enforce legislation:

Even now, nevertheless, I cannot change my mind but must needs think that, you could do the greatest good to the common weal by your advice. The latter is the most important part of your duty as it is the duty of every good man. . . . What a distant prospect of happiness there will be if philosophers will not condescend even to impart their counsel to kings! (p. 87)

Given that More had recently agreed to become a councillor at the court of Henry VIII, one of the few things which can be agreed upon concerning this most slippery and controversial of books is that the fictional More's opinions are designed to carry the day.[19] More's point is refined further to suggest that matters cannot be divided neatly into a battle between truth and falsehood as Raphael believes. Instead, More suggests, the problem of giving advice involves careful negotiation, tact, and, on occasions, disguise, pitting his understanding of philosophy against Raphael's purism: 'there is another philosophy, more practical for statesmen, which knows its stage, adapts itself to the play in hand, and performs its role neatly and appropriately' (p. 99). The counsellor must work carefully and discreetly: 'by the indirect approach you must seek and strive to the best of your power to handle matters tactfully. What you cannot turn to good you must make as little bad as you can' (pp. 99–101).

Such prefatory comment implies that the actual description of Utopia provided by Raphael in Book Two must be read with some caution and that it does contain a great deal of useful advice to those who can read it carefully; but exactly what lessons the society and customs of the Utopians can provide European readers with is by no means clear. When do the Utopians serve as negative models and when as positive? We obviously cannot take Raphael's enthusiastic endorsement of

---

[19] For details see R. W. Chambers, *Thomas More* (London: Cape, 1935), chs. 2–3; Hexter, *More's Utopia*, pp. 21–30. For a recent overview of scholarship on *Utopia*, see Thomas More, *Utopia*, ed. George M. Logan, Robert M. Adams, and Clarence H. Miller (Cambridge: Cambridge University Press, 1995), pp. xlii–xlvi.

their manner of life at face value, given his position in the debate in Book One.[20] Yet More's praise of his abilities suggests that much of what he represents may be of use to influential readers of the text. My concern is not to join in the elaborate matrix of arguments concerning the meaning of *Utopia*. Rather, its importance for this particular study is in the ways in which it represents the material it contains, inviting European readers to read accounts of the Americas—albeit here fictional—in terms of their own political questions and problems. Some of the Utopians' behaviour may well seem admirable—their disdain for the ostentatious trappings of wealth, their refusal to indulge in pointless slaughter in warfare, for example; other aspects, such as their religious beliefs and tolerance of divorce, might have appeared somewhat less obviously worthy. What is important to note is the Eurocentric focus of such concerns. Raphael's description of the Utopians' social practices even includes a discussion of colonization, a principal reason for European interest in the New World.[21] The Utopians embark on colonial expeditions if and when 'the population throughout the island should happen to swell above the fixed quotas':

on the mainland nearest them, wherever the natives have much unoccupied and uncultivated land, they found a colony under their own laws. They join with themselves the natives if they are willing to dwell with them. When such a union takes place, the two parties gradually and easily merge and together absorb the same way of life and the same customs, much to the great advantage of both peoples. By their procedures they make the land sufficient for both, which previously seemed poor and barren to the natives. the inhabitants who refuse to live according to their laws, they drive from the territory which they carve out for themselves. If they resist, they wage war against them. They consider it a most just cause for war when a people which does not use its soil but keeps it idle and waste nevertheless forbids the use and possession of it to others who by rule of nature ought to be maintained by it. (p. 137)

The Malthusian motives for colonization can be related to Raphael's often-cited comments on the problem of sheep eating men (pp. 65–71) within the text of *Utopia* itself; moreover, such fears were a commonplace of colonial propaganda.[22] Equally, the aggressive argument that under-used land could—and should—be forcibly taken from reluctant natives to help the needy of Europe was a ubiquitous feature of such works.[23] In effect, the Utopians are displaced Europeans—English, even— who have to confront exactly the same problems as their real counterparts, including the question of appropriating foreign lands to ease domestic pressures.[24] It is not surprising that a translation into English was published in 1551 during an important period of serious interest in colonial expansion (see below, p. 85, 141).

Utopia can be seen as a foundational text of early modern English travel and colonial writing. Numerous subsequent works, whether fictional or factual, can be related to More's text, either directly or indirectly, via conscious influence or intertextual borrowing. In Foucault's somewhat cumbersome terminology, *Utopia* is the 'founder of discursivity' of a self-centred discourse of the other.[25] To make this claim, of course, is not to assume that every subsequent text which represented other lands or other peoples always followed More's example, or that every text which represented others could automatically be related to *Utopia*. My point is that a significant number of works, of varying generic types, were written in the wake of More's text. What made *Utopia* so useful to subsequent writers is a union of the representation of a foreign culture with the vast generic category of the literature of counsel, an extension of the *speculum principis* tradition 'which insisted that the truly

---

[22] K. R. Andrews, *Trade, Plunder and Settlement: Maritime Enterprise and the Genesis of the British Empire, 1480–1630* (Cambridge: Cambridge University Press, 1984), 33.

[23] See e.g. Sir George Peckham, 'A true Report of the late discoveries, and possession taken in the right of the Crowne of England of the Newfound Lands, By that valiant and worthy Gentleman, Sir Humphrey Gilbert Knight', in Richard Hakluyt, *The Principal Navigations, Voyages, Traffiques & Discoveries of the English Nation*, 12 vols. (Glasgow: MacLehose, 1904), viii. 89–131.

[24] See Fox, *Thomas More*, 56–8.

[25] Michel Foucault, 'What is an Author?', in *The Foucault Reader*, ed. Paul Rabinow (Harmondsworth: Penguin, 1986), 101–20, at 111–12.

virtuous sovereign took counsel from every quarter of the political compass, testing his own inclinations against a wide range of contrary advice before finally determining the best course of action'.[26] Most early modern works, literary or otherwise, I would argue, had didactic, overtly political aims; *Utopia* channelled these in a specific direction, establishing a precedent which also usefully blurred any boundaries between imaginative and analytical writing. Utopian texts are simultaneously the most fictional and the most urgently relevant forms of writing.[27]

The general argument of this book is that much early modern travel writing and colonial writing was written, in whole or in part, in order to participate in current pressing debates about the nature of society, the limitations of the existing constitution, the means of representing the populace at large, the relative distribution of power within the body politic, fear of foreign influences undermining English/British independence, the need to combat the success of other rival nations, religious toleration and persecution, and the protection of individual liberty. To a certain extent such questions were more urgently discussed when a general crisis or an especially significant event loomed large; Mary I's attempt to re-establish Catholicism after the radical Protestant experiments of her brother, Edward VI; Elizabeth's projected marriage with François, Duc d'Alençon; the Marprelate controversy; the succession crisis in the 1590s; the earl of Essex's attempted coup; James I's battles with parliament; the void felt by many

---

[26] Greg Walker, *Persuasive Fictions: Faction, Faith and Political Culture in the Reign of Henry VIII* (Aldershot: Scolar, 1996), 22. For more specific reference to *Utopia*, see Arthur F. Kinney, *Humanist Poetics: Thought, Rhetoric, and Fiction in Sixteenth-Century England* (Amherst, Mass.: University of Massachussets Press, 1986), ch. 2.

[27] Indeed, one might usefully distinguish between texts which come under the general umbrella of a mode of writing which bears an intertextual relationship to *Utopia*, and works which are within a strictly Utopian tradition, ie, they reflect directly on contemporary politics. In these terms, *The Tempest*, I would suggest, bears many of the generic marks of a strictly Utopian work. For more general discussions of Utopian works, see Andrew Hadfield, 'Utopian/Dystopian Novel', in Paul E. Schellinger (ed.), *Encyclopedia of the Novel* (Chicago: Fitzroy Dearborn, 1998); Ruth Levitas, *The Concept of Utopia* (Hemel Hempstead: Philip Allan, 1990); J. C. Davis, *Utopia and the Ideal Society: A Study of English Utopian Writing, 1516–1700* (Cambridge: Cambridge University Press, 1981).

after the death of Prince Henry. However, the evidence would suggest that many of the presiding themes in travel and colonial literature were more structural and general than an excessive concentration on specific events would indicate. The aftermath of the Saint Bartholomew's Day Massacre in Paris (23 August 1572), for example, was not confined to the years immediately subsequent; the event cast a shadow over the Protestant imagination well into the next century. More generally, a sense that the English/British constitution was inferior to both ideal models and actual examples in contemporary Europe (most notably Venice) was articulated from the reign of Edward VI to James I, a ubiquitous criticism of domestic politics which helps define the chronological boundaries of this book (although, of course, a larger survey could have progressed from the Reformation to the Civil War). Another constant obsession was rivalry with Spain for religious domination in Europe, a competition which spilled over into the battle for colonies in the New World and trade routes to the East until the rapid decline in Spanish power in the early seventeenth century and the rise of the Dutch republic.

As a result, I have chosen not to write the book along chronological lines. Of course, I do attempt to provide all the relevant historical information necessary for my argument, and would not wish to neglect the significance of specific historical events or crises. Instead, I have divided the material up generically in order to give a sense of the broad themes and uses to which travel and colonial writing were put in the English Renaissance before foreign travel became an educational requirement for the aristocratic gentleman (another reason for the *terminus ad quem* of this study).[28] Obviously much of the material is read in similar or related ways, and the reader is urged to cross-refer and compare the representations in question. The advantages of

---

[28] I am referring to the advent of the 'Grand Tour', which, like travel writing, only became properly established as a distinct genre in the early seventeenth century; see John Stoye, *English Travellers Abroad, 1604–1667* (New Haven: Yale University Press, 1989, rev. ed.); Christopher Hibbert, *The Grand Tour* (London: Weidenfeld and Nicolson, 1969); Jeremy Black, *The British Abroad: The Grand Tour in the Eighteenth Century* (Stroud: Alan Sutton, 1992); Howard, *English Travellers of the Renaissance*, ch. 6. Howard points out that the first usage of the term was in 1670 (p. 145).

concentrating on generic distinctions is twofold; first, it enables us to distinguish between travel writing and colonial writing, rather than simply conflate the two, indicating the different ways in which each subject area develops the themes and problems outlined above; second, it means that the material is not presented to the reader *ex nihilo*, as if such conventions of reading did not—and do not—matter.[29] Accordingly, the book is divided up into two parts, each consisting of two chapters. The first studies travel and colonial writing respectively, analysing their differences and interconnections; the second examines a selection of prose fiction and dramatic texts, indicating how each kind of writing represented other cultures, enabling the reader to see how such literary forms can be related to contemporary non-fictional material as well as how they relate to each other.

I regard it as axiomatic that, just as the choices lying behind my work possess a logic which can be defended, so also they could have been different. A lot more could have been written about Fynes Moryson's *Itinerary* (1617), William Lithgow's *Totall discourse* (1614, 1632), Sir Henry Wotton's letters (1590s to 1620s), Samuel Purchas's enormous *Hakluytus Posthumous, or Purchas His Pilgrimes* (1613, 1619, 1625), or any number of literary works by other writers including Shakespeare, Jonson, Middleton, Greene, Sidney, Mary Wroth, and William Warner, author of the little-studied *Syrinx, or a Sevenfold History* (1584, 1597).[30] As my study examines the public nature of travel and colonial literature, I have chosen to concentrate on printed texts, a decision which others might not have made given the important development of a manuscript culture in early modern England.[31] Equally, my chosen period,

---

[29] A useful discussion of questions of generic reading is to be found in Tzvetan Todorov, *Genres in Discourse*, trans. Catherine Porter (Cambridge: Cambridge University Press, 1990). For an overview of Renaissance generic distinctions, see Rosalie L. Colie, *The Resources of Kind: Genre-Theory in the Renaissance*, ed. Barbara K. Lewalski (Berkeley: University of California Press, 1973).

[30] A modern edition is available, edited by Wallace A. Bacon (Evanston, Ill.: Northwestern University Press, 1950). For comment, see Paul Salzman, *English Prose Fiction, 1558–1700: A Critical History* (Oxford: Clarendon Press, 1985), 70–1.

[31] See H. R. Woudhuysen, *Sir Philip Sidney and the Circulation of Manuscripts, 1558–1640* (Oxford: Clarendon Press, 1996); Harold Love, 'Scribal Publication in Seventeenth-Century England', *TCBS* 9 (1987), 130–54.

which stretches from the aftermath of the English Reformation, (notably the interest in Italian culture and politics at the court of Henry VIII, the early literary experiments in the reign of Edward VI, and the colonial propaganda of Mary's reign) to the struggle between James I and his parliaments which arguably paved the way for the upheavals of the middle of the century, could have been extended backwards or forwards.[32] My decision to concentrate on these years is based on the significant development of colonial and travel writing in this period, as well as the transformation of the theatre away from the control of the church and state to (licensed) independence, and the evolution of a recognizably literary prose fiction which has too often been read as the putative form of the novel, rather than a body of writing with its own merits.[33] If there was no obvious need to link literary and non-literary representations of other cultures in the early 1500s, there was no way of separating the two a century later.

I cannot make any substantial claim that *All States and Princes* adheres to any particular school of criticism or follows any particular historical method. It should be obvious to the reader that I am indebted to a wide range of critics and scholarly approaches. One of my purposes is to follow through the insights of many New Historicist and Cultural Materialist theorists, and to continue the explorations they have begun into questions of power, identity, forms of cultural representation, and gender.[34] Nevertheless, I am concerned to modify the

---

[32] See Lawrence Stone, *The Causes of the English Revolution, 1529–1642* (London: Routledge, 1972), 58–117.

[33] On the changes in the production of drama, see David Bevington, *From 'Mankind' to Marlowe* (Cambridge, Mass.: Harvard University Press, 1962). On prose fiction see Robert W. Maslen, *Elizabethan Fictions: Espionage, Counter-Espionage and the Duplicity of Fiction in Early Elizabethan Prose Narratives* (Oxford: Clarendon Press, 1997). A substantial recent challenge to the still prevalent narrative of 'the rise of the novel' is Margaret Anne Doody, *The True Story of the Novel* (New Brunswick, NJ: Rutgers University Press, 1996). Doody traces the origins of the novel back to ancient Greece.

[34] I am thinking especially of Stephen Orgel, *The Illusion of Power: Political Theater in the English Renaissance* (Berkeley: University of California Press, 1975); Stephen Greenblatt, *Renaissance Self-Fashioning: From More to Shakespeare* (Chicago: Chicago University Press, 1980); Jonathan Goldberg, *James I and the Politics of Literature: Jonson, Shakespeare, Donne and their Contemporaries* (Baltimore: Johns Hopkins University Press, 1983); Louis Adrian Montrose, 'Of Gentlemen and Shepherds: The Politics of Elizabethan Pastoral Form', *ELH* 50

common, but by no means inevitable, assumption that power was a relatively homogeneous and monolithic force emanating from the centre, and that opposition was not only difficult and dangerous, but likely to be absorbed within the already-existing structures of power.[35] I have no difficulty in accepting the existence of a dominant, repressive, and self-interested locus of power, but I would argue too that early modern English writing was far more varied and lively than a simple opposition between conservatives and subversives would allow. On the contrary, if we read the evidence carefully enough, a whole range of opinion emerges, illustrating the noisy vigour with which political and religious debates were carried out, even if they often appeared in disguise. Though readers may not be persuaded by all my interpretations of the works analysed in this book, I hope they will agree that I have made enough of a case to suggest that the sphere of politics goes beyond that of the explicitly political, and that travel and colonial writing need to be read in a wider range of contexts than has been hitherto the case.

(1983), 415–59; Alan Sinfield, *Faultlines: Cultural Materialism and the Politics of Dissident Reading* (Oxford: Clarendon Press, 1992); Catherine Belsey, *The Subject of Tragedy: Identity and Difference in Renaissance Drama* (London: Methuen, 1985); Jonathan Dollimore, *Radical Tragedy: Religion, Ideology and Power in the Drama of Shakespeare and his Contemporaries* (Hemel Hempstead: Harvester, 1989, 2nd ed.). I should also acknowledge a significant debt to Norbrook, *Poetry and Politics in the English Renaissance*; Erskine-Hill, *Poetry and the Realm of Politics*; and Patterson, *Censorship and Interpretation*.

35 The so-called 'containment–subversion' debate. For details see H. Aram Veeser (ed.), *The New Historicism* (London: Routledge, 1989); Jonathan Dollimore, 'Introduction: Shakespeare, Cultural Materialism and the New Historicism', in Jonathan Dollimore and Alan Sinfield (eds.), *Political Shakespeare: New Essays in Cultural Materialism* (Manchester: Manchester University Press, 1985), 2–17. See also Howard Erskine-Hill's sceptical evaluation of the legacy of New Historical debate; *Poetry and the Realm of Politics*, 6.

CHAPTER ONE

'How harmful be the errors of princes': English Travellers in (Western) Europe, 1545–1620

THE FIRST two Tudor monarchs, acutely aware of the parochial north European reputation of their nation's culture, were keen to encourage celebrated international scholars and artists to their courts.[1] They were also prepared to sponsor intellectual traffic the other way, and send prominent courtiers to European cities, most notably Italian ones, in order to bolster the sophistication of native English arts, letters, and political theory.[2] The experiences of Sir Thomas Wyatt and Henry Howard, the Earl of Surrey, led directly to the vogue for English Petrarchanism, a naturalized, Italian-inspired poetic tradition established in the 1530s; those of Sir Richard Morison, Thomas Starkey, Thomas Lupset, Reginald Pole and others led to the introduction of a more Italianate political culture based on the dispassionate comparative analysis of different governments and states.[3]

[1] Gordon Kipling, *The Triumph of Honour: Burgundian Origins of the Elizabethan Renaissance* (Leiden: Sir Thomas Browne Institute, 1977); 'Henry VII and the Origins of Tudor Patronage', in Guy Fitch Lytle and Stephen Orgel (eds.), *Patronage in the Renaissance* (Princeton: Princeton University Press, 1981), 117–64; W. Gordon Zeeveld, *Foundations of Tudor Policy* (Cambridge, Mass.: Harvard University Press, 1948), chs. 1–2; Neville Williams, *Henry VIII and his Court* (London: Cardinal, 1973), 45; David R. Carlson, *English Humanist Books: Writers and Patrons, Manuscripts and Print, 1475–1525* (Toronto: University of Toronto Press, 1995), *passim*.

[2] T. F. Mayer, *Thomas Starkey and the Commonweal: Humanist Politics and Religion in the Reign of Henry VIII* (Cambridge: Cambridge University Press, 1989), ch. 4; Geoffrey Elton, *Reform and Reformation: England 1509–1558* (London: Arnold, 1977), 158; Zeeveld, *Foundations of Tudor Policy*, chs. 3–4.

[3] Felix Raab, *The English Face of Machiavelli: A Changing Interpretation, 1500–1700* (London: Routledge, 1965), ch. 2; J. G. A. Pocock, *The Machiavellian Moment: Florentine Political Thought and the Atlantic Tradition* (Princeton: Princeton University Press, 1975), ch. 10; Quentin Skinner, *The Foundations of Modern Political Thought*, 2 vols. (Cambridge: Cambridge University Press, 1978), i. pt. 2.

Both traditions pursued complex, interwoven courses throughout the reigns of the remaining Tudor monarchs and that of the first of the Stuarts. The enthusiasm for ambiguous politico-erotic lyrics and sonnets inspired by Petrarchan antitheses appears to have gone into abeyance during Edward VI's reign, Mary's, and the first half of Elizabeth's. The impact of the Reformation led to many writers experimenting with native models based upon medieval precursors, such as Chaucer and Langland, as a means of asserting an English independence from Rome. Such writing was often specifically targeted against the supposed privileges and vices of the Europeanized English court, and possessed a populist thrust.[4] In a related but converse way, the sophistication and access to dangerous knowledge of the Italianate Englishman made him an object of the authorities' suspicions, as well as providing him with the basis for a critical examination of his own country's failings. The most frequently cited example of such a hostile evaluation of foreign influences and foreign travel occurred in Roger Ascham's influential *The Schoolmaster* (1570), in which he devoted a long and significantly placed passage (at the end of the first book) to the malign influence of Italian culture upon his countrymen. Ascham compared Italy to the island of Circe, suggesting that more Englishmen returned with corrupted manners, forgetting all the good they had learnt before, having become dishonest and addicted to vice and pleasure, than those Ulysseses who returned ennobled.[5] The Italianate Englishman, according to Ascham, is a danger because he has been brought up 'in some free city . . . where a man may freely discourse against what he will, against whom he lust—against any prince, against any government, yea, against God himself and his whole religion'.[6] An excess of liberty and exposure to alternative methods of government could lead to the subversion of decent home-grown values.

However, the knowledge gained from sending courtiers to Italy was certainly useful to the authorities in terms of providing

---

[4] John King, *English Reformation Literature: The Tudor Origins of the Protestant Tradition* (Princeton: Princeton University Press, 1982).

[5] Roger Ascham, *The Schoolmaster* (1570), ed. Lawrence V. Ryan (Ithaca, NY: Cornell University Press, 1967), 60–75.

[6] Ascham, *Schoolmaster*, 74.

the means for writing propaganda during and after the Pilgrimage of Grace (1536–7). As Felix Raab has pointed out, Richard Morison's two treatises written in response to the rebels' use of propaganda, *A Remedy for Sedition* and *A Lamentation in whiche is shewed what ruyne and destruction cometh of seditious rebellion*, both published in 1536, owe much to Machiavelli's writings, and the former cites Machiavelli as an acute observer of political affairs.[7] Morison, who had studied in Italy, was able to employ the notorious chapter in *The Prince* on 'Ecclesiastical principalities' which observed that religion could be used to help subdue a rebellious populace, to advise Henry how to act.[8] On the other hand, such knowledge could be attacked as subversive, as was the case with Roger Ascham, who wrote of the twin evils of popery and Machiavelli (see below).[9] Crosscurrents could be complex: Cardinal Reginald Pole also condemned Machiavelli for his perceived assault on religion, but was to become a notorious traitor himself when he remained in Italy after refusing to accept Henry's break with Rome. Pole returned later as the head of Henry's daughter Mary's re-established church, and was responsible for the (brief) restoration of Papal supremacy in England.[10] The group of young intellectuals who had gathered around Pole's household in Padua in the early 1530s, debating questions of church and state, duties and rights, and the extent of the law, were thus thrown apart by the polarizing effects of the Reformation.

The most celebrated product of their labours is Thomas Starkey's *A Dialogue between Pole and Lupset* (c.1529–32),

[7] Ascham, *Schoolmaster*, 72; Raab, *English Face of Machiavelli*, 34–40. On propaganda during the Pilgrimage of Grace, see R. and M. H. Dodds, *The Pilgrimage of Grace, 1536–7 and the Exeter Conspiracy, 1538*, 2 vols. (Cambridge: Cambridge University Press, 1915), i. 280–1; A. G. Dickens, 'Wilfrid Holme of Huntington: Yorkshire's First Protestant Poet', *Yorkshire Archaeological Journal*, 39 (1956–8), 119–35.
[8] Niccolo Machiavelli, *The Prince*, trans. George Bull (Harmondsworth: Penguin, 1961), 73–6.
[9] Raab, *English Face of Machiavelli*, 33.
[10] Raab, *English Face of Machiavelli*, 31. On Pole see *DNB* article; Elton, *Reform and Reformation*, 158, 258–9, 378–85; John Guy, *Tudor England* (Oxford: Oxford University Press, 1988), 233–40.

written before Pole's defection.[11] Starkey's disputants set out to determine how a state should be ordered and how the citizens or subjects within that body politic should conduct themselves. The debate mirrors the concerns of More's *Utopia* in staging the old argument between the *vita activa* and *vita contemplentativa*, thus marking out the dialogue as a humanist work.[12] The work opens with Lupset stating the need for knowledge to be communicated in the manner of the great lawgivers of the ancient world, Solon, Lycurgus, and Plato, and chiding Pole for failing to give the benefit of his learning to others through participation in government (pp. 1–2), a criticism which presumably holds sway, given the subsequent development of the debate. The first section of the dialogue deals with the question of the health of commonwealths, how to provide workable laws, manage the economy, encourage civic behaviour from the populace, and prevent social decay. The last two discuss the much more problematic and controversial question of the rights and duties of the monarch and the form of government a state should adopt. Following Aristotle, Pole argues that man can be led astray if he relies too heavily upon his will, but that this can be controlled by the intellect and so can nullify the path towards vice.[13] The same process applies to commonwealths, and their decay can be arrested and reversed if 'dylygent instructyon & wyse consel' (p. 21) is heeded. '[W]ol lyberty' can be achieved if only ignorance is banished. The ubiquitous image of the body politic is employed, but in a way which appears to privilege the counsellors of the prince more highly than the prince himself.[14] Pole explains that 'the hart therof ys the kyng prynce & rular of the state, whether so ever hyt be one

---

[11] For the probable date see Thomas Starkey, *A Dialogue between Pole and Lupset*, ed. T. F. Mayer (London: Royal Historical Society, 1989), pp. x–xii. All subsequent references to this edition in parentheses in the text. See also the more easily usable edition of Katherine Burton (London: Routledge, 1948).

[12] Kinney, *Humanist Poetics*, ch. 2; R. S. Johnson, *More's Utopia: Ideal and Illusion* (New Haven: Yale University Press, 1969).

[13] For an argument that this aspect of Starkey's thought had a vast influence on subsequent government policy throughout the sixteenth century, see Brendan Bradshaw, 'Sword, Word and Strategy in the Reformation in Ireland', *HJ* 21 (1978), 475–502, at 492–7.

[14] On this trope see D. G. Hale, *The Body Politic: A Political Metaphor in Renaissance English Literature* (The Hague: Mouton, 1971).

or many, accordyng to the governance of the commynalty &
polytyke state', but that 'the hede wyth the yes yers & other
sensys therin resemblyd may be ryght wel the under offycerys
by pryncys appoyntyd', an analogy which, despite the use of the
qualifying noun phrase 'under offycerys', places the counsellors
in a position of superior perception and knowledge. The
body/state cannot function without the heart/prince (who may,
according to Pole, be a ruling oligarchy), who is responsible for
the 'natural powar' which runs the state, in the form of 'al laws
ordur & pollyce, al justice vertue & honesty'; but it is the
head/counsellors who 'ever observe and dylygently wayte for
the wele of the rest of thys. body' (p. 33). Certainly Starkey's
use of the metaphor is—potentially—more radical than that
used in Menenius's fable of the belly in Shakespeare's
Coriolanus (*c*.1608–9), where the 'kingly, crowned head' stands
for 'the vigilant eye' and the heart is depicted as the 'counsellor'
(I .i. 113–14).[15]

Pole continues to point out that there are various forms of
counsel which can be given to the ruler; whether this involves
'a common Consel of certayn wyse men' or 'the hole body &
multytude of pepul' depends upon 'the natur of the pepul'. The
important point is that what separates men from 'the rude lyfe
in feldes & wodys', and establishes civil society, is 'perfayt
eloquence & hye phylosophy', enabling judicious government
based on a series of commonly agreed laws. Abandoning such
commonly established principles for a rule based on men's
'owne syngular wele plesure' is to transform 'gud order' into
'hye tyrannye' (p. 36).

Although Henry VIII is frequently praised in the dialogue as
a wise ruler, Pole makes it clear that hereditary succession is not
the best way of governing a state, and that it is far better if the
ruler is chosen by the people, because arbitrary rule by one man
is 'repugnant to nature' and 'contrary to reson' (p. 72). Henry
may be capable of ruling so well and so justly that he does not
need to be subject to any laws (p. 111); nevertheless, Pole main-
tains, 'in our ordur here ys a certayn faute', which needs to be

---

[15] William Shakespeare, *Coriolanus*, ed. R. B. Parker (Oxford: Oxford
University Press, 1994). See also 'Introduction', 44–5. All subsequent references to
this series of plays. See also Pocock, *Machiavellian Moment*, 349.

remedied. The solution is that 'aftur the decesse of the prynce, by election of the common voyce of the parlyamen assembyd to chose one, most apte to that hye offyce & dygnyte wych schold not rule & governe al <at hys owne plesure & lyberty> but ever be subjecte to the ordur of hys lawys' (p. 112).

In contrast to the faulty state of England stands the 'nobul cyte of venyce, wych by the reson of the gud ordur & pollycy that therinys, usyd., hath contynuyd above a thousand yerys in one ordur & state, where the pepul . . . be as helthy and welthy as any pepul now I thynke lyvyng <apon the erth>'. Pole's advice is that such a commonwealth must be copied: 'therfor <mastur lup.> by statute made <& commynly receyvyd> . . . we must be compellyd at the fyrst to folow thes men . . . & then you schold never have any occasyon to dowte therof, nor feare the stabylyte of our prosperous state' (p. 119). In Venice no one is especially keen to fill the office of duke because 'hye is restreyned to gud ordur & polytyke'; the same should happen in England: 'so wyth us also schold be of our kyng yf hys powar were temperyd aftur the maner before descrybed' (p. 123).

Starkey's dialogue is worth quoting at length specifically because it appears to be the first work in English which is heavily indebted to the myth of Venice as the perfect constitution, and because it employs that myth as a stick with which to beat the comparatively flawed constitution of the English monarch.[16] The use of the term 'policy' further marks the text out as indebted to Italian political thought.[17] As T. F. Mayer has argued, *A Dialogue between Pole and Lupset* owes much to the Italian humanists he encountered and studied during his stay in Italy; his use of metaphors of state based on the body suggests the influence of Gaspar Contarini's *De Magistratibus et Republica Venetorum* (1543), which was later to have a major impact in England when translated by Lewis Lewkenor

[16] On this myth see Felix Gilbert, 'The Venetian Constitution in Florentine Political Thought', in Nicolai Rubenstein (ed.), *Florentine Studies: Politics and Society in Renaissance Florence* (London: Faber, 1968), 463–500; Pocock, *Machiavellian Moment*, 100–2, 318–30.

[17] Mayer, *Starkey and the Commonweal*, 205–6; Mario Praz, *The Flaming Heart* (Gloucester, Mass.: Peter Smith, 1966), 103–9; Jonathan Bate, 'The Elizabethans in Italy', in Jean-Pierre Maquerlot and Michèle Willems (eds.), *Travel and Drama in Shakespeare's Time* (Cambridge: Cambridge University Press, 1996), 55–74, at 56.

as *The Commonwealth and Government of Venice* (1599) (see below, pp. 47–58).[18] Starkey's hope for the establishment of an 'oligarchical constitution in England' is an attempt to transform England into a republic inspired by Venetian models via the reformation of the people from their luxurious sloth and the institutions of government from their potential tyranny.[19] It is perhaps not wholly surprising that the dialogue did not find its way into print, especially after Pole's decision to remain loyal to the Papacy and remain in Italy. When Starkey's contribution to government propaganda after the Pilgrimage of Grace was published, *An Exhortation to the People, instructynge them to unitie and obedience* (1540), the supremacy of Henry VIII was now asserted rather than criticized. Starkey had either changed his views, or disguised them.[20]

According to Felix Gilbert, after Thomas Aquinas in *De regimine principum* described Venice as the only state in Northern Italy which had avoided tyranny because its ruler had only limited powers, Venice became a beacon of liberty for the Italian humanists who Starkey had read and with whom he had studied.[21] The myth contained two crucial elements: first, that Venice was independent and relatively free, and, second, that its constitution had remained unchanged since it had been drafted.[22] For humanists in Italy, Venice inherited the mantle of classical republicanism; for other observers it appeared as a city-state which was able to combine the elements of monarchy, aristocracy, and democracy, either as 'a true mixed government or a true aristocracy', an ambivalence which stemmed from the application of Aristotle's categories of states, and which made Venice appear all things to all men.[23] The perception of Venice as a closed aristocracy was what caused writers such as

---

[18] Mayer, *Starkey and the Commonweal*, 61.

[19] Starkey, *Dialogue between Pole and Lupset*, ed. Mayer, p. xiii.

[20] Mayer, *Starkey and the Commonweal*, 218–19.

[21] Gilbert, 'Venetian Constitution', 467.

[22] For an account of Venice's attempt to preserve its religious liberty in the sixteenth and seventeenth centuries see Anthony Wright, 'Republican Tradition and the Maintenance of "National" Religious Traditions in Venice', *RS* 10 (1996), 405–16.

[23] Pocock, *Machiavellian Moment*, p. 100. See also Erskine-Hill, *Poetry and the Realm of Politics*, ch. 4; Peltonen, *Classical Humanism and Republicanism*, 106–7, 112–18, *passim*.

Machiavelli to turn against the positive evaluation of its constitutional framework and search for other republican ideals.[24] To its many admirers, the complex, interrelated levels of participating government were the cause of manifest virtue in the citizens, harmonious social interaction and long-term stability. As Contarini, Donato Giannotti, and others pointed out in their treatises, sovereignty resided in the Great Council on which every noble over 25 was entitled to sit, but more direct rule was carried out by the Senate, a body of about three hundred, elected for a year each by the Great Council. Above these two bodies stood the Council of Ten, able to carry out business at great speed, and the Doge (Duke), representing the sovereignty of the republic, but never ruling as a prince, as he was subject to election, bound by the laws of the commonwealth, and unable to declare war or peace without the consent of the citizens.[25]

Another admirer of Venice was William Thomas (d. 1554), whose work, unlike Starkey's dialogue, was published, but whose religious and political affiliations eventually led to his execution. Thomas was the first English speaker (he was Welsh or of Welsh extraction) to compile a grammar and dictionary of Italian specifically designed to help English readers master the works of Boccaccio, Petrarch, and Dante, having been 'constrained by misfortune' to go abroad in 1544.[26] Thomas returned to England in 1549, famous as a traveller, and became an enthusiastic supporter of Edward VI, who appears to have rewarded him handsomely, given him an elevated position within his household, and sought out his advice on numerous political issues. With the accession of Mary, Thomas lost all his influence, and he was executed after his prominent role in Wyatt's rebellion, in which he had

[24] Gilbert, *Machiavelli and Guicciardini: Politics and History in Sixteenth-Century Florence* (Princeton: Princeton University Press, 1965), 49–78; 'Venetian Constitution', 482–9; Pocock, *Machiavellian Moment*, ch. 7.

[25] William J. Bouwsma, *Venice and the Defense of Republican Liberty: Renaissance Values in the Age of the Counter-Reformation* (Berkeley and Los Angeles: California University Press, 1968), 60–3.

[26] William Thomas, *Principal Rules of Italian Grammar with Dictionarie for the better understanding of Boccace, Petrarcha, and Dante* (1550). Details of Thomas's life are from the entry in *DNB*. See also William Thomas, *The History of Italy* (1549), ed. George B. Parks (Ithaca, NY: Cornell Univ. Press, 1963), intro.

conspicuously been the most 'well-known and enthusiastic Protestant'.[27]

Although he apparently publicly defended Henry VIII in Bologna on hearing the news of the king's death, Thomas was one of the large number of intellectuals who were excited by the potential for religious and political reform at the court of Edward VI, and made most use of the freedom of the press to promote their ideas.[28] Thomas was associated with the ideas of Christopher Goodman, the most notorious defender of regicide in the mid-Tudor years. Goodman argued that a people had the right to kill a monarch who had become a tyrant, and applied the same logic to bad magistrates, asserting that no ruler was preferable to a corrupt one, and significantly going beyond Starkey's stated position.[29]

Thomas elaborated his political ideas in his *Historie of Italie* (1549), a book which no subsequent writer who desired to represent Italy could have afforded to ignore.[30] Thomas advertised his work as 'A boke excedyng profitable to be redde: Because it intreateth of the astate of many and divers common weales, how thei ben, & now be governed'. It was through this understanding of the relative merits of governments and consequent argument for the benefits of comparative study that a radical English Protestant tradition was to meet with the political ideas resulting from Italian humanism. Theorists within both camps were attracted to the ideals of classical republicanism.[31]

In his dedicatory letter to John, Earl of Warwick, Viscount Lisle, Thomas encouraged all who might have a stake in government to travel to Italy, as Italian civilization was

[27] David Loades, *Two Tudor Conspiracies* (Cambridge: Cambridge University Press, 1965), 16.

[28] King, *English Reformation Literature*, 14–15; Andrew Hadfield, *Literature, Politics and National Identity: Reformation to Renaissance* (Cambridge: Cambridge University Press, 1994), ch. 3; W. K. Jordan, *Edward VI: The Young King* (Cambridge, Mass.: Harvard University Press, 1971), ch. 4.

[29] Christopher Goodman, *How Superior Powers Ought to be Obeyed* (1558), 183–7.

[30] Erskine-Hill, *Poetry and the Realm of Politics*, pp. 127–9; David McPherson, *Shakespeare, Jonson, and the Myth of Classicism* (Newark: University of Delaware Press, 1990), 21.

[31] See Peltonen, *Classical Humanism and Republicanism*, p. 13.

pre-eminent in Europe.[32] The study of Italy could help English governors to rule better, as the various city-states and principalities either served as models of good government built up from nothing, or as negative examples of bad rule where division leads to destruction. Thomas declares himself opposed to the practice of conquering other states, and suggests that rulers should concentrate on ruling their own people well.[33] *The Historie of Italie* was clearly intended to belong to the literary tradition of the 'mirror for princes'.[34]

The text itself is divided up into a general description and history, followed by an analysis of various regions. Of these, Venice takes pride of place, as well as meriting by far the lengthiest description, followed by Naples, Florence, Genoa, and Milan, with a few pages at the end devoted to Mantua, Ferrara, Piacentia, and Parma, and Urbino. In terms of the scheme of the book outlined in the letter, Venice clearly stands as the positive example and the exception to the general rule of Italian city-states being ruled by tyrants (fo. 8) (a judgement which recalls that of Thomas Aquinas), with Naples as the counter-example.[35] The chequered histories of Florence, Genoa, and Milan, their swings between various forms of tyranny and liberty, place them somewhere in between the two extremes. Florence, for example, for whose history Thomas relies on Machiavelli's analysis, was once hopelessly divided between Guelfs and Ghibellines, but has now been united by Cosimo de Medici, who is praised, following Machiavelli, as a wise ruler, one of the notable men of the world (fos. 142, 155). Genoa has similarly been riven for much of its history by a ruinous conflict between commons and nobles and has suffered inconstant government because the will of the people has held

---

[32] William Thomas, *Historie of Italie* (1549), (sig. A2ʳ). Subsequent references in parentheses in the text.

[33] This is possibly a criticism of Machiavelli whose own criticisms of oligarchy involved the praise of a populist state based on an armed militia. As *The Historie of Italie* makes clear, Thomas was clearly familiar with Machiavelli's writings. See Pocock, *Machiavellian Moment*, 176–7; Skinner, *Foundations of Modern Political Thought*, 173–5; Gilbert, 'Venetian Constitution', 488–9.

[34] See L. K. Born, 'The Perfect Prince: A Study in Thirteenth and Fourteenth-Century Ideals', *Speculum*, 3 (1928), 470–504.

[35] For a different reading, see Erskine-Hill, *Poetry and the Realm of Politics*, 118–20.

sway (fo. 176). Only with the return of a powerful Duke has civil sedition been ended and true liberty returned (fos. 181, 187).

But if Florence and Genoa demonstrate equal but opposite political lessons, Venice, with its record of stability and liberty, has much to teach the English. Thomas's long analysis opens with an awed description of the physical appearance of the city approached from the sea, commending its striking site, and commenting on the marvellous feat of engineering which produced the city. Venice could—indeed, should—have been awful, owing to the natural disadvantages of its location. But, on the contrary, it is wonderful (fo. 73). The traveller's first impression is a quasi-religious experience, a miracle for Protestant England to emulate. In depicting the traveller's impression of Venice in these terms, Thomas may well be signalling the affinity between the experience of seeing Venice for the first time and the miraculous sights described in the pages of Sir John Mandeville's *Travels*, one of the two paradigms of European travel writing before the discovery of the New World.[36] Just as Mandeville, according to Stephen Greenblatt, refused to occupy or take possession of the wonders he saw in the name of an imperial power, so does Thomas praise the Venetians for their lack of aggression towards neighbouring states, and urges England simply to copy their example (fo. 76).[37]

Thomas's benign wonder is also applied to the buildings in Venice and fabulous wealth generated from the Venetians' pursuit of riches rather than military conquest, possibly a recollection of the purpose of Marco Polo's travels to the East.[38]

---

[36] The other being Marco Polo's *Travels* in search of the wealth of the 'Great Khan', which lay behind Columbus's plans for his voyage in 1492; see Peter Hulme, *Colonial Encounters: Europe and the Native Caribbean, 1492–1797* (London: Methuen, 1986), ch. 1; Syed Manzurul Islam, *The Ethics of Travel: From Marco Polo to Kafka* (Manchester: Manchester University Press, 1996), 120. For examples, see Mandeville, *Travels*, chs. 5, 17, 30. The veracity of Marco Polo's travels has recently been questioned, see Frances Woods, *Did Marco Polo go to China?* (London: Secker and Warburg, 1995).

[37] See Stephen Greenblatt, 'From the Dome of the Rock to the Rim of the World', in *Marvelous Possessions: The Wonder of the New World* (Oxford: Clarendon Press, 1991), 27.

[38] Marco Polo, *The Travels*, trans. Ronald Latham (Harmondsworth: Penguin, 1958).

Nowhere in Europe provides better houses for its population, and everyone, according to Thomas, lives like a prince rather than a private citizen (fos. 74–5). Thomas's voyage to Venice comes to occupy the same significance for post-Reformation Englishmen that Marco Polo's from Venice had for twelfth-century Venetians. The marvels described in the earlier book—gold and spices, but also the knowledge of the means to obtain them—led to the wealth which ensured Venice's liberty; those presented in Thomas's book—political knowledge—will lead to the establishment of the independent liberty of the citizens within the dominions of the English king. The description of the dwellings of the citizens of Venice stands out as a metonymic detail; they live like princes because the state treats them as such.

Thomas's description of the dignities and offices of the Venetians which follows stands out not only in comparison to the length devoted to the physical description of the city (seven folios, compared to four), but also when compared to the scant descriptions provided for the relevant institutions developed by the other city-states described (Naples, one folio; Florence, two folios; Genoa, one folio), where Thomas devotes far more space to the customs of the people. Here is the central passage in the book, signalled by the comment in the epistle to John, Viscount Lisle, Earl of Warwick that Italy will provide the English reader with examples of good governments built up from nothing.

The account opens with a description of the Doge as an 'honourable slave', because, although his power seems great, it is in fact strictly limited by the citizens over which he governs (fo. 77). There are ballots for everything, which means that the three citizens closest to the Doge, the Signor Capi, have greater powers than him because they are his nearest advisers (fos. 77–8). As if that were not a sufficient check and balance, there are the six elected Signori, one of whom is always with the Doge, and between them they deal with crucial matters such as the declaration of war or peace, and judicial decisions which will affect the constitution. Thomas concludes that, because the Venetians value liberty so highly, they will not meddle with such offices. Furthermore, custom has evolved such that it is considered a crime to address superiors as 'lord' or 'master'.

Thomas is keen to represent Venice as a model for England

to copy, always suggesting that its Utopian image can be adapted; that, indeed, in some respects, it already has been. Hence in his laudatory description of the Great Council the opening comment is that it serves the same function as the English parliament (fo. 80). Thomas emphasizes the danger of concentrated power, praising the widespread practice of the use of secret ballots in all votes and the fact that all offices can be revoked if the incumbent does not measure up to the task. The key question is the protection of the individual's liberty, the implication being that Edward may be able to introduce and make workable measures which will ensure a similar freedom for his own people. One of the customs of the Venetians which Thomas describes is their pride in their status and their boast that they are not 'subjects' (fo. 84). There is a related fear of a standing army, a constant preoccupation in contemporary England too, principally because of the terror, real and imagined, which disbanded soldiers caused civilian populations.[39] As a result, weapons cannot be carried within the city's boundaries without a special licence (fos. 82–3).

The history of Venice further cements the link between England and the Italian city-state. The opening sentences inform the reader that the Venetians are supposedly descended from either the Heneti, who were a people dispersed after the destruction of Troy, or the Veneti, a tribe of Britons in France (fo. 86). Given the widespread Tudor use of their own purported descent from the Trojans, both origin myths relate the Venetians to the Britons/English, representing them as a vision of what England could soon be. The history shows how the Venetians, after having agreed that they needed a proper government under one leader, have consistently opposed tyranny and deposed Doges who have attempted to infringe their liberties, without ever descending into anarchy because of the strength and fairness of their constitution and laws (fos. 108–12).

Thomas does make criticisms of the meanness and monetary greed of the Venetians, and hints at the danger of their liberty

---

[39] John Pound, *Poverty and Vagrancy in Tudor England* (Harlow: Longman, 1971), 3–5. More generally, see A. L. Beier, *Masterless Men: The Vagrancy Problem in Tudor England* (London: Methuen, 1985).

becoming excessive through the toleration of courtesans (a constant English preoccupation in descriptions of the city[40]), and the swaggering arrogance of youth (fos. 84–5), all themes which English critics of Venice, and Italy in general, would emphasize. But the overall emphasis is on the advantages of living in Venice, its security, financial success, the relative equality enjoyed by its citizens, and the liberty extended to them and to any foreigners resident there (fo. 85).

Thomas's history can clearly be related to Starkey's dialogue in terms of its attempt to use comparative studies of government within the 'mirrors for princes' tradition, itself about to be adapted and extended in another Edwardian literary project, *A Mirror for Magistrates* (c.1555, first published in 1559).[41] Yet it also clearly possesses a different emphasis to that of the former text in its use of the author's own observations and its attempt to give all the information possible about the object described, Italy, allowing the reader to relate the subject of the work to his or her own political situation (albeit with a series of hints and asides). *The Historie of Italie* is therefore an oblique work which demands an active reader who can make the connections required. Thomas's stated aim is service to the commonwealth, but in the process of serving the state, like Starkey, he provides a series of harsh criticisms which may well make the work subversive or revolutionary. The potential of the form is for disguise, for the use of material as allegory, accurately reporting a history or series of events which can be presented as innocent by the author, but which actually make a number of criticisms of the existing status quo. For Thomas this division does not occur, because he has faith that he does not have to address two opposed sets of readers, one who are supposed to decode the message, the other who, it is hoped, will fail to read it. Thomas was one of many writers who felt that Edward VI's desire was to establish a more just and liberal England— including a press which could enjoy widespread freedom—so

---

40   A. Lytton Sells, *The Paradise of Travellers: The Italian Influence on Englishmen in the Seventeenth Century* (London: George Allen and Unwin, 1964), 165; J. L. Livesay, *The Elizabethan Image of Italy* (Ithaca, NY: Cornell University Press, 1964), 13–14; Bate, 'Elizabethans in Italy', 62.

41   Hadfield, *Literature, Politics and National Identity*, ch. 3, 'Literature and History: *A Mirror for Magistrates*'.

that his service to the state did not involve the dilemma of whether to speak out or keep quiet.[42]

Thomas's use of his history of another country to promote a specific political programme at home resembles the use of English history throughout the sixteenth century. Frequently deprived of a voice within the political institutions of the realm, writers would employ material which could be read for its application to contemporary events and situations by those wishing to discover hidden meanings.[43] As Annabel Patterson has persuasively argued, Holinshed's *Chronicles*, far from being the diverse and rambling collection of materials representing the last gasp of pre-scientific history as they have usually been characterized, were the coherent efforts of a tightly knit group of intellectuals to promote their vision of a more liberal and tolerant England where matters were weighed more carefully, tolerantly, and fairly, and where individuals were able to enjoy rights which protected them instead of simply owing duties to a sovereign. In attempting to demonstrate the importance of 'indifference' in the treatment of historical material, they were also asserting that the same principle should govern the relationship between individuals and the state, especially in terms of the constitution and the law.[44] This involved the usual cat-and-mouse game with the censors—one reason why the text of the *Chronicles* appears incoherent—who insisted on the removal of a number of passages.[45]

Whereas the writers of Holinshed's *Chronicles* often had specific aims in mind in their use of material, referring to particular trials or acts of the reigning monarch, Thomas's text reads more like the programme of a man returning from exile with the knowledge which he hopes will transform the fate of his nation, centred as it is around the usefulness of the Venetian

---

[42] For details of Edward's licensing of the press in his early reign, see Clegg, *Press Censorship in Elizabethan England*, 27.

[43] 'It is clear . . . that political allusion to the present times did not depend upon a completely realistic likeness between the figure presented and the figure alluded to; it turned rather upon salient common features, problems, or issues, in situations otherwise very different, which could remind contemporary readers or audiences of their own time' (Erskine-Hill, *Poetry and the Realm of Politics*, 43).

[44] Patterson, *Reading Holinshed's Chronicles* (Chicago: University of Chicago Press, 1994), chs. 1, 8.

[45] Patterson, *Reading Holinshed's Chronicles*, chs. 3, 11.

Constitution and the liberty enjoyed in Venice. The work is unguarded, and only the most intellectually limited of readers could fail to detect its praise of liberty and hostility to tyranny. After Thomas's execution it was apparently suppressed, having been first publicly burnt.[46] Given Thomas's outspoken opinions, the fate of both book and author can hardly be regarded as surprising after the premature death of Edward VI in 1553.

It is hard to know exactly what readership *The Historie of Italie* had, or what influence it had upon later writers. The work does, however, neatly point out the liminal, potentially transgressive, status of the traveller who writes back to his native country and the suspicion with which he was regarded by the authorities, as well as the ways in which he might be transformed himself by the experience.[47] If such a creature possessed knowledge, it was always dangerous knowledge, which could be turned against the state. Even if a traveller set out with the intention of remaining loyal to the authorities he served, experience might change his mind; even if he did manage to remain loyal, his words might mean, or be read, otherwise. And, as Thomas's case demonstrates, loyalty in one reign in sixteenth-century England was often treason in the next.

Although many individual aristocrats did travel abroad during the rest of the Tudor period, inaugurating what was to be called much later 'The Grand Tour', it is noticeable that there was little effort on the part of those closest to the monarch to repeat Henry's experiment of sending a number of young intellectuals to Italy.[48] Travel abroad required a licence issued by the monarch.[49] Large numbers of books were published which gave instructions for would-be travellers, most of which emphasized the need for the traveller to serve his country through his actions.[50] Travel writing as we recognize the genre today, a series of reflections on the places visited (whether these be purely personal observations or possess a wider resonance), or more scholarly and polemical works

---

46 *DNB* entry.
47 On the status of the traveller, see Islam, *Ethics of Travel*, pt. 1.
48 On the development of the concept of 'The Grand Tour', see Intro., n. 28.
49 Howard, *English Travellers of the Renaissance*, 86–7.
50 See the list conveniently compiled, ibid. 205–6.

which owe much to the opening-out of horizons for the articulate citizen, like Thomas's *Historie of Italie*, did not appear in any quantity until the late 1590s.

Why was this? One reason was that until then there had been no intellectual sponsorship of oppositional voices. But with the rise of Robert Devereux, Second Earl of Essex, as a disgruntled ex-royal favourite who was prepared to be associated with a number of intellectual projects inspired by classical republican ideas, the growth of the genre as a form of political opposition in itself was possible. Essex encouraged the development of a Tacitean history in the late 1590s, which emphasized the problems of existing under the rule of a tyrant, a strategy which culminated in the trial of Dr John Hayward for his history of *Henry IV* (1599) in 1601, a work dedicated to Essex and which appeared to make an explicit link between Essex's relationship to Elizabeth and Bolingbroke's to Richard II (as the Queen recognized was common at the time).[51] Hayward's conclusion that Richard's deposition and death were the result of his being 'absolute in power, resolute in will, and dissolute in life', suggests that the same fate may befall the increasingly tyrannical and ineffective Elizabeth, whose later years had seen the growth of a large number of disgruntled voices complaining of her arbitrary government.[52]

The Tacitean mode of writing history owed much to the more recent works of Machiavelli and Guicciardini, providing a convenient series of associations for the English writer between admiration for another political culture and society and the interpretation of the past, a link which recalls the project of William Thomas. A figure who appears to have taken

---

[51] F. J. Levy, 'Hayward, Daniel, and the Beginnings of Politic History in England', *HLQ* 50 (1987), 1–34, at 15–21. Levy points out that Essex may not have known of Hayward before the text was written and that he eventually had the Archbishop of Canterbury remove the dedication to him from unsold copies of the work (16). See also J. H. M. Salmon, 'Stoicism and Roman Empire: Seneca and Tacitus in Jacobean England', *JHI* 50 (1989), 199–225; Erskine-Hill, *Poetry and the Realm of Politics*, 40–3; Clegg, *Censorship in Elizabethan England*, 202–5.

[52] See John Guy, 'Introduction: The 1590s: The Second Reign of Elizabeth I?', in John Guy (ed.), *The Reign of Elizabeth I: Court and Culture in the Last Decade* (Cambridge: Cambridge University Press, 1995), 1–19; Helen Hackett, *Virgin Mother, Maiden Queen: Elizabeth I and the Cult of the Virgin Mary* (Basingstoke: Macmillan, 1995), chs. 6–7.

up the mantle of Thomas—although there is no direct evidence that he had ever read his writings—is Sir Robert Dallington (1561–1637). Dallington was tutor to the Earl of Rutland in the late 1590s, and accompanied him on his tour of France and Italy; both Rutland and Dallington played parts in Essex's rebellion in 1601, the former being punished with an enormous fine.[53]

Dallington wrote a number of works based on his experiences abroad which can be read as highly critical of the political order of the late Elizabethan regime. *The View of France* (1604), based on his visit in 1598 with Rutland, opens with a series of comments which praise liberty and attack the concentration of state power in the hands of a few. Commenting on the complex civil wars in France's recent history, Dallington describes the resulting proliferation of castles as nests of tyrants to the people, and suggests that it is better to destroy them.[54] In an observation which would appear to owe much to Machiavelli's advice to rulers in *The Prince* not to allow the nobility to become too powerful—although also being a Machiavellianism which views events from the perspective of the people rather than the prince—Dallington argues that castles have three malign effects: first, they transform the inhabitants who rely on them for defence into cowards; second, they can foster civil wars when used against the incumbent ruler; and, third, they give too much power to the nobles who use them, who may be encouraged to rebel as a result (D3^r–D4^v).[55] In contrast, Dallington cites the mixed constitution of Venice as the most perfect in the world, and suggests that the frequency with which Venetian citizens change their offices guards against the danger of having to maintain citadels (D4^r). Advice which, when superficially read, could appear to praise rulers is actually targeted at the liberty and welfare of the citizens. Although

53 Levy, 'Beginnings of Politic History', 15. On Dallington, see also Karl Josef Höltgen, 'Sir Robert Dallington (1561–1637): Author, Traveller, and Pioneer of Taste', *HLQ* 47 (1984), 147–77, which, despite its thoroughness, tends to play down Dallington's political ideas. See also Roy Strong, *Henry, Prince of Wales and England's Lost Renaissance* (London: Thames and Hudson, 1986), 30–1.

54 Sir Robert Dallington, *The View of France* (1604), D3^r. Subsequent references in parentheses in the text.

55 Machiavelli, *The Prince*, 67–8, 124–5.

Dallington explicitly distances England from this analysis by stating that England has far fewer castles than France owing to the relative infrequency of civil wars at home, the criticism of excessive military power amongst a factional nobility and praise of Venice marks the work out as akin to Thomas's, albeit more oblique in approach.[56]

Dallington comments at great length on the French king, Henri IV, claiming that there was 'no Prince in Europe more perfect monarch than he' (E2^r). However, such lavish praise is immediately qualified by criticisms of the French laws which stem from the authority of the monarch. The Salic law is attacked because it was used to cheat the heirs of Edward III from their rights to the French throne, and as a modern invention rather than the ancient custom the French believe it to be (E3). The preambles to other laws are regarded as far too long, obfuscating the desired clarity of the legal process, and Dallington cites the double-edged proverb that evil customs cause good laws (E4^r). A few pages further on he appears to contradict himself when he provides a hostile description of Henri IV as a king who allows people to tell the truth about him to his face, which may be a great quality, but which also leads to the development of factions in the absence of a strong central authority. State secrets should not be exposed, but should be kept hidden to all but the initiated, like the Jewish cabbala or the rites of the druids (H1^r). Similarly, the king is too familiar with his people, which breeds contempt and which, in turn, has resulted in the development of vice at court, especially in the slavish following of fashion (H3^r–I3^v). In contrast, the greater majesty of the English, Polish, and Swedish monarchs is to be preferred (H3^r–H4^v). Elsewhere, Dallington criticizes the Grand Council as too bound up with the private affairs of its members, so that its purpose of serving the state has become obscured (Q4^v). There are frequent attacks on French religion as a divisive, many-headed hydra threatening to engulf any form of order (F4^v); on the nobility of France, for being too

---

[56] On the cult of nobility and military power in Elizabeth's reign, see Richard C. McCoy, *The Rites of Knighthood: The Literature and Politics of Elizabethan Chivalry* (Berkeley: University of California Press, 1989); Mervyn E. James, 'English Politics and the Concept of Honour, 1485–1642', *P. & P.*, Supplement, 3 (1978).

ignorant to rule, so that the state is run by a mixture of lawyers and 'penne and inkhorne' gentlemen (S3^r); and on the French commons, who are blunt and outspoken, so that they are most disloyal and unlawful, an excess of liberality which detracts from the majesty of the prince (T1^v).

Although the book concludes that England is a golden mean between France and Italy (X2^v), it is clear that *The View of France* asks a number of questions about what was and was not legitimate to observe in a country, and what a state should allow its own people to know. The criticisms of France suggest that matters are run too openly there, and that the mysteries of state have become openly circulated and hence devalued. However, there is the problem as to how one can correct this fault without further exacerbating the problem, acknowledged in Dallington's apology for including the warts of the king to his readers (H1^v).

The work announces wide reading in contemporary authorities on political history; much is taken from Jean Bodin, which would account for the apparently absolutist thrust of the argument at times.[57] Equally importantly, Dallington owes much to Florentine republican theory: Machiavelli is cited on a number of occasions, but, more often, the authority used to supplement an (apparent) observation is Guicciardini, a key writer for the political thinkers who gravitated towards Essex and whose writings Dallington made extensive use of and did much to promote (see below). Guicciardini's writings provided a convenient link between many interrelated ideas, and were massively influential in Elizabethan and Stuart England from 1560 onwards, when they were first made available.[58] His *History of Italy* provided the most useful recent example for an English audience of a Tacitean history, critical of the excessive powers of single rulers, but also acknowledging that the past was too complex to be reduced to a series of moral lessons.[59] Guicciardini was also noted as a champion of the Venetian

---

[57] See Julian H. Franklin, *Jean Bodin and the Rise of Absolutist Theory* (Cambridge: Cambridge University Press, 1973); Erskine-Hill, *Poetry and the Realm of Politics*, 32–5 passim; Skinner, *Foundations of Modern Political Thought*, ii. 286–301.

[58] Salmon, 'Stoicism and Roman Example', 201.

[59] Guy, 'The 1590s: The Second Reign of Elizabeth I?', 15–16.

constitution, regarding an aristocratic oligarchy as the best form of government (although elsewhere he was critical of Venetian greed and aloofness from the rest of Italy).[60]

Guicciardini's history had been translated by Geoffrey Fenton as *The Historie of Guicciardini containing the warres of Italie and Other Partes* in 1579, and was reprinted by Richard Field in a handsome folio edition in 1599, between Dallington's visit to France and Italy and the publication of the *View of France*. Although it was dedicated to Elizabeth, praising her as a wise governor who had brought peace and stability to her land after a period of civil wars, as Augustus had done to ancient Rome (sig. Aiii^r), the opening page rendered such praise problematic. The first paragraph argued that lessons could be learnt from history, especially when the subject was the faults of princes whose ambition and pride had led them to neglect and abuse their commonwealths, a faithful rendering of Guicciardini's prefatory words. In the margin a note drew the reader's attention to the essential message: 'How harmful be the errors of princes.'[61] In 1579 it is possible that such a juxtaposition could have seemed relatively innocent; but in 1599, with the Nine Years War in Ireland at its most threatening to the English crown (the Munster Plantation, where Fenton himself had been resident, had just been destroyed by Hugh O'Neill's forces), Elizabeth would not have resembled an Augustan emperor protecting her subjects (assuming that no irony was originally intended here).[62] The republication of the book may have had an even more topical—and aggressive—relevance if Fenton was associated with Essex, which he may have been through his connections to the Boyle family, and, through them,

[60] Gilbert, *Machiavelli and Guicciardini*, ch. 7; Bouwsma, *Venice and the Defense of Republican Liberty*, 57, 69.

[61] *The Historie of Guicciardini Containing the warres of Italie and Other Partes*, trans. Geoffrey Fenton (1599), fo. 1. A useful analysis of Fenton's translation is Rudolf Gottfried's article, 'Geoffrey Fenton's *Historie of Guicciardini*' (Indiana University Publications, Humanities Series, No. 3). I owe this reference to Willy Maley.

[62] For a recent account of the Nine Years' War see Colm Lennon, *Sixteenth-Century Ireland: The Incomplete Conquest* (Dublin: Gill and Macmillan, 1995), 292–302. On the Munster Plantation, see Michael McCarthy-Morrogh, *The Munster Plantation: English Migration to Southern Ireland, 1583–1641* (Oxford: Clarendon Press, 1986), ch. 4; A. J. Sheehan, 'The Overthrow of the Plantation of Munster in October 1598', *The Irish Sword*, 15 (1982–3), 11–22.

with Edmund Spenser, probably patronized by Essex in the late 1590s.[63] Essex was appointed Lord Lieutenant of Ireland in March 1599, where he built up his power base for his subsequent rebellion.[64]

In *The View of France* Dallington analyses the functions of the French general assemblies, concluding that they met to resolve three main tasks: first, when the future was in doubt, to decide the succession; second, when there was sedition to deal with or abuses of offices to correct; and third, to set taxation (Qi^v–Q2^r). The first on its own might explain why the publication of the treatise was delayed until 1604, just after the death of Elizabeth. Furthermore, the date advertised (1598) might be read as an aggressive act, signalling the vacillations of English monarchs in general, their scant regard for the understandable anxieties when the succession was not worked out in the case of there being no obvious heir, and the lack of proper consultation and the use of an agreed public sphere in Elizabeth's later years. Its publication might have seemed well-nigh inflammatory at that time, given how the second point was illustrated. Dallington compared the Assembly at Blois which criticized the king's poor government to that described in Holinshed, which criticized Richard II's government (Q1^r). The precedent of Richard II's overthrow by Bolingbroke (Henry IV) was endlessly invoked by Essex's supporters.[65]

The View of France is not simply caught between two competing sets of authorities; rather, these are signs of a generic confusion or ambiguity which relates it back to Thomas's *Historie of Italie*. On the one hand, the purpose of the traveller/historian is to provide useful information for his fellow countrymen. On the other, how can this take place if to do so is either to risk treason for seditious criticism, or to transform oneself into a time-serving flatterer of tyrants? Thomas's

[63] Willy Maley, *A Spenser Chronology* (Basingstoke: Macmillan, 1994), 91, *passim.*

[64] Maley, *Spenser Chronology*, 81; McCoy, *Rites of Knighthood*, 96.

[65] Levy, 'Hayward, Daniel, and the Beginnings of Politic History', 1–2. Dallington also praises Sir Philip Sidney, Essex's spiritual ancestor (Levy, 'Hayward, Daniel, and the Beginnings of Politic History', p. 9), as the epitome of English nobility (S3^v). On Holinshed's representation of the event, see Patterson, *Reading Holinshed's Chronicles*, 112–17.

history resonates with the confidence of a writer who feels able to participate in the transformation of an imperfect state with the cooperation of a wise and benevolent ruler; Dallington's is a work of sly disguise, where the allegorical message may or may not get past the censors and through to the right readers, and in which the purpose of the exercise is hard to reconstruct.

The book was reprinted in the following year (1605), in a manner which adds to the confusion of both genre and purpose. The title was altered to *A Method for Trauell shewed by Taking the View of France, As it stoode in the yeare of our Lord 1598*, with two additional prefaces; one, a letter 'To all Gentlemen that have travelled', the other, a guide entitled 'A Method for Travell', totalling some eighteen extra pages. The first expressed a solidarity with other travellers and travel writers, and provided a chart explaining how to travel. The second reiterated the common currency of travel-writing manuals, that travel writing was an ancient genre of vast use; that it provided knowledge and service to one's country; that it enabled the lazy subject to leave behind sloth and intemperance and become more useful to the state. On the other side, it warned that innovation could be dangerous in an individual as well as a state; that travellers should be careful not to reveal their religion to strangers, and that they should steer clear of undesirables, such as Jesuits; and that they should also be suspicious of excessive luggage, misleading guidebooks, clothes, and foreign wines, meat, and games such as tennis (A_1^v–C_i^v).

Why exactly had such a preface been added, transforming the expectations of the reader as to the nature of the subsequent text?[66] The answer may be that the original book was so popular that it was reprinted for a wider readership. Equally possible, however, given Dallington's political connections, is the suspicion that he felt that the book had to be disguised because it contained too many subversive comments, which might explain his seemingly innocent comment at the end of 'A Method for Trauell' that the book was a bastard which did not

---

[66] Höltgen points out that Dallington later claimed that both editions had been published without his permission and takes such a protestation at face value, a problematic assumption when dealing with works that are so heavily disguised in purpose ('Sir Robert Dallington', 159).

merit reprinting (C1^r), when it just had been so, in a significantly different manner.

The 1605 edition of Dallington's book now superficially resembled such works as Sir Thomas Palmer's *An essay of the meanes how to make our travailes more profitable* (1606), which produced a number of elablorate Ramist-inspired charts in order to map out the would-be traveller's every move and explain all types of possible and permissible travel.[67] Although Palmer is careful to distinguish travellers from spies 'who are Inquisitors or divers into the behaviours and affectations of men belonging to a State', his work pushes the notion, which opens the epistle to the reader, that the traveller should serve the state, much further towards an acceptance of the status quo than does Dallington (or Thomas).[68] Later travellers are exhorted to be careful not to be taken as spies, but to find out exactly what takes place in the country concerned, including the positions of military installations and any secret inclinations the prince may have (pp. 85–126). Like Dallington, Palmer warns the traveller against the perils of associating with those of a different religion, and is explicit about the distinct reality of becoming an infidel or unbeliever (pp. 8–9). Palmer is also clear that certain groups of people should not be allowed to travel. These include those whose religious affiliations are in doubt (all divines permitted to travel require a state licence) (pp. 11, 23), all women who should be at home (p. 17), and positive law clerks, who may be led to criticize their own legal system and so become dangerous (p. 23).

Whereas Dallington's work is explicitly troubled by the problem of who it is for, who makes up the nation at home who can learn from the observations of the traveller, Palmer is careful to excise any hint of subversion and reduce the risk of the traveller being transformed (which, of course, means that only those who know what they are going to find before they set out can be permitted to travel: hence the prophylactic function of

<hr />

[67] Höltgen, 'Sir Robert Dallington', 159. On the influence of Ramus and his system of logic, see Walter J. Ong, *Ramus, Method, and the Decay of Dialogue: From the Art of Discourse to the Art of Reason* (Cambridge, Mass.: Harvard University Press, 1958).

[68] Palmer, *An essay of the meanes how to make our travailes more profitable*, 5–6, sig.Ai^v. All subsequent references in parentheses in the text.

the charts and the symbolic use of one in the second edition of Dallington's work). Palmer also seeks to control the countries the traveller will be permitted to visit, finding most places more or less acceptable apart from Italy, specifically because it appeals to the desires of most English travellers, being a 'shop of libertie, the which to the affects of men is precious and estimable' (p. 43). Palmer's attack on the malign effects of Italian travel is set out in yet another list, which finds Italy wanting because its climate is not reason enough to go; its speech corrupts; the manners and inclinations of the people are inferior to those at the English court; it is better to read about the various forms of government than to see them; and, finally, the monuments feed the appetites rather than providing knowledge (p. 44). Palmer attacks Rome as the 'Forge of every policie, that setteth Princes at odds' (p. 44) and the 'machiedeuell of euill politickes' (p. 45), continuing his first criticism of the excess of liberty with an attack on Venice for this very reason (p. 125).

Such sentiments contrast with Dallington's praise of Venice for its liberty, and his statement in the preface to A Method for Trauell that he would rather be Italified than Frenchified because the language is more grave and demure than the latter's sudden and bold tongue (B4ʳ). More telling still is the second work which resulted from Dallington's travels, The Survey of the great Dukes State of Tuscany (1605), which is far less inhibited in its attacks on the effects of authoritarian government, and which acknowledges a specific debt to Guicciardini's works.[69] Possibly Dallington's greater boldness here results from the more certain generic tradition he was working within, as one could rely more safely on authorities for another country's history and there was no need to repeat the cliché of using one's experience to serve the state.[70] Furthermore, he articulates little which had not appeared before in Fenton's translation, a position far removed from that faced by William Thomas, who had no precedents to rely on or hide behind.

Dallington's position in The Survey is one which follows

[69] Sir Robert Dallington, The Survey of the Great Dukes State of Tuscany (1605), 1, 3, 11. Subsequent references in parentheses in the text.
[70] Levy describes Dallington's work as 'a blistering condemnation of the tyranny of the Medici Grand Dukes' ('Hayward, Daniel, and the Beginnings of Politic History', 15).

Guicciardini closely. He attacks the malign effects of rule by a prince unfettered by a constitution, criticizing not only the Medici, but also Francesco Sforza (1401–66), ruler of Milan, for his destructive ambition (p. 3), a trait which had damned him in Fenton's version of *The Historie*.[71] Dallington devotes considerable space to the fate of Florence's once-free citizens, describing the heavy burden of taxation they now have to shoulder, contrasting their penury to the relative riches enjoyed in Venice, Ferrara, and also Britain (pp. 46–9); the extensive use of torture and the proliferation of spies (pp. 57–8) (a pointed contrast to Palmer's designs on the traveller's role); and the loss of liberty through the absolute powers assumed by the Duke, who directs all court proceedings and controls magistrates (pp. 56–7).[72]

Dallington also criticizes excessive democracy and the demagogy it fosters, like that which enabled the Medici to assume power and so end any semblance of constitution that Florence had once had (the similarity to the story of the end of the Roman republic is surely not accidental).[73] Dallington alleges that the Medici rose to power through 'insinuate stealing into the peoples good opinions' (p. 35), and contrasts the lack of institutional checks and balances which enabled their coup to take place with the stability of Venice, whose founders and leaders had the wisdom to curb the powers which are infinite in Florence (p. 36). Guicciardini is cited—as he was at the start of Fenton's *Historie*—against the dangers of over-ambition and its inevitable route to tyranny. Once again the clear and aggressive message of an English traveller is that an aristocratic oligarchy is the best form of government, avoiding the twin evils of tyranny and democracy. The further suggestion is that England would benefit from a more Venetian-style government.

Dallington obviously hoped to include himself within the

---

[71] Fenton, trans., *The Historie of Guicciardini*, 2.

[72] Given Dallington's citation of Holinshed elsewhere, this suggests that he might have been familiar with the criticisms of English court procedures in the *Chronicles* and the arguments put forward for the impartial use of evidence; see Patterson, *Reading Holinshed's Chronicles*, ch. 8.

[73] See Andrew Lintott, 'The Crisis of the Republic: Sources and Source-Problems', in J. A. Crook, Andrew Lintott, and Elizabeth Rawson (eds.), *The Cambridge Ancient History*, 12 vols., vol. x: *The Last Age of the Roman Republic, 146–43 BC* (Cambridge: Cambridge University Press, 2nd edition, 1994), 1–15.

oligarchy who would surround the ruler and ensure that the constitution and legal system functioned smoothly. In 1609 he presented a manuscript to Prince Henry of *Aphorismes civill and militarie* taken from the pages of Guicciardini's history.[74] This gesture mirrored not only Guicciardini's own practice of culling maxims from his own work (*Ricordi*), an act which had Tacitean associations, but also the previous efforts of William Thomas to write his way to a position of major influence from a similar political perspective.[75] After Henry's death in November 1612 Dallington transferred his allegiance to Prince Charles, and the work was published in 1613.[76]

The work advertises itself as yet another variant on the 'mirror for princes' tradition, informing Charles in the dedicatory epistle that it will advise him how to be a good king.[77] In the address to the reader Dallington claims that everyone— public ministers, scholars, soldiers—will discover something of value in the following aphorisms (sig.A3^r). The opening maxim warns the prince that states are like bodies, in that their worst illnesses often occur after a long period of health and are all the more dangerous as a result (p. 3); the fifth warns princes not to gamble in politics (p. 7); the sixth points out that even the best princes frequently make errors and so need good councillors to advise them (p. 8), a message confirmed in the thirteenth, which urges the prince not to yield to his passions during consultations (p. 16). A more direct attack on the error of single rule is made in number 9, when Dallington argues that sovereignty is actually very nasty even though it looks good and often requires brutal behaviour to obtain it (p. 11). Number 22 remarks that tyrants will eventually suffer and be caught (p. 30).

---

[74] Prince Henry was the focus of much intellectual activity before his premature death, as authors dedicated a massive number of books to him, many of which challenged the authoritarian stance of his father; see Roy Strong, *Henry, Prince of Wales, passim.* Sir Thomas Palmer's *Essay* was also dedicated to Prince Henry, as Strong points out (46).

[75] On the former point see Salmon, 'Seneca and Tacitus in Jacobean England', 201.

[76] On the history of the publication of the *Aphorismes*, see Höltgen, 'Sir Robert Dallington', 161–7. See also Levy, 'Hayward, Daniel, and the Beginnings of Politic History', 15.

[77] Sir Robert Dallington, *Aphorismes civill and militarie, amplified with authorities* (1613), sig.A3^v. Subsequent references in parentheses in the text.

Although such comments are largely traditional pieces of wisdom, the use of examples from Italian history to illustrate each piece of wisdom, establishing Lodovico Sforza as the main villain, and the key emphasis on the results of a ruler's dereliction of his duties towards his subjects (rather than vice versa) would seem to be a pointed contrast to the focus and style of James's frequently published political writings.[78] Indeed, the *Aphorismes* could be read as a deliberate challenge to James's own advice to his son Prince Henry in *Basilikon Doron* (1598), which argues the case for a monarch answerable only to God.[79] Just as Dallington claimed that he had had no desire to see his work into print, so does James allege that the only reason that he consented to publication was because others got hold of a secret book (pp. 141–2). While Dallington's *Aphorismes* continually emphasize the need to limit the powers of the monarch, James concentrates on the need for the prince to regulate his behaviour and stand as an example to the people who, like apes, will always copy what their superiors present before them (p. 155). James advises Henry to use parliament, the highest court in the land, as little as possible, and then only 'for necessitie of new Lawes' (p. 156), a contrast to Dallington's description of the functioning of assemblies in France or virtually any account of the Venetian constitution written in the previous half-century. Henry is also advised to brook no unfair criticism of the monarch or the royal family, although he does grant that 'wee haue all our faults, which, priuately betwixt you and God, should serue you for examples to meditate upon, and mend in your person'. Henry would be well-advised to 'represse the insolence of such, as under pretence to taxe a vice in the person, seeke craftily to staine the race, and steale the affection of the people from their posteritie' (p. 158). The contrast to Dallington's open criticisms of Henri IV in *The View of France* could hardly be more marked.

[78] For details see *STC*, ii. pp. 18–21.

[79] *Basilikon Doron* in James I, *The Workes* (1616) (Hildesham and New York: Verlag, 1971), 137–92, at 148. Subsequent references in parentheses in the text. For a recent re-evaluation of James's political views in the light of developments in England in the late 1590s, see Jenny Wormald, 'Ecclesiastical Vitriol: The Kirk, The Puritans and the Future King of England', in Guy (ed.), *The Reign of Elizabeth I*, 171–91, at 185.

James advises Henry to make use of 'authenticke histories and Chronicles' where he shall 'learne experience by Theoricke, applying the bypast things to the present estate', precisely the point of Dallington's distillation of Guicciardini's writing. However, Henry should avoid the 'infamous inuectiues' of Buchanan and Knox's histories, which need to be suppressed by legal means: 'and if any of these infamous libels remaine untill your dayes, use the Law upon the keepers thereof' (p. 176). Buchanan was an influential figure within the Sidney circle, precisely the sort of constitutional theorist who made up the intellectual milieu of a writer such as Dallington, as was Knox.[80] Once again, reasons for the oblique approach and disguised nature of Dallington's political advice become apparent.

Although James did not publish *A Remonstrance for the Right of Kings, and the independence of their crowns*, his longest exposition of his defence of the divine rights of kings, until 1615, his political position could not have been hidden from anyone writing before that date. In *The Trew Law of Free Monarchies* (1598), James argued that monarchy was the form of government 'resembling the Diuinitie, approacheth nearest to perfection', because it espoused the ideal of unity.[81] James articulates a position which denies the rights of subjects to resist a monarch who has become a tyrant; using a series of biblical examples, he suggests that the only legitimate course for the disaffected is to retreat into exile (p. 199). A wicked king is simply a punishment from God for a sinful people (p. 206). Against those who argue that the king is subject to the laws, James asserts that the king is above them because kings preceded parliaments: 'it followes of necessitie, that the kings were the authors and makers of the Lawes, and not the Lawes of the kings' (p. 201). Parliament cannot make law without the permission and power of the king, so that parliament is no more than an advisory body, the conservative constitutional position since the reign of Henry VIII, but one which had

[80] James E. Phillips, 'George Buchanan and the Sidney Circle', *HLQ* 12 (1948–9), 23–55.
[81] James I, *The Trew Law of Free Monarchies*, in *The Workes*, 193–210, at 193. All subsequent references in parentheses in the text.

become significantly more prominent in the 1590s (the concomitant radical position was that the monarch could not exercise sovereignty without the assent of parliament, as the monarch only existed as monarch in parliament).[82] According to James, the monarch made no contract with his people at his coronation (pp. 207–8) and ruled over his subjects as a caring father, 'so as he is Master ouer euery person that inhabiteth the same, hauing power ouer the life and death of euery one of them' (p. 203).

That this was an aggressive attack on common-law theorists and the radical Protestant tradition of asserting the rights of the multitude against an over-mighty sovereign is clear.[83] It is also significant that James feels the need to attack the partisans of the Venetian Constitution as further deluded radicals. He argues that, contrary to appearances, hereditary monarchs actually represent a truer ideal of freedom than 'elective kings' because they can protect the rights and desires of ordinary subjects far better than other constitutions, inspire greater obedience, and hence, unite the state in question: 'I meane alwaies of such free Monarchies as our king is, and not of elective kings, and much lesse of such sort of gouernors, as the dukes of *Venice* are, whose Aristocratick and limited gouernment, is nothing like to free Monarchies' (p. 203).

James is obviously far less aggressive towards such thinkers than those who would place power with the 'headlesse multitude' (p. 208). However, it is significant that he feels the need to support his argument by mentioning Venice as a dangerous alternative form of government, indicating the common currency of its myth in British political thought in late Tudor and early Stuart Britain. The most significant expression of this

[82] Guy, 'The Second Reign of Elizabeth I?', 12–14. See also Geoffrey Elton (ed.), *The Tudor Constitution: Documents and Commentary* (Cambridge: Cambridge University Press, 1972), chs. 1, 9; Penry Williams, *The Tudor Regime* (Oxford: Clarendon Press, 1979), 399–405.

[83] See J. G. A. Pocock, *The Ancient Constitution and the Feudal Law: A Study of English Historical Thought in the Seventeeth Century* (Cambridge: Cambridge University Press, rev. ed., 1987), ch. 2; Michael Walzer, *The Revolution of the Saints: A Study in the Origins of Radical Politics* (Cambridge, Mass.: Harvard University Press, 1965); Patrick Collinson, *The Elizabethan Puritan Movement* (Oxford: Clarendon Press, 1967); A. G. Dickens, *The English Reformation* (Glasgow: Collins, 1986, rpt. of 1964), 318–30, 425–37, *passim*.

myth, for English-speaking readers at least, was Gaspar Contarini's *De Magistratibus et Republica Venetorum*, which had been published in 1543. The work was translated by Lewis Lewkenor in 1599, as *The Commonwealth and Government of Venice*, so it is exactly contemporary with James's two texts.

The publication of Lewkenor's translation also coincided with a series of moves by the authorities in England to suppress dissent and oppositional voices, and in particular to stop the use of English history as a means of criticizing the present. In June 1599 the Archbishop of Canterbury and the Bishop of London instructed the Master and Wardens of the Stationers' Company to prevent the publication of verse satires and epigrams. As Richard McCabe has pointed out, such a move was not simply designed to combat pornography, as has often been assumed, but was aimed to limit the uses of both related genres for political purposes. The discontent fostered by Elizabeth's increasingly distant and autocratic government, as well as the uncertainty as to what sort of regime would follow her death, had led to the rapid expansion of literary and historical genres as forums for political debate and for the expression of hostile views which had been excluded from more obviously public channels.[84] A Royal Proclamation of 1601 offered £100 to anyone providing information against those who slandered the royal person; a lawyer's clerk was hanged for this offence in February of the same year.[85] The same decree also stipulated that all histories must be approved by a member of the Privy Council before publication, a rule appearing in the immediate wake of the case resulting from Dr John Hayward's *The First Part of the Life and Raigne of King Henrie IIII* (see above, p. 33).[86]

Lewkenor himself was a government official. He served in Spain, translated a number of Spanish and Italian books, and

---

[84] This is the general argument of my *Literature, Politics and National Identity*.

[85] Richard A. McCabe, 'Elizabethan Satire and the Bishops' Ban of 1599', *YES* 11 (1981), 188–93. See also David Loades, 'The Theory and Practice of Censorship in Sixteenth-Century England', *TRHS*, 5th ser., 24 (1974), 141–57, 155–7; Patterson, *Censorship and Interpretation*, 47; Clegg, *Press Censorship in Elizabethan England*, 202–5.

[86] Clare, *'Art Made Tongue-Tied by Authority'*, 61–2.

later served as master of ceremonies under James I. He was also an acquaintance of Sir Robert Dallington, who dedicated some verses to him, prefacing his translation of Olivier de la Marche's *The Resolued Gentleman* (1594), and he received a dedicatory sonnet from Edmund Spenser which prefaced his translation of Contarini.[87] Both these details would seem to place him within Essex's circle.

However, the only book which actually appears in Lewkenor's name—although it is clear that he added much to many of his translations—was *A Discourse of the Usage of the English Fugitives by the Spaniard* (1595).[88] This work, which may have been published by a correspondent of Lewkenor's without his knowledge, is presented as an anti-travel work in the tradition of Ascham's famous criticism of the corrupting pointlessness of travel, as well as a means of dissuading would-be defectors to the Spanish court by one who has experienced their cruelty and treachery first-hand. The opening letter argues that all the anticipated pleasures of travel will prove to be vain and foolish, and that he hopes that Leweknor's text will prove to be a mirror to dissuade young men from being tempted by the spurious benefits of visiting foreign lands.[89]

Lewkenor's text is a contribution to the 'Black Legend', the defamation of Spain which was propagated in its most virulent form in the post-Armada years.[90] The Spanish are accused in it of a multitude of sins: they treat their own soldiers badly (B4); they are pagans and heathens (E3^r–E4^v); they commit sodomy, blasphemy, and murder (E4^v); their political society is riven by factions (D3^v); there is massive starvation owing to harvest failures (H2^r). But the main problem is the nature of Spanish society and its violent oppression of its own people, who are not only brutalized by authority, but live in constant fear of spies

---

[87] Garrett Mattingly, *Renaissance Diplomacy* (Harmondsworth: Penguin, 1965, rpt. of 1955), 248; Höltgen, 'Sir Robert Dallington', 159.

[88] An expanded version exists, entitled *The Estate of the English Fugitives under the king of Spaine and his ministers*, also published in 1595.

[89] Sir Lewis Lewkenor, *A Discourse of the Usage of the English Fugitives by the Spaniard* (1595), sig. A3^r–B1^v. Subsequent references in parentheses in the text.

[90] William S. Maltby, *The Black Legend in England: The Development of Anti-Spanish Sentiment, 1558-1660* (Durham, NC: Duke University Press, 1971), 93. See also Carol Z. Weiner, 'The Beleaguered Isle: A Study of Elizabethan and Early Jacobean anti-Catholicism', *P. & P.* 51 (1971), 27–62.

and the Inquisition (F3^v–G4^v). Although English Catholics believe that the laws in England punish them too severely, they would suffer even more as loyal subjects in Spain (F2^r–F3^v). Spain is a land of despair engendered by the Jesuits throughout the country (F3^v); at court the smiles of the courtiers disguise a constant fear in their hearts (D1^v).

A Discourse of the Usage of the English Fugitives would appear to be a straightforwardly patriotic text in terms of the contrast it establishes between England as a land of liberty and Spain as a land of oppression, right down to the conclusion that travel should only be undertaken in order to discover military knowledge and state secrets for one's own government (although this task is too dangerous in the present climate) (K2). Such an interpretation is made less secure if the text is read alongside Lewkenor's translation of Contarini. The opening pages mark the work out as a celebration of an alternative political, cultural, and aesthetic tradition, one whose success reflects badly on the current state of England; in other words, very much in the tradition of English representations of Venice. The inclusion of a map of the city, providing the reader with a view into Venice as a contemporary traveller approaching the city from the sea would have seen it, perhaps makes visible William Thomas's sense of awe on his first encounter (see above, p. 27), a message elaborated in the writings which preface the text proper.

The dedicatory letter to Anne Russell, Countess of Warwick, which prefaces *The Commonwealth and Gouernment of Venice*, would seem to suggest that Lewkenor's translation has a subversive intent, if read carefully.[91] Lewkenor describes Venice as a 'beautifull virgine, that seeing her faire picture fouely handled of an unskilfull painter, blush at the view of her wronged beauty'.[92] He urges Anne 'to be a gentle and propitious

---

[91] Anne was the daughter of Francis Russell, earl of Bedford (1527?–85), who had been imprisoned by Mary for his support of Lady Jane Grey. She was the widow of Ambrose Dudley, earl of Warwick (c.1528–90), and a prominent member of the Leicester circle, being close to the Sidneys and the Devereux. For details see Katherine Duncan-Jones, *Sir Philip Sidney: Courtier Poet* (New Haven: Yale University Press, 1991), 11–13; Rosemary O'Day, *The Longman Companion to the Tudor Age* (Harlow: Longman, 1995), 186–7, 214.

[92] Lewis Lewkenor, *The Commonwealth and Gouernment of Venice. Written by the Cardinall Gasper Contareno* (1599), fo. 2. Subsequent references in parentheses in the text.

defendresse to this renowned Commonwealth, that nothing more desireth then to bee gracious in your sight, and here frankely offreth unto your view the naked full discouerie of her faire and beautifull lineaments, not unconcealing any part of her rarest perfections' (fos. 2–3). He hopes that since Venice is to be brought into England, she 'may haue free and quiet passage' under Anne's protection.

Such comments might appear fairly standard representations of the state as a woman who has to be governed by men, a language James I was using explicitly or implicitly in the contemporary *Basilikon Doron*.[93] In the context of the late 1590s, with the frequently sardonic references in literary texts and theatrical performances to the conspicuous ageing of the virgin queen, it is hard not to observe a pointed contrast between the beauty of the naked Venice and the decaying appearance of Elizabeth.[94] The emphasis on the naked beauty of Venice provides a pointed contrast to Elizabeth's need for disguise to protect the last vestiges of her cult. Furthermore, she, Anne, is a lady protected by another lady, but, also obviously desired by men, who would seem to represent her as a combination of Diana and Venus, going one stage beyond the cult of Elizabeth.[95]

This reading might seem far-fetched, but it is corroborated in the dedicatory sonnet by J. Ashley, where exactly the same comparison is made. Ashley compares the virgin state of Venice to that of England, ruled by the virgin queen:

> In all this space of thirteene hundred yeares,
> Thy virgins state ambition nere could blot.
> Now I prognosticate thy ruinous case,
> When thou shalt from thy Adriatique seas,
> View in this Oceans Isle thy painted face,
> In these pure colours coyest eyes to please,
> Then gazing in thy shadows peerless eye,
> Enamour'd like *Narcissus* thou shalt dye.

93 James I, *Basilikon Doron*, 173.
94 See Hackett, *Virgin Mother, Maiden Queen*, ch. 6. Hackett notes that 'we should be cautious about reading idealisations of the Queen at face value' (163).
95 On representations of Elizabeth as Venus and Diana, see Philippa Berry, *Of Chastity and Power: Elizabethan Literature and the Unmarried Queen* (London: Routledge, 1989). Like Elizabeth, Anne Russell remained childless (Duncan-Jones, *Sir Philip Sidney*, 11).

Ostensibly the comparison is one of straightforward patriotic flattery: when Venice sees England she will see herself reflected as in a mirror, as Narcissus did his own reflection.[96] But the Ovidian comparison is troubling in a number of ways, not least because of the sad fate of Narcissus, who faded away as a result of his self-obsession.[97] The poem is perhaps as much a *memento mori* as a celebration of England's triumph, especially if read alongside the great wealth of literary works written in the 1590s which lamented the decline and impending death of the virgin queen.[98] Here, it is Venice which is about to die after 'thirteene hundred yeares', but surely a reader would have suspected that it was England's virgin queen who was the more likely to expire in 1599 than the Venetian republic? This had, after all, not only survived for over a thousand years already, but had also been part of a coalition which had won a major victory over the Turks, its main rivals for control of the Mediterranean, at the battle of Lepanto just under 30 years before, thus ensuring its survival as Europe's link to the riches of the east.[99] Read this way, Ashley's poem exposes the problems of a state's reliance on a mortal ruler rather than a written constitution; so that the 'ruinous case' is actually that of the 'painted face' of Elizabeth, not unconquered Venice.

The sonnet by Edmund Spenser, published posthumously and included alongside three other dedicatory poems on the sheet following, casts Venice as the third Babel which shall eclipse the first ('The antique *Babel*, Empresse of the East') and the second ('tyrant of the West'), clearly meaning Rome. In the context of Spenser's own published work, the implication is that Venice resembles Una, whose 'Royall lynage' 'stretched from East to Westerne shore', a pointed contrast to Duessa who was 'Borne the sole daughter of an Emperour, / He that the

[96] For such a reading, see Erskine-Hill, *Poetry and the Realm of Politics*, 122–3.

[97] Ovid, *Metamorphoses*, trans. Mary M. Innes (Harmondsworth: Penguin, 1955), 83–7.

[98] For details see Hackett, *Virgin Mother, Maiden Queen*, chs. 6–7.

[99] See Erskine-Hill, *Poetry and the Realm of Politics*, 120. For details of Venice's economic significance for the rest of Europe, see Lisa Jardine, *Worldly Goods* (London: Macmillan, 1996), *passim*.

wide West under his rule has'.[100] Just as Una geographically eclipses her limited rival, so does Venice eclipse hers, and, more to the point, appears to replace the symbol of Englishness as the apotheosis of earthly virtue ('Fayre *Venice*, flower of the last worlds delight').[101] In the 'Two Cantos of Mutabilitie', not published until 1609, Spenser represented the naked Queen cruelly exposed to the ravages of time:

Euen you faire *Cynthia*, whom so much ye make
Ioues dearest darling . . .
Then is she mortall borne, how-so ye crake;
Besides, her face and countenance euery day
We changed see, and sundry forms partake,
Now hornd, now round, now bright, now brown and gray:
So that *as changefull as the Moone* men use to say.

VII. vii. 50.

The lines, with the comparison in the last emphatically emphasized in the text, strike a hit at Elizabeth's vacillating political authority as well as her age.[102] It is possible that Lewkenor had seen a manuscript copy of Spenser's text; Lodowick Bryskett's *A Discourse of Civill Life* and comments by Gabriel Harvey attest that *The Faerie Queene* circulated in manuscript before its publication in 1590, as did *A View of the Present State of Ireland*.[103] Whatever the truth of such speculations, it is clear that the inclusion of Spenser among the writers of dedicatory

---

[100] Edmund Spenser, *The Faerie Queene*, ed. A. C. Hamilton (London: Longman, 1977), I, i. 5; I, ii. 22. Subsequent references to this edition in parentheses in the text.

[101] Venice appears in an apocalyptic context ('the last worlds delight'), replacing the role of England in *The Faerie Queene*; see Florence Sandler, 'The Faerie Queene: An Elizabethan Apocalypse', in C. A. Patrides and Joseph Wittreich (eds.), *The Apocalypse in English Renaissance Thought and Literature: Patterns, Antecedents and Repercussions* (Manchester: Manchester University Press, 1984), 148–74.

[102] Berry, *Of Chastity and Power*, 163–5; Hackett, *Virgin Mother, Maiden Queen*, 193.

[103] Lodowick Bryskett, *A Discourse of Civill Life* (1606), 26; Virginia F. Stern, *Gabriel Harvey: His Life, Marginalia and Library* (Oxford: Clarendon Press, 1979), 56; Josephine Waters Bennett, *The Evolution of 'The Faerie Queene'* (Chicago: Chicago University Press,1942), ch. 1; Andrew Hadfield, 'An Allusion to Spenser's Writings: Matthew Lownes and Ralph Byrchensa's *A Discourse occasioned on the late defeat given to the Arch-rebels, Tyrone and Odonnell* (1602)', *N. & Q.* n.s. 44 (1997), 478–80.

verse served further to label Lewkenor's book as a work of political criticism, given the hostility of the second edition of *The Faerie Queene* (1596) towards the cult of Elizabeth and, more ominously, perhaps, the offence it caused James I through the representation of his mother, Mary Queen of Scots, in Book V.[104]

The letter 'To the Reader' opens with words which seem to predict Othello's wooing of Desdemona through his travellers' tales (see below, pp. 227–8). Lewkenor asserts that there is no description 'that doth more beautifie the speaker or delight the hearer, then the description of forreine regions, the manners & customs of farre distant countries, the diuersitie of their complections, humor, diet and attire, and such other singularities' (A1).[105] Wise travellers can use such knowledge to further their own countries' good (A1ᵛ). Such sentiments are the staple fare of conservative travel discourse, placing the writer as a loyal servant of his regime. The following page qualifies this relationship through its assertion that no matter what any traveller has seen, 'though sundrie of them had been in the farthest parts of *Asia* and *Affrica*, yet comming once to speake of the cittie of *Venice*, they would inforce their speech to the highest of admiration, as being of the greatest worthinesse, and most infinitely remarkable, that they had seen in the course of their trauels' (A2). Again, unless Lewkenor is writing in a vacuum, the precedent appears to have been set by William Thomas's description of his ecstatic revelations—a moment repeated in the opening lines of the text proper (B1ᵛ)—even though Lewkenor confesses that he has never actually been to the city (A2ᵛ); like his predecessor, he finds the political and legal institutions of Venice to be its most praiseworthy aspects. The mixed constitution makes up the best government in the world:

---

[104] See T. H. Cain, *Praise in* The Faerie Queene (Nebraska: University of Nebraska Press, 1978), ch. 6; Richard A. McCabe, 'The Masks of Duessa: Spenser, Mary Queen of Scots and James VI', *ELR* 17 (1987), 224–42. Through the English secretary in Scotland, Robert Bowes, James demanded that Spenser be tried and punished for his offence. Bowes wrote to Burghley that he had managed to convince James that the poem had not been 'passed with privilege of Her Majesty's Commissioners'; cited in Maley, *Spenser Chronology*, 67–8.

[105] Lewkenor's translation has often been suggested as a source for Shakespeare's play, most recently in Mark Matheson, 'Venetian Culture and the Politics of *Othello*', *Sh. Sur.* 48 (1995), ed. Stanley Wells, 123–33, at 124.

the prince is 'wholy subiected to the lawes'; the council of senators are the most 'perfect and liuely pattern of a well-ordered Aristocraticall gouernment' in the world, because they 'haue not any power, mean, or possibility at all to tyranize, or to peruert their Country lawes'; the great council is 'a most rare and matchlesse president of a Democrasie or popular estate'; wherever the traveller turns his eyes, he will see justice and harmony (A3ʳ). The letter concludes with a direct link between the city-state of Venice and England:

the rest of the whole world honoureth her wyth the name of a Virgin, a name though in all places most sacred & venerable, yet in no place more dearely, and religiously to bee reuerenced, then with us, who haue thence derived our blessednesse, which I beseech God may long continue among us. (A4ᵛ)

William Thomas provided a historical link between the Venetians and the British or English; both peoples, he claimed, had been established in the wake of the diaspora following the Trojan War. Lewkenor provides a similar connection, suggesting that the virgin of England—or rather, her representatives—should copy the political and legal example of the virgin of Venice.

Lewkenor's translation, as has been noted, includes more than just Contarini's text. He also added selections from various other works: Donato Giannotti's *Libro de la Republica di Venetiani* and Sebastian Muenster's *Cosmographiae Universalis*, as well as extracts from the writings of the fifteenth-century humanist historian Bernardo Giustiniani, Sansovino's *Venetia citta nobilissima*, and a popular guidebook entitled *Delle cose notabili della citta di Venetia*. As a result, the book produced does more than simply praise the Venetian constitution (although this is its first purpose, as its early sections demonstrate); it also provides the means for curious tourists to visit the city, and for other writers to grasp its significance, presenting a whole package designed to make Venice of central significance in English cultural and political life.[106] Lewkenor also significantly modified his translation of

---

[106] David McPherson, 'Lewkenor's Venice and Its Sources', *RQ* 41 (1988), 459–66.

Contarini, making an already laudatory work even more cele-
bratory of Venetian civic values.[107]

As John Pocock has pointed out, what makes Venice pre-
eminent for Lewkenor and Contarini is not the inherent virtue
of its citizens but the regulatory effects of the institutional
framework they have constructed. It is 'an artificial angel', the
miracle of human endeavour described by William Thomas
above, struggling against the ravages of time—like Elizabeth—
and constantly having to guard against decay (but succeeding,
unlike Elizabeth).[108] The five books of Contarini's text provide,
in order, a general description of the benefits of the commonwealth; a description of the duties of the Doge (Duke) and his
councillors; the senate of 120 and the legal system; the financial
workings of the state; and government over other cities. In
essence, Contarini/Lewkenor's work presents a more detailed
picture of Venice than William Thomas's, but the basic thrust of
the argument is the same. Venice is the perfect constitution as it
has the correct balance of aristocracy, monarchy, and popular
assembly (p. 37); factionalism is avoided, as all participate in the
government of the state (p. 8); important offices and duties are
spread around, so that no one can build up a dangerous power
base (p. 33); tyranny and popular sedition are avoided (p. 11);
the laws are impartial and just (p. 25); taxes are reasonable and
fair (p. 109); and foreigners are so impressed that they flock to
the city as a haven of virtue (p. 147).

The only difference between the two is one of emphasis:
while Thomas is confident that his perceptions will assume an
importance in discussions of state, Lewkenor's work is more
aggressive and oppositional, its disguised hints designed to
focus the attention of critics and would-be reformers on an
alternative model of government. Near the start of the opening
book the stability of Venice is praised, standing out against the
calamities which have befallen the rest of Italy. What makes
Venice so successful is the fact that, while it has been materially
and politically successful, 'men enjoy a happie and quiet life'.
Beside this Lewkenor places a marginal annotation: 'Venice
hath remained untouched from the violence of any enemy since

[107] Pocock, *Machiavellian Moment*, 321.
[108] Ibid. 324; McPherson, 'Lewkenor's Venice', 461.

the first building there of, which is aboue 1100 yeares' (p. 5). The contrast with the England of religious faction described in *A Discourse of the Usage of the English Fugitives by the Spaniard* could hardly be more pointed. That work was designed to urge English Catholics to remain loyal out of self-interest, a clear understanding that the country was riven by the factions Venice has apparently managed to avoid.

A few pages further on there are two long marginal annotations which need to be considered carefully. The text attacks the notion of monarchy as a means of government because it concentrates power in the hands of one ruler (a message the work repeats again and again as a strength of Venice): 'And truely to me it seemeth exceedingly well and wisely said of them, that deemed the gouernment of men to bee unfitly granted to one alone, but that there should bee a thing more diuine to whom this office should be giuen, as out of many sorts of creatures may be gatherd' (pp. 9–10). A long marginal note contradicts this judgement:

Now soeuer the successe hath allowed the gouernment of Venice, either in regard of the smalnesse of their territory, or the strong situation of their citie: yet there was neuer any example of any other great commonwealth but that did soone perish by the plurality of commande: all great philosophers chiefly extolling the monarchy; & all course of times & examples confirming their opinion. (p. 10)

This contradiction places a considerable interpretative burden on the reader. What is the message of the text? Who is really speaking here? It seems hard to believe that the true voice of Lewkenor is that of the marginal annotator. It is simply not true to assert that all philosophers have recommended monarchy as the best form of government; Aristotle, who is cited on the following page because he could not find a more appropriate image of God than 'an authenticke law in a Citie rightly gouerned' (pp. 11–12), did not recommend monarchy in the *Politics*, but aristocracy, a form of constitution like Venice; Lewkenor's proximity to the Essex circle would certainly have alerted him to the existence of and contemporary admiration for republican Rome. Although it is possible that the annotation contains a serious point concerning the need for decisions to be made by one figure and not an endless number of councils, it would surely not have escaped the readers of *The*

Commonwealth and Government of Venice that this is what actually happens in Venice. The point is not that such power is frustrated or circumvented in Venice, but that the prince cannot become a tyrant because of the checks and balances exerted on his behaviour (p. 42). In fact, half way through the text Lewkenor/Contarini describes the beheading of the Duke, Marino Phalerio, because he had 'turned all his thoughtes to tiranny and usurpation, was likely to haue giuen a great & deadly blow to the liberty of our commonwealth' (p. 81). Only the prompt intervention of one of the chief groups of aristocratic advisers, the college of ten, saves the republic. Lewkenor's own text gives examples of the need to control the sovereign's autocratic urges, again making the marginal note on p. 10 hard to take at face value, especially as the example of Marino Phalerio, too, is highlighted by its own annotation.

Further down the page in question, Lewkenor/Contarini compounds the problem of the disclaimer. The text argues that 'euil shal that commonwealth be prouided for, that shal be committed to the gouernment of a man', because the body of one individual can become corrupted; instead, the mind, in the form of good laws agreed upon by many, should govern the state (pp. 10–11). The marginal note points to the importance of government being an active affair, as it is man's nature and right to govern: 'That ought amongest men to obtaine the place of gouernment and rule, which is in man highest, & of greatest participation with divinitie' (p. 10). The implication is that no state can be approved of by God if it does not actively solicit the participation of its citizens. Furthermore, it is monarchy, not democracy or aristocracy, which is regarded as the essentially unstable form of government:

And though in the opinion of many men, the kingly domination is of the highest esteeme and greatest account . . . if the matter be by it selfe considered, shoulde seeme of all other the best, yet in regarde of the breuitie of life, and mans fraile disposition, which for the most parte enclineth to the worser parte, the gouernment of the multitude is farre more conuenient to the assemblie of citizens, which experience the mistresse of all thinges doth elegantly teach us, because that wee haue not read that there was among auncientes any soverainty of a king, neyther haue wee in our time seene any that had not soone declyned into tiranny [.] (p. 13)

That this exactly reverses the earlier marginal annotation on monarchy is clear. The point being made is that the flesh of the monarch is weak; only placing sovereignty in the citizens can enable the government of the mind to flourish. Considered one way, this is the doctrine of the 'king's two bodies' read against the monarch.[109] The appeal to the historical record of both ancients and moderns serves to highlight the attack on the efficacy of monarchy and the republican sub-text of the translation. Monarchy will sooner or later degenerate into tyranny; perhaps in England in 1599 it already had.

A writer who made a similar use of Venice in the following reign was Thomas Coryat, who, at his own insistence and with a great deal of effort, published what was the first self-consciously styled work of English travel writing, *Coryat's Crudities*, in 1611, describing his observations of France, Savoy, Italy, Switzerland, Germany, and the Netherlands.[110] Coryat's book led to the publication of a number of other similar works in the reign of James I; Fynes Moryson, the start of whose travels predated Coryat's, produced his massive *An Itinerary, containing his Ten yeeres Travell through the Twelve Dominions* (1617); George Sandys, *A Relation of a Iourney begun An: 1610, Foure Books. Containing a description of the Turkish Empire, of Ægypt, of the Holy Land, of the Remote parts of Italy, and Islands adioyning* (1615); and William Lithgow, *The totall discourse of the rare adventures and painefull perigrations of long nineteen years travel* (1614, rev. ed., 1632).[111] Although Coryat's book includes a translation of Hermannus Kirchnerus's *An Oration . . . That young men ought to Travell into forainne Countryes*, a work which repeats many of the standard sentiments of sixteenth-century advice to

[109] For elaboration see Ernst H. Kantorowicz, *The King's Two Bodies: A Study in Medieval Political Theology* (Princeton: Princeton University Press, 1957); Marie Axton, *The Queen's Two Bodies: Drama and the Elizabethan Succession* (London: Royal Historical Society, 1977).

[110] *Coryat's Crudities, Hastily gobled up in five Monethes travells in France, Savoy, Itlay, Rhetia commonly called the Grisons country, Helvetia alias Switzerland, some parts of high Germany and the Netherlands; Newly digested in the hungry aire of Somerset, and now dispersed to the nourishment of the travelling Members of this Kingdome* (1611), (rpt. Glasgow: Maclehose, 1905, 2 vols.). All subsequent references to this edition in parentheses in the text.

[111] For details see Stoye, *English Travellers Abroad, passim.*

travellers, including the argument that they are better able to serve their princes because they can give them more useful advice (pp. 135–6), the book itself bears little resemblance to what had gone before.[112]

Indeed, it is hard to place *Coryat's Crudities* in any previously established generic form, a fact which is apparent to even the most casual reader who picks up the book. The title itself is eccentric and bears little relation to the contents, apart from the joke on the rawness of the writing as merely an *hors d'oeuvre* for what is to follow (Coryat died in India in 1617 while travelling in Asia; a subsequent work, designed to cash in on his fame, was entitled *Coryat's Crambe*, meaning 'cabbage', a plain dish to succeed the *crudités*).[113] The account of the travels is preceded by a complex frontispiece containing a number of incidents from the journey: 'An Explication of the Emblemes of the Frontispice', by Laurence Whitaker, 'certaine other Verses, as Charmes to unlocke the mystery of the Crudities', by Ben Jonson, a dedicatory epistle to Henry, Prince of Wales, an epistle to the reader, 'The Character of the Famous Odcombian, or rather Polytopian Thomas the Coryate' and an acrostic on the author's name, both by Ben Jonson, and an enormous number of 'panegyrick verses' from various writers celebrated and obscure, all of which makes up about a sixth of the complete text of the *Crudities*.

This material has been almost universally ignored by commentators, who have been more than happy to take Coryat at face value as the bizarre buffoon he represents himself to be.[114] Jonson's 'character of the author' portrays him as an obscure provincial through the mock-heroic motif of the attachment of his place of birth: 'Famous Odcombian' is an oxymoronic pairing, emphasizing the humble origins to which the author has, significantly enough, apparently returned. The description emphasizes the pointlessness of Coryat's travels:

---

[112] Howard, *English Travellers of the Renaissance*, 30–9.

[113] For the most comprehensive account of Coryat's life see Michael Strachan, *The Life and Adventures of Thomas Coryate* (London: Oxford University Press, 1962). On the titles, see Bate, 'Elizabethans in Italy', 60.

[114] See e.g. Howard, *English Travellers of the Renaissance*, 20; Strachan, *Life and Adventures of Thomas Coryate*, ch. 9; Sells, *The Paradise of Travellers*, 167; Stoye, *English Travellers Abroad*, 3.

'The word Travaile affectes him in a Waine-oxe, or a Packe-horse. A carrier will carry him from any company that hath not been abroad, because he is a Species of a Traveller. But a Dutch-post doth ravish him. The mere subscription of a letter from Zurich sets him up like a top: Basil or Heidelberg makes him spin' (i. 17). The contrast to the gravity with which arguments for the purpose of travel had been hitherto presented could not be more marked.[115] Jonson makes the author and the purpose of his journey appear thoroughly mindless: a whole series of jokes are made about the wind the author produces as an index of his wordy text, deliberately uniting man and book (i. 18).

The series of jokes is continued in the vast collection of 'Panegyrick Verses'. In his introduction to these, Coryat represents himself as a pompous and jovial fool, inventing new words which he expects the reader to find bemusing and which do not appear to add much to the text. He boasts that no book printed in England in the last hundred years has had as many dedicatory verses 'composed by persons of eminent quality and marke' who 'have vouchsafed to descend so low as to dignifie and illustrate my lucubrations without any merit of theirs (I do confesse) with the singular fruits of their elegant inventions' (a somewhat tautologous note offers the plea: 'Mistake me not reader. I referre this word to the word Lucubrations') (i. 20). The verses themselves, however, are often extremely rude and disrespectful to Coryat, giving the impression that there has been something of a pact between author and his circle (unless Coryat really is as odd as the text implies, and he has totally failed to spot any of the ironies). One of the first opens with a double-edged comparison:

> Old wormy age that in thy mustie writs
> Of former fooles records the present wits,
> Tell us no more the tale of Apuleius Asse,
> Nor Mydas eares, nor Io eating grasse.
> This worke of Toms so farre them all exceeds,
> As Phoebus fiddle did Pans squeaking reeds. (i. 27)

The question is, what kind of fool is Coryat? The poem continues to suggest that his observations are simply diverting by

---

[115] Compare e.g. the lofty tone of Sir Thomas Palmer, *An essay of the meanes how to make our travailes more profitable* (1606).

singling out his description of the great Tun of Heidelberg (ii. 218–23), honoured with an illustration and a Latin verse by a 'learned German' in the main text, with the further suggestion that the *Crudities* are the work of a clubbable drinking companion.[116] The poem's last lines hint at another reading as the reader is directly addressed: 'The care and toyle was his, thine are the gaines, / Cracke then the nut, and take the kernell for thy paines' (i. 28).

The implication is that there is more wit and intellectual substance in the work than the casual reader will find on first acquaintance, a hint also contained in the provision of a series of verses by Ben Jonson designed 'as Charms to unlocke the mystery of the Crudities' (pp. xix–xx).[117] Coryat's ludicrous persona, expressed throughout the prefatory material, may well be a disguise. He is probably more akin to the figure of folly in Erasmus's *Praise of Folly*, as is suggested by the explicit direction that the work needs to be carefully read and decoded. Coryat and his chosen poets come to appear more like co-conspirators, laughing at the ignorant reader and exposing folly rather than simply providing the reader with an object of ridicule. The classical references, including, significantly, Apuleius's golden ass, refer back to a Lucianic tradition of satire and social criticism beloved by Thomas More and Erasmus.[118] Jonson's description of Coryat as Polytopian refers to More's *Utopia*, the work closest to Erasmus's Lucianic satire, indicating that there is a serious purpose to the travels and that More's use of distant lands as a means to evaluate the worth of his own may well be a model in the author's mind.

The poem described above was written by Lewis Lewkenor,

---

[116] For another example of this representation of Coryat, see the poem by Laurence Whitaker (i. 41–3).

[117] The verses actually provide keys to the illustrations on the frontispiece where scenes from the travels are represented. Jonson himself had been under considerable suspicion from the authorities before this date, most recently for the republican subject-matter and implicit message of *Sejanus*, which brought a charge of treason against Jonson in 1603; see Patterson, *Censorship and Interpretation*, 50–8.

[118] See Kinney, *Humanist Poetics*, chs. 1–2; Walter M. Gordon, *Humanist Play and Belief: The Seriocomic Art of Desiderius Erasmus* (Toronto: University of Toronto Press, 1990). *The Golden Ass* was derived from a work attributed to Lucian.

a further indication that his own work was intended to be read as a critical assessment of the demerits of English social and political institutions, as well as a hint as to where the heart of the *Crudities* lies.[119] Coryat's 'Epistle Dedicatory' to Prince Henry—illustrating that, like Lewkenor, he may have had connections with writers such as Sir Robert Dallington, and written in a much less frivolous tone than the prefatory material following—Coryat highlights what he sees as the significance of his work.[120] Again the ubiquitous cliché that travel enables the writer to serve his country better is used; and the first aim, of describing 'many beautifull Cities, magnificent Palaces, and other memorable matters' observed in the course of his travels, seems anodyne enough. But the second aim hints at a larger purpose to the work:

I exhibite in this my Journall to your princely view, that most glorious, renowned, and Virgin Citie of Venice, the Queene of the Christian world, that Diamond set in the ring of the Adriatique gulfe, and the most resplendent mirrour of Europe, I have more particularly described, then it hath been ever before in our English tongue. The description of which famous Citie (were it done with such a curious and elegant stile as it doth deserve) I dare boldly say is a subject worthy for the greatest Monarch in the world to reade over. (i. 2)

Coryat does not mention Lewkenor's translation of Contarini; but given Henry's father's own comments attacking the significance of Venice for English and Scots writers, it would seem strange were Coryat only providing Henry with a description of the aesthetic merits of the city. If travel enlarges the mind, and Venice is 'a subject worthy for the greatest monarch in the world to read over', it is hardly likely that Coryat is recommending that Henry simply pay attention to the palaces and other memorable buildings.

Coryat's whole journey had been organized around the figure of Venice. He reproduces the letter of introduction he had from Henry Martin to Sir Henry Wotton, the English

---

[119] Next to Lewkenor's poem is one by Sir John Harington who also wrote one of the dedicatory poems to Lewkenor's translation of Contarini, further suggesting a series of shared intellectual links.

[120] On Coryat's relationship to Prince Henry and his contacts at his court, see Strachan, *Life and Adventures of Thomas Coryate*, 13–14; Strong, *Henry, Prince of Wales*, 46, *passim*.

ambassador there (and the former associate of the executed Earl of Essex).[121] His description is longer than that of any other city or area (over a sixth of the complete work), and he stayed there longer than anywhere else (six weeks out of a total of five months). As he reminds his readers before his account of the city, and again at the end of the book, Venice was the furthest point of his travels. Coryat calculated the number of miles betwen his village home of Odcombe and Venice as 1,023 (ii. 376), a detail which is eccentric and incongruous on one level, but which on another shows that the provincial fool is nearer the centre of good government than those in the English capital. In his 'Epistle to the Reader' he denies any interest in or expertise about comparative government; and as he has the habit of copying down inscriptions and epitaphs, he explains that an unnamed knight has dubbed him, rather insultingly:

a tombe-stone traveller . . . Whereas it had beene much more laudable (said he) to have observed the government of common-weales, and affaires of state. I answere him, that because I am a private man and no statist, matters of policie are impertinent unto me . . . Besides I have observed that in some places it is dangerous to prie very curiously into State matters, as divers travellers have observed by their deare experience. (i. 11–12)

It is true that Coryat is careful to avoid offering opinions on the politics and institutions of virtually all the places he visits. However, his description of Venice does contain a significant account of the politics of the city, which suggests that he knew rather more about 'policie' (a word with a specifically Italian resonance) than he pretends. Moreover, the text might be read as implying that the rest of the work is of secondary importance because English politicians have nothing to learn from other European states apart from Venice. The letter to Prince Henry almost suggests that he can ignore the rest of the work and simply pay careful attention to the Venetian passages. The last sentence cited can also be read as a piece of possible subterfuge: is it only abroad that travellers have to fear the danger of prying into state matters, a category which could, of course, include

[121] For accounts of Wotton in Venice, see Sells, *Paradise of Travellers*, ch. 3; Stoye, *English Travellers Abroad*, 113–15; Bate, 'Elizabethans in Italy', 56–9.

the suggestion that one's own country was lacking in many respects?

Coryat's actual description of Venice is perhaps of less import in terms of a development of political ideas than the fact that it is there at all.[122] His more fundamental aim appears to be to emphasize the importance of Venice in Europe as a symbolic core of democratic values and traditions. Like Lewkenor, he opens with a depiction of Venice as a glorious virgin whose beauty goes beyond his capacity to represent her (pp. 302–3); like William Thomas, he describes his sense of awe at approaching the incomparable city: 'Such is the rarenesse of the situation of Venice, that it doth even amaze and drive into admiration all strangers that upon their first arrival behold the same.' Venice is 'the richest Paragon and Queene of Christendome . . . not in respect of any sovereignty that she hath over other nations, in which sense Rome was in former times called Queene of the world, but in regard of her incomparable situation, surpassing wealth, and most magnificent buildings' (p. 303). Venice is the modern city of liberty throwing off the shackles of the magnificent but oppressive city of the old world, just as England was severing its links with the tyrannical church of Rome after the Reformation.[123]

At the end of his account of the marvellous buildings, customs, and varieties of people contained within the confines of the city, as well as his own experiences there—notably his potentially disastrous argument with some Venetian Jews (i. 370–6)—Coryat turns to 'The form of government'. He draws attention to the significance of this with a disclaimer following on from his remarks in the 'Epistle to the Reader':

Seeing I have related unto thee so many notable things of this renowned City . . . I thinke thou wilt expect this also from me, that I should discover unto thee her true form of governement, and the means wherewith shee both maintaineth her self in that glorious majesty, and also ruleth those goodly cities, townes, and Citadels that are subject to her dominion. (i. 416)

---

[122] McPherson, 'Lewkenor's Venice', describes Coryat's account as 'obligatory', suggesting that his real interest is in providing tourist information (460).

[123] Comparisons between England and Venice as 'anti-Romish islands' were frequently made; see Bate, 'Elizabethans in Italy', 59.

Coryat repeats his claim that he is unsuited to the task because he is 'a private citizen', adding further that his observations are no more than a 'superficial touch' (i. 417) because he has only spent six weeks in the city.

Such remarks serve only to highlight the comments rather than disguise them, especially considering the directions given to Prince Henry in the 'Epistle Dedicatorie'. Coryat provides a brief overview of the constitution, which might owe as much to a reading of Lewkenor's translation of Contarini (or a similar work) as actual observation. He describes the Duke's election and limited powers, the council of ten, the great council, and the principal magistrates who govern the cities under the sway of Venice, as well as the secret ballots employed in Venetian elections and account of their taxation system (i. 417–23). Overall, the proverbial judgements are applied: 'the governement of this City is a compounded forme of state, contayning in it an Idea of the three principall governements of the auncient Athenians and Romans, namely the Monarchicall, the Oligarchicall, and the Democraticall' (i. 418); and Venice is said to be 'as well governed as any City upon the face of the whole earth ever was' (i. 417).

Coryat explains that he only describes 'as much of their government as may be lawfull for a stranger' (i. 417). Taken at face value, such a statement seems innocent enough; but within the context of a book where the author is continually professing that he is no more than a 'private man' and so unable to comment on political matters, the statement appears to take on the further significance that, living under a constitution like the Venetian one, which encourages active participation from its citizens, a lot more can be said than in England, where there is a huge divide between the public and the private. In *The Trew Law of Free Monarchies*, James I had described the relationship between king and subjects as one between father and children. Love, like rights, was a force which 'useth to descend more then to ascend'. Children had no right to oppose the will of the father, and should simply obey (pp. 204–5). Under such a regime, writers like Coryat may have thought it best to disguise their criticism from hostile eyes, providing enough clues for the initiated to read the right message of the text and gauge the writer's hostility to the status quo.[124]

After his description of the constitution of Venice, Coryat relates a seemingly trivial incident. Crossing St Mark's Square he saw pictures of famous kings on the wall of the Duke's Palace, one of whom was James I. Such a sight caused him great delight ('did even tickle my senses with great joy and comfort'), especially considering the fact that James's picture was placed 'in the very middle . . . which I think was placed there not without great consideration; for I beleeve they remembered the old speech when they hanged up his picture: In medio consistit virtus' (i. 426–7). 'The middle contains virtue' might appear to be a message James would do well to heed himself, one which the city of Venice exemplifies rather better than the political institutions of the country he ruled.

Such a reading of *Coryat's Crudities* risks granting the work more coherence and conscious purpose than it perhaps has. While it is clear that Coryat's representation of himself as an obsessive buffoon is a mask—and one which is always slipping—it also appears that *Coryat's Crudities* is a work of self-fashioning, and that its mode of presenting its author needs to be taken seriously. The work is a departure in English travel writing. Nothing written in the sixteenth century remotely compares to it, whereas writers like Moryson and Lithgow produced works which not only resemble *Coryat's Crudities* in the rambling form of the travelogue they adopt, but also in the eccentric persona who holds the narrative together and the reader's interest beyond the worth of the material represented.[125] Coryat even includes a small woodcut of the shoes he

[124] On James's political views and their effect in England, see David Mathew, *James I* (London: Eyre & Spottiswoode, 1967), pt. 2, ch. 2; Conrad Russell, *The Crisis of Parliaments: English History, 1509–1660* (Oxford: Oxford University Press, 1971), 266–71, 292–7, *passim*; Alan G. R. Smith, 'Constitutional Ideas and Developments in England, 1603–1625', in Alan G. R. Smith (ed.), *The Reign of James VI and I* (London: Macmillan, 1973), 160–76.

[125] It is no accident that Moryson, whose travels began before Coryat's, had trouble editing and then publishing his manuscript. Presumably the problem was one of deciding exactly what to do with his material. For details see Charles Hughes (ed.), *Shakespeare's Europe: Unpublished Chapters of Fynes Moryson's* Itinerary (London: Sherratt and Hughes, 1903), 'Introduction', pp. xxxvi–xliv. On Coryat's difficulties in publishing his work, see Strachan, *Life and Adventures of Thomas Coryate*, ch. 9.

wore near the end of the 'Panegyrick Verses' which were eventually hung up in Odcombe church, a gesture which followed that of the famous jester, Will Kemp.[126] In one sense the fashioning of Thomas Coryat as 'a private man' through his rambling and strange book, too eccentric to fit into any recognizable categories of state control, is also a political act of resistance to an over-mighty and intrusive state. One of the 'Panegyrick Verses' was written by John Donne, who had suffered at the hands of the state for his personal beliefs and actions. Donne's verse jokes that in Venice Coryat 'wouldst seeke / Some vaster thing, and foundst a Cortizan' (i. 37). This might seem a denigrating observation until read alongside a poem like 'The Sun Rising', where the speaker tells the sun to 'Go tell court-huntsmen, that the king will ride' and so leave the lovers alone. In the final stanza the political world is eclipsed as the lovers take over the mechanics of state: 'She's all states, and all princes I.'[127] In effect, the king is banished and the world he rules is consigned to oblivion as the lovers resist the tyrannous attempts to control them. In the same way, one way of resisting for Coryat—as Donne's bawdy reference might have acknowledged—was to construct himself as a figure beyond the reach of politics. Coryat represents himself as 'a private man', a lone traveller outside the confines of his own country, a strategy which was evidently at odds with the disguised criticism of the state contained elsewhere in the same work.[128] In structuring his journey around Venice, and centring his political critique of England on that virginal city, Coryat was repeating the aggressive intent of the most important represener of Venice for an English audience, Lewis Lewkenor, who was, after all, also the author of one of the dedicatory verses which prefaced Coryat's own *Crudities*.

Through such contradictory ways was the egocentric and

---

[126] Strachan, *Life and Adventures of Thomas Coryate*, 114.

[127] John Donne, 'The Sun Rising', in *The Complete English Poems*, ed. A. J. Smith (Harmondsworth: Penguin, 1971), 80–1.

[128] As Strachan points out, Coryat provided the first account of the story of William Tell in English. William Tell's killing of the tyrant who forced him to shoot an apple placed on the top of his son's head led to the foundation of the Helvetical confederation and would seem to justify tyrannicide, a further suggestion that Coryat was less innocent of politics than he seems; Strachan, *Life and Adventures of Thomas Coryate*, 69–71; *Coryat's Crudities*, i. 101–2.

fractured field that constitutes modern travel writing brought to light. Subsequent travel writing might often be self-obsessed, insular, and, more often than not, racist, but it contained the potential for vigorous criticism of the status quo, and the added advantage of providing a voice to those who were usually denied one.[129]

[129] Reflections on this paradox, and other related contradictions, form the subject of much recent analysis of travel writing. See e.g. Islam, *Ethics of Travel*, pt. 1; Sara Mills, *Discourses of Difference: An Analysis of Women's Travel Writing and Colonialism* (London: Routledge, 1991); Mary Louise Pratt, *Imperial Eyes: Travel Writing and Transculturation* (London: Routledge, 1992); George Robertson *et al.*, (eds.), *Travellers' Tales: Narratives of Home and Displacement* (London: Routledge, 1994).

CHAPTER TWO

'What is the matter with yowe Christen men?': English Colonial Literature, 1555–1625

IF ONE of the main strands in English writing representing countries within Europe was the use of a loosely defined generic form which furthered discussion of politics at home, the same can often be said of English writing which can be designated as 'colonial', as I shall attempt to demonstrate in this chapter.[1] It should be obvious that I am not attempting to assert that this is the only way in which such writings might be read. In examining Captain John Smith's *Generall Historie of Virginia*, David Read concluded that 'we should be extremely cautious about hypostatizing a single, stable version of colonialism out of the flux that surrounds the early English activity in North America' because 'colonists imported a multiplicity of approaches which only sorted themselves out over the *longue durée*'.[2] I would suggest, moreover, that English colonial writing poses more problems of decoding than does writing describing other

---

[1] I am using 'colonial' in the specific sense of promoting colonies, i.e. a settlement of people from one country in another, as used in classical and more recent European political thought. Hence colonial literature forms a distinct sub-section of writings representing foreign peoples (in fact, colonial literature can avoid such discussions altogether, but, obviously, rarely does). 'Colonial' in this sense is inseparable from the wider phenomenon of 'colonialism', but the two terms can only be equated with the loss of important distinctions. Equally, it would be an error to suggest that colonial enterprises and their effects can be self-contained. For a lucid discussion see M. I. Finley, 'Colonies—An Attempt at a Typology', *TRHS* 26 (1976), 167–88.

[2] David Read, 'Colonialism and Coherence: The Case of Captain John Smith's *Generall Historie of Virginia*', *MP* 91 (1994), 428–48, at 446, 445. See also Myra Jehlen, 'History before the Fact: Or, Captain John Smith's Unfinished Symphony', *CI* 19 (1992–3), 677–92; Peter Hulme, 'Making No Bones: A Response to Myra Jehlen', *CI* 20 (1993–4), 179–86; Myra Jehlen, 'Response to Peter Hulme', *CI* 20 (1993–4), 187–91.

European countries. The latter becomes ambiguous when there is slippage between an intentional allegorical analysis of events or institutions at home, and the establishment of a discourse of comparative government which provides the intellectual means of criticism without necessarily being committed to it; the former has the additional problem of having to establish or help continue the establishment of government in another land in its wake. In short, colonial literature, like the colonist, occupies an ambiguous position between the motherland and the colonized land. Colonial literature is often vociferously committed to the metropolis which it has irrevocably left behind, and yet, in the face of a different location and a different culture, is obliged to acknowledge that the identity of 'home' has changed beyond recognition. Just as new identities are forged in such a process, so is there a concomitant need for new forms of government, making the colonist a radical thinker whether or not he or she accepts such a position, because colonizers have been forced to recognize the violence necessary for the formation of states.[3]

In this chapter I want to demonstrate the ways in which various forms of colonial literature, from the reign of Mary to that of James I, were forced to reflect upon the enterprises they were encouraging, and to articulate a political message which challenged the assumptions of their supporters at court. Colonial literature, like European travel writing, became yet another public forum, in which ideas were tested out and the language of sophisticated political analysis was developed when it was difficult for it to flourish elsewhere, partly because debate was suppressed, partly because dealing with colonies set problems which had not previously been encountered. In the first section of this chapter I want to examine England's colonial rivalry with Spain for the Americas, usually labelled as the 'Black Legend' because it is assumed that the main purpose of English descriptions of Spanish conquests in the New World was to promote the myth of Spanish cruelty and greed, so defending the natural English right to empire as a civilized way of spreading

---

[3] See Anthony Giddens, *The Nation State and Violence* (Cambridge: Polity Press, 1985).

trade and Christianity to the barbarians.[4] Such a monolithic
and straightforward analysis may be questioned if one takes
into account the almost total lack of success of English colonial
enterprises before the establishment of the Jamestown colony in
1607 which resulted in the desire to copy as much as discredit
the Spanish.[5] English writers used Spanish accounts of the
Americas to reflect on their own political status and to consider
exactly what the establishment of an empire could mean. In the
second section I want to look at English representations of their
own attempts at establishing colonies in the Americas, showing
how such accounts imagined and realized the creation of a new
political sphere which could go beyond the restrictive and
despotic methods which writers suggested had evolved in
England.

I

Undoubtedly one of the most influential accounts of the
Spanish conquest and colonization of the Americas was Peter
Martyr d'Anghera's *De Orbe Novo Decades* (Alcála, 1516), a
work whose popularity and influence is attested to by the fact
that it went through a bewildering variety of forms and number
of volumes throughout the sixteenth century.[6] Its importance in
an English context results from the translation made of the
1516 edition by Richard Eden (1555), which was later supplemented by a translation of decades (parts) four to eight by

---

[4] See William S. Maltby, *The Black Legend in England: The Development of
Anti-Spanish Sentiment, 1558–1660* (Durham, NC: Duke University Press, 1971),
for the most substantial account of such propaganda.

[5] For a recent analysis see Jeffrey Knapp, *An Empire Nowhere: England,
America, and Literature from* Utopia *to* The Tempest (Berkeley: University of
California Press, 1992).

[6] The first three books (decades) of *De Orbe Novo Decades* were collected
together in an edition in 1516, having been first published separately in Venice
(1504), Seville (1511), and Alcála (1516); see John Parker, *Books to Build an
Empire: A Bibliography of English Overseas Interests to 1630* (Amsterdam: New
Israel, 1965), 51, n. 22. A further expanded edition was published: *De Rebus
Oceanicis et Nove Orbe, Decades Tres, Petri Martyris Ab Angleria Mediolanensis*
(Coloniae, 1574). For details of the editions of the text, see Michael Brennan, 'The
Texts of Peter Martyr's *De orbe novo decades* (1504: 1628): A Response to Andrew
Hadfield', *Connotations*, 6 (1996/7), 227–45.

Michael Lok (1612), after Richard Hakluyt the younger had published a Latin edition in Paris (1587) for which he supplied the dedication.[7] Eden's translation, undoubtedly a work of propagandist intent designed to help establish an empire (see below, pp. 88–9), expresses many of the fundamental ambivalences of the English imperial position, complicating an already fractured and problematic text.[8]

In the third book of the second decade of *De Orbe Novo Decades* there occurs a strange and fascinating confrontation between the Spanish *conquistadores* led by Vasco Núñez de Balboa and the son of the local king, Comogrus. In the wake of Columbus's voyages and discoveries, numerous disputes took place both between colonists and the crown and amongst the colonists themselves. After a series of incidents culminating in a mutiny, Balboa was elected leader, as much out of fear as respect, because 'the best parte was fayne to give place to the greatest'.[9] In pursuit of gold, Balboa was attempting to lead his faction across Darien (Panama) from the Gulf of Uraba to the Pacific Ocean.[10] Having sacked the rich village of Poncha, they came across the court of king Comogrus, which Peter Martyr describes in some detail. In many ways it resembles European courts; the palace, despite being made of wood, 'is of no lesse strength then waules of stone'; there are civil courtiers whom the Spanish have met before under their now-deceased

---

[7] Richard Eden, *The decades of the newe worlde or west India* (1555), reprinted in Edward Arber (ed.), *The First Three English Books on America* (Birmingham: privately printed, 1885). For details see D. B. Quinn (ed.), *The Hakluyt Handbook*, 2 vols. (London: Hakluyt Society, 1974), i. 43, ii. 473.

[8] For further details see the responses to my original article, 'Peter Martyr, Richard Eden and the New World: Reading, Experience and Translation', *Connotations*, 5 (1995/6), 1–22; Brennan, 'The Texts of Peter Martyr's *De orbe novo decades*'; William Hamlin, 'On Reading Early Accounts of the New World', *Connotations*, 6 (1996/7), 46–50; Claire Jowitt, ' "Monsters and Straunge Births": The Politics of Richard Eden. A Response to Andrew Hadfield', *Connotations*, 6 (1996/7), 51–65; Andrew Hadfield, 'Richard Eden and Peter Martyr: Author's Response', *Connotations*, 6 (1996/7), 227–45.

[9] Arber (ed.), *First Three English Books on America*, 115. All subsequent references to this edition in parentheses in the text.

[10] J. H. Elliott, 'The Spanish Conquest and Settlement of America', in Leslie Bethell (ed.), *The Cambridge History of Latin America* (Cambridge: Cambridge University Press, 1984), i. 149–206, at 169; Samuel Eliot Morison, *The European Discovery of America: The Southern Voyages, AD 1492–1616* (New York: Oxford University Press, 1974), 200–4.

commander, Diego de Nicuesa; the king's huge cellar contains a wide range of wines made from dates rather than grapes, in the same way that Germans, Flemings, English, regional Spaniards, Swiss, and other Alpine dwellers 'make certayne drynkes of barley, wheat, hoppes, and apples', and 'They say also that with *Comogrus*, they droonk wynes of sundry tastes, both whyte and blacke.'

However, if this has started to make the reader feel more at home for one of the few times in the seemingly endless catalogue of exotic savagery, Spanish atrocities, and generally murderous conflicts, the narrator immediately warns us that we are about to return to that world once again: 'nowe yow shall heare of a thynge more monstrous too behoulde'. The Spanish are conducted into the bowels of the palace where 'they were browght into a chamber hanged aboute with the carkeses of men, tyed with ropes of gossampine cotton'. These, it turns out, are mummies of the ancestors of the king, 'that they tooke it for a godly thynge to honoure them religiously' and dress them up with precious stones and gold 'accordynge unto theyr estate'. Although obviously appearing 'superstitious' to the Spanish, at least this particular religious practice avoids the horrific diabolism of ritual human sacrifice and cannibalism encountered throughout the *Decades of the Newe Worlde or West India*.[11]

It is at this point that the eldest of the king's seven sons, who had an 'excellente naturall wytte', enters the frame; first he gives the Spanish four thousand ounces of gold, 'artificially wrought', and fifty slaves, veterans of Amerindian wars, as a means of flattering and pleasing 'thys wanderynge kynde of men (owr men I meane) luyvnge onely by shiftes and spoyle, least beinge offended and seekynge occasions ageynste hym and his familie, they shulde handle hym as they dyd other whiche sowght noo meanes howe to gratifie theym'. The soldiers try to divide up the booty, leaving a fifth for the crown, but fall to

[11] See Arber (ed.), *First Three English Books on America*, 50, 66, 69, 107, 110, 120, 130, 157, 187–9, *passim*, for further references. See also Bernal Díaz, *The Conquest of New Spain*, trans. J. M. Cohen (Harmondsworth: Penguin, 1963), 21, 37–8, 65, 98, 104–6, 122, *passim*. More positive encounters between the Spanish and the Amerindians do occur in *De Orbe Novo Decades*: see Arber (ed.), *First Three English Books on America*, 87–8, 95, 98, 150–2, 166, *passim*.

'brabbylynge and contention', whereupon the king's son starts to chastise them:

What is the matter with yowe Christen men, that yow soo greatly esteme soo litle a portion of golde more then yowr owne quietnes, whiche neverthelesse yow entend to deface from these fayre ouches [necklaces] and to melte the same into a rude masse. If yowre hunger of goulde bee soo insatiable that onely for the desyre yowe have therto, yowe disquiete soo many nations, and yow yowre selves also susteyne soo many calamit[i]es and incommodities, lyving like banished men owte of yowre owne countrey, I wyll shewe yowe a Region flowinge with goulde, where yow may satisfie yowr raveninge appetites. (p. 117)

He points out that they will have to contend with the fierce king Tumanama and the 'cruell Canybales, a fierce kynde of men, devourers of mans fleshe, lyving withowte lawes, wanderinge, and withowte empire'. These cannibals are also 'desyrous of golde' and have conquered the people who used to own the gold mines in the mountains. They now 'use them lyke bondmen' and force them to mine the gold they once owned and make 'plates and sundry Images luke whiche yowe see here'. The Comogruans have traded these artefacts with the cannibals for prisoners of war, 'whiche they bye for to eate', or household objects like sheets and furniture and food. The risks and rewards of such an encounter will clearly be great: the king's son informs the Spanish that in such regions all household objects are made of gold, which is as common to them as iron is in Europe.

   The Spanish marvel at the oration of the young man, 'pondered in theyr myndes, and earnestly considered his sayinges'; not, it seems, at his forthright criticisms of their inordinate greed, but at the prospect of wealth beyond their wildest dreams as they ask 'uppon what certeyne knoweleage he spake those thynges'. The king's son continues, 'stayinge a whyle with hym selfe as it were an oratour preparinge him selfe to speake of sume grave matter, and disposynge his bodie to a giesture meete to persuade': 'Gyve eare unto me o yowe Chrystians. Albeit that the gredie hunger of golde hathe not yet vexed us naked men, yet doo we destroy one an other by reason of ambition and desyre to rule. Hereof springeth mortall hatred among us, and hereof commethe owre destruction.' The natives cannot control their desire to fight wars, and so are no better than the Europeans at heart. The king's son agrees to guide Balboa's party so that they can obtain gold and the Comogruans defeat their enemies, but first the Spanish must send for another thousand troops. 'After these woordes, this prudent younge *Comogrus* helde his peace. And owre men moved with greate hope and hunger of golde, beganne to swalowe downe theyr spettle' (pp. 116–18).

Subsequently events unfold as follows: Comogrus is willingly converted and changes his name to Charles, after the Spanish king, and he appears later on as a notable friend to Christians, even though he considers himself a god when given axes, tools, and a soldier's cloak by the Spanish (pp. 148–9); Balboa undertakes the journey without waiting for the thousand relief troops from Spain (p. 137), with considerable success, until he is killed by a rival *conquistador,* Pedrarias Davila.

The narration of this encounter is multi-layered and demands some decoding, especially as we do not know exactly how Peter Martyr acquired his information: was it by way of interviews with the returning *conquistadores,* second-hand retelling, or imaginative reconstruction? It is hard to determine who is speaking at which point—the Amerindians, Peter Martyr, the *conquistadores*—or who is being addressed: the original correspondents of Peter Martyr, a general public, influential government figures, colonial Latin America, or metropolitan Spain?[12] At certain points the reader is made aware that the text exists at—to say the least—two removes, that the narrator of the book was not present at the scene but is reporting speech: 'They say that with *Comogrus,* they droonk wynes of sundry tastes.' At others, the narrator disappears and merges into the group of Spanish *conquistadores:* 'this eldest soone of Kyne *Comogrus* beinge presente, whome we praysed for his

---

[12] ' "If speaking *for* someone else seems to be a mysterious process," Stanley Cavell has remarked, "that may be because speaking *to* someone does not seem mysterious enough" '; Clifford Geertz, 'Thick Description: Toward an Interpretative Theory of Culture', in *The Interpretation of Cultures: Selected Essays* (New York: Basic Books, 1973), 3–30, at 13. *De Orbe Novo Decades* started as a series of letters to influential figures in Italy, principally ecclesiastical dignitaries, and was eventually published as a collected whole in 1530. On Richard Eden see David Gwyn, 'Richard Eden: Cosmographer and Alchemist', *Sixteenth-Century Journal,* 15 (1984), 13–34.

wisdom'. Put another way, the reader is never sure exactly what is going on and what status the statements given in the text have, because of the shifting nature of the pronouns used.[13]

In the same way it is hard to know how to read the description: as a piece of travel literature representing an alien people for the edification of a European audience, or as a specifically colonial text (the latter case would demand that cultural superiority is assumed, the former would not). Does the example of the Comogruans illustrate the superiority of European powers over the savages of the New World, a cultural clash which displays mutual incomprehension, the use of the New World as an allegory which either represents the problems of the Old World or shows a way of life which is manifestly superior? These early details appear to signify in opposite directions: on the one hand the Comogruans are recognizably similar to Europeans, with their sophisticated court where civil social intercourse takes place; on the other, they are superstitious idolators who worship the dead bodies of their ancestors.

The speech of the king's son spectacularly confirms this ambiguity. The narrator's interpretation of his motives, in what can only be an interpolation, seems to single out the Spanish as akin to one of the lowest elements of European society, the landless poor.[14] They are dismissed as 'thys wanderinge kinde

[13] Eden's translation does not differ significantly from the original Latin of Peter Martyr; the passage analysed here exists in *De Rebus Oceanicis et Novo Orbe, Decades Tres*, 146–52. There is a modern translation by Francis Augustus MacNutt, *De Orbe Novo: The Eight Decades of Peter Martyr D'Anghera* (New York: B. Franklin, 1970, rpt. of 1912), 213–23. For example, the indented quotation cited above is rendered as 'What thing then is this, Christians? Is it possible that you set a high value upon such a small quantity of gold? You nevertheless destroy the artistic beauty of these necklaces, melting them into ingots. If your thirst of gold is such that in order to satisfy it you disturb peaceable people and bring misfortune and calamity among them, if you exile yourselves from your country in search of gold, I will show you a country where it abounds and where you can satisfy the thirst that torments you' (220).

[14] On vagrancy in Europe see Beier, *Masterless Men*; Pound, *Poverty and Vagrancy in Tudor England*; Williams, *Tudor Regime*, 196–206; Angus Calder, *Revolutionary Empire: The Rise of English-Speaking Empires from the Fifteenth Century to the 1780s* (London: Cape, 1981), 22–5; J. H. Elliott, *Europe Divided, 1559–1598* (London: Collins, 1968), 67–8. On the connection between the representation of landlessness in Europe and the Americas, see Stephen Greenblatt, 'Invisible Bullets', in *Shakespearian Negotiations: The Circulation of Social Energy in Renaissance England* (Oxford: Clarendon Press, 1988), 21–65, at 49–50.

of men'—a detail which has to be reconfirmed, '(our men I mean)', presumably in case the reader mistakes Spaniards for Comogruans—and this explicitly separates them from the noble status of the Amerindian prince, so that two extremes of social rank confront each other across the cultural and racial divide.[15] This incident in early travel history shadows from afar Aphra Behn's criticism of black slavery in *Oronooko*, where the aristocratic African hero is finally executed by 'one Bannister, a wild Irishman, and one of the council, a fellow of absolute barbarity, and fit to execute any villainy'.[16] Clearly, the Amerindian prince—like Oronooko—is in the morally superior position at this point, and his hostile analysis of Spanish greed carries weight. It is not merely that the Spanish are avaricious, but that they are indifferent to and destructive of beautiful objects; whereas the natives make ornaments which are 'artificially wrought' and give them to their visitors as presents, the Spanish simply want to melt everything down into a 'rude masse'. They value gold as a monetary commodity, without valuing the labour which makes the object an aesthetic pleasure.[17]

The Comogruans, in contrast, according to the king's son, 'no more esteem rude gold unwrought, then we doo cloddes of earthe, before it bee formed by the hande of the workeman to the similitude eyther of sume vessell necessarie for owre use, or sume ouche [necklace] bewetifull to be worne' (p. 117). This is a more subtle critique of European values than that of Thomas More's ascetic Utopians, who laugh at gold chains of state and make chamber pots of gold in order to show their contempt for frivolity, and it should be read alongside that more famous account.[18] The Utopians value

---

[15] See Hulme, *Colonial Encounters*, 144.

[16] Aphra Behn, *Oronooko, The Rover and Other Works*, ed. Janet Todd (Harmondsworth: Penguin, 1992), 139–40. On the cultural stereotyping of the Irish, see Joeseph Th. Leerssen, *Mere Irish and Fíor-Ghael: Studies in the Idea of Irish Nationality, its Development and Literary Expression Prior to the Nineteenth Century* (Amsterdam: Benjamins, 1986).

[17] For a related discussion see Karl Marx, *Economic and Philosophical Manuscripts* in *Early Writings*, trans. Rodney Livingstone and Gregor Benton (Harmondsworth: Penguin, 1975), 279–400, at 377. Marx discusses speeches from Goethe's *Faust* and Shakespeare's *Timon of Athens* specifically about the greed for gold.

[18] More, *Utopia*, ed. Edward Surtz, S.J., and J. H. Hexter (New Haven: Yale University Press, 1965), 157–9.

iron more than gold because it is more necessary for human life; they respect materials only in accordance with their *intrinsic* worth. The Comogruans value the *social* worth of gold, and therefore their society stands as an exact opposite of that of the Spanish adventurers.[19]

The king's son—at least in the first part of his oration—is an early representative of a figure quite familiar from later colonial narratives and travel literature, that of the 'savage critic' who is able to perceive the excesses of the colonists and show them by word and deed what they have lost, in itself a narcissistic, Eurocentric vision.[20] The verbal echoes and rhetorical patterning in this early section of the speech make a devastating parallel between the Spanish and the cannibals, the lowest form of humanity for Europeans and their worst nightmare.[21] Both are equally 'desyrous of golde', so that the Spanish lose their own quietness while disquieting other nations (presumably those they plunder); the cannibals, on the other hand, are alienated from their own environment, and from those they conquer and ruthlessly exploit as 'bondmen' to mine the gold which they then trade for human flesh. Both are exiles, the Spanish forced to live 'like banished men owte of [their] owne countrey', 'thys wanderinge kinde of men', the cannibals 'lyving withowte lawes, wanderinge, and withowte empire'. In effect, what the king's son seems to be saying is that the Spanish are no different to what they would like to think of as their polar opposites; both restless peoples are ruled by an inordinate and destructive greed in contrast to the relative social harmony of the Comogruans; both bring appalling destruction in their wake; both are cruel, and ignorant of what really matters; neither is capable of setting down a workable and settled system of laws; both are dangerous vagabonds who threaten social stability and know no boundaries, the Spanish as colonists cut off from their homeland (which perhaps condemned many of them to a life of bondmen), the cannibals

---

[19] For comment see Marx, *Economic and Philosophical Manuscripts*, 377.

[20] Anthony Pagden, 'The Savage Critic: Some European Images of the Primitive', *YES* 13 (1983), 32–45; Bernard Sheehan, *Savagism and Civility: Indians and Englishmen in Colonial Virginia* (Cambridge: Cambridge University Press, 1980), 34.

[21] Ibid. 60–1.

as men without a nation.[22] The text recognizes that the reader will be challenged and unsettled at this point. In a crucial sense, the king's son seems to imply that both Spain and the New World work to produce what threatens their very existence, a structural imbalance which is expressed in the second half of the speech.

The reaction of the Spanish to these criticisms is similarly disturbing. They interpret them in a way which can only seem wilfully blind, and a vindication of the king's son's harsh remarks to the reader:

Owre capitaynes marveylyng at the oration of the naked younge man (for they had for interpretours those three men whiche had byn before a yere and a halfe conversant in the court of kynge *Careta*) pondered in theyr myndes, and ernestly considered his sayinges. Soo that his rashnes in scatteringe the golde owte of the balances, they turned to myrth and urbanitie, commendynge his dooinge and sayinge therin. Then they asked hym frendely, upon what certeyne knoweleage he spake those thynges. (p. 117)

The first sentence sets up expectations that are immediately thwarted in the second. The reader might think the Spaniards would consider the king's son animadversorious, while in fact they only seem to wonder whether his liberality is genuine. Even Columbus at his most pig-headed and bizarre could scarcely rival this eccentric misreading, and a huge gulf opens up between the European readers of the Latin or English text and the European protagonists of its narrative.[23] Nevertheless, his oration does succeed in restoring their good humour and stopping the fight that had started to break out: a clear irony. The laughter is, however, a false resolution which does not heal the divisions, and thus it represents a pause in the thrust of the narrative, or else a comic fissure, because the joke is really on those who are laughing.[24] The way forward for the Spanish is to confront and overcome their *doppelgängers*.

---

[22] 15. For analysis of a similar incident described in related terms see Andrew Hadfield, 'Writing the New World: More "Invisible Bullets" ', *L. & H.*, 2nd ser., 2/2 (1991), 3–19, at 13–15; Samuel Eliot Morison, *The European Discovery of America: The Northern Voyages, AD 500–1600* (New York, 1971), 237–8.

[23] See Anthony Pagden, *European Encounters with the New World* (New Haven: Yale University Press, 1993), 17–24.

[24] For further analysis, see Susan Purdie, *Comedy: The Mastery of Discourse* (London: Harvester, 1993), chs. 1, 3.

When the king's son speaks again after the Spanish ask how they can get hold of such fabulous wealth, the nature of his discourse changes dramatically and he turns his 'naturall witt' inwards in analysing how and why the Comogruans destroy themselves. They may not be afflicted by the greed of the bad savages, the cannibals, but they are by no means as serenely good as they at first appear.[25] Hate and ambition torment them:

Owre predicessours kepte warres, and soo dyd *Comogrus* my father with princes beinge bortherers abowte hym. In the wyche warres, as wee have overcoome, so have wee byn overcoome, as dothe appere by the number of bondmen amonge us, which we tooke by the over-throwe of owre enemyes, of the whiche I have gyven yowe fiftie. Lykwyse at an other tyme, owre adversaries havinge th[e] upper hande agenste us, ledde away manye of us captive. For suche is the chance of warre. (p. 117)

He then informs them that many of the Comogruans were once the captured slaves of King Tumanama who have presumably either escaped or been rescued in the course of subsequent hostilities, before making the arrangement to lead them onwards.

Just as the opening description of the court of King Comogrus oscillated between an affirmation of a shared European and New World identity—what Anthony Pagden has recently called 'the principle of attachment'[26]—and an acknowledgement of the vast difference between the two, so does the speech of the king's son, but in a more complex and sophisticated manner. In the first section the Spanish explorers and the nameless cannibals are pitted against the savage critic and, presumably, the European reader of the text; in the second, a universal malaise is affirmed, that of human aggression, a characteristic which appears to define the species.

Even though some dwellers of the New World can see through to the 'truth' of human actions and expose the false

---

[25] On this distinction, see Hulme, *Colonial Encounters*, ch. 2.

[26] Pagden, *European Encounters*, 21. See also Stephen J. Greenblatt, 'Learning to Curse: Aspects of Linguistic Colonialism in the Sixteenth Century', in Fredi Chiapelli (ed.), *First Images of America: The Impact of the New World on the Old* (Berkeley: University of California Press, 1976), 561–80.

motives and hypocrisy, they are subject to precisely the same limitations of behaviour and fall into the same traps. Ultimately both Europeans (colonists and readers) and savages (Comogruans, Tumanamans, and cannibals) blend as one. The Comogruans turn out to be exactly the sort of naked and aggressive people that they seemed to be defined against: hence the apparent schizophrenia of the savage prince. They are both savage critics and participators within the world of savagery, occupying an uneasy position within the series of discourses which represents them. They are at once noble savages (an ambiguous representation in itself, simultaneously reminding Europeans of what they have lost, but also what they should have), ignoble savages, and ordinary human beings.

This strange confrontation with its seemingly confused and conflicting messages demands to be read within the context of the whole work of *De Orbe Novo Decades*, both with and against the grain, as well as in terms of a Spanish/international Latin reader and an English one. Peter Martyr's own short preface to the expanded edition of 1516 explains that he left Italy for Spain because of a desire to record the important new discoveries in the Americas, fearing that they might be lost for ever: 'I myght particularlye collecte, these marvelous and newe thynges, which shoulde other wyse perhapps have line drowned in the whirlepoole of oblivion: forasmuch as the Spanyardes (men woorthy [of] greate commendation) had onely care to the generall inventions of these thynges.' In other words, the Spanish are good at acting but not at understanding the significance of their own actions, and a foreign narrator is required to tell the story of their deeds and interpret the meaning of them. Peter Martyr states that he left his homeland because there was nothing of significance to record: 'In Italy, by reason of the dissension among the Princes, I coulde fynde nothynge wherewith I myght feede my wytte, beinge a younge man desyrous of knowleage and experience of thynges' (p. 63).[27] Despite being tempted to return, he has not done so, partly because of the pleas of the deceased Ferdinand and Isabella, but

---

[27] For details of Peter Martyr's life, see MacNutt, *De Orbe Novo*, 'Introduction', 1–48.

also that in maner throwgh owt all Italy, by reason of the *discorde of the Christian Princes*, I perceaved all thynges to runne headelong into ruine, the countreys to be destroyed and made fatte with humane bludde: The cities sacked, virgines and matrones with theyr goodes and possessions caried away as captives and miserable innocentes without offence to be slayne unarmed within theyr owne houses. Of the which calamities, I dyd not onely heare the lamentable owtcryes but dyd also feele the same. For even the bludde of mine owne kinfolkes and frendes, was not free from that crueltie. [my emphasis] (pp. 63–4)

In marked contrast to this heartfelt lament for the fate of his patria, based on a shared sympathy and personal experience, is the extravagant praise for the Spanish monarch, Charles V, who not only has a virtually unified realm ('yowr graundefathers by your moothers syde, have subdued all Spayne under yowr dominion except onely one corner of the same'), but has expanded his territories beyond the horizons of any previous rulers:

But not offendynge the reverence due to owre predicessors, what so ever frome the begynnynge of the worlde hath byn donne or wrytten to this day, to my judgement seemeth but litle, if wee consyder what newe landes and countreys, what newe seas, what sundry nations and tounges, what golde mynes, what treasures of perles they have lefte unto yowe hyghnesse, besyde other revenues. The whiche, what they are and howe great, these three Decades shall declare. (p. 64)

The preface sets up a whole series of oppositions, many of which clearly have a bearing upon the narrated incident analysed above. These can be listed—in no particular order—as follows:

Spain/Italy
Unity/Fragmentation
Expansion/Contraction
Christianity/Paganism
Knowledge/Ignorance
Health/Illness
Nation/Regions
Centre/Margins
Empire/Colony
Wealth/Poverty
Intact/Violated
Home/Exile
Self/Other
Lack of Awareness/Awareness

Although it is easy to see that these oppositions can be related to Peter Martyr's description of the encounter between the Spanish and the Comogruans, they cannot be mapped onto it in a straightforward manner. While both the *conquistadores* and the cannibals are classified as wandering exiles, the same can, of course, be said of Peter Martyr, not just in fact, but as he chooses to represent himself. The difference is that they move away from stability, from civilization to barbarism, and he moves from the chaos of his homeland to become a subject in a more stable, powerful, and civilized country. It has frequently been noted that what holds the knowledge gained from accounts of the New World together is the rhetoric of the 'I'/eye-witness, forced to abandon all appeals to a canon of authorities and insist on the unclassifiable newness of the data which can only be described by one who has seen it in person.[28] But, in effect, Peter Martyr goes a stage further, suggesting that he alone can truly appreciate the achievements of the Spanish because he comes from a land which is contracting into small regions rather than being already unified and now expanding. Only those without a nation can come to understand the good fortune of those who have one, in perhaps the same way that the son of King Comogrus can warn the Spanish of what they might lose through their excessive greed and consequent dissension. According to Benedict Anderson, modern forms of national identity were exported back to Europe from the colonial states in the Americas; according to Peter Martyr, the exiled narrator of the colonizing voyages was in an analogous position, and able to comment on the growth of European national consciousness.[29]

This might help to explain the radical disjunction contained in the odd encounter analysed above. Ostensibly, the purpose of *De Orbe Novo Decades* is to celebrate Spanish success in the New World and the acquisition of territories, wealth, and so on; yet it is also clearly a reflection on the desirable form civil society should take. Peter Martyr cannot overlook the dissension

---

[28] Pagden, *European Encounters*, 69; Greenblatt, *Marvelous Possessions*, 31, 128–30.

[29] Benedict Anderson, *Imagined Communities: Reflections on the Origin and Spread of Nationalism* (London: Verso, 1983), ch. 4. See also 'Exodus', *CI* 20 (1993–4), 314–27.

among the Spanish without perjuring himself and ignoring the eyewitness accounts which are what constitutes the knowledge of the hitherto unknown New World, but he intervenes in his capacity as narrator to point out a moral, so that his narrative depends very much on his own credibility as an interpreter. Like the two great opponents later in the century, Sepúlvada and Las Casas, Peter Martyr was not 'an impartial neutral observer, nor did he wish to be. . . . His history belonged to a . . . political and moral project.'[30] The problem is that this project splits the narrative, pulling its narrator in two directions at once.

We cannot know the original basis of this story and how much it has been altered, whether Peter Martyr's recording of the words of the king's son are at all accurate; nevertheless, the telling bears significant marks of having been transformed to fit in with these dual, almost inevitably contradictory, aims. The incident does serve to tell Charles of the successful acquisition of new wealth and lands, as Peter Martyr announces he will do in the preface; but it also warns of the perils of civil dissension, lack of stability, and excessive greed. The narrated encounter praises Charles's vast success, but simultaneously urges him to be cautious and think carefully about how he runs his colonial policy and whom he trusts—and, if one thinks that the example of the cannibals' exploitation of neighbouring Amerindians as 'bondmen' is a reflection upon Spanish society, about domestic policy as well. King Comogrus's son serves as both type and anti-type of his Spanish opposite. In the preface Peter Martyr explicitly connects the acquisition of knowledge with his moving to the unified Spanish nation; unfortunately, part of the knowledge he gains in his attempt to complete his self-assigned task, to record the history which the native fails to understand, is that exile in the name of expansion all too often leads to the sort of civil discord that he left Italy to escape. It might well seem that what has to be excluded—a defined nation and secure identity—as a precondition of knowledge reappears as an object of knowledge. In other words, as so often in colonial narrations, we are back where we started.

The situation of Peter Martyr's English translator, Richard Eden, was in many ways analogous to that of the exiled

---

30   Pagden, *European Encounters*, 69. I have altered plurals to singulars.

Milanese historian. Eden had been active under the protectorate of Northumberland (1549–53) in translating and promoting colonial literature in order to encourage English voyages to the New World. Northumberland had gathered a formidable team, including John Dee, William Buckley, a mathematician, Clement Adams, a cartographer, Leonard and Thomas Digges, both interested in surveying, and Robert Recorde, a physician who had supervised an earlier attempt to exploit silver mines in Ireland (1551); Eden had translated part of Sebastian Muenster's *Cosmographie Universalis* as *Of the Newe India* (1553) and Ralph Robinson had produced his more famous translation of *Utopia* (1551) (again, suggesting that in England *Utopia* was read alongside non-fictional accounts of colonial voyages).[31] Northumberland was undoubtedly keen to counteract the economic depression which gripped England, and looked enviously across to the boom enjoyed in Spain fuelled by the import of gold and silver from its colonies which resulted in relative prosperity.[32]

However, when Edward VI died in 1553 many of this intellectual circle, including Richard's uncle, Thomas, had taken part in the attempt to put Lady Jane Grey on the throne, and had understandably fallen foul of Mary. Thomas and Richard's father, George, were strongly linked to English Protestant exiles in Europe, and Thomas eventually left for Strasbourg in 1554, helping in the extensive propaganda campaign against the Spanish presence in England. One of the most prominent of these exiled Protestants, John Ponet, cited Peter Martyr's *De Orbe Novo Decades* in his justification of tyrannicide, *A Shorte Treatise of Politicke Power* (1556), to condemn Spanish atrocities there and predict that soon the English would be shipped over as slaves (suggesting that Peter Martyr's work could be read in different ways in different contexts, for his work is by no means as obvious a source for the Black Legend, which sought to emphasize the cruelties of the Spanish in their empire,

---

[31] Gwyn, 'Richard Eden', 23–4. See also Parker, *Books to Build an Empire*, ch. 4, for further details on Eden.

[32] Gwyn, 'Richard Eden', 21. On Northumberland's economic problems, see C. S. L. Davies, *Peace, Print and Protestantism, 1450–1558* (St Albans: Paladin, 1977), 284–7.

as Las Casas's extensive condemnations of Spanish policy in the New World).[33]

Eden's career trajectory moved in the opposite direction, for he appears to have 'decided to throw in his lot with the new regime' and produced his translation of *De Orbe Novo Decades* in 1555, a work which also contained extracts from Oviedo's *History of the West Indies* and writings by others connected with Spanish ventures in the Americas, such as Amerigo Vespucci, Antonio Pigafetta, and Lopez de Gomara. This 'lengthy and badly-organized book', which was none the less 'readable and informative', did not fail to prevent suspicions of Eden's loyalty. In the same year he was accused of heresy and lost his job at the Treasury.[34]

Eden appended a long preface addressed to the reader to his translation, twenty-nine pages compared with the three of Peter Martyr's original; and, like that document, it is an essay beset with anxiety. Eden lavishes praise on the *conquistadores* in a manner that is alien both to Peter Martyr's preface and to his actual text:

And surely if great Alexander and the Romans which have rather obteyned then deserved immortall fame amonge men for theyr bluddye victories onely for theyr owne glory and amplifyinge theyr empire obteyned by slaughter of innocentes and kepte by violence, have byn magnified for theyr doinges, howe much more then shal we thynk these men woorthy just commendations which in theyr mercyfull warres ageynst these naked people have so used them selves towarde them in exchaungynge of benefites for victorie, that greater commoditie hath therof ensewed to the vanquisshed then to the victourers. (p. 50)

Eden does acknowledge alternative narratives—'But sum wyll say, they possesse and inhabyte theyr regions and use theym as bondemen and tributaries, where before they were free'—only to dismiss them as partial interpretations which refuse to recognize that now the natives are truly free as Christians, not pagans, and that they enjoy the benefits of land properly used. The Spanish have only killed 'suche as coulde by no meanes be brought to civilitie', and so are exonerated of any blame and charges of excessive use of violence, as in, for example, Ponet's

---

[33] Gwyn, 'Richard Eden', 27–8; John Ponet, *A Shorte Treatise of Politicke Power* (1556), sig. F7.   [34] Gwyn, 'Richard Eden', 29–31.

claim.[35] Rather, the modern Spanish heroes go beyond those of the ancient world, who are here portrayed as vicious butchers. For Eden, the discovery of the Americas is the key event which illustrates that the moderns have supplanted the ancients and established their own time through a break with the past. Once again, the discovery of the Americas is shown to be the crucial moment which defines the experience of modernity, enabling the development of a self-reflexive consciousness which does not have to refer back to previous authorities.[36]

The passage also makes play with the notion of 'exchange', suggesting that victory has been won through trade: an impressively benevolent one, as the vanquished gain more than the victors. Again, such language signals a clean break with the past; whereas, before, victory had to be won through brutal warfare and conspicuous cruelty, as in the establishment of the Greek and Roman Empires, now the peaceful bartering of commodities and spreading of true religion are all that is required. The propagandist implications of Eden's words are obvious: the conquest of the Americas will be easy, bringing untold benefits and involving no moral dilemmas (whatever others might say . . .). The English have every reason to copy their great European rivals.

Eden's comments are also notable for their partiality. He is clearly reacting to Protestant anti-Spanish sentiment and, while an alternative narrative of the history of the colonization of the Americas is dismissed, it is none the less acknowledged, shadowing his not-overly-persuasive attempt to exonerate the Spanish and transform the *conquistadores* into role models. But Eden also protests too much in his reading of the text he is translating, for what is also obvious to any scrupulous reader of his translation of *De Orbe Novo Decades* is that Peter Martyr's narrative does not support Eden's claims for it. As the encounter with King Comogrus illustrates, the natives of the New World are not always represented as straightforwardly grateful 'naked people' who will be delighted with whatever they are given, and the *conquistadores* are hardly portrayed as

---

[35] See n. 26 above. Compare Edmund Spenser, *A View of the Present State of Ireland*, ed. W. L. Renwick (Oxford: Clarendon Press, 1970), 95, for similar sentiments.   [36] Pagden, *European Encounters*, ch. 3.

saintly heroes eager to give away more than they get. The ending of the episode with the Spanish slavering over the prospect of more gold is perhaps not quite as shocking a rhetorical construction as Montaigne's conclusion to his essay 'Of The Cannibals'—'They weare no kinde of breeches nor hosen'—but it is just as graphic an image.[37]

Eden's text contains a series of marginal glosses, a mixture of shorthand pointers for the aid of readers, with a few interpretative comments.[38] Often these serve the purpose of attempting to lead the reader away from construing the incident as a criticism of European values. For example, alongside the second half of the speech of the son of King Comogrus (see above), there are three notes: at the start is 'Naked people tormented with ambition'; against the exhortation of the prince that he will lead the Spanish to the gold is printed, 'A vehement perswasion'; and at the end, as the Spanish start to drool, is 'A token of hunger'. Such comments affirm the self-confessed inability of the Comogruans to confront their defective wills,[39] linking their defects to the greed of the Spanish.

The gloss 'Naked people tormented with ambition' can be read as a contradiction of his earlier use of 'naked' in 'The Preface to the Reader' (see above, p. 86), a bad 'nature' to place beside a good, innocent one, a reading affirmed by the drooling for gold of the Spanish.[40] The point is that all people are ultimately the same and are spurred on by their desires, and, by implication, so will the English be in their search for Empire. This is confirmed by the gloss, 'A vehement perswasion', placed beside the promise of the prince to lead the Spanish on in their less-than-admirable quest. Eden's text has started to resemble later, more overtly colonial propaganda such as Thomas Harriot's *A Briefe and True Reporte of the New Found Land of*

---

[37] *The Essayes of Michael Lord of Montaigne*, trans. John Florio (1603), 3 vols. (London: Everyman, 1910), i. 229.

[38] The Latin text contains only three marginal glosses. The others are beside the description of the corpses in the temple when the king's son begins his speech; and near his concluding remarks.

[39] See Anthony Pagden, *The Fall of Natural Man: The American Indian and the Origins of Comparative Ethnology* (Cambridge: Cambridge University Press, 1982), for an analysis of European discussions of the human status of the Amerindians in the 16th century and the reasons for their 'defective' nature.

[40] On 'good' and 'bad' nature, see Pagden, *Fall of Natural Man*, chs. 3–4.

Virginia (1588) (see below). It is as if Eden is reconstructing the original conversation between the Amerindians and the Spanish for his English audience, hoping that they will choose to be inspired by the hope for gold and empire, even if the motives for gain are transparently base.

Given Eden's biography, his anxiety is perhaps understandable, and his desire to homogenize Peter Martyr's contradictory text is unsurprising. Three pages further on in the preface, a marginal note alerts the reader to an 'Apostrophe to England', following a condemnation of criticisms of Philip II who was now married to Mary and, therefore, king of both Spain and England. Eden urges his fellow-countrymen to acknowledge their 'infirmities and deformities' by rereading the book they have mangled so badly, the Bible: 'If the greefs of them bee to thee unsensible by reason of thy feeblenesse and longe sicknesse, take unto the that glasse wherein thou gloryest with the Jewe and thynkest that thou seest al thynges and canst judge all mysteries: Looke I say in that pure glasse and beholde thy owne deformities, which thou canst not or wylle not feele' (p. 53). The traditional appeal to the reading of a text as a mirror in which all vices can be seen contains a certain irony:[41] Eden's claim that the Bible ought to be read in a spirit of self-criticism, rather than directed at a Catholic monarchy ruling a Protestant people, sits uneasily with his own attempts to limit the range of meanings of *De Orbe Novo Decades*. His attempt to argue that English expansion into the New World will lead to an overall unity at home and in the newly acquired colonies is not borne out by Peter Martyr's original text where, all too often, the opposite is shown to occur (as in the tensions revealed in the encounter with the Comogruans).

For Eden, England has become a perverse and unnatural motherland: 'There is even now great talke of thee [i.e. England] in the mouthes of all men that thou hast of late yeares brought furthe many monsters and straunge byrthes.' The rhetorical manoeuvre here is an astute one: America was thought to be the land of monsters and human deformities, but

---

[41] Born, 'The Perfect Prince'; A. M. Kinghorn, *The Chorus of History: Literary–Historical Relations in Renaissance Britain, 1485–1558* (London: Blandford, 1971), 268.

in Eden's judgement they are already inside the realm.[42] He proceeds to read them for his audience and so silence the 'dyvers interpretacions more monstrous then the monsters theim selves':

> One hath well interpreted that such monstrous byrthes signifie the monstrous and deformed myndes of the people myshapened with phantastical, dissolute opinions, dissolute lyvynge, licentious talke, and such other vicious behavoures which monstrously deforme the myndes of men in the syght of god . . . What deformed beastes are more monstrous than lyinge, rebellion, strife, contention, prime malice, slaunderynge, mutteringe, conspiracies, and such other devil-ishe imaginations. But O Englande whyle time is given thee, circum-cise thy harte. (p. 53)

Eden is clearly referring to Protestant resistance to the Marian regime, notably the Wyatt rebellion of the previous year (1554), and in the process envisages a 'correct' reading of his transla-tion as a means of helping to foster unity.[43]

Ultimately, despite attempts to homogenize and simplify the text, Eden's English translation of *De Orbe Novo Decades* is as double and contradictory as Peter Martyr's Latin original. In one sense he is glorifying the Spanish in the New World and recom-mending them as heroic exemplars for the fragmented and 'monstrous' body politic of England: their actions provide a recipe for unity and expansion, and will provide both internal and exter-nal cohesion, illustrating that the forces of nationalism and colo-nialism cannot be easily separated. In another sense, however, there is an uncomfortable link between Peter Martyr's descrip-tions of the rebellious acts of the *conquistadores* in the Americas and Eden's castigations of the crimes of his fellow citizens. Either way, the speech of the son of King Comogrus addresses at least two audiences: those who recognize his criticisms as legitimate, and an affirmation that the 'other' of the New World is, in fact, identical to the sceptical, anti-colonial reader; and those who use his speech also to affirm an identity, but with the universal human desire for gold and glorious colonial conquest to which all are helpless subjects even if they can recognize the syndrome.

---

[42] Pagden, *Fall of Natural Man*, 10–11.
[43] On Wyatt's rebellion, see Loades, *Two Tudor Conspiracies*, 1–127; Anthony Fletcher, *Tudor Rebellions* (Harlow: Longman, 1968), ch. 7.

Eden's translation of *De Orbe Novo Decades* reveals the inevitable interconnection between new and old in colonial literature; the representation of the Americas as a New World which could be exploited for England's benefit had to be assimilated to the political concerns of a European nation, so that nothing is ever quite what it seems, a motif which was to run through such writings, culminating in Samuel Purchas's Augustinian sense of the world as a ubiquitous allegory (see below). In Eden's text we are not simply to choose between what is orthodox and what is subversive, but, given the unstable nature of European political society, and the uncertain forms of representing the Americas as a conspicuously 'new' site of knowledge (see above, p. 87), we find it difficult to decide what actually belongs in either category. The incident with the Comogruans might have left its first readers with the conclusion that the Spanish were successful, but, ultimately, morally wrong. Should they therefore be condemned or celebrated? Does their greed for gold serve as a condemnation of colonial enterprises, a recognition of a universal human desire necessary despite its unappealing nature, or something which ought to be—and can be—corrected in the future? In the end, perhaps, we simply do not know, just as Peter Martyr and Richard Eden seem not to have known exactly what to make of the abundance of new information coming back from the New World. European encounters with the Americas were undeniably disastrous in the short and long term.[44] However, such problems were overshadowed for early writers and readers by a whole host of self-absorbed concerns, moral, political, and national.

The same can also be said for the book which is generally taken to be the key work in spreading the legend of Spanish cruelty in the Americas in Elizabethan England. Bartolomé de Las Casas's *Short Account of the Destruction of the Indies* (*Brevissima Relación de la Destruccion de las Indias*) was the only work of his translated into English in the late sixteenth

---

[44] J. H. Elliott writes, 'If the pre-conquest population of central Mexico fell from 25 million in 1519 to 2.65 million in 1568, and that of Peru fell from 9 million in 1532 to 1.3 million in 1570, the demographic impact of the European conquest was shattering both in its scale and speed'; 'The Spanish Conquest of America', 202.

century. The original text was published in Seville in 1552—
significantly before Eden's translation of Peter Martyr's
Decades of the Newe Worlde—but was not rendered into
English until 1583 by the as yet unidentified M. M. S. as *The
Spanish Colonie, or the Briefe Chronicle of the Acts and
Gestes of the Spaniards in the West Indies, called the New
World for the space of xl. yeares*, later incorporated into
Samuel Purchas's *Purchas His Pilgrimes* in 1625.[45] Las
Casas's text was a shorter version of his *History of the Indies*,
produced for a wider audience in order to bring home the
horrific treatment of the native Americans by the *conquistadores*. He was attempting to expose the gulf between the
rhetoric of Christian conversion which justified the colonization of the Americas, and the money-grabbing reality of those
who carried out the task. He had been the editor of
Columbus's diary, and had always defended the admiral as
singled out by God to carry out the conversion of the Indies.[46]
However, since those early days when the secular and spiritual
arms of the Spanish state in the Americas had worked
together, according to Las Casas, the two had subsequently
come to oppose each other, a situation which the *Brevissima
Relación*, with its catalogue of horrifying and brutal incidents, and series of vivid representations of appalling cruelty,
seeks to expose.[47] In order to ram this message home, the
book is arranged geographically, cataloguing Spanish atrocities in each American region they have occupied, a repetitive,
almost   mnemonic   structure,   ideal   for   propaganda.
Accordingly, the priests are often the heroes of the narrative,
attempting to prevent the vicious actions of the *conquistadores*; in between, the Indians are simply victims or souls to
be saved, in effect no more than passive bodies which are

---

[45] For the publishing history in English, see Maltby, *Black Legend*, 13.

[46] Bartolomé de Las Casas, *A Short Account of the Destruction of the Indies*,
ed. and trans. Nigel Griffin with an introduction by Anthony Pagden
(Harmondsworth: Penguin, 1992), introduction, p. xv.

[47] The illustrations were not reproduced in the English translation. One shows
'the leading citizens' in Cholula, a city in New Spain (Mexico), 'roped together, tied
to stakes and burned alive' (47); another, 'pregnant women, mothers of newborn
babies, children and old men' 'thrown into pits and impaled alive' (59); and
another, 'One woman, determined that the dogs should not tear her to pieces, tied
her child to her leg, and hanged herself from a beam' (73).

dismembered by the energetic, greedy, and cruel colonizers.[48] The focus of the reader is directed towards the moral question of the legitimacy of Spanish actions, as was the case in the famous debate between Las Casas and Juan Ginés de Sepúlvada, who regarded the Indians as no more than 'natural slaves', at Valladolid in August 1550.[49]

Why was a translation not published in English until 1583, thirty years after the work's appearance in Spain? The answer must be both speculative and complex given the lack of hard, straightforward evidence, and, I would argue, the fractured and tortuous nature of colonial propaganda. One obvious reason is stated in the preface to the translation itself, where the Spanish are characterized as the most barbarous and cruel nation in the world, and the peoples of the Low Countries are urged to wake from their sleep and realize the terrible nature of the enemies they face in their struggle for independence.[50] The text can be read as having an urgent European dimension, namely, a plea for the defence of the Protestant Low Countries against the encroachments of the Spanish empire within Europe. As such, it undoubtedly aims to persuade readers of the necessity of helping their co-religionists, a frequent plea of English Protestants throughout Elizabeth's reign attacking what they saw as her dangerous parsimony in refusing to lend anything beyond the most rudimentary military aid to the Dutch.[51]

Such a reading is strengthened by the fact that the actual text of the *Brevissima Relación* is appended by a number of other relevant works; a letter from Las Casas to Philip explaining his motives in publishing his works; and a summary of the debate at Valladolid. This second work argues that the Indians should

---

[48] On Las Casas's lack of interest in and understanding of Indian culture, see Tzvetan Todorov, *The Conquest of America: The Question of the Other*, trans. Richard Howard (New York: Harper/Collins, 1984), 164–77.

[49] The fullest account of the debate and its implications is Pagden, *Fall of Natural Man*, chs. 5–6.

[50] Bartolomé de Las Casas, *The Spanish colonie, or briefe chronicle of the acts and gestes of the Spaniardes*, trans. M. M. S. (1583), sig.q2ᵛ–q3ᵛ. Subsequent references to this edition in parentheses in the text.

[51] See Maltby, *Black Legend*, 15–16. On Anglo–Dutch relations and the claims of English Protestants for greater intervention, see Guy, *Tudor England*, 281–9; Charles Wilson, *Queen Elizabeth and the Revolt of the Netherlands* (London: Macmillan, 1970), *passim*.

enjoy the same status as citizens within Spain, a desirable legal goal inherent in the 1513 document commonly known as the *Requirimento* (which, however, was read out to the native Americans in Spanish) (O1^r).[52] The fact that this ideal has not been upheld and the Indians have been treated as an inferior species means that the sins of the Spanish will be punished in turn as they were when Spain was invaded by the Moors (P1^v–Q1^v), a claim which repeats the threat that God will eventually punish the wicked, even if they succeed in the short term, made in the epistle to the reader prefacing the text (qq^v). The material surrounding the translation of the *Brevissima Relación*, selected by the translator to help the English reader interpret the text, explicitly refers the atrocities described back to a European context, a memory perhaps of the most famous atrocities in recent history, the massacres made on Saint Bartholomew's Day, 23 August 1572. For English audiences this was the story of a wicked Catholic plot against innocent Protestants, a crucial component of the Black Legend which flattened out the disputes within Catholic Spain and the unease about motives for colonialism in the Americas which Las Casas's works were seeking to exploit so that a straightforward Protestant/Catholic dichotomy could be established.[53] The reader is thus made aware that the catalogue of brutalities which make up the text—plundering gold, random massacres, feeding rebel Indians to dogs (most famously in the case of the woman who refused to submit to rape by the Spanish), dismembering, a whole variety of tortures, enslaving huge numbers, resulting in the death of more Indians than Spaniards who ever lived (q2^v)—could, in fact, be an apocalyptic vision of a future Europe overrun by the evil Spanish before they in turn meet their judgement. Las Casas claims that the wickedness of Francisco Pizarro is so great that the full extent of it will only be revealed on the Day of Judgement (K3^r), further emphasizing the apocalyptic sub-text of both Spanish and English versions; more pointed still is the claim made in the appended material that the Spanish never

[52] See Greenblatt, *Marvelous Possessions*, 97–8; Pagden, introduction, pp. xxiv–xxv.

[53] Pagden, introduction, p. xxiv; Maltby, *Black Legend*, ch. 2; Robert M. Kingdon, *Myths about the St Bartholomew's Day Massacres, 1572–1576* (Cambridge, Mass.: Harvard University Press, 1988).

condemned martyrs within Europe to greater torments than they did when forcing the Indians to mine metals for them (P3ᵛ). Mining was commonly an image of Hell, most famously in Milton's *Paradise Lost* (I. 685–92); here, it serves as a dire warning that the Spanish experience in the New World will make them return to the Old to rule it with even greater ferocity and cruelty if they are not stopped by resolute opposition.

Such opposition could take many forms. An important, half-remembered allusion to *The Spanish colonie* occurs in a colonial propagandist tract by Robert Payne designed to encourage settlement on the Munster Plantation, *A Briefe description of Ireland* (1589). Payne writes of the common fear that Ireland will be lost to the Spanish, a theme which was frequently echoed in the aftermath of the Armada, when many Spanish ships were wrecked on the Irish coasts and survivors were slaughtered for fear of them leading rebellions, and again, often in more overtly apocalyptic mode, after their intervention in the Nine Years' War.[54] Although it is true, he admits, that there are traitors in Ireland as there are in England, 'all the better sorte doe deadly hate the Spaniardes' even if 'they beare them faire wether, for that they are the popes champions' and many Irish 'are greatly inclined to papistrie'.[55] The situation described in *The Spanish colonie* has been reversed—as both Las Casas and the translator predicted—so that the Spanish fear the Irish 'who so lately imbrued their handes in their [i.e. Spanish] blood, slaying them as dogges in such plentifull manner' (pp. 5–6). Given the following sentences, this simile can hardly not be a recollection of Las Casas's work:

If you haue not the said booke of the Spanishe cruelties, I praye you buy it, it is well woorth reading, I haue forgotten the title. but it is of a small volume in quarto: it is written by a learned Bishop of their owne country about forty yeeres sithens in the *Castalian tonge*, and dedicated to theire King for reformation of those cruelties: afterwardes translated into English and diuers other languages, to make their monstrous tirannie knowen to the world. (p. 6)

---

[54] See J. J. Silke, *Ireland and Europe, 1559–1607* (Dundalk: Dundalgan, 1966); Ralph Byrchensa, *A Discourse occasioned upon the late defeat, giuen to the Arch-rebels, Tyrone and Odonnell, by the right Honorable Lord Mountjoy* (1602).

[55] Robert Payne, *A Briefe description of Ireland: Made in this yeere. 1589* (1590), ed. Aquilla Smith (Dublin: Irish Archaeological Society, 1841), 5. Subsequent references to this edition in parentheses in the text.

Payne suggests that the readers addressed (in the first instance, his neighbours in Nottinghamshire who he hoped would join him in Munster[56]) 'commende it to our Catholickes' in order to persuade them to be loyal, thus reinforcing the message that the problem is one of an international conflict between Catholics and Protestants, with the Irish, like Las Casas's Indians, balanced between the two sides.

The use of the work in an Irish context also points out the ambivalence of the discourse of the Black Legend and its divided points of reference. Just as Ireland was frequently represented as caught between the Old and the New Worlds, simultaneously a European outpost, a sovereign territory ruled by the English monarch, and a land which was as alien to the English—and Spanish—who sought to govern there as they did in parts of the Americas, so was fear of and rivalry with the Spanish a war fought on two fronts, in two different continents.[57] Regarded one way, the fear was that Spain was becoming too powerful within Europe and its brand of tyrannical Catholicism might come to dominate the continent.[58] Looked at the other way, the fear was that Europe could become like the New World if Spain were not stopped, a fear based in part on the power to rule and the consequent technologies of conquest and domination developed in the Americas, in part on the legitimate concern that the Spanish acquisition of gold was making them too powerful to be challenged by any other European power.[59] Unless colonies were developed in the

[56] See the entry in the *DNB*.

[57] On the ways in which Ireland was represented see Nicholas P. Canny, 'The Ideology of English Colonisation: From Ireland to America', *WMQ* 30 (1973), 575–98; Andrew Hadfield, 'Crossing the Borders: Ireland and the Irish between England and America', in Paul A. S. Harvey (ed.), *Rethinking Cultural Encounter: The Diversity of English Experience, 1550–1700* (Amherst, Mass.: University of Mass. Press, forthcoming, 1999).

[58] Wiener, 'The Beleaguered Isle'; R. B. Wernham, *After the Armada: Elizabethan England and the Struggle for Western Europe, 1588–1595* (Oxford: Clarendon Press, 1984).

[59] See Geoffrey Parker, 'The Emergence of Modern Finance in Europe, 1500–1730', in Carlo M. Cipolla (ed.), *The Fontana Economic History of Europe: The Sixteenth and Seventeenth Centuries* (Glasgow: Collins, 1974), 527–89, at 528; R. Trevor Davies, *The Golden Century of Spain, 1501–1621* (London: Macmillan, 1967, rpt. of 1937), 62–4. Reports of the Spanish greed for gold are legion, culminating in the famous woodcut which accompanied Girolamo Benzoni's account of his travels in South America, published in Theodor De Bry's *America*

Americas by rival European powers, Spanish power would become unassailable.

Therefore it is not without significance that the *Brevissima Relación* was translated as *The Spanish colonie*, or that it appeared in 1583 when the first concerted efforts to establish colonies in the New World were being made by the English, backed up by a significant number of exhortatory and propagandist treatises, an outburst of intellectual activity which served to point out the conspicuous lack of interest in the Americas since the reign of Mary. Between 1576 and 1578 Martin Frobisher made three unsuccessful voyages in search of the North-West Passage; Francis Drake circumnavigated the globe (1577–80); and Humphrey Gilbert wrote a *Discourse of a Discoverie for a New Passage to Cataia* (published in 1576), and made voyages to Newfoundland, where he attempted to establish colonies (1582–3). In order to publicize these, George Peckham published his *A true Report of the late discoveries, and possession taken in the right of the Crowne of England of the Newfound Lands, By that valiant and worthy Gentleman, Sir Humphrey Gilbert Knight* (1583); Richard Willies published a *History of Trauayle in the West and East Indies* (1577), a new edition of Peter Martyr's *Decades of the New World*; John Florio published *A short and Briefe Narration of the two Navigations and Discoveries to the North-west Partes called New Fraunce* (1580);[60] and in 1582 Richard Hakluyt the younger published his first book, *Divers Voyages touching the discoverie of America*. After the publication of *The Spanish colonie*, Richard Hakluyt wrote his pioneering and hugely influential 'Discourse of Western Planting' (1584), aimed at promoting colonization in the Americas; the first attempts to transplant English and Irish subjects to the Americas took place when colonies were established first on Roanoke Island (1585–6) and then on mainland Virginia (1587), followed by the publication of Thomas Harriot's *Briefe and True Report of*

(1594), where the Indians of Darien pour molten gold down the throat of a bound Spanish soldier taunting the dying man with the words, 'Eat, eat gold, Christian'; conveniently reproduced in Michael Alexander (ed.), *Discovering the New World, Based on the Works of Theodor De Bry* (London: London Editions, 1976), 137.

[60] I owe this reference to Willy Maley.

the New Found Land of Virginia (1588, 1590), and the first edition of Hakluyt's major compilation of English voyages, *Principall Navigations, Voyages, Traffiques, and Discoveries of the English Nation*, the two most significant Elizabethan publications on the Americas (see below).[61]

The Spanish colonie appears chronologically and ideologically central to such a list of publications. Moreover, given the fact that the first colony on Roanoke was undoubtedly established as a privateering base to help carry back treasure ships captured from the Spanish, the propaganda importance of the text becomes much more obvious.[62] The prologue to the text, faithfully translated from Las Casas's Spanish, emphasizes the benign character of the people, their delicate and simple nature, their desire to learn and serve God, their total lack of guile and malice, their faithfulness and obedience to their own superiors as well as to the Spanish, and their lack of interest in worldly power (A1^r–A2^v). In short, they are the *tabulae rasae* which constitute European notions of the 'good savage', disappearing from view as a race apart, becoming blank projections for the debates carried out in their name or the colonial rivalry of competing European empires.[63] The New World is represented as an earthly paradise (F4^r), a common enough depiction which could have been found in such ubiquitous texts as *The Travels*

[61] Publications dealing with the English colonization of America are extensive. This list is based on the information provided in Morison, *The European Discovery of America: The Northern Voyages*, chs. xv–xx; William Gilbert Gosling, *The Life of Sir Humphrey Gilbert, England's First Empire Builder* (London: Constable, 1911); Parker, *Books to Build an Empire*, ch. 8; Mary C. Fuller, *Voyages in Print: English Travel to America, 1576–1624* (Cambridge: Cambridge University Press, 1995); David Beers Quinn (ed.), *The Roanoke Voayages, 1584–1590: Documents to Illustrate the English voyages to North America under the Patent Granted to Walter Raleigh in 1584*, 2 vols. (London: Hakluyt Society, 1955); and Karen Ordhal Kupperman, *Roanoke: The Abandoned Colony* (Totowa, New Jersey: Rowman and Allanheld, 1984).

[62] See Kupperman, *Roanoke*, 20, 26; Quinn (ed.), *Roanoke Voyages*, p. 173; K. R. Andrews, *Elizabethan Privateering: English Privateering during the Spanish War, 1585–1603* (Cambridge: Cambridge University Press, 1964), 192–5. In 1585, during attempts to establish the first colony at Roanoke, Sir Richard Grenville managed to capture the richly laden *Santa Maria de San Vicente* (Kupperman, *Roanoke*, 26–7).

[63] Sheehan, *Savagism and Civility*, 1–2; Hayden White, 'The Noble Savage: Theme as Fetish', in Chiapelli (ed.), *First Images of America*, 121–35; Tzvetan Todorov, *The Conquest of America: The Question of the Other*, trans. Richard Howard (New York: Harper/Collins, 1984), 176–7.

of Sir John Mandeville, but one which was clearly not dependent on any specific source.[64] For Las Casas, the crime is that
the Spanish have ruined the nearest place to heaven they will
ever find; for the English, the text provides evidence of an
opportunity to outdo their colonial rivals, building anew in the
recently discovered continent which was also a reclamation of
their past. This is its key message.[65]

M. M. S.'s translation, *The Spanish colonie,* assumes an
obvious importance beyond its value as a faithful English reproduction of Las Casas's *Brevissima Relación.* Read one way, the
book shows the cost of abandoning the Americas to the
Spanish; as the letter to the reader prefacing the summary of
Las Casas's and Sepúlvada's debate puts it, leaving the Spanish
in charge of the Indians is like trusting a child to a madman
holding a razor (P1^r). But such horrific visions are never simply
driven by commendable moral indignation; many contemporaries
noted how badly the English often behaved towards the natives
in the Americas.[66] As in so many other colonial texts, the focus
is turned inwards rather than outwards, the fear being that
unless England is vigilant in both Europe and the Americas then
their own fate could be that of the Indians. They too could be
reduced to savages exploited by the agents of the Antichrist if
they did not defend their faith vigorously enough. The link
between the vivid woodcuts which represented Spanish atrocities in the Americas, the barbarous cruelty of the Indians,
resulting from their own isolation from God's true civilization
and their resistance to the violent European invaders, and
representations of devilish torture in Hell, are by no means
accidental. Theodor De Bry, whose massive collection of

---

[64] *Travels of Sir John Mandeville,* 182–4; J. H. Elliott, *The Old World and the New, 1492–1650* (Cambridge: Cambridge University Press, 1970), 24–5.

[65] J. H. Elliott, 'Renaissance Europe and America: A Blunted Impact?', in Chiapelli (ed.), *First Images of America,* 11–23.

[66] See e.g. Philip Edwards, 'Edward Hayes Explains Away Sir Humphrey Gilbert', *RS* 6 (1992), 270–86. According to Edwards, Hayes regards Gilbert as undermining the purpose of discovery and colonization by his undue greed, which he pays for with his death. One might compare Hayes' account with Sir Walter Raleigh's picture of the grasping Spanish in his *The discoverie of the large, rich, and beautifull Empire of Guiana* (1596); reprinted in Richard Hakluyt, *The Principal Navigations, Voyages, Traffiques & Discoveries of the English Nation,* 12 vols. (Glasgow: MacLehose, 1903), vii. 338–431, at 346–8.

American voyages (1590–1634) included a multitude of gory pictures of Indian and Spanish mutilations, was a Belgian Protestant who had had to flee his native land to Strasbourg in 1570; Jacques Le Moyne De Morgues, who supplied many of the drawings for De Bry's volume, was a Huguenot who had escaped from the Spanish when they destroyed the French colony in Florida in 1564 and eventually settled in England in about 1580 specifically because of his religion.[67] Both had lived through the Massacre of Saint Bartholomew's Day, an event frequently represented as the consequence of the burgeoning power of the Antichrist.[68]

The relationship between courtiers who favoured a more interventionist policy in the Netherlands against Spain as a means of furthering Protestantism as an international movement as well as fostering a more reformed religion at home, and who argued for the importance of colonial expansion in the Americas (partly as a means of stopping the flow of gold to Spain), is well attested. The pivotal figures are Sir Francis Walsingham, his son-in-law Sir Philip Sidney, Sir Walter Raleigh, and Richard Hakluyt the younger, all of whom took a strong anti-Spanish line in their writings.[69] The first version of Hakluyt's collections of English overseas exploration, *Divers voyages* (1582), was dedicated to Sidney; Hakluyt's edition of Peter Martyr's *De Orbe Novo Decades* (1587) was dedicated to Raleigh.[70] Walsingham had been ambassador in Paris, and had sheltered Sidney when he had visited during the massacre of Saint Bartholomew.[71]

[67] For biographical information see Alexander (ed.), *Discovering the New World*, 8; Paul Hulton, 'Jacques Le Moyne De Morgues: A Biographical Sketch', in Hulton (ed.), *The Work of Jacques Le Moyne De Morgues: A Huguenot Artist in France, Florida and England*, 2 vols. (London: British Museum, 1977), i. 3–12.

[68] See A. G. Dickens, 'The Elizabethans and St. Bartholomew', in Alfred Soman (ed.), *The Massacre of St. Bartholomew: Reappraisals and Documents* (The Hague: Martinus Nijhoff, 1974), 52–70; Sylvia Lennie England, *The Massacre of Saint Bartholomew* (London: John Long, 1938), ch. 6; Kingdon, *Myths about the St. Bartholomew's Day Massacres*.

[69] See Carol Shammas, 'English Commercial Development and American Colonization, 1560–1620', in K. R. Andrews, N. P. Canny, and P. E. H. Hair (eds.), *The Westward Enterprise: English Activities in Ireland, the Atlantic and America* (Liverpool: Liverpool University Press, 1978), 151–74, at 153; Quinn (ed.), *Hakluyt Handbook*, 133–4, 269, 286–7; *Roanoke Voyages*, 77–9, 197–200, passim.   [70] Quinn (ed.), *Hakluyt Handbook*, 293, 338–9.

[71] Katherine Duncan-Jones, *Sir Philip Sidney: Courtier Poet* (New Haven: Yale University Press, 1991), 60–2, 233–4.

Therefore, it is not surprising that Hakluyt's apparently influential attempt to further colonization in the Americas, the text which has subsequently been known as 'A Discourse of Western Planting' (1584), makes a direct link between the need to supplant Spain's empire in the New World and the spread of Protestantism. For Hakluyt this is not simply a case of converting the natives, but also using the wealth from the Americas to increase the population of England, expanding through the establishment of colonies and correcting the disadvantages of English society by putting idle hands to work in these colonies.[72] Hakluyt quotes directly from a number of Spanish, Portuguese, and French works to make his case (Francisco Lopez de Gomara's *The pleasant historie of the Conquest of West India*, translated by T. Nicholas (1578), Jean Ribault's *The whole and true discovery of Terra Florida*, translated in 1563, Dr. Monardes' *Historia Medicinal . . . de nuestras Indias*, translated in 1577, and others), significantly including descriptions of massacres from M. M. S.'s translation of Las Casas (pp. 257–61), published in the previous year, illustrating that, even if Hakluyt had little to do with the actual publication of that work, it formed an important part of English colonial propaganda.

Hakluyt commences his argument with the need to establish the reformed religion in the Americas, but, in doing so he draws attention to England's inadequacies. While the Spanish have managed to convert numerous Indians, 'Of wch acte they more vaunte in all their histories and Chronicles, then of anythinge els that ever they atchieved' (p. 216), the ministers of the gospel sent by the French into Florida, the Genevans into Brazil, and 'also those of our nation that went wth ffrobisher, S^r ffraunces Drake, and ffenton', had less success: 'yet in very deede I was not able to name any one Infidell by them converted' (p. 217). Hakluyt makes the connection between material success and the conversion of the infidels, neatly eliding the spiritual and the economic: 'Unto the Prince and people that shalbe the occasion of this

[72] Richard Hakluyt the younger, 'Discourse of Western Planting', in E. G. R. Taylor (ed.), *The Original Writings and Correspondence of the Two Richard Hakluyts* (London: Hakluyt Society, 1935), 211–326. All subsequent references to this edition in parentheses in the text.

worthie worke, and shall open their coffers to the furtheraunce of this most godly enterprise, God shall open the bottomles treasures of his riches and fill them wth aboundance of his hidden blessinges' (p. 216). The 'hidden blessinges' promised, as chapter 13 makes clear, include 'the Revenewes and customes of her Matie' (pp. 268–70): moral righteousness and wealth need not be at odds.

The problem is that England is failing on two counts, and that matters at home are impeding hopes of glory abroad. First, there has been no state encouragement for colonization: Hakluyt points out that God 'hath his tyme for all men, whoe calleth some at the nynthe, and some at the eleventh hower', suggesting that the time for converting the Indians is imminent if it is to happen at all (a concern that the apocalypse is impending). Hence the desperate need for the Queen to act: 'And if it please him to move the harte of her Matie to put her helping hande to this godly action she shall finde as willinge subjectes of all sortes as any other prince in all christendome' (p. 217). However, not all blame can be directed at the queen. As in Eden's preface to his translation of Peter Martyr, Elizabeth's subjects' lack of success in expanding overseas also results from a divided nation:

But also many inconveniences and strifes amongest o^rselves at home in matters of Ceremonies shalbe ended: For those of the Clergye wch by reason of idlenes here at home are nowe alwayes coyninge of newe opynions, havinge by this voyadge to sett themselves on worke in reducinge the Savages to the chefe principles of our faithe, will become lesses contentious, and be confined with the truthe in Relligion alreadie established by aucthoritie: So they that shall beare the name of Christians shall shewe themselves worthye of their vocation, so shall the mouthe of the adversarie [i.e. the Spanish] be stopped, so shall contention amongest Bretheren be avoyded, so shall the gospell amonge Infidells be published (pp. 217–18).

As for Eden, national renewal and the colonial enterprise were interrelated goals (although the way ahead is more straightforward in Hakluyt's text).[73] The establishment of colonies in the

---

[73] See the reading of Hakluyt's enterprise in Richard Helgerson, *Forms of Nationhood: The Elizabethan Writing of England* (Chicago: Chicago University Press, 1992), ch. 4, 'The Voyages of a Nation', 149–91.

Americas would force idle ministers to direct their energies towards a more productive enterprise, making into an impossible luxury the destructive disputes which, according to Hakluyt, had torn the nation apart.[74] Just as Elizabeth would have to speculate in order to accumulate wealth, so would the nation have to expand in order to unify itself.

The key word in Hakluyt's analysis is 'idlenes', a theme he develops in the fourth chapter of the text, which argues that 'this enterprise will be for the manifolde ymployment of nombers of idle men, and for bredinge of many sufficient'. Hakluyt alleges that Spain and Portugal have managed to expand despite being 'poore and barren and hardly able to susteine their inhabitaunts' (p. 233), which has eliminated harmful social problems such as the proliferation of pirates. In contrast, England has 'growen more populous than ever heretofore' through peace and general good health, blessings from God which have their drawbacks:

> nowe there are of every arte and science so many, that they can hardly lyve one by another, nay rather they are readie to eate upp one another: yea many thousands of idle persons are w[th]in this Realm, w[ch] havinge no way to be sett on worke be either mutinous and seeke alteration in the state, or at leaset very burdensome to the common wealthe, and often fall to pilferinge and thevinge and other lewdnes, whereby all the prisons of the lande are daily pestred and stuffed full of them, where either they pitifully pyne awaye, or els at lengthe are miserably hanged. (p. 234)

The hard work of colonial life would discipline them, as it would stop the divisive doctrinal disputes of ministers, transforming creatures who would undermine the state into solid citizens.[75]

But the phrasing of this passage means that it cannot simply be read as a solution to a pressing economic problem. Hakluyt describes idle Englishmen as cannibals, ready to consume each other, a trope which recalls Thomas More's description of sheep

---

[74] For a similar argument used with respect to Irish colonies, see *CSPD, Addenda, 1566–79*, pp. li–liv. A convenient overview of contemporary religious developments and Elizabeth's reactions to them is described in W. P. Haugaard, *Elizabeth and the English Reformation* (Cambridge: Cambridge University Press, 1968).   [75] See Williams, *Tudor Regime*, 196–206.

becoming man-eaters, a subject which leads onto the very same problem of the debilitating effects of idleness on the community.[76] Implicit in Hakluyt's comparison is the fear that if nothing is done to tackle social problems at home, then the English will become—literally, or metaphorically—man-eating savages similar to those which inhabit the Americas.[77] English society stands delicately balanced: either it can expand and unify, absorbing and converting savages as it does so, or it can stagnate, let Spain dominate, and risk becoming a savage land itself.

The apocalyptic dimension of this analysis—in line with other contemporary texts which represented Spanish behaviour in the Americas—becomes much more explicit towards the end. Hakluyt attacks the division of the world into Spanish and Portuguese spheres of influence by Pope Alexander VI (1493–4) using John Bale's *Acta Romanorum Pontificum* (1558), one of the many works in which he outlined his apocalyptic reading of European history (p. 302).[78] Philip II is denigrated as 'the supporter of the greate Antechriste of Rome' (p. 315); a further function of English colonies will be to act as sanctuaries for those 'people from all partes of the worlde that are forced to flee for the truthe of gods worde' (p. 318); and the treatise concludes with the express injunction that only Protestant artisans are to be permitted to travel to the New World, as Catholics will undermine colonial projects 'for the speciall inclynation they have of favour to the kinge of Spaine' (p. 326). For Hakluyt, due care and attention paid to colonial government will enable the grey compromises of English society to be sorted out into the black and white divisions of religious truth.

---

[76]   More, *Utopia*, 46–8.

[77]   More's discussion of the man-eating sheep set on the populace by greedy, idle aristocrats may be hyperbolic and, possibly, ironic (see Kinney, *Humanist Poetics*, 83; Johnson, *More's Utopia*, 53–4); nevertheless, the fear that civilized Englishmen could easily become savage enough to eat each other was often expressed, and, indeed, often happened: see Sheehan, *Savagism and Civility*, 60–2; Andrew Hadfield, 'Writing the New World'; Hulme, *Colonial Encounters*, ch. 2. Numerous accounts of English man-eating are described in George Percy, ' "A Trewe Relacyon": Virginia from 1609 to 1612', *Tyler's Magazine*, 3 (1922), 259–82.

[78]   Katherine Firth, *The Apocalyptic Tradition in Reformation Britain, 1530–1645* (Oxford: Oxford University Press, 1979), ch. 2.

Hakluyt's interest in promoting English colonialism led him to publish a number of Spanish accounts of their experiences in colonizing the Americas.[79] A work he may have been connected with is Edward Grimstone's translation of José de Acosta's *The Natural and Moral History of the Indies* (*Historia Natural y Moral de las Indias* (1590)) (1604), portions of which Hakluyt had translated himself in the 1598 edition of the *Principal Navigations*.[80] Grimstone's translation is dedicated to Sir Robert Cecil, the courtier who was the central focus of colonial efforts after the death of Sir Francis Walsingham in 1590, and to whom the second edition of the *Principal Navigations* was also dedicated.[81]

Grimstone's translation of Acosta provides a pointed contrast to the religious focus of Hakluyt's earlier work on colonialism and his use of Spanish material available.[82] Little is known of Grimstone's life: in the dedication to his translation of Pierrre d'Avity's *The Estates, Empires and Principalities of the World* (1615), a handsomely produced folio, to Thomas Howard, Earl of Suffolk, Lord High Treasurer, refers to his service in France, subsequent travel there, as well as in the Netherlands and Spain, and refers to his work as the last labours of an old man.[83] Grimstone's prefatory comments to

---

[79] For a list of Hakluyt's publications, those he sponsored and those where his influence is acknowledged or apparent, see Quinn (ed.), *Hakluyt Handbook*, 461–575.   [80] Ibid. 235, 308, 603–4.

[81] Parker, *Books to Build an Empire*, 167. The 2nd edition of Hakluyt's *Principal Navigations* was dedicated to Cecil.

[82] Hard experience dictated that the stated religious motive for establishing colonies receded after early hopes in the late 1580s and early 1590s; see Parker, *Books to Build an Empire*, 70, 84, 87; Parker, 'Religion and the Virginia Colony, 1609–10', in Andrews *et al.* (eds.), *Westward Enterprise*, 245–70. See also K. R. Andrews, *Trade, Plunder and Settlement: Maritime Enterprise and the Genesis of the British Empire, 1480–1630* (Cambridge: Cambridge University Press, 1984), 31–2, where it is argued that religious motives were never a significant factor in the establishment of colonies.

[83] Pierre d'Avity, *The Estates, Empires and Principalities of the World*, trans. Edward Grimstone (1615), n. p. Subsequent references to this edition in parentheses in the text. Grimstone's dedication to Suffolk and his Spanish experience may signify a political allegiance with a Catholic, pro-Spanish faction at court; his last translation, of Philippe Bethune's *The Counsellor of Estate* (1634), was dedicated to Sir Richard Weston, another prominent Catholic. However, the dedications to two Lord Treasurers may signal a more straightforward hope for financial gain. Given that Grimstone's translation of Acosta's work is dedicated to the undoubtedly Protestant Sir Robert Cecil, and that he may have had connections with Hakluyt at

his translation of d'Avity may shed light on the ways in which his earlier translation of Acosta can be read. In his address as translator to the reader, Grimstone confesses that he has added a great deal to the translation, has omitted sections where d'Avity is mistaken, and has altered some religious descriptions. He also repeats the ubiquitous claim that travel and travel writing are intended to teach, a claim repeated at length in d'Avity's own address to the reader. D'Avity argues that we cannot know ourselves unless we have knowledge of other nations because we cannot judge our own estate until we have seen that of our neighbours. Hence his aim is to provide a science of the world, a task which will make his book more useful than any other scientific inquiry undertaken. He will show a whole range of nations for the reader to compare, providing details of the legal and political systems of governments, their histories, and religions, so that the book can be used by all estates of men, from princes and noblemen to soldiers and merchants. In the 1,234 pages d'Avity surveys most countries known to Europeans at the time: the three kingdoms of the British Isles (placed first), most nations in Europe itself, as well as Eastern nations (Calicut, China, and Japan), North African nations (Morocco and Turkish North Africa), and the legendary kingdom of Prester John.[84]

Significantly enough, d'Avity/Grimstone praises Venice in the strongest terms as the best of all commonwealths, repeating the myth of the Venetian golden age, admiring its stable oligarchy, the relatively equitable treatment of all its citizens, and its avoidance of tyranny (pp. 526–30). Equally important is the praise given to England because of the sovereignty of Parliament and gradual diminution of the role of the monarch over the centuries, so that the sovereign is not even required to

this point, political motives for the last two dedications appear less likely. On the importance of Suffolk and Weston, see Conrad Russell, *The Crisis of Parliaments: English History, 1509–1660* (Oxford: Oxford University Press, 1971), 286, 311. For further details of Grimstone's life, see Father Joseph De Acosta, *The Natural and Moral History of the Indies*, trans. Edward Grimstone, ed. Clements R. Markham, 2 vols. (London: Hakluyt Society, 1880), intro., p. xiv.

[84] A significant feature in Mandeville's *Travels*, 167–72, *passim*, hence included also in the first edition of Hakluyt's *Principal Navigations* (1589), although omitted for the second.

attend sessions of Parliament until they are nearing their end (pp. 10–11). Also to the nation's credit is the notable absence of torture for crimes (p. 12) and the flourishing of Protestantism under James (pp. 12–13). Grimstone's much later translation of Bethune's *The Counsellor of Estate*, is a handbook advising the ways and means of good government. Bethune/Grimstone's projected audience is both princes and counsellors, so that the work can be seen to belong to the tradition of 'mirrors for princes' literature opened out by later works such as *A Mirror for Magistrates*. The dedication advises Lord Weston that princes require counsellors for the health of the state: without them, the people will suffer.[85] The text itself, which is prefaced by a list of chapter summaries appropriate to a work designed for consultation, details the various forms of government possible, concluding that an oligarchy ruled by a prince, although by no means perfect, is best (pp. 10–11: again, Venice is the model, p. 9). There is an extensive discussion of colonization, which undoubtedly owes much to Machiavelli (pp. 297–300), as does the recommendation that a prince can use cunning and fraud when necessary (p. 8), and the suggestion that good order is easier to maintain with the help of religion (pp. 28–9).[86]

Grimstone's labours indicate that, as the careers of many Renaissance Englishmen illustrate, there was a close connection between the theory and experience of travelling within Europe and plans to colonize the New World, and it is in the light of conceptions of comparative government that Grimstone's translation of Acosta can be read.[87] Much of Acosta's text, like Harriot's (see below, pp. 112–26), is devoted to a description of the natural world of the Americas, as well as the perplexing

[85] Philippe Bethune, *The Counsellor of Estate*, trans. Edward Grimstone (1634), sig.A3ʳ. Subsequent references to this edition in parentheses in the text.

[86] Niccolò Machiavelli, *The Prince*, trans. George Bull (Harmondsworth: Penguin, 1961) 73–6, 99–101, 114–19.

[87] In addition to Sidney, who completed an extensive tour of Europe (1572–5) (see Duncan-Jones, *Sir Philip Sidney*, ch. 4), and Walsingham, the career of Sir George Sandys is important: see Richard Beale Davis, *George Sandys, Poet Adventurer: A Study in Anglo-American Culture in the Seventeenth Century* (London: Bodley Head, 1955). One should also note that numerous colonists and colonial organizers had European military experience (e.g. Sir Richard Grenville, Sir Humphrey Gilbert, Sir Walter Raleigh). Grimstone also wrote a history of France and pieced together a history of the Netherlands (Acosta, *History of the Indies*, intro., p. xiv).

question of how the Indians evolved in apparent isolation from the rest of humanity.[88] The first four books deal with natural history; the last three tell the moral history of the Indians. Book 5 argues that Mexican religion reveals that the Indians have some knowledge of a supreme deity, but are infected by the sin of idolatry; Book 6 examines Peruvian and Mexican society and government; Book 7 narrates the history of Mexico up to the Spanish conquest under Cortés and the murder of Montezuma, a story which refigures the eyewitness account and defence of Cortés' actions given in Bernal Díaz's *The Conquest of New Spain*.[89]

Acosta's text was the first attempt to systematize the cultures discovered by Europeans in the Americas. To this end, his aim was to understand rather than condemn, even though he had a lower estimate of the Indians' capacities than Las Casas, regarding them as servile, like European peasants or children, because of the malign effects of their cultural isolation. Like Grimstone and other defenders of travel writing, Acosta hoped to educate his readers by presenting them with evidence of diverse societies.[90]

Acosta examines Peruvian and Mexican society in Book 6 in conceptual terms familiar to readers of European political discourse. He divides Indian societies into three types: monarchy, which is 'first and best', although often degenerating into tyranny; 'Comminalities, where they are governed by the advice and authoritie of many, which are as it were Counsellors'; and the barbarous government 'composed of Indians without law, without King, and without any certaine place of abode, but go in troupes like savage beasts'.[91] Acosta's understanding of government is both hierarchical and historical in its teleology:

---

[88] It is not beyond the bounds of possibility that there is a historical relation between the two works. Harriot's *Briefe and True Report* was published in 1588, then again in 1590 as the first part of De Bry's *America* (see below, pp. 113–15); Acosta's *Historia Natural* was first published in Seville in 1590, before going through a number of editions. It is possible that Grimstone's translation was intended to make up for the promised work which Harriot never completed. On the theological problems created by the discovery of the Indians and Acosta's role in subsequent debates, see Pagden, *Fall of Natural Man*, ch. 7.

[89] Díaz, *Conquest of New Spain*. See also Greenblatt, *Marvelous Possessions*, 128–45.   [90] Pagden, *Fall of Natural Man*, 153–62.

[91] Acosta, *History of the Indies*, 426–7. Subsequent references to this edition in parentheses in the text.

It is apparent that the thing wherein these barbarous people shew their barbarisme, was in their governement and manner of command: for the more that men approch to reason, the more milde is their governement, and lesse insolent; the Kings and Lords are more tractable, agreeing better with their subjects, acknowledging them equall in nature, though inferior in duetie and care of the commonwealth. But amongst the Barbarians all is contrary, for that their government is tyrannous, using their suiects like beasts, and seeking to be reverenced like gods. (pp. 409–10)

Such comments are double-edged, recalling Hakluyt's fear that a stagnant European society which refused to expand could degenerate into savagery. Tyranny is equated with barbarism, the implication being that the same standards can be applied to unreasonable forms of government within Europe, especially one where the king is reverenced like a god and does not acknowledge the equality of his subjects, opinions which James had voiced in the 1590s (see above, pp. 44–7).

Acosta's tale of the destruction of the Aztec empire of Montezuma is a particular example of such general observations on the nature of government, theory being illustrated by practice very much in line with a Guicciardinian use of history, the aim being to draw a useful political lesson from the information given.[92] Montezuma is represented as a remote and ineffective leader, a grand figure and impressive orator, but fatally cut off from his people. When appointed, Montezuma withdraws to the chapel in the Temple, which according to Acosta, is a hypocritical and cynical manoeuvre designed to 'show that he desired not Empire' (p. 500).[93] More seriously damaging is Montezuma's refusal to listen to any advice: his elderly schoolmaster warns him that dismissing 'all the plebians from their charges and offices' and positions at court, and replacing them with nobles, will leave the emperor dangerously isolated from the majority of his nation (p. 503). Acosta acknowledges Montezuma's military success against the

---

[92] Fenton's translation of Guicciardini's *History of Italy* had just been republished (1599) (see above, p. 37).

[93] Montezuma's actions resemble those of Richard III in Shakespeare's play when he pretends that he has no interest in accepting the crown in order to inspire public approval (*Richard III*, III. vii).

Spanish, as other accounts testify (p. 506), but clearly sees a lesson to be learnt in the emperor's haughty grandeur. Montezuma demanded that he be 'worshipped as a god', refusing to allow plebians to look directly at him on pain of death; he was always carried by noblemen, so that his feet never had to touch the ground; after returning from wars he often disguised himself (like the Duke in *Measure for Measure*) and went among the people to make sure that nothing was omitted from the planned feast or reception, punishing any who neglected their duties; most significantly, he often spied on his ministers, disguising himself after victories in war, 'offering giftes and presents to the iudges, provoking them to do iniustice' and if they were found wanting, 'they were presently punished with death, without remission or respect' (p. 505). The responsibility for Montezuma's death remains something of a mystery, both Spanish and Indians blaming the other. Such ambiguity enables Acosta to reinforce the moral point of his story: 'But howsoever, Montezuma died, miserably, and paied his deserts to the judgement of our Lord of heaven for his pride and tyranny: his body falling into the Indians power, they would make him no obsequeies of a king, no, not of an ordinarie person, but cast it away in great disdaine and rage' (p. 522).

It is, of course, extremely difficult to evaluate exactly how relevant to English politics or subversive of received orthodoxies Grimstone's translation of Acosta's work is. Grimstone is generally a faithful translator of Acosta;[94] there are no significant marginal annotations to guide the reader, as there are in Eden's translation of Peter Martyr. The date of the work's publication (1604) may be significant in terms of the recent accession of James I, but it is more likely that Grimstone had been working on his translation for a few years. What can be concluded is that *The Natural and Moral*

---

94 The few changes which have been made do not appear overly significant; the reply of Montezuma to the old man has been altered from the direct speech of the original version into indirect speech and somewhat intensified in the process; odd phrases are omitted and there are one or two interpolations. See José de Acosta, *Historia Natural y Moral de las Indias* (1590) (Mexico: Fondo de Cultura Economica, 1940), 569–70, 565, 584–5. I am extremely grateful to Robert Stone for help with comparing the Spanish and English texts.

History of the Indies cannot be read simply as a work of colonial propaganda, or as a contribution to the Black Legend (which it obviously is not).[95] Instead, the later books would appear to fit into a tradition of studies of comparative government—one in which Grimstone himself played an important role—developed throughout the sixteenth century, and assuming increasing importance in the latter years of Elizabeth's reign. The story of Montezuma's defeat and death, which differs markedly from the account given in Bernal Díaz,[96] illustrates a government which resembles those of China, Japan, or the Congo as described in *The Estates, Empires and Principalities of the World*, where rulers aspire to be revered as gods. It stands as the antithesis of the Venetian constitution, which solicited the participation of all citizens, insisted on elected rulers and counsellors, and remained stable and prosperous precisely because advice was the central principle of its government.[97] As English writers frequently recognized, much could be learnt from Spain's experience in the Americas.

II

In marked contrast to Spanish success in the New World was the abject failure of English enterprises in the late sixteenth and early seventeenth centuries before the advent of the Jamestown settlement in 1607, when the demands of propagandists like Hakluyt, that colonial enterprise on a massive scale should be backed up by government funding, were met with the establishment of the

---

[95] As the historian of the legend acknowledges without offering any other suggestion as to how Acosta's work might be read (Maltby, *Black Legend*, 28).

[96] See Díaz, *Conquest of New Spain*, 294–5. Díaz claims that Montezuma died after being hit by stones during an Aztec attack when the soldiers who were guarding him 'momentarily neglected their duty'. Indians and Spanish alike mourn the death of 'the best king they ever had in Mexico'.

[97] See d'Avity, *Estates, Empires and Principalities of the World*, 731, 747–8, 1104, 526–7. The Mexican king, Acamapixtli, refuses to leave his kingdom to his lawful children, suggesting instead that his people should 'choose him that seme fittest for their good government', an act described by Acosta as 'one memorable thing' (*History of the Indies*, 470–1).

Virginia Company in 1606.[98] However, an English text did become one of the most influential works of early ethnohistory in Europe after its publication (1588, 1590), namely, Thomas Harriot's *A Briefe and True Reporte of the New Found Land of Virginia*.[99] Harriot's enigmatic text, like Acosta's, displays as much interest in the problems of comparing cultures and the significance of doing so as it does in the representation of the Indians for a European audience.[100] Put another way, such a division results from the conflict between a comparative political science and a putative anthropological discourse.[101]

As with many other colonial works, Harriot's motives in writing his report are not clear. While the observations of the natural world of the Americas, Indian society, and customs are undoubtedly intended as scientific recordings which will help Europeans understand the recent enlargement of their intellectual and geographical horizons, the tract was also written as propaganda to persuade sceptics in England that the Roanoke colonies were worthwhile enterprises.[102] More specifically, it was an attempt 'to counteract the evil rumours surrounding Ralegh's colonizing ventures'.[103] Interpretation is made complicated by the number

---

[98] See Calder, *Revolutionary Empire*, 130–9; D. B. Quinn, *Raleigh and the British Empire* (London: Hodder and Stoughton, 1947), ch. 7; Andrews, *Trade, Plunder and Settlement*, ch. 14. Even the success of Jamestown was only relative to earlier disasters; Knapp, *Empire Nowhere*, 2–3; James Axtell, *After Columbus: Essays in the Ethnohistory of Colonial North America* (New York: Oxford University Press, 1988), 219.

[99] On Harriot's influence, see David B. Quinn and John Shirley, 'A Contemporary List of Harriot References', *RQ* 22 (1969), 9–26.

[100] A case most famously argued by Stephen Greenblatt in 'Invisible Bullets', in *Shakespearian Negotiations: The Circulation of Social Energy in Renaissance England* (Oxford: Clarendon Press, 1988), ch. 2. See also Fuller, *Voyages in Print*, 40–54, 91–5; Knapp, *Empire Nowhere*, 141–6. For assessments of the value of Harriot's observations as ethnographic study, see Axtell, *After Columbus*, 133–5; Quinn (ed.), *Roanoke Voyages*, 314–89; D. B. Quinn, 'Thomas Harriot and the New World', in John Shirley (ed.), *Thomas Harriot: Renaissance Scientist* (Oxford: Clarendon Press, 1974), 36–53.

[101] See Edward Rosen, 'Harriot's Science, The Intellectual Background', in Shirley (ed.), *Thomas Harriot*, 1–15; Allen G. Debus, *Man and Nature in the Renaissance* (Cambridge: Cambridge University Press, 1978); Margaret T. Hogden, *Early Anthropology in the Sixteenth and Seventeenth Centuries* (Pennsylvania: Philadelphia University Press, 1964).

[102] John W. Shirley, 'Sir Walter Raleigh and Thomas Harriot', in *Thomas Harriot*, 16–35, at 19; Hadfield, 'Writing the New World', 10.

[103] Quinn (ed.), *Roanoke Voyages*, 314, 548; Shirley, 'Raleigh and Harriot', 10.

of early editions of various forms of the work, and the fact that it is also unclear who authorized which version.

The *Report* first appeared in 1588, published by Robert Robinson. This edition was a quarto, probably commissioned by Raleigh, and no record of it having been entered in to the Stationers' Register survives. Harriot advertises himself as a servant to Raleigh in the colony, and there is a letter addressed to the reader by Ralph Lane, governor of the colony, recommending Harriot as a reliable eye-witness, 'as that I dare boldly auouch it may very well passe with the credit of trueth euen amongst the most true relations of this age', even though Lane himself cannot endorse all that Harriot has written.[104] This defensive tone is continued in the address of the text itself 'To the Adventurers, Fauourers, and Welwillers of the enterprise for the inhabiting and planting in Virginia', indicating the propagandist purpose of the edition.[105] However, given that Harriot probably wrote the work in February 1587, it is unclear why publication was delayed for so long, unless it was held over to solicit support for the expedition Sir Richard Grenville was planning in 1588.[106]

The *Report* was reprinted with minor editorial changes in Hakluyt's *Principal Navigations* of 1589, and subsequently included in the expanded version of 1598.[107] The most important edition was undoubtedly that published by the exiled Belgian printer, Theodor De Bry, as the first part of his multivolume collection of New World voyages, *America*. Harriot's *Report* was published in a folio edition, separately reproduced in four languages—Latin, English, French, and German—as the first part of De Bry's massive project in 1590. Appended were a series of drawings by the English artist, John White, who had sailed with Grenville's expedition in 1585, and who had become governor of the Roanoke colony in 1587, before being

---

[104] David Beers Quinn (ed.), *The Roanoke Voyages: Documents to Illustrate the English Voyages to North America under the Patent Granted to Walter Raleigh in 1584*, 2 vols. (London: Hakluyt Society, 1955), 319.

[105] Quinn (ed.), *Roanoke Voyages*, 320.

[106] Ibid. 37–9, 317–18. On Grenville's activities in the Americas, see A. L. Rowse, *Sir Richard Grenville of the Revenge* (London: Jonathan Cape, 1937), chs. X–XIII.

[107] Quinn (ed.), *Roanoke Voyages*, 38, 318; *Hakluyt Handbook*, 376.

persuaded to return to England by his charges to plead for supplies and support.[108]

De Bry's edition was dedicated to Raleigh, as originator of the Roanoke colony, and he had probably been persuaded to publish Harriot's *Report* as the first volume of his series by Hakluyt, whom he had met in London in 1587. Hakluyt was in pursuit of the exiled French Huguenot artist Jacques Le Moyne de Morgues, whose drawings of the Florida Indians he wished to include as engravings to accompany the text of René de Laudonniere's account of the French colony in Florida (1562–5), where Le Moyne had been the official artist.[109] Harriot had written Latin captions to accompany White's drawings, which Hakluyt translated into English.

Harriot's text remains virtually the same in all editions, but its significance clearly alters according to the context. While the text published by Robert Robinson appears to have an exhortatory function, displaying scientific learning in order to encourage backers to provide more money and persuade new colonists to undertake the voyage to the Americas (although the delay in publication may suggest that such assumptions are by no means secure), De Bry's magnificent edition aims as much to perform the double function of celebrating English success in the Americas and assessing the importance of the discovery of the new continent. De Bry's work has a strongly anti-Spanish bias— hardly surprising, given his own religious views, his nationality, his narrow escapes from persecution, and his age at the time of the Bartholomew's Day massacre (early forties)—and his framing of Harriot's narrative is explicitly theological.[110] Given that

[108] For an account of White's life and importance, see Paul Hulton, 'Images of the New World: Jacques Le Moyne de Morgues and John White', in Andrews *et al.* (eds.), *Westward Enterprise*, 195–214; Kupperman, *Roanoke*, ch. 7, *passim*; Paul Hulton and David Beers Quinn (eds.), *The American Drawings of John White, 1577–1590*, 2 vols. (London: British Museum, 1964), 12–24.

[109] For an account of Le Moyne's life, see Hulton, 'Images of the New World'; Paul Hulton (ed.), *The Work of Jacques Le Moyne De Morgues*, i. 3–16. On the probable sequence of events which led to De Bry's publication of Harriot's *Report* and the close relationship between Harriot, Raleigh, Hakluyt, De Bry, and White, see Quinn (ed.), *Roanoke Voyages*, 39; Alexander (ed.), *Discovering the New World*, 64; Paul Hulton (ed.), *America 1585: The Complete Drawings of John White* (London: British Museum, 1984), 17–21.

[110] Something of an irony given Harriot's scandalous reputation in England; see Greenblatt, 'Invisible Bullets', 22–3; Shirley, 'Raleigh and Hakluyt', 23–4.

De Bry's multilingual volume was probably the most important—certainly the most comprehensive—survey of European voyages and attempts to colonize the Americas in the late sixteenth and early seventeenth centuries, the ways in which he frames the narratives he included is evidently significant.[111]

White's drawings have generally been accepted as an accurate record of the now vanished Algonkian Indians of Virginia.[112] De Bry is, as a rule, reasonably faithful in his reproduction of John White's original drawings as engravings— although he does have a tendency 'to idealize the features and soften the more awkward gestures', and he adds important details to the drawings of the ancient inhabitants of Great Britain (see below).[113] The former alterations are perhaps as much the result of the problems of reproducing drawings as book plates and fitting them into an acceptable and recognizable style as they are consciously motivated and significant changes. However, it is clear that there is more than simple accuracy at stake in his reproduction of representations of the native Americans, especially in the additions to the backgrounds to White's drawings.

The introduction to the collection of appended drawings makes the religious context clear, perhaps demanding that the reader return to Harriot's text and interpret Harriot's words in a deeper, more allegorical manner.[114] The series is introduced by an engraving of Adam and Eve before the Fall, attributed to De Bry himself, with the serpent entwined around the tree between them as they reach up to pick the apples (Fig. 1).[115] In

[111] For a compelling analysis of the iconography of the whole of *America*, see Bernadette Bucher, *Icon and Conquest: A Structural Analysis of the Illustrations of De Bry's Great Voyages*, trans. Basia Miller Gulati (Chicago: University of Chicago Press, 1981).

[112] For the most comprehensive analysis, see Hulton and Quinn (eds.), *American Drawings of John White*.

[113] Paul Hulton, 'Introduction', Thomas Harriot, *A Briefe and True Report of the New Found Land of Virginia* (New York: Dover, 1972), p. xi.

[114] De Bry published other works which placed such demands upon the reader, and was clearly well-versed in the modes of Protestant allegory; see e.g. the emblem book he published, *Iani Iacobi Boissardi Vesvntini Emblematum* (Frankfurt, 1593).

[115] Another analysis of the engraving can be found in B. J. Sokol, 'The Problem of Assessing Thomas Harriot's *A briefe and true report* of his Discoveries in North America', *Annals of Science*, 51 (1994), 1–16, at 6.

the foreground a lion lies next to a mouse, and a panther prowls on one side of the tree with a rabbit on the other, symbolizing the harmony of nature before the Fall. The background is divided into two sections by the tree: on the left, a mother nurses a baby; on the right, a man tills the ground with a staff, symbolizing the division of the sexes after the Fall and God's injunction in Genesis 3: 19, that 'In the sweat of thy face shalt thou eat bread, till thou return unto the ground.' The meaning of the picture is ambiguous, as are its implications: has mankind rediscovered the Garden of Eden in the Americas, even if Indian society is more georgic than pastoral? And if so, is the European discovery of the peoples of the New World a violation, a forced entry into an earthly paradise which will eventually lead to its destruction? The question is posed at the start of the sequence of images, and needs to be borne in mind by the reader, providing an interpretative frame for what follows. As the iconography of the developing project makes clear, Protestant colonialism has the potential to establish the first possible future of the world, through peaceful coexistence with the natives and their conversion to the true faith; Spanish Catholic colonialism can lead only to dark visions of hell.[116] Of course, either vision depends on the cooperation of the Indians in question; but it is notable that De Bry represents those colonized by the Spanish as far more ferocious than those colonized by French or English Protestants.

De Bry's epistle 'To the gentle reader' serves as a companion piece to the engraving, further emphasizing the theological framing of the colonial voyage and the hope for the recovery of the Golden Age:

Although (frendlye Reader) man by his disobedience, weare depriued of those good Gifts wher with he was indued in his creation, yet he was not berefte of wit to prouyde for hym selfe, nor discretion to deuise things necessarie for his use, except suche as appartayne to his soules healthe, as may be gathered by this sauage nations, of whome this present worke intreateth. For although they haue noe true

---

[116]   See e.g. the engraving of the natives of Darien feeding liquid gold to the greedy Christians; or the Spanish atrocities reminiscent of the illustrations accompanying Las Casas's text (reproduced in Alexander, ed., *Discovering the New World*, 137, 136, 144–5). De Bry reproduces the story of Balboa narrated in Peter Martyr (146).

knoledge of God nor of his holye worde and are destituted of all lerninge, Yet they passe us in many thinges, as in Sober feedinge and Dexteritye of witte[.][117]

These opening remarks establish a number of complex, interrelated themes which overshadow interpretation of the pictures which follow. The key phrase within the lines is probably 'except suche as appartayne to his soules healthe', which here can be read to indicate that the Indians' lack is relatively insignificant and can easily be rectified by the English Protestant colonists.[118] Elsewhere in De Bry's anthology the gap between the civilized man and the (often cannibal) savage is rather more significant, making the explanation seem more defensive than secure. The passage also establishes the Indians as 'savage critics' of European society, similar to More's Utopians, and able to point out the excesses resulting from the European departure from the virtues of the simple life of pastoral living (as represented in the engraving).[119] The implication is that if both societies can learn from each other, then a radically different society will really have been established, combining Old World sophistication and New World purity. The Protestant colonization of the Americas will be the dawn of a new age, offsetting the effects of man's original sin.

The engravings and commentaries establish Virginia as a land of plenty which is administered in a civil and sophisticated manner by the natives.[120] Plate IX (Fig. 3) shows 'An ageed manne in his winter garment', standing in front of a well-ordered, fortified village. To either side are fields of abundant corn and, in the background, a line of carefully planted and

---

[117] Thomas Harriot, *A Briefe and True Report of the New Found Land of Virginia* (1590), ed. Paul Hulton (New York, Dover, 1972), 41. All subsequent references to this facsimile edition are in parentheses in the text.

[118] The question of the origin of the newly discovered peoples in the Americas was often discussed, whether they were different from Europeans or had migrated from Asia many years previously, had been cut off, and so had been oblivious to God's revelations (and, indeed, whether this was their fault); see Pagden, *Fall of Natural Man, passim*; Acosta, *Natural History*, i.

[119] Anthony Pagden, 'The Savage Critic: Some European Images of the Primitive', *YES* 13 (1983), 32–45.

[120] For commentary, see Karen O. Kupperman, *Settling with the Indians: The Meeting of English and Indian Cultures in America, 1580–1640* (Totowa, New Jersey: Rowman & Allanheld, 1980).

pruned trees separates the village from the river on which Indian canoes are paddled (details not present in the original John White drawing, (Fig. 5)); they may have been transferred from a drawing such as that of the village of Secoton (Fig. 6). The accompanying commentary describes the garment of the old man, but concludes with an acknowledgement that the surrounding details bear considerable significance: 'The contrye abowt this plase is soe fruit full and good, that England is not to bee compared to yt' (p. 52). Similar praise of Indian life and virtues is expressed in the commentary to Plate XII, 'The manner of makinge their boates'. The engraving shows two Indians hollowing out a boat from a tree trunk by burning out the centre. The last sentence of the commentary reads, 'This god indueth thise savage people with sufficient reason to make thinges necessarie to serve their turnes' (p. 55).

However, the following illustration, Plate XIII (Fig. 4), depicting 'Their manner of fishynge in Virginia' (thus serving as a companion piece to the previous engraving) provides a less optimistic representation of the Indians. The illustration shows a canoe in the foreground with two Indians using nets to catch the abundant supply of various fish in the water, a number in the background wading in the water using spears, and a series of large nets designed to force the fish nearer to their doom. Although Harriot's commentary recognizes the skill of the Indians ('Ther was neuer seene amonge us soe cunninge a way to take fish with-all'), the conclusion reveals that the question of religion, so lightly dismissed in De Bry's opening epistle, is an ever-present problem:

Dowbteles yt is a pleasant sighte to see the people, somtymes wadinge, and goinge somtymes sailinge in those Riuers, which are shallowe and not deepe, free from all care of heapinge opp Riches for their posteri-tie, content with their state, and liuinge frendlye together of those thinges which god of his bountye hath giuen unto them, yet without giuinge hym any thankes according to his desarte. So sauage is this people, and depriued of the true knowledge of god. For they haue none other then is mentionned before in this worke. (p. 56)[121]

_____

[121] For other disparaging comments on the Indians' lack of religion (which increase as the sequence continues), see Plates XXI, 'Ther Idol Kivvasa' (a plate which appears to be based on the observations of Le Moyne in Florida rather than White in Virginia, and which may have been incorporated by De Bry to end the sequence of engravings with an attack on the Virginian Indians' idolatry: see

Evidently the primitive georgic mode of life enjoyed by the Indians has severe limitations as well as obvious advantages.[122] The commentary to Plate XII represents the Indians as possessing 'sufficient reason'; that to Plate XIII points up the very strict boundaries to such sufficiency. Together they demonstrate the complex and ambiguous ways in which the Indians are represented in Harriot's text as published by De Bry, an indication of the difficulty of reading the whole sequence, as well as the interactive nature of the written and visual representations.

The sequence concludes with a group of five engravings, 'Som Pictures of the Pictes which in the Olde tyme dyd habite one part of the great Bretainne'. These are advertised as by 'The Painter of whom I have had the first Inhabitans of Virginia' (i.e. John White), found in an old English chronicle, 'for to showe how that the Inhabitants of the great Bretannie haue bin in times past as sauuage as those of Virginia' (p. 75).[123] The engravings show three pictures of Picts; a naked warlike man, covered in body-painting, holding a spear and the severed head of a vanquished enemy in one hand (as the commentary makes clear), with another severed head beside his feet in the foreground (Fig. 7); a Pictish woman, similarly naked and body-painted, carrying three spears; and the daughter of the Picts, legs crossed at the calf, reclining on a spear and staring to her left in a wary and aggressive manner (Fig. 8).[124] The two neighbours of the Picts are not identified, but they appear to be more civilized than the Picts (Figs. 10–11); they wear clothes which

Hulton (ed.), *Work of Jacques Le Moyne*, 216; Hulton and Quinn (eds.), *American Drawings of John White*, i. 93–4), and XXII, 'The Tombe of their Werowans or Cheiff Lordes'. Positive comments on their temperance, which Europeans would do well to imitate, accompany Plates XV and XVI.

[122] Perhaps the key concept which differentiates georgic from pastoral literature is the necessity of work in the former; for further details see John Chalker, *The English Georgic: A Study in the Development of a Form* (London: Routledge, 1969).

[123] Engraving III, 'The Truue picture of a yonge dowgter of the Pictes', is actually based on a painting by Jacques Le Moyne: Hulton (ed.), *Work of Jacques Le Moyne*, ii. Pl. 7. De Bry probably confused the collections he had acquired from the two artists, and the remaining 4 pictures may well be based on lost work by Le Moyne; Hulton, 'Le Moyne and John White', 211.

[124] Hulton argues that this change has been made to 'give it [her face] a more classical appearance' ('Le Moyne and John White', 211). It might also be argued that the change makes the woman more threatening.

cover their genitals; the man does not retain the severed heads of his enemies; they look out to the side of the engraving rather than staring directly at the observer in a hostile manner.

Furthermore, it could be argued that the Picts are all seen to have turned their backs on the civilization which is represented in the background to their pictures: the man has no obvious connection to the village or the ships which sail in the river behind him; the woman would appear to be excluded from the castles on the hills behind her, which may have been erected to keep her out (especially if one bears in mind that the stated purpose of the engravings was to show that the Picts were as savage as the Virginian Indians: savage peoples do not, as a rule, build castles); the daughter of the Picts could also be regarded as a contrast to the orderly village behind her. Conversely, the 'neigbours unto the Picts' are integrated with their backgrounds; the three figures in the background wear the same clothes as the main figure, indicating that they may all come from the village on the far shore and have built the large ocean-going boats (significantly larger than those in the first two pictures) sailing away on the sea (towards new lands?); the woman is also obviously from the village behind her, a settlement which may be intended to recall the shelter in the prefatory engraving of Adam and Eve.

What is the point of De Bry's comparison of the savagery of the Virginian Indians with the peoples of ancient Britain? The evidence from the engravings is ambiguous (once again leaving aside the problem of interpreting the details as simply changes made for the convenience of the engraver or printer),[125] partly because we are not told the identity of the neighbours of the Picts, a deliberate omission given that they are clearly identified in John White's drawings (Fig. 12).[126] Undoubtedly the neighbours are Britons, as they are in White's drawings, although it

[125]   I have also left aside the question of the controlling intellect behind the text. De Bry may have worked in collaboration with Hakluyt, Harriot, or even Raleigh. Raleigh's belief in the existence of the Amazons, described in *The discoverie of the large, rich, and beautifull Empire of Guiana* (1595), may be connected to this engraving (Richard Hakluyt, *Principal Navigations*, x. 338–431, at 366–8).

[126]   Denise Albanese argues that 'the Pict is brought in as a proximate avatar for the precursors of the English race' ('Humanism, Colonialism, and the Gendered Body', 28), which appears to ignore the presence of the Britons.

is significant that De Bry does not choose to name them. Holinshed, in the first edition of his *Chronicles of England, Scotland and Ireland* (1577), describes the Picts as invaders who are descended from the Scythians, 'a cruell kind of men and much giuen to the warres . . . more desirous of spoyle than of rule or gouernment'.[127] Having invaded Britain at the suggestion of the Scots inhabiting Ireland, they are eventually defeated by the British king, Marius, who allowed those that remained to live in Scotland. Holinshed includes an engraving of the armoured, civilized and anachronistically armoured Britons (one fires a musket) defeating the savage hordes of Picts and Scots (Fig. 13).[128]

Holinshed's contrast between Picts and Britons is exaggerated in this illustration to make the point that a vast gulf separated civil and savage; De Bry's distinction between the two peoples is less dramatic, more subtle, and more problematic. However, the iconography of the engravings clearly indicates that one group of peoples, the Picts, are savages in need of civilizing; the other, the Britons, have established the rudiments of agricultural life and look out towards the New World (is the man in Fig. 7 looking Westward?), ready to colonize and civilize others, if not now then in the future.

Such an interpretation of ancient British life suggests a number of possibilities for the cultural encounter between the new Britons (English) and the Virginian Indians. The Indians may be compared to the Picts; much is made of the body painting of both peoples, a practice which provides a link between the two sequences of pictures, as the last one in the series of Indian life shows the tattoos used by the Virginians (Plate XXIII, 'The Marckes of sundrye of the Cheif mene of Virginia', Fig. 2). This would suggest that the English are like the Britons,

---

[127] Raphael Holinshed, 'The Historie of Englande', in *The Chronicles of England, Scotland, and Ireland* (1577), 67. On the reputation of the Scythians as the most savage of all peoples, see Andrew Hadfield, 'Briton and Scythian: Tudor Representations of Irish Origins', *IHS* 112 (Nov. 1993), 390–408, at 400–5.

[128] Holinshed's expanded collection of 1587 dispensed with the large number of illustrations included in the first; it is certainly arguable that these illustrations had a considerable influence on the contemporary English imagination. The woodcut depicting the Scots and Picts fighting the Britons is reproduced in the same chronicle (123) to show the Britons defeating the Irish, indicating that what is important is the contrast between civilized and savage peoples.

and they have to build a new Britain in the Americas by conquering and absorbing the Indians (their ancestors were shown building ships and sailing westwards).[129]

But this does not accord with the representation of the Indians in the sequence, who are shown to be quite civil, often possessing many superior aspects to the English which their old-world counterparts would do well to imitate (notably, their moderate consumption of food, a vital requirement, especially given the notorious agricultural inefficiency of early English settlers in America).[130] The point is, perhaps, that the possibilities for the future of 'New Britain'—and, indeed, the world—are not fixed, as the engraving of Adam and Eve suggested. Britain's past may well be a guide to the future; alternatively, the future may point back even further to the harmony experienced by mankind at the world's beginning in the Garden of Eden. The civilized but pagan inhabitants of the Americas may explode the old dichotomies between civil and savage enshrined in the Holinshed engraving, leading to a future society beyond the brutalities of the old world. On the other hand, the possibility that such divisions will simply be rediscovered and reinforced should not be ruled out of court. Either way, the discovery of the Americas is represented by De Bry as an apocalyptic event (as in Hakluyt's 'Western Planting'), the discovery of new wonders which cannot be quantified or classified within the realms of Western knowledge, scientific or otherwise.[131] The content has gone beyond the form; the identities of the colonizers are called into question as much as those of the colonized.[132]

[129] The concept of a New Britain is implicit in the name 'Virginia' named after Elizabeth; later treatises such as William Strachey's *The Historie of Travell into Virginia Britania* (1612), ed. Louis B. Wright and Virginia Freund (London: Hakluyt Society, 1953) made the comparison explicit. Strachey refers to Virginia as 'Nova Britania' (10).

[130] For comment see Sokol, 'The Problem of Assessing Thomas Harriot's *A briefe and true report*', 8–12; Greenblatt, 'Invisible Bullets', 29.

[131] Greenblatt, *Marvelous Possessions*, introduction.

[132] On this—frequently discussed—question in post-colonial theory, see Homi K. Bhabha, 'Articulating the Archaic: Cultural Difference and Colonial Nonsense', in *The Location of Culture* (London: Routledge, 1994), 123–38; Albert Memmi, *The Colonizer and the Colonized*, trans. Howard Greenfield (New York: Orion, 1965), conclusion; Robert Young, *Colonial Desire: Hybridity in Theory, Culture and Race* (London: Routledge, 1995).

De Bry's framing of Harriot's report can arguably be seen to be very much in line with the implications of Harriot's text. Although the first two parts catalogue the crops, commodities, and animals which benefit Indian society (clearly designed to attract would-be colonists), the third part, which describes the 'nature and manners of the people', registers this awareness of a knowledge which has changed all certanties, demanding that the English rethink their own identities and historical genealogy in order to meet the challenge of the New World. The Indians are represented as open to be persuaded that their explanations of events are not necessarily the best. Harriot describes their religion and comments: 'Wherein they were not so sure grounded, nor gaue such credite to their traditions and stories but through conuersing with us they were brought into great doubts of their owne, and had no small admiration of ours' (p. 27). This open-mindedness leads to a moment of great embarrassment after Harriot has explained the contents of the Bible to the Algonkians. Their excessive zeal for the truth makes them profane the book as a sexual rather than a religious object, as if somatic sensation can replace intellectual effort:

And although I told them the booke materially & of it self was not of anie such vertue, as I thought they did conceive, but onely the doctrine therein contained; yet would many be glad to touch it, to embrace it, to kisse it, to hold it to their brests and heades, and stroke ouer all their bodie with it; to shewe their hungrie desire of that knowledge which was spoken of. (p. 27)

While the first trait illustrates a tolerance which contrasts favourably with the brutal zeal of internecine European politics, the second opens out the problem once again, representing the Algonkians as a benign, confused, and inferior people in need of the guidance of their cultural superiors. One moment the Indians are savage critics, morally superior to their European counterparts, the next, they are helpless savages. The gap between the two peoples extends and contracts in a series of rapid movements.

However, the report ends, quite deliberately, with a phenomenon which no-one can explain; the death of hostile Indians after the visits of the English.[133] In fact, events would seem to confirm the simultaneous bemusement of both English and Indians alongside an efficacious serendipity, leaving the text balanced between success and failure (the actual position of English colonial ventures in the period). The Algonkians are convinced that the English can kill whom they please without weapons, and ask them to help them destroy their enemies. Although the English refuse, arguing that such entreaties are ungodly, that all should try to live together and wait for God to act, what the Indians want is what actually happens, leaving the colonizers in a more powerful position than before and allowing them to retain the moral high ground:

Yet because the effect fell out so sodainly and shortly after according to their desires, they thought neuerthelesse it came to passe by our meanes, and that we in using such speeches unto them did but dissemble the matter, and therefore came unto us to giue thankes in their manner that although wee satisfied them not in promise, yet in deedes and effect we had fulfilled their desires. (p. 29)

Although the two peoples misunderstand each other, events conspire to leave both satisfied; the Algonkians get rid of their enemies and the English affirm their colonial power. Nevertheless, the gratitude of the Indians depends upon their perception of the English as duplicitous, hinting that future discord may result between the two peoples, thus leaving the encounter in a state of precarious balance.[134]

Perhaps the most important point for the European reader is that the report does not conclude with a discussion of the identity of the newly discovered peoples, but the identity of the English colonizers, linking the text neatly to the series of pictures which conclude with representations of the ancient inhabitants of Britain. The final page of Harriot's report lists the various opinions of the Indians as to the nature of the

---

[133] The most famous explanation of Harriot's text is Stephen Greenblatt's argument that Harriot is testing out Machiavelli's hypothesis that religion is best used as an instrument of control over subject populations; 'Invisible Bullets', 24–39. Greenblatt's essay is too well-known to require further comment. It suffices to say that my argument here complements Greenblatt's analysis.

[134] Compare the story of the death of Captain James Cook; see Neil Rennie, *Far-Fetched Facts: The Literature of Travel and the Idea of the South Seas* (Oxford: Clarendon Press, 1995), 129–36.

English: some suggest that they are not born of women but are a series of immortals; some prophesy that more English will come to kill the Indians in future years (a chillingly accurate prediction); others that these creatures are ethereal, and shoot invisible bullets at the hapless Indians who anger them. It is the Indians who ask the questions, not the English, a surprising reversal of expected norms indicating that what is at stake in the text is the future of the world after the discovery of the New World, not simply colonial domination.

The last two paragraphs reinforce this message, exhorting the reader to pay heed to the importance of the author's observations, however unsettling they may be. The penultimate paragraph points to a potentially bright future for the powerful English in the Americas: 'there is godd hope they [The Algonkians] may be brought through discreet dealing and gouernement to the imbracing of the trueth, and consequently to honour, obey, feare and love us' (p. 29). If the text ended here it would be a straightforward plea for English rule under the banner of civilization, trade, and religion.[135] The last paragraph of the text proper ('The Conclusion' is not a narrative, but advice as to how to survive the first year in the Americas) qualifies such hopes and strikes an ominous note: 'And although some of our companie towardes the end of the yeare, shewed themselves too fierce, in slaying some of the people, in some towns, upon causes that on our part, might easily enough have been borne withal: yet notwithstanding because it was on their part iustly deserued, the alteration of their opinions generally & for the most part concerning us is the lesse to bee doubted' (p. 30).[136] Here, both peoples are in danger of appearing as the descendants of the fierce, warlike Picts rather than the civilized Britons.

Harriot's report shows how colonial society must go beyond the acceptable flaws and weaknesses of metropolitan English

[135] Compare Sir George Peckham, 'A true report of the late discoveries, and possession taken in the right of the Crowne of England of the Newfound Lands, By that valiant and worthy Gentleman, Sir Humphrey Gilbert Knight', in Hakluyt, *Principal Navigations*, viii. 89–131.
[136] These comments may be a veiled criticism of Ralph Lane's attempts to run the colony along military lines; Quinn (ed.), *Roanoke Voyages*, 381. Compare Lane's 'Discourse on the First Colony', ibid. 255–94.

society, how colonists must go back to first principles if they are to survive, in the process challenging their conceptions of themselves if they are not to reinforce old dichotomies which will undoubtedly prove lethal. Perhaps, as Greenblatt has argued, Harriot's text is informed by Machiavellian political theory.[137] Nevertheless, whatever the truth of such a claim, *A Briefe and True Report* does, as Greenblatt suggests, attempt to show the need to build English society anew in the colonies and, in doing so, challenges the ideological certainties of official dogma.[138]

Harriot's argument, range of reference, and conclusions might usefully be compared with another colonial tract, Richard Beacon's *Solon His Follie* (1594), written by a near neighbour of Harriot's on the Munster Plantation.[139] Beacon's tract, the only serious work to have been published on Ireland in the 1590s, is heavily indebted to Machiavelli, as well as Justus Lipsius, Guicciardini, and Jean Bodin, and aims to advise the incoming Lord Deputy, Lord William Russell, and other significant figures at court (the dedication is to the Queen) on how to make Ireland amenable to English rule.[140] Ireland's status as a colony was

---

[137] Greenblatt, 'Invisible Bullets', 26–8. If nothing else, Harriot's relationship with Raleigh suggests that he must have been aware of Machiavelli's political writings; see Shirley, 'Harriot and Raleigh'. On Raleigh's knowledge of Machiavelli, see Raab, *English Face of Machiavelli*, 70–3.

[138] See e.g. 'An Homily against Disobedience and Wilful Rebellion', in *Certain Sermons Appointed by the Queen's Majesty* (1574) (Cambridge: Parker Society, 1850), 551–601. However, one should note that official propagandists such as Richard Morison and Thomas Starkey were well-versed in Machiavellian political theory (see above, p. 19).

[139] Harriot, as one of Raleigh's Irish colonists, possessed an estate connected with the Abbey of Molanna, a former Augustinian priory, from c.1589 to c.1597 (Shirley, 'Raleigh and Harriot', 21; Spenser refers to Molanna in *The Faerie Queene*, VII. vi. 38–55). How long he lived at Molanna is a matter of conjecture. Beacon possessed lands in Waterford and Cork, became Queen's Attorney-General on the plantation and was resident there from 1589; see Vincent Carey, 'Introduction, Part 1: Richard Beacon's Irish Experience', in Richard Beacon, *Solon His Follie, or a Politique Discourse touching the Reformation of common-weales conquered, declined or corrupted* (Binghamton, NY: MRTS, 1996), ed. Vincent Carey and Clare Carroll, pp. xiii–xxv. See also MacCarthy-Morrogh, *Munster Plantation*, 43, 56, 58, *passim*.

[140] See Clare Carroll, 'Introduction, Part 2: The Text, Its Sources, and Traditions', in Beacon, *Solon his Follie*, pp. xxvi–xliii; Sydney Anglo, 'A Machiavellian Solution to the Irish Problem: Richard Beacon's *Solon His Follie* (1594)', in Edward Chaney and Peter Mack (eds.), *England and the Continental Renaissance: Essays in Honour of J. B. Trapp* (Woodbridge: Boydell and Brewer, 1990), 153–64. On the state of publishing regarding Ireland in the 1590s, see

ambiguous in contemporary political theory, though not in practice: Elizabeth's title usually included Virginia as well as Ireland among her kingdoms from the 1590s.[141]

While Beacon's first two books depend heavily upon a rhetoric of moderation (even though Beacon was prepared to recommend the extensive use of force when the rule of law broke down, along with other colonists with more ferocious reputations like Edmund Spenser),[142] the last book, as Clare Carroll points out, owes much to the millenarian theology of the *Geneva Bible* (1560), the translation which served as 'a handbook for the judgement of God upon nations and powers of the world'.[143] The second chapter, 'The times wherein commonweales doe usually fall and decline', borrows its title from the prophecy of the four kingdoms in Daniel 11, and the accompanying marginal gloss in the Geneva translation which interpreted these as the 'enemies to the Church of God'.[144] The struggle between English Protestants in colonized Ireland and the native Irish, Catholic Old English, and their Spanish and Papal allies, is cast—yet again—as the battle for the future of the world. On one level, *Solon His Follie* is a work which explains how Ireland may be reclaimed from its perilous state by the English who ostensibly rule there; on another, Ireland is merely a geographical location or example for a more general discussion of how to rule which develops into the all-encompassing problem of the perpetual battle between good and evil.[145] The

Andrew Hadfield, 'Was Spenser's *A View of the Present State of Ireland* Censored? A Review of the Evidence', *N. & Q.* n.s., 41 (1994), 459–63. On Russell's deputyship and the state of Ireland in 1594, see Steven G. Ellis, *Tudor Ireland: Crown, Community and the Conflict of Cultures, 1470–1603* (Harlow: Longman, 1985), 299–301.

[141] On Ireland's status, see Ciaran Brady, 'Court, Castle and Country: The Framework of Tudor Government in Tudor Ireland', in Ciaran Brady and Raymond Gillespie (eds.), *Natives and Newcomers: The Making of Irish Colonial Society, 1534–1641* (Dublin: Irish Academic Press, 1986), 22–49.

[142] See Andrew Hadfield, *Spenser's Irish Experience: Wilde Fruit and Salvage Soyl* (Oxford: Clarendon Press, 1997), 42–6.

[143] Carroll, 'Introduction, Part 2', p. xl; Katherine R. Firth, *Apocalyptic Tradition*, 125. See also Collinson, *Elizabethan Puritan Movement*, 164–5, *passim*; Hardin Craig, Jr., 'The *Geneva Bible* as a Political Document', *PHR* 7 (1938), 40–9.   [144] Cited in Carroll, 'Introduction, Part 2', p. xl.

[145] Compare Spenser's 'Two Cantos of Mutabilitie' (analysed in Hadfield, *Spenser's Irish Experience*, ch. 6).

means whereby Ireland is to be reformed can clearly be applied to other purportedly Protestant countries such as England, a reading made rather more likely given the dire apocalyptic warnings of the first chapter, and the extensive and general nature of the final—and longest—chapter, 'The sundry waies and meanes lefte unto us for the suppressing of every distemperature raigning in this polliticke bodie'. Like Harriot's report, Beacon's political allegory leaves the reader poised between a sense of hope and a feeling of impending disaster if the nature of English identity does not change by returning to the purity of basic principles.

Among the signs of imminent decline are a popular neglect of religion and a departure from the right principles of government, signalled more forcefully by 'Great earthquakes . . . hunger, pestilence, and fearfull thinges'.[146] 1594 was the first year of a series of dreadful harvests in England (1594–7) which led to widespread unrest (a previous dearth had occurred in 1586); a comet had been observed in 1577 and widely reported; and there had been an earthquake, the tremors of which had been felt in London, on 6 April, 1580.[147] It is clear that the portents do not just refer to events in Ireland, but are part of a wider conflict which is signalled throughout the work, which becomes much more explicit in the final book.

Beacon's dialogue between the religious leader and prophet Epimenides and Solon, the Athenian lawgiver, concentrates on the Machiavellian subject of the means of persuading people to do what one wants. Exactly which people Solon should aim to persuade varies: but the most frequently targeted audience is an

---

[146] Beacon, *Solon His Follie*, 90–2. Subsequent references in parentheses in the text.

[147] See Jim Sharpe, 'Social Strain and Social Dislocation, 1585–1603', in Guy (ed.), *The Reign of Elizabeth I*, 192–211, at 201–2; Edward Grant, *Planets, Stars, and Orbs: The Medieval Cosmos, 1200–1687* (Cambridge: Cambridge University Press, 1994), 353–7; H. R. Woudhuysen, 'Letters, Spenser's and Harvey's', *Spenser Encyclopedia*, 434–5. The comet had been discovered by Tycho Brahe, to whom Thomas Harriot refers in his mathematical work (see Jon V. Pepper, 'Harriot's Earlier Work on Mathematical Navigation: Theory and Practice', in Shirley (ed.), *Thomas Harriot*, 54–90, at 63); Edmund Spenser, a contemporary Munster planter, refers to the earthquake in his published correspondence with Gabriel Harvey: *Three Proper, and Wittie, Familiar Letters* (1580), letter 1, in *The Poetical Works of Edmund Spenser*, ed. J. C. Smith and E. de Selincourt (London: Oxford University Press, 1912), 609–32, at 613–22.

English one rather than an Irish one, so that the means of effecting a change in the commonwealth is perceived as a problem of colonial administration, one which inevitably reflects back upon government at home. Solon is praised for his skilful oratory in persuading the Athenians (English) 'to make warres with the *Megarians* [Spanish] for the possessing of *Salamina* [Ireland], contrarie to their former liking, publike lawes, and proclamations made in their behalfe' (p. 49), illustrating that the real battle is between rival colonial powers for the possession of a subject territory. Later, Epimenides reminds Solon of the time when he had to use force 'to suppresse the ambition of *Pisistratus* [Robert Devereux, second Earl of Essex?[148]]' because his persuasive skills were not sufficient, again demonstrating the real audience addressed in the dialogue and who has to change policy in order to ward off impending disaster.

As the last example suggests, ruling Ireland well involves rethinking the means of ruling England; and, following Machiavelli's *Discourses*, Beacon asserts that a more republican constitution in England would result in swifter, sterner, and more just actions in Ireland.[149] The best way to effect a reformation is with 'the consente of the people', which 'doth give so great furtheraunce unto this action of reformation' (p. 48). Although strong monarchs are to be welcomed, they must not rule with absolute power. Epiminides advises Solon that powerful rulers are necessary to implement policies and sort out problems, 'Therefore more wisely did the *Lacedemonians* give great authority to their kinges; and likewise did the *Venetians* to their Dukes, but yet with certaine limits and bondes, not lawfull for them to exceede; and farther did appoint certaine watchmen, as daily beholders and observers of all their actions and doings' (p. 44). England would be a more succesful colonial power if it had a more republican constitution; and the dialogue ends with a plea for the usefulness of establishing colonies and garrisons throughout Salamina (Ireland) as a means of controlling the

---

[148] See Beacon, *Solon His Follie*, 13, n. 27. Nicholas Canny argues that Pisistratus is Elizabeth: Richard Beacon, 'From *Solon His Follie*', *The Field Day Anthology of Irish Writing*, 3 vols., ed. Seamus Deane (Derry: Field Day Publications, 1991), i. 203–10, at 203.

[149] On Machiavelli's radical republicanism, see Pocock, *Machiavellian Moment*, chs. 6–7.

people (pp. 135–43), a plea that the counsel of people like Beacon be implemented to offset the manifest dangers of tyranny.

Beacon's combination of millenarian fears and republican politics can be read alongside Richard Hakluyt the younger's patriotic desire to reconstitute the English nation through his arduous collecting of materials.[150] Hakluyt is conscious of the need to defend and explain his decision to limit his material to voyages undertaken solely by Englishmen. In the dedicatory epistle to Sir Francis Walsingham in the first edition (1589), he expresses his sense of shame when other countries (presumably Spain in particular) are 'miraculously extolled for their discoveries and notable enterprises by sea, but the English of all others for their sluggish security, and continuall neglect of all the like attempts especially in so long and happy a time of peace, either ignominiously reported, or exceedingly condemned'.[151] Hakluyt answers such criticisms with a seemingly positive confirmation that his labours have laid all misconceptions to rest:

it can not be denied, but as in all former ages, they have bene men full of activity, stirrers abroad, and searchers of the remote parts of the world, so in this most famous and peerlesse government of her most excellent Majesty, her subjects through the speciall assistance, and blessing of God, in searching the most opposite corners and quarters of the world, and to speake plainly, in compassing the vaste globe of the earth more then once, have excelled all the nations and people of the earth. (p. xx)

However, Hakluyt is clearly speaking anything but 'plainly' to Sir Francis Walsingham and other readers here. The purpose of the *Principal Navigations* was not simply to record the obscured but glorious deeds of the heroic nation, but to encourage further voyages and, arguably, colonization, in order to counter the threat of Spain.[152] Hakluyt's prefatory material

---

[150] See Helgerson, 'The Voyages of a Nation', in *Forms of Nationhood*, 149–91; Fuller, *Voyages in Print*, ch. 4.

[151] Hakluyt, *Principal Navigations*, p. xviii. Subsequent references in parentheses in the text.

[152] See Louis B. Wright, *Middle-Class Culture in Elizabethan England* (Chapel Hill, NC: University of North Carolina Press, 1935), ch. 14; Fuller, *Voyages in Print*, 149. I would suggest that Parker, *Books to Build an Empire*, 139 and Helgerson, *Forms of Nationhood*, 181–7, take Hakluyt far too much at face value in arguing that his principal aim was the encouragement of trade rather than colonialism in the Americas given Hakluyt's involvement in the Roanoke ventures and the publishing of Harriot's *Report*.

demonstrates that his collection revolves around the question of the nation, constructing an identity through a re-remembered past of activity outside its boundaries.[153] Exile becomes the criterion for possessing a homeland, literally as well as figuratively.[154] Hence Hakluyt informs the 'favourable Reader' (1589) that he includes voyages 'onely of our owne nation' (p. xxiv); in the corresponding preface to the second edition he writes of his painful labours in the service of his country, comparing his editing to the perils faced by those included within the volume on the seas, in order to 'preserve certaine memorable exploits of late yeeres by our English nation atchieved, from the greedy and devouring jawes of oblivion' (p. xxxix). Just as Beacon fears that if England does not reform itself then it will not simply lose its Irish possessions but be in danger of losing its identity altogether, so does Hakluyt suggest that if these valiant deeds are not preserved and England not transformed into a nation unafraid to venture beyond its own boundaries, then it may well cease to exist at all.

Hakluyt's work opens with reference to a map and a Biblical text, both brought to him by his cousin Richard Hakluyt the elder when the former was a scholar at Westminster School, which serve as inspiration for his collection: 'From the Mappe he brought me to the Bible, and turning to the 107 Psalme, directed mee to the 23 & 24 verses, where I read, that they which go downe to the sea in ships, and occupy the great waters, they see the works of the Lord, and his woonders in the deepe' (p. xvii). The religious allegory is no more than implied in the *Principal Navigations*, as the concept of the English nation forms a means of controlling the boundaries of the narrative(s). When Hakluyt's papers were expanded and re-edited by Samuel Purchas, his sometime assistant, as *Hakluytus Posthumus or Purchas His Pilgrimes: Contayning a History of the World in Sea Voyages and Lande Travells by Englishmen and others* (1625), the figure of the nation has disappeared as an organizing principle, and an apocalyptic religious allegory of man's pilgrimage—possibly triggered by Hakluyt's opening comments concerning the generational transfer of inspirational stories—has taken its place.

---

[153] Hadfield, *Literature, Politics and National Identity*, 59.
[154] Anderson, 'Exodus'.

Purchas starts with the story of King Solomon's navy and the voyage to Ophir (I Kings 9: 26–8).[155] He interprets this as an allegory of individual life ('Every Christian man is a ship, a weake vessell, in this Navie of Solomon, and dwelling in a mortall body' (i. pp. 6–7) and the history of the world, through Solomon's use of the gold brought back by Hiram to adorn his Temple. Purchas reads this holy building as a prefiguration of the new Jerusalem of the Apocalypse ('all is brought to Solomon, that God may bee all in all, as the Alpha which sets them forth, so the Omega, who hath made all things for himselfe, for whose will and glories sake, all things are and were created': p. 7). When Purchas writes of the 'Tropologicall use of the Story', with Solomon becoming 'a wise guide', teaching 'the lawfulnesse of Navigation to remote Regions' (p. 9), we understand that widespread travel and discovery occur only in the last days of mankind. The concluding chapter of allegorical decoding and expansion based on Solomon's voyage is entitled 'The glorie of Apostolicall Conquests: the hopes of enlarging the Church in this last Age, by knowledge of Arts and Languages through the benefit of Printing and Navigation' (pp. 166–78), which yet again contrasts the Satanic behaviour of the Catholic Spanish to the hopes for a beneficent empire under Protestant suzerainty, an empire which will prefigure the second coming. Spanish domination is all part of God's overall design:

Spaine hath as is said, in Navigation best deserved (in leading the way to others, some of which have since in the Art equalled, in attempts perhaps exceeded her) and by divine Providence hath beene bountifully rewarded in the East and West, both overshadowed under her wings: is also one of the ten hornes . . . which together with the beast receive power as Kings, out of the ruins of the Romaine Empire . . . God put into their hearts to be thus truly Catholike, and able to discerne the whoredoms and many witchcrafts of their mother Jezebel, the mother of fornications of the earth. (p. 175)

Purchas repeated the link, made often enough before, between 'the bloudy effects of their Inquisition in Europe, and their

---

[155] Samuel Purchas, *Hakluytus Posthumus or Purchas His Pilgrimes*, 20 vols. (Glasgow: MacLehose, 1905), i. 4. Subsequent references to this edition in parentheses in the text.

inhumanity in America' (p. 176). The arts of navigation and printing have taken the world beyond that of the first apostles and helped to establish the monstrous success of the Spanish empire (albeit, now obviously in decline).[156] After the Reformation, the ignorance of the dark ages is at last over, argues Purchas, and the truth of Protestantism can be spread via the printed word, exported to other nations through the benefit of the newly established arts of navigation. The time has come, he says, to replace the evil empire with a holy one.

Purchas, in abandoning the notion of a body politic as addressee of his text, surrenders to an absolutist politics (it is appropriate that the work is dedicated to Prince Charles, whose authoritarian politics eventually precipitated the civil war; and this is also a measure of how far travel and colonial writing had altered since the proliferation of works dedicated to the late Prince Henry). In expounding the tropological allegory of Solomon's navy, Purchas argues that although our duty of obedience to princes is not the same as to God, political opposition is to be ruled out. Instead 'subjection to God is absolute; to Princes as they are called Gods, and yet die like men, with reservation . . . we must by suffering doe the will of Superiors, thereby to shew our fidelitie in keeping Gods Proviso, though with losse, of our Wils where we love, and our lives where wee feare' (pp. 16–17). In making his work an all-encompassing religious allegory, Purchas had gained the whole world (in print, at least), an obvious move, given the logic of English colonial battles from the Reformation onwards. *Purchas His Pilgrimes* serves as a fitting culmination of the colonial writing of the first English empire. In writing it, however, Purchas had lost sight of the object which had precipitated such efforts as a means of preserving itself both within and beyond the printed word: the English nation itself.

---

[156] See Davies, *Golden Century of Spain*, chs. 9–10.

CHAPTER THREE

'The perfect glass of state': English Fiction from William Baldwin to John Barclay, 1553–1625

IT IS probably still true that prose fiction is the poor relation of poetry and drama as far as modern critical interest is concerned, despite the number of recent challenging studies which have urged readers to alter their ingrained preferences.[1] At least it has become far less acceptable to read such works as immature literary precursors of fully grown generic forms, worthy only as a prelude to a study of the 'rise of the novel' in the second half of the following century, or as sources for Shakespeare's plays.[2] Far from being undeveloped, sixteenth-century prose fiction, on the contrary, consists of a vast number of works by a large number of writers who were imitating and adapting a myriad of literary forms: pastoral, romance, (Menippean) satire, Terentian comedy, Utopian fiction, humanist allegory, Biblical exegesis, beast fable, journalistic accounts of the Elizabethan underworld, Italian novella. To read such a

---

[1] See e.g. Paul Salzman, *English Prose Fiction, 1558–1700: A Critical History* (Oxford: Clarendon Press, 1985); Caroline Lucas, *Writing for Women: The Example of Woman as Reader in Elizabethan Romance* (Milton Keynes: Open University Press, 1989); Reid Barbour, *Deciphering Elizabethan Fiction* (Newark, Del.: University of Delaware Press, 1993); Lorna Hutson, *The Usurer's Daughter: Male Friendship and Fictions of Women in Sixteenth-Century England* (London: Routledge, 1994); Constance C. Relihan, *Fashioning Authority: The Development of Elizabethan Novelistic Discourse* (Kent, Oh.: Kent State University Press, 1994); Pamela Benson (ed.), *Italian Tales from the Age of Shakespeare* (London: Everyman, 1996). The most significant re-evaluation of early Elizabethan fiction is Robert W. Maslen, *Elizabethan Fictions: Espionage, Counter-Espionage and the Duplicity of Fiction in Early Elizabethan Prose Narratives* (Oxford: Clarendon Press, 1997). See also G. K. Hunter, *John Lyly: The Humanist as Courtier* (London: Routledge, 1962).

[2] Lorna Hutson, 'Fortunate Travelers: Reading for the Plot in Sixteenth-Century England', *Representations*, 41 (1993), 83–103, 83.

complex range of material as if it could all be subsumed under one goal is to indulge in the worst excesses of teleological literary history. As often as not, authors were performing experiments for a variety of purposes: advertising their worth to the commonwealth as reformed prodigals who knew how to combat the vice they once embraced; adapting humanist theories of rhetoric and education to a new medium; reflecting on social and legal changes; commenting on their own invidious position as landless men in search of patrons and riches in the big city; entertaining; trying to produce a new literary form which could express the desires and frustrations of their class.[3] Equally, it is by no means clear that authors were always in control of the works they produced and that what they intended to write was what they actually ended up writing.[4]

My purpose in this chapter is to argue that one of the manifold uses of the relatively new form of prose fiction was as a vehicle to explore contemporary political problems, invariably setting the individual fiction in question in a distant land or a distant time. Sometimes this self-reflection is not sustained throughout a whole text, but exists as one of a number of functions of the writing, whether explicitly articulated or not. Given too that many early fictions were translations from and/or adaptations of other European works—mainly Italian—this latter tendency was further encouraged. Exactly why writers of prose fiction dealt with political subjects, and why they often set their fictions in foreign settings is another complex question to answer. At times the motive undoubtedly was that of disguising potentially subversive material which could not be introduced into the public sphere directly, making the fiction a coded allegory—such, I will argue, is the case with Robert Greene's *Gwydonius. The Carde of Fancie* (1584) and, in a slightly different manner, Mary Wroth's *Urania* (1621)—at others, the relationship between vehicle and message was reversed, the

<hr />

[3] Richard Helgerson, *The Elizabethan Prodigals* (Berkeley: University of California Press, 1976); John Dover Wilson, 'Euphues and the Prodigal Son', *The Library*, 10 (1909), 337–61; Rebecca W. Bushnell, *A Culture of Teaching: Early Modern Humanism in Theory and Practice* (Ithaca, NY: Cornell University Press, 1996); Hutson, *Usurer's Daughter*, pt. II; Relihan, *Fashioning Authority*.

[4] See Hadfield, *Literature, Politics and National Identity*, 'Introduction', for further reflections on this problem.

story affording the author/translator the chance to reflect on domestic politics, as is the case with Geoffrey Fenton's *Tragicall Discourses* (1567). Elsewhere, authors tried to establish the novel as a more overt means of political reflection and satire: John Barclay's *Argenis* (1621; 1624) is the most obvious example. All three types owe much to the example of Thomas More's *Utopia* (1516; 1551), and that work's use of travel writing, set in Europe or the Americas, to combine political reflection and fiction. Through the selection of a series of pertinent examples rather than the problematic reconstruction of a sub-genre or 'line' within English fiction, I shall try to show how authors from the reign of Edward VI to that of James I performed literary experiments similar to More's.

On a more empirical level of argument, it is undeniable that many of the authors involved had obvious reasons to want to write about political subjects. Indeed, given the precarious career prospects for young men who did not inherit land or possess independent wealth, it is by no means self-evident that all wrote literary texts because they were bent on pursuing a literary career. Richard Rambuss has recently argued that many of Edmund Spenser's works were actually covert advertisements for his suitability as a secretary, one of whose duties was to keep secrets, and that Spenser was at least as keen on a bureaucratic career as a literary one.[5] It is worth bearing in mind that Geoffrey Fenton (?1539–1608), a prolific author and translator of literary and political works, became a secretary to Lord Grey when he became Lord Deputy of Ireland, at the same time that Spenser obtained an identical post.[6] Spenser continued his literary endeavours, but Fenton abandoned his. William Baldwin was a prominent figure at the court of Edward VI,

[5] Richard Rambuss, *Spenser's Secret Career* (Cambridge: Cambridge University Press, 1993), and 'Spenser's Lives, Spenser's Careers', in Judith H. Anderson, Donald Cheney and David A. Richardson (eds.), *Spenser's Life and the Subject of Biography* (Amherst, Mass.: University of Massachusetts Press, 1996), 1–17.

[6] Geoffrey Fenton, *Certain Tragicall Discourses of Bandello* (1567), 2 vols., ed. Robert Langston Douglas (London: Nutt, 1898), i. introduction, p. xxxiv; Maley, *Spenser Chronology*, 12. Fenton and Spenser were both later related through marriage to Robert Boyle, the first Earl of Cork; Fenton was Boyle's father-in-law; Spenser married Elizabeth Boyle, a relation (probably a cousin) of the earl's. For details of Fenton's life see Douglas's introduction, pp. xxxi–xliii; *DNB* entry.

writing a treatise on moral philosophy, planning the first edition of *A Mirror for Magistrates*, as well as writing the first prose fiction in English, but he appears to have abandoned his writing career as well to become a relatively obscure divine in the reign of Elizabeth.[7] Thomas Lodge (?1557–1628), author of numerous plays, prose romances, and poems, graduated as a doctor of medicine in 1602, and wrote little thereafter. Lodge converted to Catholicism early in his life, was summoned before the Privy Council in 1581, and subsequently spent long periods abroad, especially after the Gunpowder Plot (1605). Many recusants were doctors, as contemporaries noted.[8]

It would be surprising if none of these three writers had chosen to consider political questions in their fictions, given their knowledge of and close involvement in contemporary politics, even if they had wished to draw a strict dividing line between their fictional and non-fictional works.[9] Fenton was resident in Paris in the 1560s as part of Sir Thomas Hoby's entourage, and was closely involved with the Sidney circle. Soon after completing his translation of Bandello/Belleforest, he produced three works on contemporary French politics: *A discourse of the Ciuile warres & late troubles in France* (1570); *Acts of conference in religion* (1571); and *A forme of Christian pollicie* (1574).[10] The first work, the most extensive published report on France in the late 1560s before the Massacre of Saint Bartholomew, catalogues the violence of Catholics against Protestants, warns of the threat of the Duke of Guise, and

---

[7] See Stephen Gresham, 'William Baldwin: Literary Voice of the Reign of Edward VI', *HLQ* 44 (1980–1), 101–16.

[8] N. Burton Paradise, *Thomas Lodge: The History of an Elizabethan* (New Haven: Yale University Press, 1931), 53–4.

[9] Such strict divisions of texts were not generally made in the sixteenth century: to take just one example, the works of Chaucer and Gower were cited in the *Acte for thadvauncement of true religion and for thabbolishment of the contrarie* (1542–3) alongside chronicles, religious texts, legal works and biographies as guarantors of a separate English identity. As Kevin Pask comments, 'their authority remained symbolically embedded in the "truth" of their texts': *The Emergence of the English Author* (Cambridge: Cambridge University Press, 1996), 25). See also Michel Foucault, 'What is an Author?', in *The Foucault Reader*, ed. Paul Rabinow (Harmondsworth: Penguin, 1984), 101–20, at 108–9.

[10] Geoffrey Fenton, *A discourse of the Ciuile warres & late troubles in France . . . 1568 and 1569* (1570); *Acts of conference in religion . . . drawen out of French into English* (1571); *A forme of Christian pollicie drawne out of French* (1574). All subsequent references to these works in parentheses in the text.

advises against any toleration of religion in England. The dedication to Sir Henry Sidney argues that history has a providential design, in which wickedness can be seen to get its just deserts—eventually—and should be valued for the tales it tells (Aiii^r).[11] The work itself, according to Fenton, provides a looking-glass in which the queen will be able to see which policies to follow, a claim also made in literary works such as Lyly's *Euphues and his England*, John Barclay's *Argenis*, and Edmund Spenser's *The Faerie Queene* (VI: proem) (see below). *A forme of Christian pollicie*, dedicated to William Cecil (like Ralph Robinson's translation of *Utopia*: see below, p. 141), states on the frontispiece that the work will be useful for magistrates and governors of commonwealths. The dedication argues that no government can work well without the use of true religion, and that any divisions will lead to disaster (qii^r–Aiii^v). Fenton's non-fictional works can be seen to mirror the concerns of his literary efforts in matters of both form and content.

John Lyly (1554?–1606) spent a large part of his early adulthood attempting to secure a position at court, eventually succeeding when Edward de Vere, Earl of Oxford, became his patron. Lyly also came to the notice of William Cecil, Lord Burghley, championed the cause of the bishops in the Marprelate controversy, writing *Pappe with an Hatchet* (1589), and was a member of the parliaments of 1589, 1593, 1597, and 1601.[12] John Barclay (1582–1621) was born in France, where his Scottish father was Professor of Civil Law. He was probably educated by Jesuits, and made numerous attacks on them in his early Latin poems and translations, notably the *Satyricon* (Paris, 1607). He spent his adult life moving between London, Paris, and Rome, hoping for reward from both the English crown and the papacy, with limited success. His works include an attack on the usurpations of medieval popes, as well as an

---

[11] It is arguable that Sir Philip Sidney was responding to Fenton's comments when he claimed that poetry was superior to history because of the truth which it taught: *An Apology for Poetry*, ed. Geoffrey Shepherd (Manchester: Manchester University Press, 1973, rpt. of 1965), 105. For details of Henry Sidney's extensive patronage see Michael G. Brennan, *Literary Patronage in the Renaissance: The Pembroke Family* (London: Croom Helm, 1988), ch. 3.

[12] For details of Lyly's life see *DNB* entry.

adaptation of Petronius and a satirical Latin novel, *Argenis* (1621), translated into English in 1625.[13] Barclay's biography links him to Thomas Lodge, who also had a knowledge of the law, having studied at Lincoln's Inn, and who had spent time moving between countries owing to his Catholicism. Like Barclay, Lodge was a classical scholar, translating Flavius Josephus's works (1602) as well as writing a political play based on Appian's history of the Roman civil wars (which had been translated into English in 1578), *The Wounds of Civil War* (published 1594). His only other extant play, written in collaboration with Robert Greene (1560?–1592), was a didactic work which also bore a significant relation to the tradition of 'mirrors-for-princes' literature, entitled *A Looking Glasse for London and England* (published 1594, probably written in 1588 or 1589) and indicating both writers' concern with politics and the literature of counsel (see above, pp. 8–9, 19–20).[14] Lady Mary Wroth (1580?–1641?), the only woman writer included in this chapter, undoubtedly experienced politics in a different way to such aspiring male writers from the trading classes (Lodge's father was a grocer and financier of the crown who had risen to become Lord Mayor of London before going bankrupt; Greene was born in Norwich, still the main commercial centre outside London in the late sixteenth century). She was the daughter of Sir Robert Sidney, and so was privy to the political position of the Leicester–Sidney group at court, who were significant sponsors of much of the literature discussed in this book. She patronized a number of writers herself, and was friendly with Ben Jonson in the early 1600s, soon after he had been in trouble for writing *Sejanus* (see above, p. 61). Jonson's poem to her husband Sir Robert Wroth, published in *The Forest* (1616), ironically praised him for avoiding the vices of the court, and he later referred to her as 'unworthily married to a jealous husband'.[15] *Urania*

---

[13] For details of Barclay's life see *DNB* entry. On the editions of *Argenis* see Salzman, *English Prose Fiction*, 149–55.

[14] For details of Lodge's life see *DNB* entry; Paradise, *Thomas Lodge*. On Greene's, see *DNB* entry; John Clark Jordan, *Robert Greene* (New York: Columbia University Press, 1915).

[15] 'To Sir Robert Wroth', in Ben Jonson, *Poems*, ed. Ian Donaldson (Oxford: Oxford University Press, 1975), 91–4. Jonson's epigrams to Lady Mary (57–8, 59) offer far less equivocal praise of the addressee.

(1621), her prose romance written in the wake of her uncle Sir Philip Sidney's success with *Arcadia*, and the first published English romance written by a woman, offended a number of James's courtiers, one going so far as to respond in kind despite her denial of the work's contemporary relevance and her fulsome apologies.[16] Wroth clearly had good reason to reflect on contemporary political allegiances at court, and, more importantly, on gender politics.

Biographical detail of many early modern writers is often notoriously sketchy. Conyers Read's comment that outside what Edmund Spenser wrote himself 'all that is positively known about his life could probably be written in a few short paragraphs' so that all else 'is inference, surmise, and conjecture', should be regarded as a general warning.[17] Nevertheless, my argument is that what information we do have—and I have only rehearsed a small amount here—both inside and outside what writers tell us themselves in their fictional and nonfictional works, indicates beyond any reasonable doubt the desire of authors to engage in political reflection on their own freedoms and the pros and cons of political life in England, whether this was an easy task or not.

The first significant experiments in prose fiction took place during the reign of Edward VI, when there was a concerted attempt to inaugurate new literary forms, many sponsored by the Lord Protector Edward Seymour, Duke of Somerset (*c.*1506–52), including *A Mirror for Magistrates* (1555).[18] This important and often reprinted work transferred the well-established genre of 'mirror-for-princes' literature from the monarch to the magistrate, and was openly critical of despotic rulers who failed to obey the rule of law.[19] As a political work it should be read alongside the similar political sentiments voiced

---

[16] For details of Wroth's life see Josephine Roberts, 'Mary Wroth', in M. Thomas Hester (ed.), *Seventeenth-Century British Nondramatic Poets* (Detroit: Gale Research, 1992), 296–309.

[17] Cited in Maley, *Spenser Chronology*, p. xiv.

[18] See King, *English Reformation Literature*, 106–12. On the complex publishing history of the text see Lily B. Campbell, 'The Suppressed Edition of *A Mirror for Magistrates*', *Huntington Library Bulletin*, 6 (1934), 1–16; Eveline Iris Feasey, 'The Licensing of the *Mirror for Magistrates*', *The Library*, 4th ser., III (1923), 177–93.

[19] See Hadfield, *Literature, Politics and National Identity*, ch. 3.

in William Thomas's *The Historie of Italie* (see above, pp. 24–32), as an indication of the freedoms of political expression and publication encouraged in Edward's reign.[20]

Most of the literary works sponsored by the regime or allowed to see their way into print were poetic or dramatic. However, Ralph Robinson produced the first translation of More's *Utopia* into English (1551), dedicating the work to William Cecil (1520–98) later Lord Burghley, Elizabeth's principal secretary, but at the time one of Seymour's secretaries and an important dedicatee of literary works during Edward's reign. As John King has pointed out, Robinson reduces the balanced complexity of More's text to 'an unambiguous guide to statecraft', indicating how keen writers were to present counsel to the monarch or governors in print without the need for elaborate disguise.[21] Two years later William Baldwin, the presiding genius behind the project of *A Mirror for Magistrates*, wrote what is probably the first prose fiction in English, *A Marvelous Hystory Intitulede, Beware the Cat.*[22] This work was not published until 1570, probably because, like *A Mirror for Magistrates*, it fell foul of the Marian authorities after Edward's death on 6 July 1553, when it was either in the press or not yet submitted for publication.[23] Baldwin's multi-layered text combines a whole series of types of writing—satire, beast fable, dream vision, proverb, hymn, chronicle—further indicating the experimental and essentially 'mixed' genesis of English fiction in the second half of the sixteenth century.[24]

It is hard to pin down Baldwin's elaborate satire with any confidence. In many ways it satirizes the excesses and blindness of Catholics within and outside the realm, which is why it was probably published at a similar time to Wilfrid Holme's poem,

---

[20] For details see King, *English Reformation Literature*, 76–94.

[21] Ibid. 111.

[22] I am not including Sir Thomas Elyot's extended retelling of the story of Titus and Gisippus from an Italian *novella* in *The Boke named the Governour* (1531). For comment, see Hutson, *Usurer's Daughter*, 57–64.

[23] Gresham, 'William Baldwin', 113.

[24] For comment see King, *English Reformation Literature*, 387–406; William A. Ringler, Jr., '*Beware the Cat* and the Beginnings of English Fiction', *Novel*, 12 (1979), 113–26; Gresham, 'William Baldwin', 113–15. King points out that the narrative structure of *Beware the Cat* bears some resemblance to that of *Utopia* (394–5).

The Fall and Evill Successe of Rebellion. That work was first published in 1536 as part of a government sponsored attack on the Pilgrimage of Grace (1536–7), but was republished in 1573 as part of a similar propaganda assault designed to keep subjects loyal after the shock of the Northern Rebellion (1569–70).[25] Baldwin's text is divided up into three sections, all dealing in different ways with the problem of understanding and controlling the cats which roam throughout the dominions of the English monarch. The first part is set in Ireland, and includes the story of an unfortunate Irish kern (foot-soldier) who accidentally kills Grimalkin, the chief of the cats. This episode is an obvious piece of anti-Catholic satire, as is made clear by the subsequent comments in the first part.[26]

The story, told to the reader at third hand via an English soldier, official, or traveller in Ireland, is set in the aftermath of a successful Irish cattle raid. The kern involved, aided by his boy, escapes with a cow and a sheep. Not believing themselves to be pursued, they rest in a churchyard and start a fire over which they roast a sheep. When the meal is ready a cat sits beside them and, addressing them in Irish, demands some of the food, which they give her until the whole sheep is consumed. The cat eats the cow too, and the two men flee. However, after they have gone a mile or two, the boy spots the cat chasing them on his master's horse, and the kern kills it with his spear. Immediately a whole host of cats appear, attack them, and kill and eat the boy. The kern only just escapes, but when he returns home and tells his wife of his misfortune his cat exclaims, 'Hast thou killed Grimalkin!', and strangles him (pp. 32–3).

This episode suggests that, like the dangerous cats, Catholicism functions in a manner akin to the hydra.[27]

---

[25] For details see Dickens, 'Wilfrid Holme of Huntington'.

[26] Grimalkin is compared to the Pope who plunders on behalf of his subjects, and then a witch; there is a satire of transubstantiation; the section concludes with a description of the malign effects of witches on the superstitious population in Ireland: William Baldwin, *Beware the Cat / The Funerals of Edward VI*, ed. William P. Holden (N. London, Conn.: Connecticut College, 1963), 34–6. Subsequent references to this edition in parentheses in the text. On anti-Catholic satire, see John N. King, *Spenser's Poetry and the Reformation Tradition* (Princeton: Princeton University Press, 1990), ch. 1.

[27] One might compare the Red-Cross Knight's killing of Error (*Faerie Queene*, I. i, 19–26).

Grimalkin can be destroyed, but her death only leads to further destruction and confusion as the obvious target disappears, to be replaced by a series of more slippery, but equally dangerous, figures. Much is made of the Irish reverence for churches (p. 32), and it is in the churchyard that Grimalkin approaches the two Irishmen. However, *Beware the Cat* does not fit easily into straightforward models of anti-Catholic satire. The section opens with a description of the wilderness existing in contemporary Ireland, resulting from civil strife among the king's subjects, pointing specifically to the conflict between Cahir Mac Art Kavanagh and John Butler, whom the kern who slays Grimalkin serves (p. 31). The dissension, therefore, predates sectarian division. Grimalkin is not slain by an obviously loyal Protestant subject of the king's, but as part of a local power struggle between the Old English, descendants of Anglo-Norman settlers from the twelfth century (the Butlers), and the native Irish chieftains (the Kavanaghs (MacMurroughs)).[28] Given the adoption of Irish customs and law (or a hybrid form of English and Irish law) in such areas, it is not easy to tell Irish from English, the loyal from the disloyal, or the Protestant from the Catholic.[29]

In the second part of the novel the principal narrator, Streamer, concocts a potion using the magical works of Albertus Magnus, which he applies to his ears in order to enable him to understand what beasts are saying. What he at first hears is an assault to his senses:

barking of dogs, grunting of hogs, wawling of cats, rumbling of rats, gaggling of geese, humming of bees, rousing of bucks, gaggling of ducks, singing of swans, ringing of pans, crowing of cocks, sewing of socks, cackling of hens, scrabbling of pens, peeping of mice, trulling of dice, curling of frogs, and toads in the bogs . . . with such a sort of commixed noises as would a-deaf anybody to have heard. (p. 46)

---

[28] See T. W. Moody, F. X. Martin, and F. J. Byrne (eds.), *A New History of Ireland*: III. *Early Modern Ireland, 1534–1691* (Oxford: Clarendon Press, 1976), 7, 9. On the ethnographic divisions in early modern Ireland, see pp. xlii–xlvii; on Cahir Mac Art Kavanagh (*d*.1554), see 47.

[29] The same problem besets John Bale's much more assertive autobiographical text, *The Vocacyon of Johan Bale to the Bishopricke of Ossorie* (1553), which tries to separate the English Protestants from the Irish Catholics; see Andrew Hadfield, 'Translating the Reformation: John Bale's Irish *Vocacyon*', in Bradshaw *et al.* (eds.), *Representing Ireland*, 43–59.

What Streamer is forced to recognize is that beneath the apparently united appearance of English life there is a whole cacophony of voices which only rise to the surface and become apparent when they pose a threat to the powers that be. In other words, what took place in Ireland is also happening in England.[30] The fundamental divisions within society are already there, waiting to be exploited, as Grimalkin was able to aggrandize his own position in Ireland because of what had taken place before (although Grimalkin's fate indicates that he was by no means any more secure than those he menaced and exploited). The point is that the (Catholic) threat to England may well come from Ireland, as was often the fear throughout the sixteenth century after the Reformation, but it would have no chance of success without a number of already-established divisions within the body politic.[31]

The story of Grimalkin functions in two crucially interrelated ways: in one sense it is a traveller's tale of a (relatively) remote land which can serve as an Aesopian beast-fable, warning England that it too can become a land as divided as Ireland and subject to the superstitions which abound there if a vigilant policy is not pursued at home. In another, it is a more direct warning of what is taking place within the king's own dominions after 18 June 1541, when Henry VIII was declared king of Ireland in the Irish Parliament and England was committed to asserting its control over the whole island of Ireland, uniting the kingdoms and establishing a homogeneous rule of law.[32] If colonialism in the Americas demanded a radical rethinking of English identity, so too did the assumption of power over a

[30] My analysis is indebted to that of Robert Maslen's in *Elizabethan Fictions*, ch. 2. I am extremely grateful to Dr Maslen for allowing me to see his important work in typescript. Maslen points out that much of the action of *Beware the Cat* 'takes place on the roof of the Aldgate, where the limbs of dismembered rebels—including, from 1549 to 1551, participants in the Prayerbook Rebellion—were displayed for the edification of the English public' (79). On the Prayerbook Rebellion, see Dickens, *English Reformation*, 301–7.

[31] On the threat from Ireland, see Dickens, *English Reformation*, 425.

[32] For details, see G. A. Hayes-McCoy, 'The Royal Supremacy and Ecclesiastical Revolution, 1534–47', in Moody *et al.* (eds.), *Early Modern Ireland*, 39–68, at 46–8.

multiple kingdom within the British Isles, with its own attendant 'internal' colonialism.[33]

In Part 3 Streamer listens in to the world of the cats one night, overhearing the trial of Mouse-Slayer, who has broken their laws. What emerges from the trial further reinforces the reader's sense of confusion, unease, and inability to control a threat which is as much from within as without. Mouse-Slayer has to defend herself by narrating the story of her life in order to prove that she has remained faithful to the principles of cat morality. Her story is a picaresque adventure through England of which the reader only obtains a part, the story of the first four years of her life having been told on the previous evening, and the potion Streamer has taken in order to decipher the language of the cats wearing off before the trial reaches a conclusion. Mouse-Slayer lists the humans with whom she has lived; first, there was an old lady who believed that her blindness had been cured by the priest's mass-wafer, a trick which Mouse-Slayer warns the other cats does not work when they ask whether it can be practised on their kittens. Next, she lives with a pious hypocrite who says her beads before a statue of the Virgin every day, but actually makes her living by keeping a brothel and receiving stolen goods. She feeds Mouse-Slayer mustard, which makes her weep, and tricks a credulous local beauty into sleeping with a young man when she claims that her daughter has been turned into a cat for refusing his advances, and has wept constantly as a result of her misfortune. After this she is mistaken for a devil and makes an old priest look ridiculous when he tries to exorcize her. Finally, she takes her revenge on the old bawd and the young lecher by revealing him in compromising circumstances to the wife's husband.

Just as it is extremely difficult to establish obvious boundaries between sides in Ireland, or to blame all division on clear religious differences, so is it difficult to separate human foibles from those of the cats. As Robert Maslen has pointed out, Baldwin never allows readers to equate the term 'cat' with 'Catholic'.[34]

---

[33] On the concept of a 'multiple-kingdom', see Conrad Russell, 'The British Problem and the English Civil War', *History*, 73 (1988), 395–415. The concept of 'internal colonialism' is developed in Michael Hechter, *Internal Colonialism: The Celtic Fringe in British National Development* (Berkeley: University of California Press, 1975).   [34] Maslen, *Elizabethan Fictions*, 79–80.

Although the cats are by turns promiscuous, superstitious, tyrannical, greedy, and spitefully vindictive on occasions, they are no worse than the humans encountered, and often show themselves to be manifestly superior, having established a relatively benign legal system (which might be contrasted to the grim fate of the Prayerbook rebels, for example).

Beware the Cat works by never allowing the reader to settle for easy answers and rest assured that the world can be neatly split up into sheep and goats. Although it has been read as a work supporting the government's religious policies, it carries hints of criticism, and should be read alongside projects such as *A Mirror for Magistrates* and William Thomas's *The Historie of Italie*, which were concerned with establishing a vigorous public forum for debate by pushing the limits of what could be said, attempting to manipulate government policy, and reserving the right to be critical when it was desirable. A crucial component of the work's challenging nature is its rapid movement from an Irish to an English setting. *Beware the Cat* starts as a travel narrative to another world, one which involves both a voyage across the sea to England's first overseas colony and a fantastic journey into the parallel universe of the cats. Simultaneously, the relevance of these foreign worlds to the situation in England is apparent from the start (as is the case, I would argue, in much of the travel and colonial writing proper which was written in the subsequent decades of the sixteenth century), becoming ever more obvious as the text continues, and culminating in Mouse-Slayer's picaresque tale of her adventures through English social life. Overall, the effect of Baldwin's writing is to challenge the reader's sense of certainty, of a tangible distinction between inside and outside.[35] The text deliberately shrouds its epistemological status in mystery; although Cahir Mac Art Kavanagh and John Butler were real people, the story told about their followers is not only fantastic, but also reaches the reader in a complex and untrustworthy way, like the transmission of pre-Reformation saints' legends.[36] A man

[35] Reid Barbour, although he does not discuss Baldwin, argues that this was the general effect of Elizabethan prose fiction, even in a writer such as Greene who was keen to argue that clear distinctions between truth and falsehood could be maintained; *Deciphering Elizabethan Fiction*, ch. 2.

[36] Ringler, '*Beware the Cat* and the Beginnings of English Fiction', 117.

FIG. 1. Frontispiece to Theodor Be Bry, 'The True Pictures and Fashions of the People in that Parte of America now called Virginia, Discovered by Englichmen'.

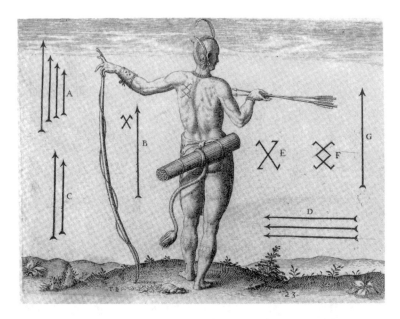

FIG. 2. De Bry, 'True Pictures', Plate XXIII, ' The Marckes of sundrye of the Cheif mene of Virginia'.

FIG. 3. De Bry, 'True Pictures', Plate IX, 'An ageed manne in his winter garment'.

The manner of their fishing.

FIG. 4. De Bry, 'True Pictures', Plate XIII, 'Their manner of fishynge in Virginia'.

Fig. 6. John White, 'Indian Village of
Secoton' (c.1585–6)

Fig. 5. John White, 'Old Indian Man'
(c.1585–6)

Fig. 7. Thoedor De Bry,'Som Pictures of the Pictes which in the Olde tyme dyd habite one part of the great Breatainne', Plate I, 'The truue picture of one Picte'.

Fig. 8. De Bry, 'Som Pictures of the Pictes', Plate III, 'The Truue picture of a yonge dowgter of the Pictes'.

FIG. 9. John White, 'Pictish Man Holding a Human Head' (1580s)

FIG. 10. De Bry, 'Som Pictures of the Pictes', Plate IV, 'The truue picture of a man of nation neighbour unto the Picte'.

FIG. 11. De Bry, 'Som Pictures of the Pictes', Plate V, 'The Truue picture of a women neighbour to the Pictes'.

FIG. 12. John White, 'Ancient British Man' (1580s)

Fig. 13. Raphael Holinshed, insert engraving of the Scots and Picts fighting the Britons, *Chronicles of England, Scotland and Ireland* (1577).

from Staffordshire informs the company that 40 years ago a man from his county had been told by a cat that Grimalkin was dead; another then tells the story told to him 33 years ago by an Irish churl, who seven years previously had been told the story reproduced in the novel. Add to such teasing narrative strategies the unreliability of Streamer as a narrator (he frequently reveals his ignorance, notably in the second section, where his knowledge of astrology is shown to be wanting), and the fact that the received text has been further edited by the unknown G. B., and Baldwin's methods of placing a series of barriers between himself as a writer and the reader are apparent. *Beware the Cat* does not fit into any straightforward model of Protestant propaganda; rather, it refuses to rest with any easy answers, throwing up a series of disturbing questions which demand further debate. In breaking down a number of binary oppositions, most importantly, any attempt to distinguish confidently between self and other, it struck a note of profound paranoia, arguably the definitive mood of the early English novel.

A similar sense of uncertainty, desire to expand the public sphere, and fear of the consequences of writing openly pervade the collections and translations of stories produced in the 1560s, the next significant literary experiment in English prose fiction. The two major works which inaugurated a trend for Italianate fiction throughout Elizabeth's reign were William Painter's *The Palace of Pleasure* (1566, 1567, and 1575) and Sir Geoffrey Fenton's *Certaine Tragicall Discourses* (1567).[37] It was almost certainly either or both of these works which occasioned Roger Ascham's famous outburst in *The Schoolmaster* against the Italianate Englishman and the malign influence of 'fonde bookes, of late translated out of *Italian* into English, sold in every shop in London, commended by honest titles the soner to corrupt honest maners'.[38]

Ascham's fears were not necessarily based on a reading of the text. His complaint is Socratic: what he appears to be lamenting

---

[37] Salzman, *English Prose Fiction*, ch. 2.

[38] Cited in Salzman, *English Prose Fiction*, 7. See also Fenton, *Certain Tragicall Discourses of Bandello*, i. pp. xlvi–lvii; William Painter, *The Palace of Pleasure*, 3 vols., ed. Joseph Jacobs (Hildesheim: Georg Olms Verlagsbuchhandlung, 1968, rpt. of 1890), i. p. xxiv. Subsequent references to these two editions in parentheses in the text.

is the neglect of sound humanist works of learned study and counsel in favour of frivolous romances which pander only to the senses of readers who should know better than to damage their educational development in such an irresponsible manner.[39] Yet Painter's prefaces to his massive and various collection of stories attempt to place the work within a tradition of humanist literature of counsel rather than the irresponsible pleasures of romance. The letter 'To the Reader' emphasizes the didactic benefits of 'reading and perusing a variety of Hystories' (p. 10), whether this be through positive or negative examples:

Profitable they be, in that they disclose what glorie, honour, and preferment eche man attaineth by good desert, what felicitie, by honest attempts, what good successe, laudable enterprises do bring to the coragious, what happie ioy and quiet state godly loue doth affecte the imbracers of the same. Profitable I say, in that they do reueale the miseries of rapes and fleshy actions, the ouerthrow of noble men and Princes by disordered gouernment, the tragical ends of them that unhappely do attempt practices vicious and horrible. (p. 11)[40]

The emphasis is placed on the duty of the individual to behave well: the suspicion that this might be a moral imperative which works against the rich and powerful occurs in the second example, which Painter cites as a guide to the reader.[41] Painter asks, 'Wilt thou understande what dishonour and infamie, desire of libidinous lust doth bring, read the rape of Lucrece?' (p. 11). The well-known story of Tarquin's ravishment of Lucrece not only represented the brutal disregard of weaker subjects by an arrogant tyrant, but also, given its political consequences, the ultimate triumph of the abused republic over the Roman monarchy.[42]

---

[39] See Barbour, *Deciphering Elizabethan Fiction*, ch. 3; Lorna Hutson, *Thomas Nashe in Context* (Oxford: Clarendon Press, 1989). Socrates' ideas are disussed in dialogues such as *Ion*, *Theatetus* and *The Republic* which include discussions of the question of true and false art.

[40] Compare the comments in the preface to the 1559 preface to *A Mirror for Magistrates*, ed. Lily B. Campbell (Cambridge: Cambridge University Press, 1938), 64–5; for analysis see Hadfield, *Literature, Politics and National Identity*, 91–5.

[41] The first concerns the ability 'to behaue thy selfe with modestie after thou hast atchieued any victorious conquest' (11).

[42] The story appeared in numerous versions in late medieval and early modern English, most notably in Chaucer's *Legend of Good Women*, John Gower's *Confessio Amantis*, and Shakespeare's *The Rape of Lucrece*. For comment on the republican significance of the poem, see Jonathan Bate, *Shakespeare and Ovid* (Oxford: Clarendon Press, 1993), 73.

The work is dedicated to Ambrose Dudley, Earl of Warwick (to whose widow Lewkenor's translation of Contarini was dedicated: see above, p. 49), a known Protestant and brother-in-law of Lady Jane Grey, whose claim to the throne he had supported.[43] Painter explains the genesis and purpose of his work in the dedicatory letter to his patron.[44] Hoping to repay his benefactor for his generosity, Painter claims that he searched for a suitable literary task until he happened upon a volume of Livy, 'In whom is contayned a large campe of noble facts and exploites atchieued by valiaunt personages of the Romaine state. By whom also is remembered the beginning and continuation of their famous common wealth' (p. 4). Such comments would seem to mark out Painter's first plan (or his representation of his first plan in the published version) as a political work which might have been read alongside such comparable works as Sir Thomas Elyot's *The Boke Named the Governour* (1531), *The Defence of Good Women* (1540), or, given its concentration on the acts of noble persons rather than the ruler, *A Mirror for Magistrates*. The choice of Livy as a source, an author of marked republican sympathies, may have been somewhat subversive in two related ways; first, Livy was associated with Tacitus, and hence was important for writers keen to explore the possibilities of a more republican form of constitution, notably those intellectuals associated with Essex in the 1590s; second, he was one of Machiavelli's principal sources, and, to a lesser extent, was also associated with Guicciardini and other Italian politic historians.[45] The original title of the work was *The Cytie of Cyuelitie*, and it was entered into the Stationers' Register under this name in 1562.[46]

---

[43] For details of Dudley's life, see *DNB* entry; Rosemary O'Day, *The Longman Companion to the Tudor Age* (Harlow: Longman, 1995), 186; Duncan-Jones, *Sir Philip Sidney, passim*.

[44] Warwick was general of the Queen's Ordinance where Painter worked from 1560 until his death in 1594; for details of Painter's life, see *DNB* entry; Painter, *Palace of Pleasure*, ed. Jacobs, i. pp. xxv-vii, xxxvii-xliv.

[45] For further details see Gilbert, *Machiavelli and Guicciardini, passim*; Richard Tuck, *Philosophy and Government, 1575-1651* (Cambridge: Cambridge University Press, 1993), 8.

[46] Robin Kirkpatrick, *English and Italian Literature from Dante to Shakespeare: A Study of Sources, Analogy, and Divergence* (Harlow: Longman, 1995), 242; Painter, *Palace of Pleasure*, ed. Jacobs, i. p. xxvi.

However, this volume never appeared, and the tales from Livy were supplemented by a host of other stories derived from classical authors such as Herodotus, Cicero, and Apuleius, Italian authors such as Giovanni Boccaccio and Matteo Bandello, and their French translators, François de Belleforest, Margaret of Navarre, and Pierre Boiastuau.[47] Painter claims that he had translated all that he 'deemed most worthy the prouulation in our native tongue', and that, considering the small number of these, he planned to embark upon a further batch. However, 'when I considered mine owne weakenes, and the maiestie of the Author, the cancred infirmitie of a cowardly minde, stayed my conceyued purpose, and yet not so stayed as utterlye to suppresse mine attempt' (p. 12). Instead he turned to the modern French and Italian authors listed above, and in his description of the resulting volume he emphasizes the hybrid nature of the project:

In these histories (which by another terme I call Nouvelles) be described the liues, gestes, conquestes, and highe enterprises of great Princes, wherein also be not forgotted the cruell actes and tiranny of some. In these be set forth the great valiance of noble Gentlemen, the terrible combates of couragious personages, the vertuous mindes of noble Dames, the chaste hartes of constant Ladyes, the wonderful patience of puissant Princes, the mild sufferaunce of well disposed gentelwomen, and in diuers, the quiet bearing of aduers Fortune. In these Histories be depainted in liuelye colours, the uglye shapes of insolencye and pride, the deforme figures of incontinencie and rape, the cruell aspectes of spoyle, breach of order, treason, ill lucke and ouerthrow of States and other persons. Wherein also be intermixed, pleasaunte discourses, merie talke, sportinge practises, deceitfull deuises, and nipping tauntes. (p. 5)

This long and involved list, which illustrates the reluctance to separate fact and fiction (history and novel) when a useful moral can be extracted from a narrative, leads the reader to expect a diverse, heterogeneous collection of tales which will deal with both good and bad actions and, as the last sentence indicates, more diverting material (presumably the target of Ascham's ire).

---

[47] Painter provides a list of authors used in the prefatory material (9). For details of Painter's sources and adaptations, see Kirkpatrick, *English and Italian Literature*, 241–6.

Nevertheless, the first thirty of the hundred tales which make up the completed volume (altogether they form less than a tenth of the overall narrative) concentrate on the bad behaviour of rulers, the malign effects such behaviour has on their subjects, their noble resistance and Stoic calm in the face of adversity, and the need for the impartial administration of justice. There is far greater emphasis on 'the cruell actes and tiranny of some' than the 'high enterprises' of others.

I shall discuss only a few of Painter's tales in any detail, as they are not all directly relevant to my argument. The first story concerns an incident in the Roman–Alban war. The Alban dictator, Metius Suffetius, eager to end the fighting, suggests that the war be decided via a combat between three champions of either side. Eventually, only one of the Romans, Horatius, remains alive, so the Romans are able to enforce their rule over the Albans. However, Horatius's sister was espoused to one of the dead champions. As the victors marched triumphantly into Rome, she tore her hair and loudly lamented the death of her beloved. Horatius, angered by what he saw as her disloyalty, publicly slew her and was promptly condemned to death. However, an appeal by his grieving father, who, having lost one child, was understandably not keen to lose another, led to his acquittal against the strict legal code of the Romans.

The story, which is a version of the judgement of Solomon (that is, a seemingly insoluble case), concludes with a meditation on the nature of law and justice from the narrator. Observing that Horatius has been spared death 'rather through the admiration of his vertue and valiance, then by iustice and equity of his cause', Painter comments:

Such was the straite order of iustice amonges the Romaines, who although this yonge gentlemen had vindicated his countrie from seruitude and bondage (a noble memorye of perfecte manhode) yet by reason of the murder done uppon his owne sister, were very straite and slacke to pardon: because they would not incourage the posteritie to like inconuenience, nor prouoke wel doers in their glorye and triumphe, to perpetrate thinges unlawfull. (p. 21)

Readers of this opening story can hardly be left in any doubt where the translator's sympathies lie. Horatius deserves honour for his noble deeds in preserving the independence of Rome

(Painter describes the agony of those watching the combat, aware of the huge stakes involved: 'For the losse consisted in neither those three, *but the publique gouernement or common thraldome of both the cities*' [my emphasis], pp. 18–19). Yet, however sympathetic one might be towards his fate, justice demands his death, and the people are acting against their own interests in failing to implement their legal code. The story is a militant defence of the need for a rule of law, however difficult it might be to administer, because the consequences of failing to establish an agreed set of rules will eventually be anarchy. Although the motives involved in making exceptions might well be honourable, the effects are likely to be malign, leaving future generations with problems ('incourage the posteritie to like inconuenience') and allowing mighty subjects who have benefited the commonwealth to ignore the restraints of the law.

This particular story aims its criticisms at the unstable nature of the populace as much as at the danger of over-mighty subjects. I would suggest, however, that the story of Horatius needs to be read alongside the second novel which tells the much more well-known story of the rape of Lucrece, signposted in the introduction. The consequence of Tarquin's crime and Lucrece's suicide is the deposition and formal banishment of the king after an armed uprising led by her widowed husband, Brutus. Two consuls are appointed, and the city changes from a tyrannous monarchy to a republic. Before this occurs there is a moment of dangerous anarchy: Brutus urges the populace to take up arms and show themselves to be men, not children. Many do follow him, but not before 'the lustiest and most desperate persons within the citie, made themselves prest and readie, *to attempte any enterprise*' [my emphasis] (p. 24). Tarquin, significantly enough, is murdered after the gates have been shut against him and he is on his way into exile.

The rape of Lucrece can be read as a synecdoche for Tarquin's tyrannous rule over the city. The effects of his misgovernment and the lack of any existing constitutional checks and balances are rectified in the end with the founding of a republican state, but not before a moment of serious danger has passed. As in the story of Horatius, the people break the rules; just as Horatius was pardoned against the strict legal code, so was Tarquin murdered by an uncontrollable and armed people after he had been banished. Indeed, Tarquin's death might well have been perceived by the Elizabethan reader as a consequence of the first exception to the rule, which 'incourage[d] posteritie to like inconuenience'.

Painter's first two tales have made a strong case for the need for an agreed legal code and the rights of citizens to be protected from a hastily swayed mob-rule on the one hand and the tyranny of unconstrained rulers on the other. Together they articulate an attack on the dangers of the 'common-law mind', the resistance to codifying the legal system and reliance upon custom which, at its worst, enabled the government to defend whatever was in its interests as the law.[48] It is more than likely, given Painter's comments in the dedication, that these two tales would have opened the never-published *Cytie of Cyuelitie*, which would help to explain its transformation into *The Palace of Pleasure*. The subsequent tales adapted from Livy argue a similar political case: the third, set during the seige of Rome inspired by the banished followers of Tarquin, tells how a gallant Roman soldier, having failed in his attempt to assassinate the enemy king, saves his life through his bold words and deeds; the fourth is the story of Coriolanus, which concludes when the aristocratic rebel's mother persuades him to spare the city; the seventh concerns a dialogue between the powerful king of Lydia, Craesus, and the philosopher Solon, who persuades him that the life of the individual subject is happier than that of the ruler, a democratic message which eventually leads to the mighty ruler listening to others; the eighth concerns a father who pleads for his wayward son's death and, as a result, is made a judge by the admiring king who remarks, 'Hee that dare thus seuerely and iustly pronounce sentence upon his owne child, doubtles he wil shew himselfe to be an incorrupt and sincere Iudge upon the offences of other' (p. 53); and the thirteenth concerns the eloquent plea of the Scythian ambassadors to Alexander the Great that he check his desire for empire and leave their country alone, which he duly ignores.

The Palace of Pleasure is by no means the frivolous work it has been frequently represented as being: assuming that

---

[48] Pocock, *Ancient Constitution and the Feudal Law*, 47–8; Patterson, *Reading Holinshed's Chronicles*, ch. 8.

Ascham was referring to Painter's work in his infamous statement, we might conclude that he either misread (or did not
read) its contents, or objected to its Italianate 'policie', which
he regarded as subverting the English constitution. Certainly
based on its first thirty tales, *The Palace of Pleasure* reads as a
book of humanist counsel—albeit a rather radical one, resembling the products of the court of Edward VI rather than that
of his father—providing advice to the mighty and powerful,
warning them not to abuse their power, and making a strong
case for equality before the law. The subsequent Italian tales are
designed, I would argue, to dilute and disguise the original
republican purpose of *The Cytie of Cyuelitie*, consisting more
of 'pleasante discourses, merie talke, sportinge practises' than
political advice, as Painter himself acknowledged in the dedication. In his words, the text is 'intermixed', diverting enough to
satisfy one type of reader, but containing enough serious
content to warrant more sophisticated decoding for those
prepared to play the cat-and-mouse game of recognizing potentially subversive material. The Italianate novels immediately
succeeding those derived mainly from Livy are conspicuously
tame in comparison; the thirty-first novel tells how Ermino
Grimaldi, a mean Genoese gentleman, was embarrassed into
becoming more liberal with his wealth; the thirty-third tells
how Rinaldo of Esti was kindly served by a lusty widow after
he had been robbed by three thieves; the thirty-eighth tells how
Giletta of Narbona demanded the hand of Beltramo, count of
Rossiglione, after she healed the French king, and how she
eventually won him away from his wife, having already borne
two of his children; the forty-second tells how Valencia murders
her husband, Didaco, after he has discarded her because of her
base origins, and how she eventually confesses to the magistrates and is executed for her crime.

   Such stories do, of course, often have morals appended. But
these are not of the same order or significance as those which
conclude the first series of Roman stories. The forty-first novel,
which tells the story of a steward who falsely accused his
master's wife of adultery after she rejected his advances being
devoured by lions instead of her, concludes that 'he which
diggeth a ditch, and setteth up a Gallowes, is the first that doth
fall, or is stretched thereuppon', the just fate of those who

'without reason, not measureing their own abilty, doe suffer themselves to be guided and led into their sensual lustes and appetites' (i. pp. 216–17). The forty-third, which tells a similar tale of the grim punishment of a lady of Turin who commits adultery and is locked in a room with the dead body of her lover, does not append any moral (i. pp. 240–8). The majority of the Italianate stories narrate tales either of adultery or chastity, some highly serious, others, like that of Philenio Sisterno, a Bolognian scholar who takes his revenge on three gentlewomen who ridicule his attempts to seduce them (ii. pp. 18–28), is essentially a fabliau. It is hard to imagine that such stories would have been included in *The Cytie of Cyuelitie*.

The Palace of Pleasure is a strange hybrid miscellany, the exotic Italian tales which make up the bulk of its contents being as much a disguise or a distortion of its first incarnation as a radical, humanist text. Nevertheless, it would be foolish to dismiss all the Italianate tales in this way. Some do deal with the problems of government, often telling stories of heroic resistance to tyrannous intrusion into the lives of private individuals. One example is the story of Hyrenee, the beautiful Greek woman captured by the Turkish emperor, Mahomet, which consists mainly of a long discussion between captor and victim in which she urges him to 'Attend to the gouernment of your Empire: leave of this effeminate life: receive againe the smell of your generosity and virtue' (i. p. 195), before he cuts off her head in front of his assembled nobles to show that he will eventually triumph over anything that binds his earthly senses. Such stories are probably best read as variations on that of Lucrece.

The most significant—and ambiguous—of such stories is that of the Duchess of Malfi, which explores the problems of private (specifically, erotic) desire and public life.[49] Painter begins his story with a warning that the fall from a high estate to a lower one is painful and hard to endure, so that the deposition of Dionisius, the tyrant of Sicily, was far worse to endure than the banishment of Milo from Rome. 'The one was a

[49] I shall read Painter's tale without reference to Webster's much later play (c.1613) as it is by no means clear that each tells the story with the same emphasis and Painter's important account is only ever read in terms of Webster's retelling of the story.

Soueraygne Lorde, the sonne of a Kynge, a Iusticiary on Earth, and the other but a simple Citizen of a Citty, *wherein the People had Lawes, and the Lawes of the Magistrates were had in reuerence*' [my emphasis]. In other words, where the laws are agreed and understood, there should be no particular resentment if they are infringed. Accordingly, the mighty and powerful, especially those in government, must live an honest life: 'Wherefore it behooueth the Noble, and sutch as haue charge of Common wealth, to lyue an honest Lyfe, and beare their port upright, that none haue cause to discourse uppon their wicked deedes and naughty life' (iii. p. 3).[50]

Such comments sit easily with Painter's earlier reverence for the rule of law. However, the situation is made more complex when the reader's attention is immediately turned to the problem of women rulers and their relationship to such attempted distinctions of private life and public virtue:

And aboue all modesty ought to be kept by Women, whom as their race, Noble birth, aucthority and name, maketh them more famous, euen so their vertue, honesty, chastity, and continencie more praye worthy . . . a woman being as it were the Image of sweetnesse, curtisie and shamefastnesse, so soone as she steppeth out of the right tract, and abandoneth the sweete smel of hir duety and modesty, besides the denigration of hir honour, thrusteth her selfe into infinite Troubles, causeth ruine of sutch whych should bee honoured and praysed, if Womens Allurementes solicited theym not to Folly. (p. 4)

Such comments require explanation, especially as they preface a story which seemingly casts the Duchess as an innocent abused by her corrupt brothers when she makes a match with Antonio Bologna, her steward, which will secure her happiness. While they do not explicitly preclude the possibility of female rule, they come perilously close to suggesting that women should not be trusted with positions of power because they are unable to control their emotions when they have to. Painter's story should perhaps be read as a contribution to the debate on

[50] As Gunnar Boklund points out, Painter actually changes very little of the story from the version he translated in François de Belleforest (*The Duchess of Malfi: Sources, Themes, Characters* (Cambridge, Mass.: Harvard University Press, 1962), 11). Boklund argues that 'To all intents and purposes Belleforest and Painter constitute one version' [of the story of the Duchess], but does not consider the possible significance of the story in Painter's text.

the question of female rule inaugurated at the end of Mary's reign and, as if to reinforce such possible connections, the Duchess tells Antonio in her first speech that although she is 'no Queene, endued with the greatest reuenue, yet with that little portyon I haue, I beare a Pryncely heart' (p. 6).[51] Certainly the commentary on the problems women have in controlling their emotions recalls Hyerenee's criticism that Mahomet's passion for her was impeding his ability to govern his empire because he was leading an 'effeminate life'.

The story proper starts with the attempt of Antonio to retire from his life at various French and Italian courts in order to exert control over his own destiny. Accordingly he 'went home to his house to lyue at rest and to auoyd trouble, forgetting the delicates of Courtes and houses of great men, to bee *the only husband of his owne reuenue*' [my emphasis] (p. 5). Painter's use of the word 'husband' is by no means without resonance: Antonio's reputation has gone before him, and he is sought out by the Duchess, who has learnt of his loyalty to the house of Aragon, to enter her service. However, her initial respect for Antonio soon grows into a burning passion, and she desires him for her husband. Antonio is not to be allowed to be 'husband of his owne reuenue' (a husbandman?); his administration of the Duchess's accounts starts him on a journey which leads to his becoming her lover, a fugitive, and, ultimately, to his meeting his death at the hands of insane and corrupt courtiers, precisely the sort of fate he was anxious to avoid. The Duchess, being a young woman recently widowed, is still likely to feel the pangs of desire, especially as she lives at court. Painter encourages the reader to acquiesce in his judgement and adopts a familiar, knowing posture: 'Now consider hir personage being sutch [i.e. young and handsome], her early life and delycate bringing up, and hir daily view of the youthly trade and manner of Courtiers lyfe, whether she felte hir selfe pryckt wyth any desire, which burned hir heart the more incessantly, as the flames were hidden and couert' (p. 7).

---

[51] For recent analyses, see Constance Jordan, 'Woman's Rule in Sixteenth-Century British Political Thought', *RQ* 40 (1987), 421–51; Melanie Hansen, 'The Word and the Throne: John Knox's *The First Blast of the Trumpet against the Monstrous Regiment of Women*', in Kate Chedgzoy, Melanie Hansen, and Suzanne Trill (eds.), *Voicing Women: Gender and Sexuality in Early Modern Writing* (Keele: Keele University Press, 1996), 11–24.

The Duchess is indeed a virtuous character, but her position is problematic given the inherent weakness of her sex. She does not resemble Mahomet in character (her brothers are more obviously culpable), but passion burns as brightly in her as in him, and the effects of her secret marriage to Antonio are not in the interests of her duchy. In terms of abstract laws and the need for justice her story resembles that of Horatius in the very first story; we might sympathize with the duchess's predicament, but we feel obliged to find against her anyway. Their marriage creates a vacuum at the heart of the state, leaving the Duchess vulnerable to the attacks of her brothers and unable to offset the effects of such familial power struggles on the population at large.

As the story progresses and the danger to the couple and their two children increases, the Duchess longs time and again to be a private and obscure citizen away from the prying eyes and malice of the court. When Antonio leaves Naples, fearing for his life if he stays, the Duchess assents with the hope that: 'hereafter we may lyue at rest together, ioyning our selues in the companye of our Chyldren and Famylye, voyde of those troubles, whych great Courts ordinarily beare within the compasse of their Palaces' (p. 23). Such apparently sympathetic wishes betray a serious naivety, because what the brothers fear is the loss of the state itself through the Duchess establishing an unsuitable match to a commoner.[52] When the Duchess gives birth to a daughter the rumours of her secret marriage reach the brothers. The narrator comments that although they are angry at the 'dishonest fame' she has brought upon the family, their more serious worry is for the fate of the dynasty, which they regard as 'defamed by one of their Bloude': 'farre greater was their sorrow and griefe for that they did not know what hee was, that so curteously was allied to their house, and in their loue had increased their Lineage' (p. 21).[53]

[52] A theme explored in much recent criticism of Webster's play. See e.g. Frank Whigham, *Seizures of the Will in Early Modern English Drama* (Cambridge: Cambridge University Press, 1996), ch. 4; Richard McCabe, *Incest, Drama and Nature's Law, 1550–1700* (Cambridge: Cambridge University Press, 1993), 248–56.

[53] On the contemporary legal implications of defamation, see Lisa Jardine, ' "Why should he call her whore?": Defamation and Desdemona's Case', in *Reading Shakespeare Historically* (London: Routledge, 1996), 19–34.

Painter makes it clear that he sympathizes with the brothers on this particular point, although he condemns their brutal actions and tyranny (p. 37). He frequently criticizes the Duchess for the 'libidinous appetite' (p. 27) which causes her downfall and leads to the tragedy which unfolds in the story. The Duchess places her own private desires over her service to the state and, however much one might sympathize with her dilemma, she has to be condemned, a harsh conclusion which recalls the moral of the opening story of *The Palace of Pleasure*. It is quite acceptable for Antonio to desire a private life, but not the Duchess, whose body and its issue can never simply be her own (one reason why it is hard for women to govern). Given her sense of priorities, she is unfit to govern properly; she has become one of those who 'gouerne them selues by carnall desires' (p. 24) instead of governing the duchy. A telling moment occurs when Painter, in describing the Duchess's understandable paranoia after her husband's departure, represents her as 'voide of Counsel and aduise' (pp. 24–5). Her folly has left her isolated and vulnerable, unable to fulfil her duties of state.

Painter's novel concludes that the reader has witnessed a morality tale of 'Notable Folly': 'You see the miserable discourse of a Princesse loue, that was not very wyse, and of a Gentleman that had forgotten his estate, which oughte to serve as a lookinge Glasse to them which bee ouer hardy in making Enterprises, and doe not measure their Ability wyth the gretanesse of their Attemptes' (p. 43). Who, it needs to be asked, was this looking-glass for in the England of the late 1560s? Obviously, on one level the story is a simple tale of knowing one's place in society, and is directed to the over-ambitious. But the main narrative crux is the question of the dynastic issue and inheritance through the Duchess, which suggests a much more complex and aggressive moral.[54] An aristocratic woman in the mid- to late sixteenth century 'could expect to be married for the benefit of her male relations', something the Duchess resolutely refuses.[55]

[54] Lorna Hutson has pointed to the ubiquity of inheritance themes in early Elizabethan fiction; *Usurer's Daughter, passim*.

[55] David Loades, *Mary Tudor: A Life* (Oxford: Basil Blackwell, 1989), 4.

The story, certainly in Belleforest, demands to be read as a misogynist tirade against women flouting conventions and destabilizing the social order. More specifically, it is hard not to read the story as informed by the complex dynastic politics of the English throne in the 1550s and 1560s, even if there is no clear resemblance between the cases involved and the foolish match of the Duchess of Malfi. Mary Tudor's marriage to the leading Catholic sovereign in Europe, Philip II, had led to Wyatt's rebellion in 1554, after which Sir Henry Dudley, Lord Guildford, the younger brother of *The Palace of Pleasure*'s dedicatee, had been executed as a leading conspirator.[56] Ambrose Dudley had been pardoned by Mary after he had supported the claim to the throne of his sister-in-law, Lady Jane Grey, who was also executed after the failed rebellion.[57] The unpopular marriage of a monarch was hardly likely to have been forgotten by someone whose family had been so closely involved in trying to support a rival—Protestant—claimant as a means of opposing her religious policies.[58] It is also worth noting that the first English translation of Foxe's *Actes and Monuments* which chronicled the numerous martyrdoms of Mary's reign in great detail, was published only three years before *The Palace of Pleasure* (1563).

The threat to Elizabeth's Protestant regime was as acute in the 1560s as it was throughout her reign.[59] The principal fear was that if Elizabeth died childless, the throne would go to another Catholic, Mary Queen of Scots, as she was the heir of the eldest sister of Henry VIII.[60] Elizabeth was already 33 in 1563, well beyond the age when most women had given birth to their first child.[61] The fear of a return to a Catholic regime

[56] Loades, *Two Tudor Conspiracies*, *passim*.

[57] Loades, *Two Tudor Conspiracies*, 115.

[58] On the unpopularity of Mary's marriage and its influence in Elizabeth's reign, see Hackett, *Virgin Mother, Maiden Queen*, 52–3.

[59] Details of Elizabeth's religious settlement can be found in Haugaard, *Elizabeth and the English Reformation*.

[60] On the problem of Mary Queen of Scots and contemporary literary texts, see Erskine-Hill, *Poetry and the Realm of Politics*, 15–29, 65–7, *passim*.

[61] Peter Laslett calculates that most women married at the age of 25 or 26 and so gave birth to their first child almost immediately afterwards; *The World we have Lost* (London: Methuen, 2nd ed., 1971), ch. 4. See also David Cressey, *Birth, Marriage and Death: Ritual, Religion, and the Life-Cycle in Tudor and Stuart England* (Oxford: Oxford University Press, 1997), pt. 1.

similar to that of the previous reign was common enough among Protestants, like the Dudleys, so concern about the Queen's marital status was intense. But, equally understandably, Elizabeth was reluctant to sanction any such discussion, which, arguably, could be construed as treasonable.[62] She forbade legal argument concerning the validity of Henry's contested will which had forbidden the succession being transferred to the Stuart line of his sister should his children die without issue. She also issued a proclamation on 16 May 1559 which decreed that no plays concerned with matters of religion or the 'gouernaunce of the estate of the common weale' could be performed, because both were 'no meete matters to be wrytten or treated upon, but by menne of aucthorities, lerning and wisedome'.[63] Against such a background of threats and censorship it is highly unlikely that Painter would have attempted any overt exhortation to the Queen or her potential advisers, and the non-appearance of *The Cytie of Cyuelitie* would further suggest either caution in the face of a real or imagined threat, or hostile intervention by the authorities. Painter's discussion of the dangers of a bad female marriage and the tendency of women to ignore reason when confronted by the force of passion were probably intended, first, for the eyes of his patron, whom Painter praises lavishly in his dedication, where he also refers extensively to the need to repay debts with gratitude (i. pp. 4–5); and second, to a wider Protestant audience amenable to the medium of print as a means of disseminating messages.[64] Of course, expecting Painter to have control over the possible uses and functions of his experimental work would be asking a great deal in the still-early days of the printing press.[65]

Painter's disguised and heterogeneous work undoubtedly had a major influence upon subsequent developments in

[62] See John Bellamy, *The Tudor Law of Treason: An Introduction* (London: Routledge, 1979), 61–2.

[63] Cited in Marie Axton, *The Queen's Two Bodies: Drama and the Elizabethan Succession* (London: Royal Historical Society, 1977), 11–12. My comments are indebted to Axton's painstaking analysis of the succession question in Elizabeth's early reign. See also Hackett, *Virgin Mother, Maiden Queen*, ch. 2 and on proclamations in general, Clegg, *Press Censorship in Elizabethan England*, ch. 3.

[64] Elizabeth Eisenstein, *The Printing Press as an Agent of Change* (Cambridge: Cambridge University Press, 1979), ch. 4.

[65] See Clegg, *Press Censorship in Elizabethan England*, ch. 10.

English fiction, as Ascham's comments suggest, not least in associating the representation of foreign locations (usually Italian or French) with political criticism. A year after the first part of *The Palace of Pleasure* was published the young Geoffrey Fenton published his first work, a series of translations from Belleforest entitled *Certain Tragicall Discourses of Bandello* (1567).[66] Fenton's text is by no means as complicated as Painter's, and it is unlikely that his intentions were as subversive or critical. Yet the thirteen novels were dedicated to Lady Mary Sidney, Countess of Pembroke and sister of Sir Philip, so the text would probably have been aimed at much the same immediate readership as Painter's.

Fenton was to become a significant translator of political and Protestant works within a few years of translating Belleforest, and *Certain Tragicall Discourses* are peppered with his own interventions and marginalia, directing the reader to the relevant moral of each story in a didactic fashion. In his dedicatory epistle he exhorts the reader to learn from history which provides a whole fund of examples for every possible reader in every possible situation: 'Yf a man be a magistrate, or beare authoritie in publicke affaires, what labor is better bestowed then in searchinge the actes of suche as have supplied equall dignitye and place, to accomodate himselfe to their vertues? And, to the privat person, antiquitie gives choice of admonicions for obedience to his superiors, with charge to applie and employe all his care for the commoditye of his countreye' (p. 4).[67] Fenton presents his translations to Mary Sidney as 'the frutes and effecte' of his work in France and Italy (his service with Hoby), arguing that they are 'benefyciall to the common welthe, do expose so common a profitt to the generall commoditie of all men' (pp. 6–7), thus defending his foreign travel in the usual fashion.

Nevertheless, Fenton's choice of tales from Belleforest, his translations, and his interpolations, are often at odds with the resolutely conservative message propounded here. *Certain*

---

[66] Fenton was about 28. Fenton's translations are actually all via Belleforest not directly from Bandello; see *Certain Tragicall Discourses*, p. ix. Subsequent references to this edition in parentheses in the text.

[67] Fenton writes as if his work were simply factual and later asserts the superiority of historical over feigned examples (5–6).

Tragicall Discourses often celebrates the virtue of private citizens who oppose the oppressive forces of mighty princes and their attempts to intrude into the lives of their subjects. The first discourse tells the story of a noble friendship between two Sienese gentlemen, Salymbyno and Montanyn, former enemies, the first of whom saves the other from being executed after he has infringed manifestly unjust laws and is rewarded with the hand of Montanyn's sister. The story celebrates the virtues of friendship and liberality; Fenton's introductory comments castigate ingratitude via a series of examples from ancient history (pp. 18–20).

Fenton's narrative invites the reader to apply the example of Montanyn and Salymbyno to political and personal situations in England, making *Certain Tragicall Discourses* a work which duplicates the purpose of Painter's *Palace of Pleasure*: 'I wishe chiefly a perticipacion of the fruite of such examples to all sortes of our countriemen in Englande' (p. 20). At certain points in the text, Fenton's interventions are particularly pointed and quite possibly based on personal experience. He marks the law which leads to Montanyn's imprisonment, whereby anyone who purchases property from a banished subject is liable to a huge fine and execution if unable to pay it within ten days, as 'An ungodlie lawe' in the margin, informing the reader that it was only passed because 'mutuall quarels and civil dyscentions' have led to the nobility being driven out of most urban areas, being replaced as legislators by 'town clarks and catchepowles', a 'villanous set of cursed caterpillars'. Fenton's vituperative attack on this 'tyrannous statute' suggests not simply principled opposition to injustice, but a warning that such laws undermine the integrity of the commonwealth:

Who markes well the misterye of this law, maye easely judge the viperous meaninge of those wretches [i.e. the 'town clarks and catchepowles'], who rather resemble the barbarous tirants and infidels without faith then seame to have the hartes of true Christians. And happye is hee that is not borne under the governemente of suche a state; where they doo not onyle shutte the gates of compassion against their innocent neighbours and frends, habandoned their countrey for peculiar grudges one against another, but also punished, by an unnaturall cruelty. (p. 30)

Fenton's comments are highly suggestive in a number of ways for readers attempting to reconstruct the context in which they were written; first, they hint at an experience of a similar injustice, whether via personal affront or legal proceeding;[68] second, they imply a certain aristocratic disdain for the rule of the populace who are regarded as just as tyrannical as a despot;[69] third, they pose the tantalizing question of whether England actually resembles the corrupt Italian city, or whether Englishmen are those happy few 'not borne under the governemente of suche a state'.

Fenton's further comments on the administration of law and government in Siena suggest that, like Painter, his novels were used as a means of arguing the case for the importance of the rule of law. The suit against Montanyn is brought by 'a long nosed marchaunte' (p. 29) covetous of his neighbour's lands, an 'oppressour of innocents' who 'was bothe one of the lawe makers and chiefe minister and commaunder of the same' (p. 30).[70] Clearly, such duplication of interests compromises the independence of the judicial process, which relies upon the impartiality of those involved to administer it in an even-handed manner. Is this a criticism of the ways in which law and government functioned in England? After all, many of Fenton's contemporaries had suggested that the English people—or, at least, those who counted—laboured under the burden of a flexible constitution which hid its mechanisms from sight rather than revealing them for all to see. Montanyn's sister, Angeliqua, makes such a complaint more explicit. She laments that her brother's fate lies in the hands of 'a peltynge marchaunt, never norrished in anye skole of cyvill or curteous education', and other inferior subjects not fit to bear office or sit in judgement on their superiors. More just are states where 'kynges gyve lawes, and princes use respect of favor to suche as resemble

<hr />

[68]   Despite the best efforts of Richard Ireland, I have been unable to trace any particular instance of Fenton's involvement in a relevant law case.

[69]   One might compare Fenton's comments with the attempt by Robert Devereux, second Earl of Essex, and some of his followers, to revitalize aristocratic codes of honour and chivalry in the 1590s; see James, *English Politics and the Concept of Honour*; McCoy, *Rites of Knighthood*.

[70]   The Jewish identity of the merchant suggests very specific allusions to the story of Ahab and Jezebel, who murdered Naboth when he refused to sell them his vineyard (1 Kings, 21).

them in condicion and vertue'. She wishes that 'oure predeces-
sours . . . by reducynge this countrye into a monarke, had
established a seat royall of a kynge, wythe authoritye that only
his seede and succession shoulde governe the whole, rather then
by leaving it thus dispersed into diverse confuced liberties, to
make us a mutuall praye one to another' (pp. 33–4).

Angeliqua's political comments make the novel into a robust
defence of hereditary monarchy as the best means of defending
the peoples' liberties; the threat to a decent way of life comes
from the uneducated rabble and, most specifically, an alien Jew.
The novel develops into a battle between individual virtue and
the corrupt authorities, and ends with the triumph of virtue and
honour over worldly obstacles, but it is clear that Fenton's
distaste is for the more democratic constitutions of the Italian
city-states rather than anything closer to home. Fenton's choice
of the tale of the two gentlemen of Siena to open his collection
and his significant additions to Belleforest's narrative place him
as an ambitious, somewhat embittered young careerist, eager to
defend traditional virtues and the status quo (although the text
exhibits a certain fear, paranoia even, that separating the wheat
from the chaff is by no means as easy as it should be).[71] *Certain
Tragicall Discourses*, although it adapts similar material, serves
as a contrast to the political stance of Painter's *Palace of
Pleasure*. Taken together, the two works represent equal but
opposite possibilities in early English fiction. Both use the novel
form to articulate political positions and contribute to current
debates; both dedicate their works to patrons from the same
circle of courtiers; most importantly, perhaps, both employ
similar discourses and styles while adopting radically divergent
positions.

---

[71] Like Painter's collection, Fenton's translations of Belleforest are heterogeneous in function and moral seriousness: e.g. Discourse 3 tells the story of Pandora,
a wicked and badly brought up young Milanese woman, who eventually procures
a horrifyingly described abortion and comes to a suitably miserable end; Discourse
5 tells the story of Cornelio, a young Milanese gentleman, and his pursuit of
Plaudyna, is basically a fabliau, but ends with a highly moral conclusion about the
sin of adultery; Discourse 6 exposes the evils of Catholicism via the story of a
villainous abbot. Fenton's translations often tell of the debilitating effects of love on
men, which makes them lose their reason, become effeminate and tyrannous, and
also stress the need to secure a legitimate and healthy succession; for further
comment see Hutson, *Usurer's Daughter*, 111–13.

Although there were a number of other collections of Italianate novels published in the 1570s and 1580s, the next most significant development in English prose fiction was John Lyly's two prose romances, *Euphues. The Anatomy of Wit* (1578) and *Euphues and his England* (1580), among the best-selling works in Renaissance England.[72] G. K. Hunter has remarked, 'Every aspiring author in the period must have read *Euphues*,' and Lyly's distinctive style—later labelled 'Euphuism'—came to define a dominant form of literary English.[73] As late as 1632 Edmund Blount, editor of Lyly's plays, commented, 'Our nation are [*sic*] in his debt for a *new English* which hee taught them' [my emphasis].[74] Lyly's characteristic style, consisting predominantly of balanced shorter clauses and antitheses, made the 'Petrarchan paradox into the capstone of a whole view of life'. Lucilla, when infatuated with Euphues, for example, endures 'termes and contraries', her heart caught 'betwixt faith and fancie . . . hope and fear . . . conscience and concupiscence'.[75] It is perhaps not too far-fetched to describe this style as a means of vernacularizing Latin and of successfully finding a 'structural principle in English which would enable the language to deal adequately and in an ordered fashion with complex material, and thus do the work formerly done by the inflected endings of Latin'.[76] It also became the courtly style *par excellence*.[77] So dominant did Euphuism become that any author of prose seeking to thrust himself forward as the literary spokesman of Englishness had either to copy Lyly's writing or define his own in opposition to it. This is exactly what Sidney felt obliged to do in *An Apologie for Poetrie*, as he pitted the periphrasis he employed as a

---

[72] The principal examples being George Pettie's *The Pettie Palace of Pettie his Pleasure* (*c*.1576) and Barnaby Riche's *His Farewell to his Militarie Profession* (1581). For details see Relihan, *Fashioning Authority*, ch. 2; Salzman, *English Prose Fiction*, 14–19.   [73] G. K. Hunter, *John Lyly*, 259.

[74] R. W. Bond (ed.), *The Works of John Lyly*, 3 vols. (Oxford: Oxford University Press, 1902), iii. 3; William Ringler, Jr., 'The Immediate Source of Euphuism', *PMLA* 53 (1938), 678–86, at 679.

[75] Bond (ed.), *Works of Lyly*, i. 205. All subsequent references to this edition in parentheses.

[76] Jonas A. Barish, 'The Prose Style of John Lyly', *ELH* 23 (1956), 14–35, at 24, 27; Hunter, *John Lyly*, 264; Catherine Bates, *The Rhetoric of Courtship in Elizabethan Language and Literature* (Cambridge: Cambridge University Press, 1992), 97–8.   [77] Bates, *Rhetoric of Courtship*, 97.

structural principle in the *Arcadia* against Lyly's balanced antitheses.[78]

Lyly—like Fenton, Painter, Pettie, and others—was in many ways writing in a vacuum, and the experimental nature of his work must once again be taken into account.[79] Just as his style has precursors—William Pettie, John Rainolds' Latin[80]—but is clearly not simply derivative, so the form and generic identity of *Euphues. The Anatomy of Wit* and *Euphues and his England* have models: courtesy books of varying modes, like Stefano Guazzo's *The Civil Conversation* (1574, translated into English by William Pettie in 1581 after the publication of Lyly's two books) and Sir Thomas Elyot's *The Boke Named the Governour* (1531), Roger Ascham's *The Schoolmaster* (1570), and, in the corpus of classical and Renaissance literature, the Greek romances of Heliodorus (*c.* third century AD), Terentian comedy, Boccaccio's *Decameron* (mid-fourteench century), as well as contemporary Italian prose romances, without actually resembling any individual one.[81]

Symptomatic of this mixed, experimental mode of writing is the fact that Lyly's conception of his project in his two prose works seems to have changed between the writing of the one and the other.[82] *Euphues. The Anatomy of Wit* tells the straightforward story of a witty but arrogant and morally suspect young Athenian who chooses to reside in Naples, where he betrays his friend, Philautus, in love, is himself then betrayed by the young woman, Lucilla, who dies in suitably miserable circumstances later, becomes reconciled to Philautus, realizes that he has not behaved very well so far, and returns to Athens to study moral philosophy, where he proceeds to lecture all and

---

[78] Sidney, *Apologie for Poetrie*, 139–40; Hunter, *John Lyly*, 286–7.

[79] Walter N. King, 'John Lyly and Elizabethan Rhetoric', *SP* 52 (1955), 149–61, at 161.

[80] J. Swart, 'Lyly and Pettie', *ES* 23 (1941), 9–18; Ringler, 'The Immediate Source of Euphuism'.

[81] Hunter, *John Lyly*, 53–4; John Leon Livesay, *Stefano Guazzo and the English Renaissance, 1575–1675* (Chapel Hill, NC: University of North Carolina Press, 1961), 78–83; Samuel Lee Wolff, 'A Source of *Euphues: The Anatomy of Wit*', *MP* 7 (1910), 577–85; John Dover Wilson, 'Euphues and the Prodigal Son', *The Library*, n.s. 10 (1909), 337–61. This variety of sources accounts for the problems critics have had classifying the works: see Theodore L. Steinberg, 'The Anatomy of *Euphues*', *SEL* 17 (1977), 27–38.

[82] Hunter, *John Lyly*, 65.

sundry on the ins and outs of moral behaviour. Appended to the third edition of *Euphues* is a letter to the gentlemen scholars of Oxford. Here, Lyly acknowledges that his work had been read allegorically and that criticisms he had made of the University in Athens (Athens is represented as effectively one giant university) had been read as criticisms of Oxford (i. 324). The text itself ends with Euphues crossing the sea to England, where he expects to 'see a courte both braver in shewe and better in substance, more gallaunt courtiers, more godlye consciences, as faire Ladyes and fairer conditions' (i. 323).

In the letter Lyly imputes these criticisms to 'the envious . . . the curious by wit . . . [and] the guiltie by their own galled consciences'; he promises that 'Euphues at his arrival I am assured will view Oxforde, where he will either recant his sayinges, or renew his complaintes' (pp. 324–5). Such comments—and the title—probably lead the reader to expect a survey of the realm which only actually occurs at the end of *Euphues and his England* in passages which owe a great deal to William Harrison's well-known *Description of England* (1577), included in Holinshed's *Chronicles*.[83] The bulk of the story casts Philautus as the principal actor, who suffers in love and courtship until he eventually woos and wins the chaste and beautiful Camilla. Euphues, alongside various other moral guides whom they meet during their stay, serves as a moral instructor, returning to Athens before the end of the book, where he pens his 'Glasse for Europe', a description of England and the English for the edification of 'the Ladyes and Gentlewomen of Italy': 'I am come out of Englande with a glasse, wherein you shall behold the things which you never sawe, and marvel at the sightes when you have seene. Not a Glasse to make you blush, yet not at your vices, but others vertues' (ii. 189).

All of which implies that the relationship between the two texts and reflections on English political life is both undeniable and undeniably problematic. *Euphues and his England* has been taken at face value and read as a celebration of England

---

[83] Euphues arrives in England armed only with Caesar's *De Bello Gallico* and experience shows him that more up-to-date accounts are required; Helgerson, *Elizabethan Prodigals*, 76.

and Englishness.[84] However, its inherently mixed generic nature would seem to preclude such a naive empiricist reading and use of evidence beyond context, as would the question of its readership. The 'Glasse' is addressed to Italian ladies, but within a work which is prefaced by two letters, one 'To the Ladies and Gentlewomen of *England*' [my emphasis] and one 'To the Gentlemen Readers' (*Euphues. The Anatomy of Wit*, in contrast, is addressed to a singularly male audience). While the former promises to correct the misogyny of the previous volume and, most importantly, advertises itself as a work for female consumption—'*Euphues* had rather lye shut in a Ladyes casket, then open in a Schollers studie' (ii. 9)—the latter is explicitly clubbish, using comparisons to denigrate women and bind a male audience together in recognizing such tropes as means of sexual exclusion. Euphues is described 'as long in viewing of London, as he was in comming to it, not farre differing from Gentlewomen, who are longer a dressing their heads then their whole bodyes' (ii. 11). Lyly draws attention to the complexities of reader response in this openly diacritical act of splitting up his audience into two separate groups.[85] What does connect them is their Englishness, so that when a section is addressed to Italian ladies within a fiction which openly acknowledged that it had been interpreted allegorically, the English reader must surely entertain the probability that things are not what they seem. Not only is 'Euphues' Glasse for Europe' really a glass for England to read itself, but when the fictional author specifically protests that the text is designed to make the reader blush 'not at your vices, but other's virtues', it should be apparent that the vices and the virtues are both English. When, towards the end of the treatise, Euphues informs his audience that '*we can see our faults only in the English Glass*' [emphasized in the text] (ii. 202), the mirror is clearly self-reflexive. England is forced to take a hard look at itself isolated from the rest of Europe.

[84] E. D. Marcu, *Sixteenth-Century Nationalism* (New York: Abaris, 1976), 79–81; Salzman, *English Prose Fiction*, 42.

[85] For some reflections on the sexualizing of national identity see Andrew Parker *et al.* (eds.), *Nationalisms and Sexualities* (London: Routledge, 1992); Partha Chaterjee, *The Nation and its Fragments: Colonial and Postcolonial Histories* (Princeton, NJ: Princeton University Press, 1993), chs. 6–7.

However, the precise relationship between 'Euphues' Glasse for Europe', the rest of the text, and the world outside that text, has to be puzzled out by the reader; and there is not necessarily one right answer or right way of reading. Ostensibly, the 'Glasse' reads as a long eulogy to the virtues of England. Careful inspection, however, reveals much that demands closer scrutiny. For example, early on Euphues attacks English attitudes to attire as 'the greatest enormity that I coulde see in England', and comments, 'There is nothing in England more constant, then the inconstancie of attire, nowe using the French fashion, nowe the Spanish, then the Morisco gownes, then one thing, then another' (p. 194). Strangely enough, the last description we have of Euphues before his departure for Athens is that he was 'commonlye in the court to learne fashions' (p. 185), a seeming discrepancy which is not explained. Is Euphues merely learning about fashions? Does the word 'fashions' refer to something other than clothes despite the verbal echo? Is Euphues' leaving after this comment merely a coincidence? Or does the attack on the vagaries of English fashion refer to something more serious?

A similarly troubling passage occurs two pages later and needs to be quoted at greater length:

Their Aire is very wholesome and pleasant, their civilitie not inferior to those that deserve best, their wittes very sharpe and quicke, although I have heard that the *Italian* and the *French*-man have accompted them but grose and dull pated, which I think came not to passe by the proofe they made of their wits, but by the Englishmans reporte.

For this is straunge (and yet how true it is there is none that every travailed thether but can reporte) that it is always incident to an English-man, to thinke worst of his owne nation, eyther in learning, experience, common reason, or wit, prefereing alwaies a straunger rather for the name, then the wisdome. I for mine owne parte thinke, that in all *Europe* there are not Lawyers more learned, Divines more profound, Phisitions more expert, then are in *England*. (ii. 196)

This also seems to read fairly straightforwardly as extravagant self-praise for an internal audience under the guise of correcting an undue modesty for the benefit of other nations (in some ways that is obviously the witty joke). Nevertheless, certain things do not appear to add up. Euphues provides no answer to his initial question as to whether the English are witty or not. He first gives an explanation for the poor reputation of the English—foreigners believe their bad accounts of themselves. He comments on the lack of English self-confidence. Finally, he sidesteps the issue by praising learned lawyers, profound divines, and expert physicians. The question of the wit of the English is not solved.

Such a reading might seem unduly pedantic. However, it needs to be remembered that the first volume's full title is *Euphues. The Anatomy of Wit*, and it is in essence the story of a young man who abuses his natural wit at court (from where, incidentally, he has just come in *Euphues and his England*) and the place in which he is really interested is the 'Glasse'. Wit is nothing if not an ambiguous quality as represented in the text. Near the start of the book, Euphues is observed by a wise old Neapolitan gentleman, who respects his potential but fears for his future:

an old Gentleman in *Naples* seeinge his pregnant wiytte, his Eloquent tongue somewhat tauntinge, yet wyth delight, his myrthe wythout measure, yet not wythout wytte, hys sayinges vaineglorious, yet pythie, beganne to bewayle hys nurture; and to muse at his Nature, beeinge incensed agayunste the one as moste pernicious, and enflamed wyth the other as moste precious: for hee well knewe that so rare a wytte woulde in tyme eyther breede an intollerable trouble, or bringe an incomperable Treasure to the common weale: at the one hee greatly pittied, at the other he rejoysed. (i. 186)

Euphues stands poised between two extremes here: his story will either be that of national glory—for if Athens was read as Oxford, Naples was read as a representation of the English court[86]—or of waste and shame. Unfortunately he uses his wit to bad purposes,[87] abusing the elderly gentleman with a series of clever logical reversals, and going on to betray his friend before his deserved come-uppance, retreat into scholarship, and the study of general ethics.

It would be false, I suggest, to read a simple dichotomy of good English court against bad Neapolitan court as represented in the behaviour of the sexually loose Euphues and Lucilla.

---

[86]   Hunter, *John Lyly*, 59; Helgerson, *Elizabethan Prodigals*, 75.
[87]   King, 'Lyly and Elizabethan Rhetoric'.

Instead, the question of English wit is quite deliberately left open and the reader forced to weigh up the advantages and disadvantages of witty conduct—whether it will bring 'intollerable trouble' or 'incomparable Treasure' to the nation—in the light of the story of Euphues' conduct.

In a sense what Lyly is arguing for, I believe, is that his work be read as a conduct book on a national level. In 'Euphues' Glasse', the fictional author heaps praise upon the 'grave and wise Counsellors':

whose foresight in peace warranteth saftie in warre, whose provision in plentie, maketh sufficient in dearth, whose care in health is as it were a preparative against sicknesse, how great their wisdome hath been in all things, the twentie two yeares peace doth both shew and prove. For what subtilty hath thir bin wrought so closely, what privy attempts so craftily, what rebellions stirred up so disorderly, but they have by policie bewrayed, prevented by wisdome, repressed by justice? What conspiracies abroad, what confederacies at home, what injuries in anye place hath there beene contrived, the which they have not eyther fore-seene before they could kindle, or quenched before they could flame? (ii. 196–7)

This description becomes more disturbing as it continues. We move from a depiction of an ordered and happily stable nation to an almost nightmare vision of a paranoid panoptican state with threats from both within and without the realm. The suggestion is of a nation which needs to be vigilant against the wiles of its enemies, rather than the celebration of English virtue which many uncritical readers observe.

Indeed, the reader might be forgiven for asking why 'Euphues' Glasse for Europe', purportedly a description of the continent's pre-eminent nation for the others to copy, is actually based on such outdated sources (Harrison, Julius Caesar), texts which could in any case be readily obtained elsewhere. In a sense, 'Euphues' Glasse for Europe' is as much a refusal to engage in the sort of descriptive travel literature encouraged by Sir Thomas Palmer or Sir Robert Dallington, as it is an example of the type of writing they wished to encourage. One learns nothing of the English constitution, political practice, or laws, certainly in comparison to the informative nature of Dallington's own *View from France*, Fenton's *Discourse of the Civile warres ... in France*, or Lewkenor's translation of

Cotarino's *Commonwealth and Government of Venice*, all works produced in Elizabeth's reign. The praise of Elizabeth's clemency may well be backhanded, especially the description of her treatment of private bills:

This mightie and mercifull Queene, hauing many bils of priuate persons, y^t sought before time to betray hir, burnt them all, resembling *Iulius Caesar*, who being presented with ye like complaints of his commons, threw them into ye fire, saying that he had rather, not knowe the names of rebels, then haue occasion to reueng, thinking it better to be ignorant of those that hated him, then to be angrie with them. (ii. 207)

Superficially this seems reasonable, but there is a dangerous slippage between legitimate criticism or complaint, and treason, precisely the sort of hazy distinction which worried many travel writers. Elizabeth as portrayed by Euphues appears not to want to face up to any criticism from the commons, and merely rejects their pleas. Not only is the comparison with Julius Caesar double-edged—for no sixteenth-century reader would have been ignorant of his fate—but the resonance of the term 'commons' may suggest not merely a contempt for the lower orders, but also a refusal to listen to the elected representatives of the lower House of Parliament. Elizabeth herself may not be too bad, and may indeed feel a strong bond with her subjects; but the fact that too much power is invested in her personal rule leaves her subjects unrepresented and so subject to her foibles, whims, and moods.

Immediately after this passage, Euphues cites an example to illustrate the clemency of the Queen, which he actually witnessed. While out in the royal barge on the Thames one day, a gun 'was shotte off though of the partie unwittingly'. Although the royal person was in danger, Elizabeth 'graciously pardoned' the culprit and accepted his 'iust excuse', worrying more about the bargeman who was slightly hurt (ii. 207). Again, this appears to show the fine qualities of the queen who is lavishly praised by Euphues ('O rare example of pittie, O singular spectacle of pietie'), but actually raises two awkward questions. First, what if the queen had been killed, whether by accident or design? With so much power concentrated in her person and with no heirs apparent, is she not acting irresponsibly and putting them in danger as much as herself (a neglect which corresponds to her dismissal of their pleas)? Second, does the incident not imply that there may well have been people who wanted to kill the queen—cementing the comparison of Elizabeth and Julius Caesar—and that her pardon in this instance is just as likely to have been misplaced as judicious? Without a proper constitution it is impossible to sort such matters out in any satisfactory way.[88]

Euphues had, in fact, been warned that he would be strictly circumscribed in what he could write about England. After landing at Dover, he and Philautus head towards London on foot. Soon after passing through Canterbury, and keen to find an inn to rest in, they encounter an old beekeeper, whom the narrator calls Fidus, with whom they rest and refresh themselves. Their conversation turns to the object of their visit, their wish to observe the queen and her court, and Euphues asks Fidus to tell him what he knows. He receives a long-winded but ultimately firm answer from Fidus: 'Cease then Gentle-men, and know this, that an English-man learneth to speake of menne, and to holde his peace of the Gods. Enquire no farther then beseemeth you, least you heare that which can-not like you' (ii. 38).

The subsequent discussion between Euphues and Fidus revolves around this problem, whether it is desirable or even permissible to represent the monarch or discuss the functions of his or her office, and what role the subject/citizen should be expected to assume in a commonwealth. Euphues argues that 'A cleere conscience needeth no excuse, nor feareth any accusation' (p. 40) and that even if they cannot represent the queen with perfect accuracy, there is still virtue in doing so as they, foreign admirers, can learn from her example. Fidus will have none of this, claiming, with rather world-weary logic, that they are too young to examine the affairs of state, and that he has learnt through the wisdom of his years that 'to reason of Kings or Princes, hath euer bene mislyked of ye wise' (p. 41). Subjects

---

[88] Compare the attacks on Elizabeth's excessive pity in attempting to spare the life of Mary Queen of Scots, who was involved in plots against the Queen's life, in Spenser's *Faerie Queene*. For details see Colin Burrow, *Epic Romance: Homer to Milton* (Oxford: Clarendon Press, 1993), 132–9.

should not enquire into the works of princes, just as princes should not pry into the works of God: 'as Kings pastimes are no playes for euery one: so their secretes, their counsells, their dealings, are not to be either scanned or enquired off any way' (pp. 42–3). He concludes with the fable of the bees, who all know their place ('office') and obey the dictates of rational hierarchical order to the extent that any who disobey the commandments of the king, 'hee kylleth hym-selfe with his owne sting, as executioner of his own stubbornesse'.[89]

Fidus's fable can be read as a rather nightmarish vision of contemporary England which parallels what Euphues later finds to be the case. Fidus explains that the bees are helpless if their prince dies: 'they know not how to liue, they languish, weepe, sigh, neither intending their work, nor keeping their old society' (pp. 44–5). Their dependence on their monarch mirrors exactly the dependence of the English on Elizabeth. Although the bees do have a parliament which has the power to create the monarch, pass laws, appoint officers of state, and determine penalties, a 'bad' representative causes 'such ciuill war and dissention' that there can be no 'friendship' until he is 'ouerthrowne' (p. 45). Fidus concludes his political fable by referring back to his own life and experience. He has chosen to live his life in rural retreat, 'contented with a meane estate, and neuer curious of the high estate', trusting in the powers that be: 'I was neuer busie in matters of state, but referring al my cares unto the wisdom of graue Counsellors, and my confidence in the noble minde of my dread Souereigne and Queene, neuer asking what she did' (p. 46).

Fidus's peace of mind is at the cost of his adopting a quietist politics, which appears to be a logical bargain, even if in doing so he has become rather like the animals he tends and so diminished in his humanity. However, it is clear that if all power is invested in the queen—or the prince of the bees—then disaster strikes if they perish without having secured their succession. When *Euphues and his England* was published, this very problem was a burning political issue. From 1578 onwards Elizabeth had been considering the marriage proposal of

---

[89] Bond notes that although the fable is adapted from Pliny's *Natural History*, this is an added detail (ii. 498).

François, Duke of Alençon, a diplomatic manoeuvre which might lead to a lasting Anglo-French alliance against Spain, as well as curb the influence of the Guise faction in France and make easier a rapprochement between England and France after the Massacre of Saint Bartholomew's Day.[90] Negotiations were still in progress when *Euphues and his England* was being written, and had not been resolved when it was published.

Many English Protestants—most notably the Leicester–Walsingham circle—were particularly worried about two inter-related potential developments: a loss of English sovereign integrity, and the Catholic corruption of the English reformed church.[91] In 1579 Sir Philip Sidney wrote, and circulated at court, a *Letter to Queen Elizabeth touching her marriage with Monsieur*, suggesting that such a marriage would endanger Elizabeth's relationship with her subjects and risk infecting her native Protestant religious policy with alien Catholicism.[92] A more spectacular attack on the Queen's alliance was John Stubbs's polemical pamphlet, *The Discoverie of a Gaping Gulf whereinto England is like to be swallowed* (1579), probably encouraged—like Sidney's letter—by the Walsingham–Leicester circle.[93] Stubbs makes a forceful case that Elizabeth ought to heed good counsel and listen to the voice of the people who really wanted to preserve English independence because England has always been 'divided from the world'.[94] The event Stubbs most frequently alludes to in order to make his case is the Massacre of Saint Bartholomew's Day, referring to the

---

[90] See J. E. Neale, *Queen Elizabeth* (London: Cape, 1934), ch. 15; Guy, *Tudor England*, 282–5. More generally, see Berry, *Of Chastity and Power*, ch. 3–6; Axton, *Queen's Two Bodies*.

[91] Bond (ed.), *Works of John Lyly*, i. 74; Geoffrey Elton, *England under the Tudors* (London: Methuen, 1965, rpt. of 1955), 324–5.

[92] See Duncan-Jones, *Sir Philip Sidney*, 162–4, for details. Alençon was, in fact, a Protestant who served with some distinction for the Dutch against the Spanish.

[93] Walsingham successfully pleaded for the printer, Hugh Singleton, which suggests that he was in some way involved in the production of the book; Duncan-Jones, *Sir Philip Sidney*, 161; Clegg, *Press Censorship in Elizabethan England*, ch. 6.

[94] *John Stubbs's* Gaping Gulf *with Letters and Other Relevant Documents*, ed. Lloyd E. Berry (Charlottesville, Va.: University of Virginia Press, 1968), 30, 36, 57. Subsequent references to this edition in parentheses in the text. The quotation is clearly an echo of Virgil's description of the Britons as 'penitos toto divisos orbe Britannos' (*Eclogues*, i. l. 66).

slaughter as God's punishment of an unfaithful church in the last days of the world (p. 14); conjuring up the spectre of Guise (p. 24); leading up to the claim that if English Protestants do not stand firm then 'we shall be taught by late experience and go the way of our Parisian bretheren' (pp. 27–8). A *Gaping Gulf* 'remains in effect a commentary on St Bartholomew and its infamous perpetrators'.[95] For his forthright stand Stubbs, along with his publisher, William Page, had his right hand severed on 30 October 1579.[96]

Stubbs's text and the events surrounding its publication offer a useful interpretative context for Lyly's two romances. The fear outlined in *A Gaping Gulf* goes some way towards explaining the drastic and confusing generic change between *Euphues. The Anatomy of Wit* and *Euphues and his England*. 'Euphues' Glasse for Europe'—possibly the germ of an original plan for the sequel; possibly a sign that such a 'Glasse' could not be written in England in 1579/80—presents what could be seen as a hopeful but fragile ideal of a happy and successful England, one which current events threatened to engulf in various ways; indeed, the reproduction of such archaic material suggests that this is already starting to happen. Lyly uses the survey not as an unqualified jingoistic celebration of England and its institutions, but as a stick with which to beat the present and spur it into action. In effect, Lyly, an aspiring courtier, is pushing himself forward as a sage counsellor—precisely like those who Fidus chooses to trust to act on his behalf—whose literary offering is more valuable than the empty wit of court.[97] It is surely an obvious irony that Euphues' wisdom emerges only when he has returned to the university world of Athens and left the Court, exactly the opposite journey to the one Lyly himself was hoping to make.[98] Symbolically, the wisdom of the ancients is being ignored, as is contemporary counsel.[99] Like Euphues' wit at the start of his tale, England has the potential

---

[95] Dickens, 'Elizabethans and Saint Bartholomew', 69.

[96] For details see Berry (ed.), *Stubbs's* Gaping Gulf, pp. xxx–xxxvi; Christopher Haigh, *Elizabeth I* (Harlow: Longman, 1988), 76, 160.

[97] Helgerson, *Elizabethan Prodigals*, 6–7, 77.

[98] Bates, *Rhetoric of Courtship*, 102–3.

[99] In a letter Euphues explicitly warns Philautus to 'avoyde solitariness, that breedes melancholy' (i. 256), an ironic reflection on his own status.

for disaster or spectacular success, and a careful look into the 'Glasse' will reveal, if not the answers, then at least the right sort of questions to ask.

But, one might well ask, what exactly is the advice being proferred in *Euphues and his England*? Was Lyly as violently opposed to the Alençon match as Stubbs and Sidney were? The text provides no clear answer to this second question—which is, of course, significant in itself—but an oblique answer to the first can be deciphered by the alert reader.[100] The 'Glasse for Europe' actually provides no useful advice at all, despite its resemblance to the abundant supply of 'mirror-for-princes' literature and its numerous variant sub-generic forms;[101] and the style of travel writing which was to emerge later in the century (see Chapter 1). Rather, by providing a gaping hole at the centre of the narrative—a possible witty allusion, if not to Stubbs's title, then to the implications of his fate for other would-be critics of Elizabeth's secret policies—Lyly is pointing out the difficulties of political life in an English public sphere which observed unpredictable and violently policed limits.[102] The glass is, in fact, one in which the reader/viewer sees only darkly;[103] the substance of the message lies elsewhere, in the story of the prodigal son, now reformed and fit to advise the commonwealth; in Euphues' use and abuse of his witty abilities to serve or hinder the state; and, perhaps most importantly, in the debates Euphues has with Fidus concerning the nature of the monarchy, a theme which was to become almost an obsession in Elizabeth's last years and the first years of the Stuart court.

The fact that Lyly concluded his fiction with 'Euphues' Glasse for Europe' might suggest that he was in favour of the

---

[100] For more general analyses of the problem of 'deciphering' see Barbour, *Deciphering Elizabethan Fiction*; Hutson, 'Fortunate Travellers'; Kinney, *Humanist Poetics*, introduction. Helen Hackett argues that *Euphues and his England* 'hovers between wishing for Elizabeth's marriage and accepting that her virginity is perpetual' (*Virgin Mother, Maiden Queen*, 119).

[101] For an analysis of various forms such literature could take, see Walker, *Persuasive Fictions*; *Plays of Persuasion*.

[102] Stubbs's title refers to the vortex into which England will be swept if the French marriage goes ahead. It may also allude to the gap between the monarch and her subjects, a problem Lyly's prose fictions make clear.

[103] A possible suppressed allusion to 1 Cor. 13: 12.

French match; certainly the fear expressed in *Euphues* is more that the succession has not been secured rather than that England might be engulfed by an alien religion.[104] Whereas Stubbs rested his case on the need for England to be separate from Europe, *Euphues and his England* argues the opposite case. Euphues addresses the 'Ladyes and Gentlewomen of Italy' with a glass which will make them blush at others' virtues, not their own vices (p. 189), implying that mutual cooperation between European nations might be beneficial to all concerned (especially if it is borne in mind that the Athens represented in *Euphues. The Anatomy of Wit* was an allegorical version of England). Just as Europe could learn much from England's virtues (although these are actually absent rather then present), so could England learn from Europe, or, at least, be open to the possibility of a dialogue (again, details are absent).[105]

Both prose romances demand to be read in terms of the national form they attempt to produce and flesh out, the suppressed context not just for a circumscribed work like *Euphues*, but, I would argue, a significant sub-text for virtually all travel writing, colonial writing, and literary representations of other cultures in Tudor and Stuart England. Lyly, forced to manoeuvre around his central problem without ever discussing it directly, was caught between conflicting desires and discourses, as, indeed, the idiosyncratic development of his hybrid prose works illustrates. At one level form and content appear to be out of sympathy: while Lyly develops a sophisticated courtly style to rival other European literatures, the logic

---

[104] It should be noted that Elizabeth was already in her early forties by the time negotiations with Alençon were under way, so it is unlikely that an heir would have resulted from the match.

[105] Stubbs's and Lyly's subsequent political careers are almost a model of symmetry. Stubbs, according to Camden, 'having his right hand cut off, put off his hat with his left and said with a loud voice, "God save the Queen" '. He was later employed by Lord Burghley to defend the latter's book justifying the execution of Edmund Campion against the attacks of Cardinal Allen, and became an MP in 1588, helping to draft a bill designed to protect puritan ministers from the attacks of bishops (Stubbs, *Gaping Gulf*, pp. xxxvi, xlv). Lyly became an MP in 1589, and was also employed by the authorities as a propagandist, but against the puritans during the Martin Marprelate controversy, publishing *Pappe with an Hatchet* in the same year (*DNB* entry). Criticism of the monarch's actions clearly did not preclude further official employment, or indicate implacable hostility to the mechanisms of state.

of the text demands the ability to decode narratives in a more straightforward, allegorical manner. Rhetorical elaboration confronts logical analysis, and Lyly appears both to enjoy the copiousness of his style and simultaneously to be suspicious of it (as the praise of the counsellors who can see through the masks of conspiracies perhaps illustrates). One celebrates the achievements of an increasingly sophisticated court display, while the other impulse values a more obvious moral truthfulness and fear of the present. Courtly virtues are set against those of the university, to say nothing of the suspicion that, at the court of a Queen, there is a feeling that excessive *politesse* and flowery language are feminine values and therefore cannot represent the whole of the nation. As the two prefatory letters to *Euphues and his England* recognize, a fractured text will have a fractured audience; the nation cannot be united, but will consist of different groups who will read the texts in different ways.[106] Such an awareness conflicts dramatically with the desire of the author to serve as a spokesman for the nation and advise the monarch at court. *Euphues*, like so many sixteenth-century English literary texts, attempts to mould and fix a national identity and, inevitably, becomes entangled in the logic of that slippery problem. In this sense, the text is both about the national question and defined by it.

Lyly's vast influence on subsequent literature has usually been attributed to his style. However, it might also owe much to the oblique, somewhat sly relationship between surface narrative and political critique enshrined in the story of Euphues, an important link for authors who were prepared to experiment with various kinds of writing at a time when travel writing itself was not yet an established generic form which they could adopt.

As is well attested, *Euphues* and the Euphuistic style did spawn numerous imitators and disciples in the 1580s and 1590s. These were often writers who experimented with various types of writing in order to make a living or to project their ideas into the public sphere. Many such works, like *Euphues* and its sequel, represented exotic, distant, or fictional lands as a means of discussing English politics. Robert Greene's

---

[106] Helgerson, *Elizabethan Prodigals*, 68.

Gwydonius. The Carde of Fancie (1584) is one intriguing example of this disguised relationship between text and subtext. It tells the story of Gwydonius, the only son of the tyrant Duke Clerophantes of Metelyne, who is a gifted but prodigal youth.[107] After a dispute with his father, Gwydonius determines to leave the court and devote his life to travel, a decision which pleases Clerophantes, who proceeds to praise the virtues of travel as a means of transforming 'vanitie to vertue', replacing the folly of youth with the wisdom of age.[108] However, Clerophantes does warn that there can be no profit without danger: 'there is nothing *Gwydonius*, so precious, which in some respect is not perillous, nor nothing so pleasant which may not be painefull'.[109]

After an unpleasant interlude in the city of Barutta, where he squanders all his money and is thrown into prison, specifically because the magistrates are suspicious of his conspicuous consumption, Gwydonius travels to Alexandria, where he enters the service of the good Duke Orlanio, 'who was so famous and fortunate, for the peaceable government of his Dukedome, administering justice with such sinceritie, and yet tempering the extremitie of the law with such lenitie', that both his own subjects and strangers are content to serve him (p. 174). Orlanio serves as a pointed contrast to Gwydonius's own father, who used 'such mercilesse crueltie to his forraine enemies, and such modelesse rigour to his native citizens, that it was doubtfull whether he was more feared of his foes for his crueltie, or hated of his friends for his tyrannie' (p. 165).

---

[107] For further comment see Helgerson, *Elizabethan Prodigals*, 84–7; Helmut Bonheim, 'Robert Greene's *Gwydonius. The Carde of Fancie*', *Anglia*, 96 (1978), 45–64; René Pruvost, *Robert Greene et ses Romans (1558–1592): Contribution à l'Histoire de la Renaissance en Angleterre* (Paris: Faculté des Lettres d'Algier, 1938), ch. 4; Jordan, *Robert Greene*, 65–6. Robert W. Dent points out that *Gwydonius* was taken from a story in George Pettie's *The Pettie Palace of Pettie his Pleasure*, alleging (not terribly convincingly) that Greene's borrowings go well beyond even what was considered acceptable in Elizabethan times; 'Greene's *Gwydonius*: A Study in Elizabethan Plagiarism', *HLQ* 24 (1960–1), 151–62.

[108] Richard Helgerson points out that Gwydonius's responses to his father resemble those of the arrogant young Euphues to Eubulus, illustrating how closely Greene followed Lyly's text; *Elizabethan Prodigals*, 84.

[109] Robert Greene, *Gwydonius. The Carde of Fancie*, in George Saintsbury (ed.), *Shorter Novels: Elizabethan* (London: Dent, 1966, rpt. of 1929), 157–260, at 169. Subsequent references to this edition in parentheses in the text.

Ironically enough, it is Orlanio who has delivered an oration in praise of travel when he has most to fear of his subjects experiencing other regimes and better forms of government.

Gwydonius starts to prosper in Orlanio's service, falls in love with his daughter, Castania, and, after a long courtship, they come to a mutual understanding in secret. At this point the larger political world intervenes, because Orlanio (unwisely) has not paid the tribute he owes to Gwydonius's father. Despite diplomatic manoeuvres, during which Orlanio's son, Thersandro, falls in love with Gwydonius's virtuous sister, Clerophantes marches on Alexandria. A full-scale battle fails to sort matters out, and so it is decided to resort to single combat. Clerophantes chooses to fight for his cause, but the less virile Orlanio promises to give his daughter to whoever will act as his champion. Gwydonius, who has been forced into exile, having been exposed by a disgruntled former suitor of Castania, performs this duty in disguise, unhorses his father, who repents of his tyranny, and marries Castania.

The novel is not a straightforward Terentian prodigal-son story, and its distinctive elements suggest that it had a topical relevance in the manner of *Euphues*. First, it is not the son who has to be reformed at the end of the story, as Gwydonius's repentance and rehabilitation is over as soon as he enters the service of Orlanio, but the father. Clerophantes' words about the efficacy of foreign travel prove more applicable to himself. The Duke of Metelyne enters the final combat against his unknown foe 'as a balefull wretch thirsting after bloud, and glorying in the hope of his supposed conquest' (p. 259), but ends the novel having to surrender in humiliating fashion. However, he still emerges in credit for his belligerence when Orlanio embraces him and promises to give him half his Dukedom as a dowry for his daughter's wedding.

This apparent lacuna may well simply be a case of Greene's prolific output not resulting in finished or polished literary products.[110] But it may take on significance when the second structurally unusual feature of the novel is considered.

---

[110] Helgerson, *Elizabethan Prodigals*, 86–7. Helgerson argues that Greene fails to combine his romantic and didactic themes in any coherent design, ending the novel with love conquering and subsuming all.

Gwydonius's situation as an alien in the benevolent but beseiged city of Alexandria leads to a serious conflict of interests for the protagonist, which he eventually manages to solve when given the opportunity. However, before the eventual happy resolution of the plot, Gwydonius suffers terrible agony: 'for he feared death if hee were knowen to *Orlanio*, and hee doubted despight-full hate at the least, if he bewraide himselfe to *Castania*' (p. 232). Like Euphues, who suffers for love, he retires and so-liloquizes on his impossible dilemma: 'And what if *Castania* were privie to thy state, doest thou thinke her so constant as to consent to her father's foe? Doest thou thinke she wold wish the sonnes weale, when the father wisheth her mishap?' (p. 241). As it turns out, Castania is distraught by Gwydonius's betrayal, and decides that the only way she can continue to live is if she plans to 'rigorouslie revenge the villanie of *Valericus* [who betrayed Gwydonius], and by bathing in his bloude, she might both satis-fie her selfe and signifie to *Gwydonius* how entirely shee loved and liked him' (p. 250). Gwydonius could not have been expected to have known this, of course.

The difficult choices which the romance provides for its readers do not end here. It is clear that Clerophantes' military tyranny is by no means an ideal form of government, but the Dukedom of the goodly Orlanio is also far from perfect. When Clerophantes threatens Alexandria, Orlanio's attempts to deal with such hostility are comically inept. He manages to make a rousing speech to his troops before the battle, arguing that right will prevail whatever the odds because Clerophantes 'invadeth our realme without reason, and we defend but our owne right: he cruelly seeketh to deprive us of freedome, and we law-fully doe maintain our own liberty' (p. 251), and his troops achieve an honourable—if bloody—draw. However, when Clerophantes suggests that they decide the issue by single combat, Orlanio, 'finding himselfe farre unfit to resist his furi-ous force', discovers that all his nobility share a similar opinion of Clerophantes' martial prowess. This leaves Orlanio 'greatlie perplexed' and his realm in considerable danger of revolt:

for assembling his nobilitie together, amongst whom he appointed the champion should be chosen. They not onelie with one consent with-stood his command, but began to murmure and mutinie against him, condemning him of follie that he would so unadvisedlie commit his own state and their staie to the doubtful hazard of one mans hap. *Orlanio* seeing that it was now no time to chastise this their presumption, unlesse he meant to raise civill dissention in the citie, which were the next waie to confirme the enimie, and breed his owne confusion, he dissembled his cholar, and began to work a new waie. (p. 253)

Orlanio's new strategy is to promise the hand of his daughter to whoever tries to defeat Clerophantes, a ploy which solves none of the problems of relying on a single person's success to determine the fate of nations, but which, fortunately enough, works. However, just as it is not clear that Clerophantes has actually been transformed into a good ruler at the end of the novel, neither is it obvious that Orlanio, a man who can only react to hazards, but who cannot foresee or forestall them, is at all fit to govern.

Gwydonius. The Carde of Fancie contains a number of reflections on contemporary political problems which it resolutely refuses to unravel, as the title might suggest (*The Carde of Fancie* undoubtedly refers to the random game in which fortune deals each person a hand, implying that, just as not all card players are of equal skill, neither are players in the game of life). Gwydonius is caught in a classic moral conflict of loyalties between commitment to a father and commitment to a lover. Any argument that he should throw his lot in with the state he serves is made problematic because first, such loyalty might be considered treacherous, and, second, it is unclear that Orlanio is any better as a ruler than the tyrannical Clerophantes. Whichever way one turns, moral pitfalls are lurking.

It would be odd if these quite deliberately staged conflicts were not related to contemporary problems in the 1580s, especially given the allusions to *Euphues* in the text, most significantly the reproduction of the importance of travel as a crucial plot motif. Alexandria may not be a straightforward allegory of England, but what the characters in the novel have to endure strongly implies that their situation relates to that of many Englishmen and women in the early 1580s.[111] Greene's political

---

[111] Such an equation may be strengthened by a conversation Gwydonius and Castania have in which she is equated with Diana and he with Acteon, perhaps alluding to contemporary allegorical representations of Elizabeth (206). See Berry, *Of Chastity and Power*, chs. 1–3; Hackett, *Virgin Mother, Maiden Queen*, 174–7, 191–6, *passim*.

and religious views are not easy to determine, but the evidence suggests that he inclined towards Catholicism. *Gwydonius* is dedicated to Edward de Vere, Earl of Oxford (1562–1604), known for his Catholic sympathies and his bitter quarrel with Sir Philip Sidney.[112] He was notably hostile to Puritanism throughout his writing career, and he collaborated with Thomas Lodge, whose Catholic loyalties were quite explicit, on a play entitled *A Looking Glasse for London and England*, published in 1594 but probably written in 1588–9.[113]

The early 1580s were a particularly fraught and dangerous time for Catholics within England. There had been a significant problem since Pope Pius V's bull, *Regnans in Excelsis* (1570), had excommunicated Elizabeth and called on her Catholic subjects to rise up and depose her, placing English Catholics in a difficult position of divided loyalties, exactly the sort of conflict which Gwydonius has to undergo when forced to choose between bonds of state, kinship, and love. However the situation became increasingly tense after the arrival of the Jesuits Edmund Campion and Robert Parsons in 1580, who secretly conducted Mass for Catholic families. A series of harsh penalties were passed through Parliament in 1581, punishing recusants with heavy fines and approving the death penalty for priests caught administering Mass, enshrined in the Act to Retain the Queen's Majesty's Subjects in their True Obedience and the Act against Seditious Words and Rumours. Campion was captured and executed in December with two other priests, and Parsons, who had fled to France, was condemned to death *in absentia*. In November 1583 Francis Throckmorton, a Catholic nobleman, confessed that he had been instrumental in a plot inaugurated by the Duke of Guise to invade England and

---

[112] See Duncan-Jones, *Sir Philip Sidney*, 166, 202, *passim*; Collinson, *Elizabethan Puritan Movement*, 198–9. Greene also wrote an elegy on the death of Sir Christopher Hatton (1540–91), a defender of the established church against the attacks of the Puritans (*DNB* entry; Collinson, *Elizabethan Puritan Movement*, 193–4).

[113] On Greene's hostility to Puritanism and his role in the Marprelate controversy, see E. H. Miller, 'The Relationship of Robert Greene and Thomas Nashe (1588–92)', *PQ* 33 (1954), 353–67. On *A Looking Glasse for London*, see Paradise, *Thomas Lodge*, 142–57; Jordan, *Robert Greene*, 177–9, for details. Helgerson, however, claims that Greene gradually moved towards a radical Protestant position in his later years; *Elizabethan Prodigals*, 102.

place Mary Queen of Scots on the throne in Elizabeth's place with the help of other prominent English Catholics, thus reviving fears of the Saint Bartholomew's Day Massacre. Throckmorton was duly tortured and executed. The new Archbishop of Canterbury, John Whitgift, issued a series of articles aimed to curb the activities of both Puritans and Catholics and bring all within the range of acceptable beliefs established by the Church of England. It should also be added that Pope Gregory XIII (1572–85) was keen to provide aid to Elizabeth's enemies, and had financed both Sir Thomas Stukeley's bizarre attempts to invade Ireland and, eventually, England (1578), and the much more serious threat of James Fitzmaurice Fitzgerald, who invaded Ireland in 1579 with the papal legate, Nicholas Sander, sparking off one of the most significant threats to English control over Ireland in Elizabeth's reign.[114]

Greene's novel is not a straightforward treatment of these events, but it is hard not to read the text in terms of the attempts of the Elizabethan authorities to regulate the lives of their subjects and enforce an outward conformity by policing their spirituality (in the same year that Campion and two priests were executed, three separatists were executed in Bury St Edmunds for attacking the Queen as 'Jezebel').[115] Greene was a prolific author, even by the standards of many of his contemporary prose writers, so to expect consistency and depth in his treatment of complex issues might be asking rather too much.[116] Clerophantes' speech to Gwydonius concerning the efficacy of travel is undoubtedly a key moment which defines the action of the novel, although the irony of his faith is not exploited in the conclusion. One trajectory of *Gwydonius*

[114] For details, see Guy, *Tudor England*, 284–5; Russell, *Crisis of Parliaments*, 232–3. A useful overall perspective is provided in Williams, *Tudor Regime*, ch. 8. On the figure of Guise, see Kingdon, *Myths About the St. Bartholomew's Day Massacres*, 73–4, 207–8, *passim*. For details of Campion's execution, see Bellamy, *Tudor Law of Treason*, *passim*. For details of the Desmond Rebellion, see Moody *et al.* (eds.), *New History of Ireland*, III. 104–9. For details of the harsh treatment of Puritans in the same period, see Collinson, *Elizabethan Puritan Movement*, pts. 4 and 5; Clegg, *Press Censorship in Elizabethan England*, 183–4.

[115] O'Day, *The Tudor Age*, 63.

[116] For one reading of the contradictions in the novel, see Helgerson, *Elizabethan Prodigals*, 87.

appears to be towards a realization that it is not the prodigal son who needs to be educated but the prodigal state, governed by a tyrant. However, this has to be set against another growing awareness that the individual is caught between balancing forces which he or she cannot evade or work through in a satisfactory manner (*The Carde of Fancie* one is dealt by life). Both narrative movements can be related to the contemporary religious background elaborated above, just as both can be related to the meaning and purpose of travel writing (travel as a means of moral discovery; travel leading to experience of other cultures and governments and, hence, comparative evaluation). Ultimately, the two structuring motifs cannot be harmoniously reconciled, and the conclusion to *Gwydonius* is abrupt, delivering rather less than has been promised. Nevertheless, the novel articulates a profound disquiet with actions of the mighty which directly intervene in the lives of their subjects in order to limit their freedom, or fail to protect them from external threats. Placed in either situation, the ordinary citizen will struggle to know how to act loyally and to whom.

Gwydonius can usefully be compared with Thomas Lodge's much more well-known and successful novel, *Rosalynd* (1590), a work which has suffered unfortunate distortion because it served as the main source for Shakespeare's *As You Like it*.[117] Lodge's novel is also a Euphuistic work. Its subtitle describes it as 'Euphues Golden Legacy: found after his death in his cell at Silexedra. Bequeathed to Philautus' sons, nursed up with their father in England.'[118] Also, like *Gwydonius*, it concerns the need to escape from a tyrannous land and experience others in order to bring about moral and political reform. Furthermore, if Greene's religious and political affiliations are somewhat shadowy, Lodge's are quite clear and frequently voiced. Lodge was summoned before the Privy Council to defend his beliefs in 1580, and his brief prison sentence soon after this may have been due to his recusancy.[119] He was further in trouble in the first two decades of the seventeenth century.[120] The year before

---

[117] See Charles Whitworth, '*Rosalynde*: *As You Like It* and As Lodge Wrote It', *ES* 58 (1977), 114–17.

[118] Thomas Lodge, *Rosalynde*, ed. Brian Nellist (Keele: Keele University Press, 1995), 23. Subsequent references to this edition in parentheses in the text.

[119] Paradise, *Thomas Lodge*, 17, 22.   [120] Ibid. 54.

Rosalynd appeared he had published a series of satires, one of which, 'Truth's Complaint over England', lamented the absence of truth from a land in which 'Justice sore I fear by power is led'.[121] Another, 'The Discontented Satyre', more pointedly attacks the moon-goddess, Cynthia, alleging that her 'borrowed beauties merit no regard: / Boast, discontent, naught may depress thy power / Since in thyself all grief thou dost devour' (l. 40–2).[122] It is hard to read the poem as anything other than a negative portrait of Elizabeth, given the frequent representation of her as Cynthia/Diana in the last two decades of her reign.[123] Cynthia's all-encompassing power means that nothing can be achieved without her favour, and all significant activity—literary, military, courtly—depends upon her whims, indicating that the poem is yet another attack on the vagaries of life in over-centralized Elizabethan England.[124]

The same hostility to the queen and court life is undoubtedly present in *Rosalynde*. The title itself may well be a deliberate echo of the lady who rejects Colin Clout's advances and causes him so much melancholy in Edmund Spenser's *The Shepheardes Calender* (1579). Spenser's work was also notably hostile to Elizabeth (albeit from a rather different religious perspective from that of Lodge), an antagonism Lodge may have sought to recall for his readers.[125] Although the story has a precedent in the form of the medieval romance, *Gamelyn*, a similar story of a wronged younger brother, much of what Lodge writes is new.[126]

---

[121] K. W. Grandson (ed.), *Tudor Verse Satire* (London: Athlone, 1970), 85. Compare those of another ambitious young writer of Catholic family, John Donne, especially Satire 3 (probably written between 1593 and 1598); Donne, *Complete English Poems*, 161–4.

[122] Grandson (ed.), *Tudor Verse Satire*, 87.

[123] Hackett, *Virgin Mother, Maiden Queen, passim.*

[124] For further comment on this poem see Lodge, *Rosalynde*, ed. Nellist, 15. For further examples of attacks on Cynthia, see Hackett, *Virgin Mother, Maiden Queen*, ch. 6.

[125] Collinson, *Elizabethan Puritan Movement*, 200–1; Hadfield, *Literature, Politics and National Identity*, 174–88; Paul E. McLane, *Spenser's* Shepheardes Calender: *A Study in Elizabethan Allegory* (Notre Dame, Ind.: Notre Dame University Press, 1961).

[126] See *Gamelyn*, in Walter Hoyt French and Charles Brockway Hale (eds.), *Middle English Metrical Romances*, 2 vols. (New York: Russell & Russell, 1964), i. 207–35; Lee C. Ramsey, *Chivalric Romances: Popular Literature in Medieval England* (Bloomington, Ind.: Indiana University Press, 1983), 93–5; Lodge, *Rosalynde*, ed. Nellist, 8–13.

The novel is set in France, a departure from the unspecified location of *Gamelyn* and, paradoxically, an indication that its subject matter is probably of relevance to English readers but needs to be disguised. The text is prefaced by a schedule (a codicil to a will) from the dying Euphues which Lodge has purportedly discovered with the novel. Euphues addresses his work to Philautus's family, urging them to pay careful attention to his 'golden legacy', as the 'counsel' provided in the text must serve 'instead of worldly goods' (pp. 26-7). Philautus, the attentive reader would have recalled, remained behind in England when he married Camilla at the end of *Euphues and his England*, when Euphues wandered off to disappear in obscurity. Within the first layer of its fictional framework, *Rosalynde* is very deliberately addressed to English readers.

As with *Gwydonius*, it would be unwise to try to force the events of the narrative into a straightforward allegory of events in the late 1580s. But equally, it would be a blinkered reading which refused to acknowledge a possible relationship between fiction and politics. *Rosalynde* shares with many other early English novels, particularly the group which came in the wake of *Euphues*, an atmosphere of intense paranoia and fear that all is not as it seems. When John of Bordeaux dies his lands are distributed among his sons, with the largest portion being left for the youngest and most virtuous, Rosader. He is promptly cheated out of his inheritance by the eldest brother, Saladyn, who is in turn cheated by the usurping king, Torismond. Rosader flees to join the exiled good and true monarch, Gerismond, in the forest of Arden, where he is joined by Rosalynd, Gerismond's daughter, disguised as a man, Ganymede, and, later his brother. Rosader and Rosalynd have fallen in love and she, still disguised as Ganymede, helps him express his passion for her real self until she reveals her identity at the end of the novel, when all the political and personal intrigues are conveniently sorted out. Torismond is killed in battle and Gerismond restored to his kingdom; Saladyn marries Alinda, Torismond's good daughter who has remained faithful to her companion, Rosalynd; Montanus, a shepherd, marries Phoebe and is made 'lord over all the forest of Arden' (p. 126).

The setting of the novel is only French in name, and nothing of significance that happens can be tied to that specific location.

It is clear that life under the rule of Torismond is dangerous and unjust; when it suits him he cheats Saladyn of his lands; when he feels that Rosalynd's virtuous beauty is a potential focus of resistance to his rule, he has no compunction in banishing her, although it means the departure of his own daughter too, 'the tyrant rather choosing to hazard the loss of his only child than anyways to put in question the state of his kingdom, so suspicious and fearful is the conscience of an usurper' (p. 46). He lives in constant fear of the people turning against him, so much so that a wrestling tournament provides the opportunity to distract the commons from political thought and keep the 'French busied with all sports that might breed their content' (p. 36) and 'busy his commons' heads, lest being idle their thoughts should run upon more serious matters and call to remembrance their old banished king' (p. 37).[127]

Given Lodge's own situation as a recusant constantly in danger of persecution by the Elizabethan authorities, and Pope Pius V's bull declaring the Queen a usurper who could legitimately be deposed by loyal Catholics, it is easy to understand the anxiety which pervades the novel. Given also that it was written just after the defeat of the Spanish Armada (1588) at a time when attempts to root out Catholics had increased to new levels, that paranoia is all the more simple to explain. In 1588 thirty-one priests were executed, and the 1589 Parliament had opened with a speech from Sir Christopher Hatton which denounced both Catholics and Puritans. 1588 also saw the start of the anti-episcopal propaganda wars concerning the subversive Marprelate tracts, which led to a number of prosecutions for sedition.[128] It is thus tempting to read *Rosalynd* as the utopian story of a retreat from the cares of the world into a pastoral idyll where all is as it seems.[129] But the novel, like *Gwydonius*, refuses to provide any such straightforward contrast. Rosalynd and Rosader's courtship, which occupies much of the narrative of the second half of the work, remains

---

[127] Compare the fears of Orlanio in *Gwydonius* (see above, pp. 183–4).
[128] O'Day, *The Tudor Age*, 64; Collinson, *Elizabethan Puritan Movement*, 391–6, *passim*.
[129] See Walter R. Davis, 'Masking in Arden: The Histrionics of Lodge's *Rosalynde*', *SEL* 5 (1965), 151–63, reworked in *Idea and Act in Elizabethan Fiction* (Princeton: Princeton University Press, 1969), 83–93.

one of misrecognition, disguise, and intrigue until the very end. Equally significant, especially when read in the light of Lodge's 'The Discontented Satyre', is the fraught relationship between Montanus and Phoebe, the latter being interchangeable with Cynthia or Diana and therefore standing for Elizabeth.

As *Rosalynd*'s editor, Brian Nellist, points out, the forest of Arden has no magic about it and Alinda and Rosalynd 'are only momentarily free from the pressures of power' (p. 12).[130] Every positive sentiment to the contrary is undercut by immediate events or contrary statements from other characters. The focus for such disillusion is inevitably the relationship of Phoebe and Montanus; as Alinda and Rosalynd plan to live 'quiet, unknown and contented' among the shepherds' flocks, the reader is reminded of the plight of Montanus, 'in a muse thinking of the cruelties of his Phoebe', whom he had wooed long but was in no hope to win' (p. 57). Phoebe, in love with Ganymede, only agrees to marry Montanus when Ganymede/Rosalynd agrees that he will marry Phoebe unless 'I can by reason suppress Phoebe's love towards me' (p. 122), which, of course, the reader knows will happen easily enough. As in Greene's *Gwydonius*, the novel ends with this problem left unresolved, although one assumes that the union does go ahead.

The unrequited love Montanus feels for Phoebe serves as a counterpoint to the political anxieties of the novel, dramatizing the interrelationship between personal and public loyalty which Lodge, like any other recusant, evidently felt so keenly. Ganymede/Rosalynd warns Montanus that 'in courting Phoebe thou barkest with the wolves of Syria against the moon, and rovest at such a mark with thy thoughts as is beyond the pitch of thy bow, praying to Love when Love is pitiless and thy malady remediless' (p. 112). The comparison of Montanus to a wolf surely alludes to contemporary Protestant satire which cast Catholics as wolves and Protestants as innocent sheep on whom they would prey.[131] However loyal Montanus tries to be,

---

[130] On this reading, *Rosalynd* fits into the tradition of pastoral literature mapped out by Judith Haber in *Pastoral and the Poetics of Self-Contradiction: Theocritus to Marvell* (Cambridge: Cambridge University Press, 1995).

[131] See John N. King, *Tudor Royal Iconography: Literature and Art in an Age of Religion* (Princeton: Princeton University Press, 1989), 173.

Phoebe/Elizabeth will turn her back on him and refuse his love and loyalty, exactly the situation of her Catholic subjects for the best part of her reign after the Papal bull of 1570. *Rosalynd* ends with Montanus inheriting the right to rule the (formerly) outlawed kingdom in the forest of Arden and so being able to force Phoebe to marry him. Phoebe, significantly enough, is silent after she has agreed to Ganymede/Rosalynd's duplicitous promise. In effect, a circle has been squared and a trick resolves matters in the fantasy kingdom; only Phoebe's lack of speech enables the ending to preserve the appearance of happy resolution, with the maligned 'wolf' achieving both power and (qualified) acceptance. In the real world outside the forest, we know that matters are very different.

Rosalynde exhibits a profound pessimism; nevertheless, it still remains within a humanist tradition of fictional text as advice book, employing a foreign location in order to provide a disclaimer of any direct relationship between narrative and contemporary politics.[132] Such possibilities are directly challenged in Thomas Nashe's *The Unfortunate Traveller* (1594), a work which is keen to lay the ghost of the Euphuistic tradition to rest. Nashe achieves this by virtue of his overt cynicism as well as his brutally and gratuitously realistic style, as many critics have noted.[133] More pertinently for the argument here, *The Unfortunate Traveller* directly confronts the question of foreign travel, the usefulness of acquiring knowledge from abroad and, as a result of this scepticism, the ability of the text to teach the reader anything of use.

The Unfortunate Traveller is a work suffused with paranoia even by the standards of much Elizabethan fiction. The protagonist, Jack Wilton, is 'a certain kind of an appendix or page, belonging or appertaining in or unto the confines of the English Court' during Henry VIII's wars with the French.[134] Wilton is

---

[132] Kinney, *Humanist Poetics*, ch. 10.

[133] Most recently in Robert Weimann, *Authority and Representation in Early Modern Discourse* (Baltimore: Johns Hopkins University Press, 1996), ch. 12. See also Kinney, *Humanist Poetics*, ch. 9; Hutson, *Thomas Nashe in Context*, ch. 6; David Kaula, 'The Low Style in Nashe's *The Unfortunate Traveller*', *SEL* 6 (1966), 43–57.

[134] Thomas Nashe, *The Unfortunate Traveller*, in *The Unfortunate Traveller and Other Works*, ed. J. B. Steane (Harmondsworth: Penguin, 1972), 251–370, at 254. Subsequent references to this edition in parentheses in the text.

an involuntary traveller, a picaresque rogue, able to thrive in his environment by exploiting the possibilities which distance from the social edifices of home provides for transgression of accepted norms as a means of self-protection and, when possible, self-advancement. The pieties of humanist education count for little in the brutal world of military conflict. In the first paragraph Wilton signals his conscious inversion of established patterns of learning: 'What strategical acts and monuments do you think an ingenious infant of my years might enact? You will say, it were sufficient if he slur a die, pawn his master to the utmost penny, and minister the oath of the pantofle artificially' (p. 255). In other words, a good page learns how to cheat, expropriate money, and, most significantly, lie.[135]

Jack Wilton's first two 'jests' illustrate how he intends to use his experience of travel. First, he dupes the cider-maker by playing on his fears of the treacherous world they inhabit, where spying and lying are the norm. Wilton informs him, 'It is buzzed in the King's head that you are a secret friend to the enemy, and, under pretence of getting a licence to furnish the camp with cider and suchlike provant, you have furnished the enemy, and in empty barrels sent letters of discovery and corn innumerable' (p. 259). The cider-maker's error is that he is wise enough to believe that treachery is omnipresent—as *The Unfortunate Traveller* demonstrates is the case time and again—but foolish enough to trust Jack Wilton, a lesson which obviously also unsettles the reader, who does not know how far to trust the narrative of the text, or how secure any interpretation of it can be. In one sense, this is the logic of the novella pushed to its extremes and exploded from within its own sceptical conventions. Whereas the writer of Euphuistic fiction could always claim that no subversive meaning was ever intended when foreign lands were represented, and that such settings bore no relation to life in England, Nashe's Wilton writes as if this were literally the case, via the paradoxical argument that travel is such a subversive and dangerously uncertain activity that it cannot bear any relation to life in England.

[135] R. B. McKerrow notes that the oath on an old shoe ('pantofle') was used to initiate a freshman at university; it may have performed a similar function at court: *The Works of Thomas Nashe*, ed. R. B. McKerrow, rev. F. P. Wilson (Oxford: Oxford University Press, 1958), 5 vols., iv. 256.

In this first example, little harm is done. The drunk cider-maker pledges his loyalty to the king, the jest is exposed, and Wilton is whipped, 'though they made themselves merry with it many a winter's evening after' (p. 261). The second jest Wilton undertakes is potentially more disturbing, a pattern which structures the novel's narrative until he eventually flees back to England after the bloody torture and execution of Cutwolfe, having finally realized the potential consequences of his actions. Wilton dupes 'an ugly mechanical Captain' whom he serves into believing that he has been chosen to assassinate the King of France by pretending to be an English traitor and bluffing his way into the French camp in order to gain his trust. Needless to say, he is easily exposed and only escapes torture on the wheel because his story is too preposterous to take seriously as a threat. The captain is whipped and sent back to the English camp, so that Wilton has inflicted his suffering on another. The French send back a boast to the English: 'they were shrewd fools that should drive the Frenchman out of his kingdom, and make him glad, with Corinthian Dionysius, to play the school-master' (p. 269). The story of Dionysus, the tyrant who was transformed into a proper king after he became a humble schoolmaster for a while, was a standard example in English humanist treatises, illustrating the power of education to quell the excesses of over-mighty government.[136] In Nashe's text the moral force of the fable is negated as it becomes merely a military boast; only a nation more powerful than the French can make them trade their weapons for school books.

Wilton stands as a figure of the untrustworthy and malign counsellor whose advice can only bring disaster to those who listen, a further sign that Nashe is attacking the claims frequently made in Euphuistic fiction and travel writing for the pedagogical and political value of their messages. Wilton sees himself, like Tamburlaine in Marlowe's play, as 'God's scourge from above' (p. 271) for fools; his advice to the cider-maker he describes, insidiously, as 'counsel' (p. 260). When flattering the mechanical captain he claims, 'I see in your face that you were born, with the swallow, to feed flying, to get much treasure and honour by travel' (p. 266). Such words return to haunt Wilton

---

[136] Bushnell, *Culture of Teaching*, 35–7.

towards the end of his own travels. He encounters 'a banished English earl' (p. 340) who warns him of the harmful effects of European travel, which, he claims, teach the traveller nothing he could not learn 'without stirring [his] feet out of a warm study' (p. 343). The earl's diatribe consists of a series of prejudiced stereotypes against diverse European national characters; the French are untrustworthy, addicted to fashion and fine living; the Italians are atheists, lecherous, addicted to sodomy and poisoning; the Danes and Dutch are habitually drunk.[137] He starts by exhorting his fellow countrymen never to leave England, and concludes by bursting into tears at his unfortunate fate. Wilton, with the virtue of hindsight, laments his refusal to listen to the earl: 'Certainly if I had bethought me like a rascal as I was, he should have had an Ave Marie of me for his cynic exhortation. God plagued me for deriding such a grave fatherly advertiser' (p. 347). Only when he witnesses the horrific execution of Cutwolfe, who is torn limb from limb so that he is left 'on the wheel as in hell, where, yet living, he might behold his flesh legacied amongst the fowls of the air' (p. 369), does Wilton decide to reform himself and return home.

Wilton, although he tells the earl that he 'took his counsel in worth' (p. 347), does not appreciate the full force of his words until he witnesses Cutwolfe's vision of hell. It would, of course, be naive to take the earl's words at face value. Jack Wilton's endorsement of them in the light of his future experience suggests that his cynicism, too, has its limits, and that the fear of the afterlife persuades him to reform himself. Nevertheless, such strategic ironies only serve to show that the biter has been bitten; they do not enable the reader to return to the model of reading posited by the Euphuistic novel with any confidence. At the end of *The Unfortunate Traveller*, Jack Wilton has indeed learnt nothing that he could not have encountered in 'a warm study': simply that one should avoid the pains of hell-fire at all costs, something he might more easily have gleaned from a

---

[137] Such stereotypes can be found in numerous contemporary travellers' accounts and plays; see e.g. Fynes Moryson, *An Itinerary Containing His Ten Yeeres Travell through the Twelve Dominions* (1617), 4 vols. (Glasgow: MacLehose, 1907), *passim*; Coryat, *Crudities, passim*. The earl's opinions could also have been verified from reading the works of Geoffrey Fenton, William Thomas, William Painter, etc.

book (this, of course, applies also to the reader of the novel). On the other hand, is it not the case that the experience of the author makes the book in question more readable and persuasive, or do all books simply relate to other books? In the end, we simply do not know, just as we do not know whether the experiences represented in the novel have any independent existence outside the text. In the same way, whether we can take Wilton's conclusion that there is no point in travelling abroad at face value, or whether he is not to be trusted on this issue, is left open. Neither reading holds out much hope for the possibility of serious political lessons being learnt from the representation of foreign lands and cultures. Jack Wilton may be a fortunate rather than an unfortunate traveller in some respects, in that he does manage to return to his native land with his life intact; but the novel would appear to align Nashe alongside Ascham as a hostile critic of the supposed values of European travel.

The use of a foreign or exotic location as a means of representing domestic events and politics continued to be a frequent ploy in English fiction of the early seventeenth century, despite Nashe's hostility. Often, the narratives of such works could be decoded much more directly and straightforwardly than in earlier novels, because authors were keener to represent recent events in their texts, many of them notorious scandals which caused offence to readers involved.[138] A case in point is John Barclay's *Argenis*, published in Latin in 1621, an overtly politicized romance which dealt with the religious conflicts in late-sixteenth-century France by way of a straightforwardly decoded allegory. The work was very popular in England, and met with the approval of James I, who asked Ben Jonson to translate it into English. After Jonson's work was lost in the fire

---

[138]   The most famous case was probably that of Mary Wroth's romance, *Urania* (1621), which angered Sir Edward Denny for its portrait of his daughter's adultery and his own alleged reaction to her conduct; see Josephine Roberts, 'An Unpublished Literary Quarrel Concerning the Suppression of Mary Wroth's "Urania" ', *N. & Q.* 222 (1977), 532–5; Paul Salzman, 'Contemporary References in Mary Wroth's *Urania*', *RES* 24 (1978), 178–81; Helen Hackett, 'Courtly Writing by Women', in Helen Wilcox (ed.), *Women and Literature in Britain, 1500–1700* (Cambridge: Cambridge University Press, 1996), 169–89, at 181. On the general character of early seventeenth-century fiction, see Salzman, *English Prose Fiction*, chs. 9–10.

which destroyed his library (November 1623), two translations appeared: one by Kingsmill Long (1625), which was conveniently divided up into chapters and was the more popular of the two, and one by Sir Robert De Grys (1628), which was dedicated to Charles I.[139]

Argenis is a long romance of some 400 pages, which deals with the relationship between Argenis, daughter of the good king, Meleander, and Poliarchus, a young knight who helps Meleander, the legitimate king, defeat the rebellion inaugurated by the duplicitous Poliarchus. Appended to De Grys' translation was a key which glossed all the characters in the text; the Sicilian setting was a representation of France; Meleander stood for Henri III; Licogenes, the Duke of Guise; and Hyanisbe, Elizabeth.[140] Such correspondences would have served to distance the reader from the immediate significance of the historical material, as all references are to events which took place at least a quarter of a century before the translation was published. They also demonstrate the continuing relevance of the events surrounding the Massacre of Saint Bartholomew's Day, despite James' much more diplomatic relationship with Spain, as then Europe was neatly divided into two easily defined halves.[141]

Both translations point out the contemporary political relevance of the romance. Kingsmill Long concludes his preface by drawing the attention of the reader to the seriousness of the work's purpose:

It is so full of wise and politique Discourses, and those so intermixed and seconded with pleasing accidents, so extolling Vertue and depresing Vice, that I have sometimes compared it to a greater Globe, wherein not onely the World, but euen the businesse of it is represented; it being (indeed) such a perfect Glasse of State, that I cannot suppose, but euery Reader will be drawne by the delight of something in it, to read the whole.[142]

---

[139] John Barclay, *Barclay his Argenis or the loves of Poliarchus and Argenis*, trans. Kingsmill Long (1625); John Barclay, *Argenis*, trans. Sir Robert Le Grys (1628). Barclay's Latin text is Io. Barclaii, *Argenis* (Paris, 1621).

[140] Barclay, *Argenis*, trans. De Grys, 485–9.

[141] For details of James' diplomatic relationship with Spain in the early 1620s, see David Mathew, *James I* (London: Eyre & Spottiswoode, 1967), ch. 24; Russell, *Crisis of Parliaments*, 297–8.

[142] Barclay, *Argenis*, trans. Long, A3ʳ.

Such comments invite readers to reflect on their own political experience and to use the work as a didactic treatise, placing *Argenis* firmly within the tradition of the literature of 'mirrors for princes' and so, generically, as a close relative of Euphuistic novels.

But why were James and, apparently, Charles, so keen on such material, given the general suspicion with which fictional writing had often been regarded by the authorities? It is, of course, dangerous to assume that Charles was necessarily enthusiastic about the work just because it was dedicated to him. However, the fact that two translations, one actual and one projected, were associated with the monarch must surely be a significant indication of the ways in which the novel was perceived by readers, suggesting that *Argenis* was regarded as a royalist novel.

The second chapter outlines the situation which has to be resolved in Sicily. Meleander is a ruler who is the victim of his excessive trust in others because 'hee thinketh by his owne goodnesse, all men to stand so affected to him'. His reign had been an easy one to start with, which made him indulge his harmless pleasures rather too much (the one mentioned is hunting), and in his feelings of bonhomie he became 'slow to revenge iniuries with fitting iustice'.[143] As a result the tyrannous Lycogenes was allowed to gain significant power until he was able to transform his faction into a rebellious force which challenged the power of the lawful monarch. Whereas Meleander is guilty of being overly straightforward in his dealings with his subjects, Lycogenes is devious and dissimulating, badly advising the king and 'pretending (after the menner of Tyrants) redresse of abuses' (p. 6).

The political thrust of the novel leads the reader towards an acceptance of the value of the independence of the monarch free from the control of parliament, an argument James himself had made in *Basilikon Doron* and *The Trew Law of Free Monarchies* (p. 202) (see above, pp. 44–7).[144] Hence any resemblance between Meleander and James which sets the

---

[143] Barclay, *Argenis*, trans. Long, 5. All subsequent references to this edition in parentheses in the text.

[144] See Salzman, *English Prose Fiction*, 149–50.

British monarch in a more critical light—both are keen on hunting, both are rather over-keen on certain favourites (pp. 14–16)—is not only offset by the French allegory explicitly signalled in the appended key to De Grys' translation, but is also rendered positive because of the eventual happy outcome of the novel, with Meleander becoming a wiser ruler without forfeiting any of his personal powers.[145] *Argenis* is, yet again, a work which is suffused with an atmosphere of paranoia and mistrust, where nothing is ever what it seems. Meleander resembles Duncan in *Macbeth* (*c*.1606), another literary work intimately bound up with the political debates of James' reign, who laments his inability to read his subjects deeply: 'There's no art / To find the mind's construction in the face' (I. iv. 12–13). Unlike Duncan, Meleander survives to learn the lessons of his naïveté, and becomes adept at distinguishing the fine line between the practice of *realpolitik* necessary in order to rule the state and the surrender to the Machiavellian deceptions of a tyrant.[146] *Argenis* does not occupy an exalted place in the literary canon today, but in a crucial sense it achieved the political influence in high places which few other works of prose fiction had managed in spite of their pretensions: something of an irony, given that its Franco-Scots author was already dead when the first edition was published. In gaining the attention of the king, *Argenis* provided a belated riposte to the cynicism of *The Unfortunate Traveller*, as well as a vindication of Nashe's sense that works of travel writing teach you nothing either that you don't already know or that you can't discover more easily elsewhere.

[145] On James' notorious promotion of favourites, see Mathew, *James I*, pt. 2, ch. 12, *passim*. A contemporary literary reflection on James's love of hunting is found in the first stanza of the Donne poem, 'The Sun Rising', which also provides this book with its title: 'Go tell court-huntsmen, that the King will ride' (l. 7); Donne, *Complete English Poems*, 80. Smith notes that 'King James's passion for the sport was a byword' (402), indicating that any king who was represented as loving hunting in the early seventeenth century was likely to remind the reader of James.

[146] Salzman, *English Prose Fiction*, 153.

CHAPTER FOUR

'All my travels' history': Reading the Locations of Renaissance Plays

THE SUGGESTION that many plays written in the late sixteenth and early seventeenth centuries dealt with contemporary political issues, or that dramatists used foreign locations in order to effect such engagement, has been made often enough by various critics to make both claims uncontroversial.[1] Plays performed at the court of Henry VIII more often than not aimed to persuade the king to take a specific course of action; throughout Elizabeth's reign, a significant number of plays performed at court and in public theatres proffered advice on how the succession might be secured; many plays performed from the late 1590s to the early 1620s clearly reflected on the nature and status of the English court in representing the courts of Italian city-states. Various works commented on particular diplomatic relations with France or, more frequently, Spain, most notoriously in Thomas Middleton's *A Game at Chess* (1624).[2] My purpose in this chapter is not to provide an

---

[1] See e.g. J. W. Lever, *The Tragedy of State* (London: Methuen, 1971); Gordon McMullan and Jonathan Hope (eds.), *The Politics of Tragicomedy: Shakespeare and After* (London: Routledge, 1992); Walter Cohen, *Drama of a Nation: Public Theater in Renaissance England and Spain* (Ithaca, NY: Cornell University Press, 1985); Jonathan Dollimore, *Radical Tragedy: Religion, Ideology and Power in the Drama of Shakespeare and his Contemporaries* (Hemel Hempstead: Harvester, 2nd edn., 1989); R. Helgerson, *Forms of Nationhood: The Elizabethan Writing of England* (Chicago: University of Chicago Press, 1992), ch. 5; J. R. Mulryne, 'Nationality and Language in Thomas Kyd's *The Spanish Tragedy*', in Maquerlot and Willems (eds.), *Travel & Drama in Shakespeare's Time*, 87–105; J. R. Mulryne and Margaret Shewring (eds.), *Theatre and Government under the Early Stuarts* (Cambridge: Cambridge University Press, 1993); Ivo Kamps, *Historiography and Ideology in Stuart Drama* (Cambridge: Cambridge University Press, 1996); Curtis Breight, *Surveillance, Militarism and Drama in the Elizabethan Era* (Basingstoke: Macmillan, 1996), 78–81, *passim*.
[2] Walker, *Plays of Persuasion: Drama and Politics at the Court of Henry VIII* (Cambridge: Cambridge University Press, 1991); M. Axton, *The Queen's Two Bodies: Drama and the Elizabethan Succession* (London: Royal Historical Society,

overview of a subject which has been treated extensively and intelligently elsewhere; moreover, such a project would require a large volume to itself, not a solitary chapter. Rather, my hope is that in carefully selecting a small sample of dramatic works, I can provide some sense of the manifold uses to which English Renaissance dramatists put the locations in which they chose to stage their plays.

Accordingly, I have chosen to highlight four plays (although my discussion necessitates the consideration of others) which deal with the various issues I have outlined so far in this study. First I shall discuss Christopher Marlowe's *The Massacre at Paris* (*c*.1592), because it is one of only two plays which deal directly with the Massacre of Saint Bartholomew's Day, an event which, so I have argued, was a defining moment in English Protestant consciousness, and which produced the horrified fear that similar apocalyptic violence could easily explode in England if measures were not taken to prevent it.[3] Second, I shall outline the multiple contexts of *Othello* (*c*.1604), a play which represents the ideal republic of Venice as the last bastion of European civilization pitted against the lure and danger of the barbarous and exotic Orient, but which can also be read as an allegory of contemporary England struggling against the dangers of savage Ireland. Third, I shall attempt to show that *The Tempest* (*c*.1611)—a text which has been subject to a heated battle between those who insist on the relevance of the play's colonial context and those who seek to deny any such relationship—can best be read as an attempt to negotiate between the question of European and colonial forms of government. In my reading of the play the problems of governing old kingdoms are described through the instance of the acquisition of new territories, a form of political analysis which

---

1977); P. Berry, *Of Chastity and Power: Elizabethan Literature and the Unmarried Queen* (London: Routledge, 1989), *passim*; H. Hackett, *Virgin Mother, Maiden Queen: Elizabeth I and the Cult of the Virgin Mary* (Basingstoke: Macmillan, 1995), *passim*; Alexander Leggatt, *English Drama: Shakespeare to the Restoration, 1590–1660* (Harlow: Longman, 1988), 7–8; Richard Dutton, *Mastering the Revels: The Regulation and Censorship of English Renaissance Drama* (Basingstoke: Macmillan, 1991), 237–46; Janet Clare, *'Art made Tongue-Tied by Authority': Elizabethan and Jacobean Dramatic Censorship* (Manchester: Manchester University Press, 1990), 190–99.

3 The other play is George Chapman's later *Bussy D'Ambois* (1600–4).

recalls Machiavelli's comments in *The Prince*, and, significantly enough, *Utopia*. Finally, I shall argue that John Fletcher's *The Island Princess* (*c*.1620–1), a work heavily indebted to Shakespeare's later comedies and romances (notably *The Tempest*), represents Portuguese colonialism in order to discuss the issues confronting contemporary English colonists. Not surprisingly, questions of national identity and colonial expansion are seen to be intertwined, in a relationship similar to that between domestic and foreign politics.

Obviously other works could have been selected; *The Merchant of Venice*, *Measure for Measure*, *The Spanish Tragedy*, *Bussy D'Ambois*, *The Maid's Tragedy*, *Tamburlaine*, to name just a few which could easily have been substituted for those analysed here. In a sense, the ubiquity of shared concerns makes my point for me. Dramatists were just as keen to enter the public sphere and stage political debates as other writers. Indeed, given the ephemeral nature of dramatic performance at a time before plays had obtained the literary status of other types of writing, they were arguably more politically topical, subversive, and reached out to a wider public than other forms, necessitating more significant attention from official channels designed to control potentially treasonable discourse.[4] The four chosen here illustrate the use of European, African, and East Indian locations as vehicles to consider English domestic, colonial, and foreign policy, indicating the ingenious range of political concerns to be found in English Renaissance drama.

'Thus Caesar *did goe foorth*': The Republican Sub-Text of The Massacre at Paris

Any discussion of *The Massacre at Paris* is rendered problematic owing to the almost certainly corrupt nature of the published octavo text (*c*.1602).[5] The surviving text is short, amounting only to 1250 lines (i.e. half the length of either part

---

[4] Clare, '*Art made Tongue-Tied by Authority*', Introduction.

[5] For discussion of textual problems, see Christopher Marlowe, *Dido Queen of Carthage and The Massacre at Paris*, ed. H. J. Oliver (London: Methuen, 1968), pp. xlvii–lxi.

of *Tamburlaine the Great*, *The Jew of Malta*, and *Edward II*),
and the discovery of the fragment of a manuscript indicates that
Marlowe's original text—whatever the relationship of that
work to the performed text—was probably significantly
longer.[6] The octavo is probably, as H. J. Oliver suggests, 'a
corrupt text put together by memorial reconstruction', possibly
by an actor, a company of actors working together, or the
prompter.[7] It is therefore even more speculative than usual to
attempt to read the play in terms of Marlowe's other writings
and the known facts of his life, as his part in 'authoring' the
surviving text may be tangential in the extreme.

Nevertheless, as some recent critics have pointed out, the
play does appear to bear the stamp of distinctly Marlovian
obsessions.[8] The plot itself is simple enough: after the wedding
between Margaret, daughter of the Catholic Queen-Mother,
Catherine De Medici, and the Protestant King of Navarre,
hopes are high that France will finally end her bitter civil wars
of religion and be united peacefully.[9] However, such hopes are

[6] J. Q. Adams, 'The Massacre at Paris Leaf', *The Library*, 4th ser., 14 (1934),
447–69; J. M. Nosworthy, 'The Marlowe Manuscript', *The Library*, 4th ser., 16
(1946), 158–71.

[7] Oliver (ed.), *The Massacre at Paris*, pp. lix–lx. Mark Thornton Burnett
points out that Guise's lines are more fully recorded than those of Margaret probably because the actor playing the first part remembered them better than the boy
actor who would presumably have played the latter role; Christopher Marlowe,
The Complete Plays, ed. Mark Thornton Burnett (London: Everyman, 1998, forthcoming), introduction. While cautioning the reader that the play is seriously
corrupt, Dr Thornton Burnett argues that the play does provide 'a provocative
judgement upon the French wars of religion'. I am grateful to Dr Thornton Burnett
for allowing me to see this edition in typescript.

[8] Judith Weil, 'Mirrors for Foolish Princes', in *Christopher Marlowe: Merlin's
Prophet* (Cambridge: Cambridge University Press, 1977), 82–104; Julia Briggs,
'Marlowe's *Massacre at Paris*: A Reconsideration', *RES*, n.s., 34 (1983), 257–78;
Thomas Healy, *Christopher Marlowe* (London: Northcote House, 1994), 68–71;
David Potter, 'Marlowe's *Massacre at Paris* and the Reputation of Henri III of
France', in Daryll Grantley and Peter Roberts (eds.), *Christopher Marlowe and
English Renaissance Culture* (Aldershot: Scolar Press, 1996), 70–95.

[9] On the large number of works translated into English on the Massacre of
Saint Bartholomew and the French wars of religion, see Vivien Thomas and
William Tydeman (eds.), *Christopher Marlowe: The Plays and their Sources*
(London: Routledge, 1994), 249–92. See also Paul H. Kocher, 'François Hotman
and Marlowe's *The Massacre at Paris*', *PMLA* 56 (1941), 349–68; 'Contemporary
Pamphlet Backgrounds for Marlowe's *The Massacre at Paris*', *MLQ* 8 (1947),
151–73, 309–18. On Geoffrey Fenton's works on the French wars of religion in the
early 1570s, see above, pp. 137–8.

dashed by the Machiavellian designs of the Duke of Guise, who, supported by Queen Catherine, is determined to purge the realm of all Protestants and make himself King of France. Guise, aided by the Catholic aristocracy (including the Duke of Anjou, the future King Henri III), carries out the Massacre of Saint Bartholomew's Day, disposing first of the old Queen of Navarre by means of some ingeniously poisoned gloves, then murdering Coligny, Lord High Admiral, before turning his attention to a series of less exalted victims in the frenetic scenes which make up the middle of the play.

After the sudden death of King Charles IX, who mysteriously confesses that he has 'deserv'd a scourge', his brother, the Duke of Anjou, returns from Poland, where the prince electors have offered him the crown, to become King Henri III.[10] From now on the play changes significantly, moving from the events of 1572 to narrate incidents from 1587–9, culminating in the murder of Henri III and the accession of Henri IV.[11] Whereas the Guise had been the instigator of events in the first half of the play, he now becomes the victim, reminding the reader of the octavo that the subtitle of the play is 'With the Death of the Duke of Guise'. At Henri IV's coronation (sc. xii), a cutpurse who dares to steal the buttons from the cloak of one of the king's servants has an ear cut off, a sign that Henri's reign will be no less bloody than his predecessor's. The Duke of Guise is shown to be fallible when the Duchess conceives a passion for Mugeroun, the courtier who administered such brutal justice in the previous scene (who is promptly murdered on the Guise's instructions). Meanwhile the crown forces confront the army of the King of Navarre, but are defeated. The Guise assembles an army of his own as part of the Holy Catholic League and is declared a traitor by Henri III, who now plots the Guise's death. The King of Navarre orders his army to fight for the crown against the Guise's Catholic forces. The Guise is brutally murdered, as is the Cardinal of Lorraine, and the King of

[10] Christopher Marlowe, *The Massacre at Paris*, in *The Complete Works of Christopher Marlowe*, ed. Fredson Bowers (Cambridge: Cambridge University Press, 1973), 354–417, sc. xi, l. 544. Subsequent references to this edition in parentheses in the text.

[11] As pointed out by Briggs, 'Marlowe's *Massacre at Paris*', 262–3. My reading is indebted to her incisive analysis of the play.

Navarre and Henri III are reconciled. However, the play concludes no more hopefully than it began, with Henri III being murdered in turn by a friar, and Navarre succeeding as Henri IV, vowing 'to revenge his death, / As *Rome* and all those popish Prelates there, / Shall curse the time that ere *Navarre* was King, / And rulde in *France* by *Henries* fatall death' (sc. xxii, ll. 1248–50).[12]

The Massacre at Paris has usually been read as either a militantly Protestant work, or as a balanced satire on the cruel excesses of sectarianism, recalling similar representations of religious hypocrisy in *The Jew of Malta* and *Tamburlaine*.[13] But it might be better read as a warning of the dangers of an arbitrary government cut off from a more solid base in a wider public, in line with much contemporary political reflection, and also consistent with other attempts to make sense of the traumatic events of 23 August 1572. Marlowe provided similar political criticisms in his historical drama, *Edward II*—as did numerous other plays written in the 1590s which used English history as their subject matter.[14] *The Massacre at Paris*, I would argue, graphically represents the terrible effects of government which loses control because it is either unable or unwilling to protect and honour the rights of the citizens over which it rules. Sectarian conflict and personally motivated feuds run riot.

It might not be irrelevant to recall that Marlowe had recently been employed as part of Sir Francis Walsingham's (*d.*1590) spy network, providing him with a direct link to an eyewitness of

[12] If the play was written in 1593 these lines are shrouded in irony, given that Henri converted to Catholicism in that year (compare the allegorization of this historical event in Edmund Spenser, *The Faerie Queene*, V. xi. 44–65. For commentary, see Anne Lake Prescott, 'Burbon', *The Spenser Encyclopedia*, 121). See Healy, *Christopher Marlowe*, 70–1. Compare the anti-papal sentiments in *Edward II*, ed. Charles R. Forker (Manchester: Manchester University Press, 1994), I. iv. 94–105. I owe this last reference to Mark Thornton Burnett.

[13] For the former type of reading, see Wilbur Sanders, *The Dramatist and the Received Idea* (Cambridge: Cambridge University Press, 1968), ch. 2; Kocher, 'François Hotman and Marlowe'; and, to a lesser extent, Healy, *Christopher Marlowe*, 68–71. For the latter, see Briggs, 'Marlowe's *Massacre at Paris*'; Weil, 'Mirrors for Foolish Princes'; Potter, 'Marlowe's *Massacre at Paris*'; Marlowe, *Massacre at Paris*, ed. Oliver, pp. lxiv–lxxiv; Breight, *Surveillance, Militarism and Drama*, 114–16.

[14] See Clare, '*Art made Tongue-Tied by Authority*', ch. 2.

the massacre.[15] More importantly, the directly—and quite unusually—topical nature of the play should be borne in mind, circumstances which might well explain why it was not printed until the relative safety of 1603.[16] *The Massacre at Paris* was written only three or four years after the events which it represented in its final scenes had taken place. During the 1590s there were enduring fears of a second Spanish invasion after the Armada of 1588, if not on the coast of England, then in Ireland; there had been a large number of Catholic plots and subsequent executions; the Marprelate controversy had only just subsided; English troops had been despatched to the French wars, and legislation had been passed to counter the perceived threat of 'masterless men' terrorizing the countryside.[17]

The balance that is exhibited in *The Massacre at Paris*, with the use of Catholic League sources in the second half of the play to undermine any sense of moral superiority the Huguenots might have had in the first, makes it hard to read the work as Protestant propaganda.[18] Little is made of the murder of Admiral Coligny, one of the principal episodes in contemporary Protestant propaganda; the Duke of Anjou, the future Henri III, is shown to be a henchman of the Duke of Guise until he is offered the Polish throne, overly partial to his courtier, Epernoun, in a manner which resembles the king's blind devotion to Gaveston in *Edward II*, and just as scheming and sectarian as pretenders of opposite religious persuasions (his reign, significantly enough, opens with the mutilation of the

[15] For analysis of Marlowe's career as a spy and his links to Walsingham, see Constance Brown Kuriyama, 'Marlowe's Nemesis: The Identity of Richard Baines', in Kenneth Friedenreich, Roma Gill, and Constance B. Kuriyama (eds.), *'A Poet and a Filthy Play-Maker': New Essays on Christopher Marlowe* (New York: AMS Press, 1988), 343–60; Charles Nicholl, *The Reckoning: The Murder of Christopher Marlowe* (London: Picador, 1993, rpt. of 1992); Breight, *Surveillance, Militarism and Drama*, ch. 5.

[16] Although it should also be noted that *Dr Faustus* was not published until 1602 and 1616 and *The Jew of Malta* in 1633.

[17] The most thorough overview, especially regarding English intervention in France, is R. B. Wernham, *After the Armada: Elizabethan England and the Struggle for Western Europe, 1588–1595* (Oxford: Clarendon Press, 1984). See also Beier, *Masterless Men*, 93–5, *passim*, and Mark Thornton Burnett, '*Edward II* and Elizabethan Politics', in Paul Whitfield White (ed.), *Marlowe, History, Sexuality: New Essays on Christopher Marlowe* (New York: AMS Press, 1998, forthcoming), 114–30. I am grateful to Dr Burnett for allowing me to see this essay in typescript.

[18] See Briggs, 'Marlowe's *Massacre at Paris*', 268–77.

cutpurse); the play concludes with the promise of further sectarian violence, bloodshed which, as the audience undoubtedly knew, would involve English troops and so link English fortunes to those of war-torn France.[19] The one Protestant martyr who engages his murderers at any length is the famous Professor of Logic, Peter Ramus.[20] When Ramus asks the Dukes of Guise and Anjou how he has offended them, Guise engages him in a logical dispute. Guise claims that Ramus has scoffed at Aristotle's treatises on logic and has tried to reduce logical argument to a series of mutually exclusive dichotomies, 'To contradict which, I say *Ramus* shall dye: / How answere you that? your *nego argumentum* / Cannot serve, sirra: kill him' (sc. vii, ll. 396–8). Ramus insists in answering Guise's criticisms of his scholarship as if that were the prime issue at stake here: 'Not for my life doe I desire this pause, / But in my latter houre to purge my self' (l. 401–2). He insists that Aristotle's logic was confused and that he 'reduce'd it into better forme', and attacks the 'Sorbonests' because they 'Attribute as much unto their workes, / As to the service of the eternall God' (ll. 407, 412–13). Notwithstanding these philosophical niceties, Anjou stabs and kills Ramus.

This scene undoubtedly reveals the murderous irrationality of the Guise. However, it is also grimly comic in revealing Ramus to be myopically obsessed with arid intellectual debate. In their discussion neither interlocutor does more than assert a position based on the value of authorities or supposed achievements, exactly the sort of argument Ramus's works were supposed to eliminate.[21] Marlowe's Ramus can thus provide no effective opposition to the power and energy of the Catholics, either in physical, dramatic, or emotional terms. Accordingly, his murder fails to register any significant human sympathy in

---

[19] On Coligny as a Protestant hero, see Kingdon, *Myths about the Saint Bartholomew's Day Massacres*, ch. 2. Kocher describes the Admiral in Marlowe's play as 'querulous and naive'; 'François Hotman and Marlowe', 367. On the link between Gaveston and Epernon, see Briggs, 'Marlowe's *Massacre at Paris*', 264. On English involvement in France, see Wernham, *After the Armada*, ch. 22.

[20] On Ramus's life and influence, see Walter J. Ong, *Ramus, Method, and the Decay of Dialogue* (Cambridge, Mass.: Harvard University Press, 1958). For a very different reading of this scene, see John Ronald Glenn, 'The Martyrdom of Peter Ramus in Marlowe's *The Massacre at Paris*', *PLL* 9 (1973), 365–79.

[21] Ong, *Ramus*, pt. 3.

reader, or, presumably, audience, and does not stand out against the background of 'telescoped' frenetic murder scenes which constitute the Massacre itself.[22] These, too, are remarkable for their grim humour, especially the interchanges between Guise and Anjou, notably in the following parody of a Protestant church service:

> GUISE. *Loreine, Loreine,* follow *Loreine.* Sirra,
>   Are you a preacher of these heresies?
> LOREINE. I am a preacher of the word of God,
>   And thou a traitor to thy soule and him.
> GUISE. Dearely beloved brother, thus tis written.
>   *He stabs him.*
> ANJOY. Stay my Lord, let me begin the psalme.
> GUISE. Come dragge him away and throw him in a ditch.
>
>   (v. 339–45)

In marked contrast is the murder of Guise, who is lured to his death when summoned by the king, and then dispatched by three rather apologetic murderers. Guise meets his end through his ambition and over-confidence, not realizing that he is about to become the victim of an underhand plot. In the previous scene, Henri III had pretended to offer the crown to Guise out of exasperation after the Duke had threatened to crush the Huguenots: '*Guise,* weare our crowne, and be thou King of *France,* / And as Dictator make or warre or peace, / Whilste I cry *placet* like a Senator' (sc. xvii, ll. 859–61). Guise now enters, assuming the role outlined for him by the incumbent monarch: 'So, / Now sues the King for favour to the *Guise,* / And all his Minions stoup when I commaund: . . . / So will I triumph over this wanton King, / And he shall follow my proud Charriots wheeles' (ll. 976–84). His murder, some thirty lines later, assumes the dignity of Aristotelian *hubris,* and Guise's impressively stubborn pride at the point of death serves to mark his fate as spectacular, in contrast to the murders of Admiral Coligny and Ramus. Here it is the murderers who beg Guise for pardon, implore him to make his peace with God, and ask the king for forgiveness, to which he replies:

---

[22] Although this may, of course, be the result of textual corruption.

GUISE. Trouble me not, I neare offended him,
Nor will I aske forgiveness of the King.
Oh that I have not power to stay my life,
Nor immortalitie to be reveng'd:
To dye by Pesantes, what a greefe is this? . . .
Vive la messe, perish Hugonets,
Thus *Caesar* did goe foorth, and thus he dyed. *He dyes.*

(xix. 1009–19)

Guise's consistency is impressive, and the comparison to Julius Caesar undoubtedly apt.[23] Indeed, Guise has been shown explicitly modelling his actions on a comparison between himself and Caesar. In his Machiavellian soliloquy (sc. ii, ll. 91–165), where he professes his ambition to gain the throne ('mount to the top with aspiring winges, / Although my downfall be the deepest hell', (ll. 103–4), and confesses to the audience that policy is more important to him than religion (ll. 122–3), Guise shows that he has been studying the beliefs and career of Caesar: 'first lets follow those in *France*, / That hinder our possession to the crowne: / As *Caesar* to his souldiers, so say I: / Those that hate me, will I learn to loath' (ll. 153–6). In other words, the actions of Guise are framed in the extant play text by the figure of Julius Caesar.

It is more than likely that when Marlowe completed *The Massacre at Paris* he was also working on his unfinished translation of Lucan's *Pharsalia*, eventually published in 1600 by Thomas Thorpe (who also published Shakespeare's *Sonnets*), with a dedicatory letter to Edward Blount.[24] Lucan's epic poem emphasizes the horrors of civil war and deplores the loss of civil liberty resulting from Caesar's seizure of power, a theme also emphasized in Thomas North's translation of Plutarch's *Life of Caesar* (1579), another work Marlowe was likely to have known.[25] In the seventeenth century it was clearly associated

[23] For the possibility that Marlowe's play might contain echoes of Shakepeare's *Julius Caesar* (c.1599), see Marlowe, *Massacre at Paris*, ed. Oliver, pp. lvii–viii.

[24] Edward Blout (*fl.* 1588–1632), stationer and translator. For further details see *DNB* entry.

[25] Plutarch, *Life of Julius Caesar*, in *Shakespeare's Plutarch*, ed. T. J. B. Spencer (Harmondsworth: Penguin, 1964), 21–101. See esp. 26, 77, 79–81. On the use of Lucan in Elizabethan schools, see T. W. Baldwin, *Shakespeare's Small Latin and Lesse Greek* (Urbana, Ill.: University of Illinois Press, 1944), i. 103–8, *passim*.

with the republican cause, as an attack on the excesses of tyrannical monarchy, after it was translated by Thomas May, the
historian of the long parliament, and published in 1626–7.[26]

Marlowe's translation only covers the first book, which
recounts the opening moves in the civil war between Caesar
and Pompey.[27] Marlowe, following Lucan, emphasizes the
destructive effects of civil war and the tragedy of the imperial
city tearing itself apart: 'Rome, if thou take delight in impious
war, / First conquer all the earth, then turn thy force / Against
thyself: as yet thou wants not foes.'[28] Marlowe's rendition of
the poem can therefore be read as a criticism of the unnecessary
slaughter caused by war, and, more specifically, not just civil
war but also imperial conquest, both of which are treated in
The Massacre at Paris. When Guise is threatening Henri III that
he means to use his power 'To overthrow those sectious
Puritans', he asserts that if the Catholic cause is ever in danger
of failing, not only will the Pope 'sell his triple crown', but 'the
catholick *Philip* of *Spaine*, / Ere I shall want, will cause his
Indians, / To rip the golden bowels of America' (sc. xvii, ll.
850–4), a boast which relates to current English fears that
unless the Spanish were stopped from exporting gold and silver
from the Americas by a rival Protestant empire Europe would
be in danger of falling prey to a Spanish/Catholic hegemony, a
fear explicitly related to the Massacre of Saint Bartholomew's
Day (see above).[29] Guise's lust for power, and the sectarian
struggles within Europe, are explicitly related to exploitation
and misery in the New World, signalling not only a direct link
between French Catholicism, Spain, and the papacy, but, more
terrifying for a Protestant audience, a pan-Catholic venture
which threatened to engulf the Old and New Worlds.

An epic simile which describes Caesar immediately before he
crosses the Rubicon, and thus makes civil war an inevitability,

---

[26] Peltonen, *Classical Humanism and Republicanism*, 275, 282–3, 289.

[27] See also Plutarch, *Life of Julius Caesar*, 49–68.

[28] Christopher Marlowe, *Lucan's First Book*, in *The Poems*, ed. Millar
Maclure (London: Methuen, 1968), ll. 21–3. Subsequent references to this edition
in parentheses in the text.

[29] See also the boast in Guise's opening soliloquy: 'For this [i.e. to assume the
throne], from Spaine the stately Catholickes / Sends Indian golde to coyne me
French ecues' (ii. 118–19).

indicates his grand but fatal pride, and the terrible effects which his actions will have on the Romans and other peoples. Caesar witnesses a vision of 'fearful Rome' (l. 188), which urges him not to proceed with his military campaign. Caesar replies that it is not Rome which he hates, as his conquests have made Rome great, arguing instead that 'He, he afflicts Rome that made me Rome's foe' (l. 205), aggressive logic which flies in the face of the narrator's comments on Rome's violence and ultimate self-destruction after conquering other nations (ll. 125–7).[30] After he has resolved to cross the Rubicon and continue his campaign, Caesar is described as being

> Like to a lion of scorch'd desert Afric,
> Who, seeing hunters, pauseth till fell wrath
> And kingly rage increase, then having whisk'd
> His tail athwart his back, and crest heav'd up,
> With jaws wide open ghastly roaring out
> (Albeit the Moor's light javelin or his spear
> Sticks in his side), yet runs upon the hunter.
>
> (208–14)

The trope casts Caesar simultaneously as a tragic figure of noble stature, hemmed in by a series of less impressive figures (the hunters), resolving to fight to the bitter end despite overwhelming odds, and as a bestial savage (an African lion), who will wreak as much havoc and destruction as possible in order to save his own pride.

Assuming that the two apparently carefully placed references comparing Guise to Caesar in *The Massacre at Paris* are not later additions, but that they either approximate to or recall lines which were in the manuscript of the play or the acted version of 1593, then it seems likely that a link can be made between the portrayal of Caesar in Marlowe's translation of Lucan and Guise's self-representation as Caesar.[31] Like Julius Caesar, Guise may be a suitably heroic and fascinating creature who will seize the imagination of the audience, but the effects of his actions are horrendous. In emphasizing the link between the dictator from ancient Rome who triumphed

---

[30] Compare the logical arguments in the scene which depicts the murder of Ramus (see above, pp. 207–8).

[31] See Marlowe, *Massacre at Paris*, ed. Oliver, pp. lvii–iii, for further comment.

through popularity and the support of a powerful army and a similar figure from contemporary European history, Marlowe's play demands to be read alongside other late Elizabethan and early Jacobean Roman plays.[32] As in *Julius Caesar* (*c.*1599), *Sejanus* (1603), *Coriolanus* (*c.*1608), and *Catiline* (*c.*1611), political commentary is often directed at weak and ineffective government and applied to contemporary problems in British politics, a possible reason why *The Massacre at Paris* was not published until nearly ten years after it was first performed.[33]

If *The Massacre at Paris* has a cogent political message, it is perhaps less an obviously Protestant polemic, or attack on sectarianism *per se*, than an indictment of the failures of a central, manifestly unrepresentative ruling élite. The text exposes a regime which refuses to countenance the inclusion of an informed and responsible political class into the process of government, so subjecting the people entrusted to its care to a series of arbitrary and contradictory demands, partly as a result of the petty power struggles which assume disproportionate importance because there are no checks and balances to prevent such instability. Such criticisms bear a striking resemblance to those implicitly and explicitly articulated in contemporary travel literature—most notably descriptions of Venice—and a historical setting which bears an uncomfortable resemblance to the sectarian nature of recent English history.

Hence Guise, the pretender with the most conspicuous power base, allows his energies to be taken up with his plans to kill the courtier Mugeroune because the Duchess, unbeknown to Mugeroune, has taken a fancy to him. Guise laments the fickleness of women ('O wicked sexe, perjured and unjust, / Now doe I see that from the very first, / Her eyes and lookes sow'd seeds of perjury': sc. xiii, ll. 693–5) in legal language ('perjured and unjust', 'perjury'), seemingly oblivious to the effects his own actions will have on a wider public under a

---

[32] Guise is represented as hugely popular in Paris, a Catholic stronghold, as Henri III has to admit (xvii. 879–910).

[33] For details of official reactions to such plays, see Clare, '*Art made Tongue-Tied by Authority*', 74, 111–14; Dutton, *Mastering the Revels*, 10–14, 155, *passim*.

government which has no means of implementing justice other than by the salutary influence of great men. Equally culpable is Henri III, the former Duke of Anjou, who helped Guise perform the massacre of Saint Bartholomew's Day: stage directions indicate that it is Anjou who stabs Ramus. Henri III accepts the Polish crown on the understanding that he can assume the French one if circumstances so decree, and rules exclusively through his favourite, Epernoun.[34] Henri goes so far as to dismiss his council and be advised only by Epernoun (sc. xvii, ll. 882–5), a clear indication that his personal relationships have come to determine his public office. Hence there is a certain rather obvious irony when Henri blames Guise for sectarianism in France after he has had him treacherously murdered in a manner which recalls their former actions (sc. xix, ll. 1020–44), as there is when Henri pretends to offer the crown to Guise (sc. xvii, ll. 859–64) because it is not absolutely clear that the violence of Guise will be that much more destructive of French political institutions than the underhand and cowardly methods of Henri. Epernoun stands as the king's bad counsellor. In his first scene as the principal courtier he urges Henri to have Guise slain because he is powerful and popular, and because he threatens the king ('I think for safety of your riyall person, / It would be good the *Guise* were made away': sc. xvii, ll. 887–8). It is clear, then, that a narrow political interest now asserts itself over the more idealistic hopes with which the play opened.

Arguably, Navarre, the future Henri IV, is a less repellent figure. Certainly he is represented more sympathetically than his religious opponents at the start of the play, but when he assumes the leadership of a Protestant faction fighting against the king—who, after all, is now significantly distanced from Guise—the costs of his actions are no less onerous for the common people than those of Guise. Celebrating his victory against the leader of the crown forces, Duke Joyeaux, Navarre appears only slightly less fanatical than Guise:

---

[34] For further comment on the relationship between Henri III and Epernoun, and the similarity to that between Gaveston and Edward II, see Potter, 'Marlowe's *Massacre at Paris* and the Reputation of Henri III'.

> How many noble men have lost their lives,
> In prosecution of these cruell armes,
> Is ruth and almost death to call to minde:
> But God we know will alwaies put them downe,
> That lift themselves against the perfect truth,
> Which Ile maintaine so long as life doth last[.]

> (xvi. 795–800)

The Massacre at Paris concludes with Navarre, about to become Henri IV, promising to revenge his predecessor's death by turning against Catholics in France, thus perpetuating the cycle of violence.[35]

It might be stretching a point to argue that France in *The Massacre at Paris* stands for contemporary England, and that events in the play can be related to recent significant events in England (although the rapid changes in official religious policy inaugurated by each new monarch—partly achieved by the play's telescoping of historical events—must have appeared familiar to students of recent English history).[36] Nevertheless, there are a number of links between the two countries, which appear to be as deliberately placed within the text as references comparing Guise to Caesar. When explaining to Henri III that he cannot be expected to cease his crusade to rid France of Protestants, Guise refers to them as 'those sectious Puritans' (sc. xvii, l. 850), a word which could only have meaning in an English context.[37] Elsewhere Guise refers to French Protestants as Huguenots (such as immediately before he dies, sc. xix, l. 1018), a name synonymous with radical theories of contractual government, who were regarded in a scarcely less positive light than Catholics by the

---

[35] For the terrible effects of military campaigns on enlisted men, see Breight, *Surveillance, Militarism and Drama*, pt. III.

[36] On the conflation and juxtaposition of separate historical events, see Briggs, 'Marlowe's *Massacre at Paris*', 262–3. On contemporary uses of the recent past in drama, see Lily B. Campbell, *Shakespeare's Histories: Mirrors of Elizabethan Policy* (San Marino, Calif.: Huntington Library, 1947); Kamps, *Historiography and Ideology in Stuart Drama*.

[37] See Patrick Collinson, 'A Comment: Concerning the Name "Puritan" ', *JEH* 31 (1980), 483–8, *Elizabethan Puritan Movement*, 13; Dickens, *English Reformation*, 422–60. The Cardinal also speaks of Guise's plan to 'kill the Puritans' (xii. 643).

English authorities.[38] The sectarian troubles which erupted in France are shown to be close to home.

A notable absentee from the play is the Duke of Anjou/Henri III's younger brother, the Duke of Alençon, who does not appear on stage, but is referred to by Catherine de Medici, the Queen Mother, when she informs the Cardinal that she will persuade Henri to dispose of all the Puritans/Huguenots: 'And if he doe deny what I doe say, / Ile dispatch him [Henri III] with his brother [Alençon] presently, / And then *Mounser* weare the diadem' (sc. xii, ll. 645–7). Given Elizabeth's courtship of Alençon and, the huge extent of contemporary opposition to the projected match, most notably by John Stubbs (see above, pp. 176–9), which was primarily religious in motivation and directly related to the events represented in *The Massacre at Paris*, it is easy to understand why the play chose to omit Alençon from the historical record.[39] What is more significant is the fact that he is referred to at all, a reminder of the possible links between France and England through the sort of unrepresentative dynastic matches which the play is at pains to criticize. The use of the term *Mounser* is especially appropriate. Although here Catherine is referring to Guise—one of Marlowe's inventions in the plot is to invent Catherine's affection for Guise, a relationship not developed in any of the sources he is likely to have used[40]—it was well known that this was Elizabeth's term of affection for Alençon. In effect, the play implies that the English Queen's passion for a younger man resembles a similar relationship which led to the darkest day in Protestant history.[41]

---

[38] Skinner, *Foundations of Modern Political Thought*, ii. 8; Owen Chadwick, *The Reformation* (Harmondsworth: Penguin, 1985, rpt. of 1964), 158–60, *passim*; Dickens, *English Reformation*, 449.

[39] Potter, 'Marlowe's *Massacre at Paris* and the Reputation of Henri III', 85, 93; Briggs, 'Marlowe's *Massacre at Paris*', 269.

[40] Kocher, 'François Hotman and Marlowe's *Massacre at Paris*', 368; Briggs, 'Marlowe's *Massacre at Paris*', 272.

[41] Neville Williams, *The Life and Times of Elizabeth I* (London: Weidenfeld and Nicolson, 1972), 123; Susan Doran, *Monarchy and Matrimony: The Courtships of Elizabeth I* (London: Routledge, 1996), 155. Doran points out that some Protestant aristocrats feared that the marriage of Elizabeth and Alençon would lead to 'a repetition of the St Bartholomew's Day Massacre within their own shores' (156). See also Potter, 'Marlowe's *Massacre at Paris* and the Reputation of Henri III', 93. It is also worth noting that Guise is called 'Monsieur' in Chapman's *Bussy D'Ambois*.

Such references could be dismissed as incidental. However, the ending of the play makes the link between the two countries quite explicit.[42] As soon as Henri III has been stabbed by the friar under pretence of delivering a letter to the king, he summons the 'English Agent' so that Elizabeth can be informed and so that, if Henri lives, an alliance can be formed to combat international Catholicism. This Protestant League will also include the King of Navarre, to whom Henri now turns: 'And heere protest eternall love to thee, / And to the Queene of *England* specially, / Whom God hath blest for hating Papestry' (sc. xxii, ll. 1206–8). Unfortunately Henri's wound proves fatal, thus aborting plans for the alliance; but Henri reaffirms his commitment at the point of death: 'I dye *Navarre*, come beare me to my Sepulchre. / Salute the Queene of *England* in my name, / And tell her *Henry* dyes her faithfull freend' (ll. 1242–4).

What is to be made of such links? One possible reading is to see *The Massacre at Paris* as a Protestant play, affirming the need to combat the Catholic threat as Henri alleges, a reading many previous critics have accepted.[43] Such an interpretation has to face the obvious question of Henri's characterization within the play as a scheming Machiavel who changes sides according to which way the wind is blowing, as well as his obviously inadequate means of governing through Epernoun, both problems which Marlowe is at pains to represent else-where in his drama. It is more feasible that Henri stands as a warning to Elizabeth of the sectarian conflict which could engulf a nation which failed to bridge its religious and political divides. Elizabeth's religious settlement may well have been a successful means of negotiating between the two extremes and establishing a peculiarly English *via media*—although it is arguable that the Civil War of the 1640s was a conflict along the same lines as other European wars of religion fought in the previous century.[44] However, the main thrust of *The Massacre*

[42] Julia Briggs points out that Catholic League propaganda emphasized Henri III's anglophilia; 'Marlowe's *Massacre at Paris*', 271.

[43] See above, n. 11.

[44] For details, see Haugaard, *Elizabeth and the English Reformation*, *passim*; John Morrill, *The Nature of the English Revolution* (Harlow: Longman, 1993), pt. 1.

at Paris's criticism of the French monarchy is less to do with the question of its failure to deal with religious hostilities, and more concerned with the limited means of political expression which are granted a wider public, restrictions which, as the play demonstrates, help to escalate the crisis. The sole plan which the regime has to unite a divided society is the marriage between Catherine's daughter, Margaret, and Navarre, a marriage which will clearly fail because powerful elements at court—including the bride's mother—are committed to undermining any fragile sense of unity which can be established. Guise is hugely popular, especially in Paris, and his grand Roman ambitions cannot easily be resisted because the opposition is weak, divided, and uncertain. Charles IX and Henri III are inept rulers, Henri conspicuously so in his reliance on Epernoun and his dismissal of the one public forum for debate, the council. In short, probably the most serious weakness which the play exposes is the absence of an articulate political class in France. The court is cut off from any sense of the people represented in a national debating chamber where crucial issues can be made public, a criticism made time and again of Elizabeth's means of ruling throughout her reign. The exclusion of vast numbers of different people from the visible structure of the body politic means that they have no method of representing themselves other than through violence, and there is a destructive alliance between court factions and the ambitions of self-interested men such as Guise and Anjou, and the enormous numbers of disenfranchised sections of the populace. The link between Henri and Elizabeth with which *The Massacre at Paris* ends is one which emphasizes the close proximity of England to Europe, a reminder that what has taken place across the Channel only a few years earlier can easily plague England too unless measures are taken to prevent such bitter conflict breaking out, the logical conclusion of most English writing on the Massacre of Saint Bartholomew's Day.

The 'gross clasps of a lascivious Moor': The Domestic and Exotic Contexts of Othello

The significance of the geographical locations of *Othello* is contradictory and disturbing. The play exposes the close relationship between the most noble political and cultural achievements of European civilization and the constant threat to the continent's uncertain boundaries. As John Gillies has observed, Contarini's Venice is represented as an uncomfortable contradiction in the play, its reputation for liberty stretched to the limit: 'The image of the "pure and untouched virgin" was haunted by its opposite, the image of Venice as the whore of Babylon, the universal courtesan whose legs were perpetually open.'[45] I want to comment later on both the specificities of this doubleness and the relationship between Europe and Africa in the play. What I would like to suggest first is that the liminal status of the Venetian colonial outpost of Cyprus, where Othello is employed as military governor, and where his tragedy unfolds, resembles a problematic territory closer to home, Ireland, a logical correlative of the often-assumed comparison between England and Venice as guardians of European liberty (see above, p. 64). To make such a case, which I anticipate will be controversial, I need to establish Shakespeare's enduring interest in Ireland.

Shakespeare was clearly aware of Ireland and referred to the kingdom and its inhabitants regularly—albeit usually briefly— in many of his earlier works. In *The Comedy of Errors* (*c.*1593), Dromio of Syracuse provides a humorous geographical description of Luce (Nell), Adriana's kitchen maid. He suggests that her forehead is France; England, her chin; Spain, her hot breath; America, her nose; The Netherlands her nether parts, and Ireland, 'in her buttocks. I found it out by the bogs' (III. ii. 115–16).[46] This might well signal a familiarity with John Derricke's *The Image of Ireland* (1581), one of the few books on Ireland published during Elizabeth's reign, and apart from the sections on Ireland in Holinshed's *Chronicles* (1577, 1587), the only description of Ireland readily available to English readers. Derricke explicitly connects the Irish with dirt as an inversion of the clean and proper established order, specifically with the anus. One of the accompanying woodcuts in his work represents figures publicly defecating at a feast, and he tells the

---

[45] John Gillies, *Shakespeare and the Geography of Difference* (Cambridge: Cambridge University Press, 1994), 140.

[46] All references are to the relevant Arden editions.

story of the Irish eagles (who clearly stand for the Irish people) preferring life in 'the Deuills Arse, A Peake' and the desolate bogs to that at court.[47]

Related assumptions occur elsewhere in other plays. In *Richard III* (*c*.1594), the usurping king confesses to Buckingham that 'a bard of Ireland told me once / I should not live long after I saw "Richmond" ' (IV. ii. 104–5), a detail which serves to label the Celtic nations as inherently superstitious, addicted to prophecy and in touch with the forces of darkness (like the witches in *Macbeth*).[48] In *Henry IV, Part One* (*c*.1597), Hotspur reacts to the prospect of a Welsh song with the words, 'I had rather hear Lady my brach howl in Irish' (III. i. 230), a prejudice which labels Irish as an unmelodious and incomprehensible language. A similar sentiment—but with far more serious reverberations—is expressed by Rosalind in *As You Like It* (*c*.1599), when she describes the wordplay of the would-be lovers as being 'like the howling of Irish wolves against the moon' (V. ii. 110–11); since Elizabeth was invariably associated with the moon, this is possibly a reference to Hugh O'Neill's rebellion against her.[49] In *The Merry Wives of Windsor* (*c*.1597), Frank Ford opines that he would 'rather trust . . . an Irishman with my aqua-vitae bottle' (II. ii. 292–3) than his wife alone with another man, alluding to the intemperate reputation of the Irish. Altogether such references provide a picture of Ireland and the Irish as brutish, dirty, primitive, savage, eccentric, and unreliable, an overall description which was common currency in Elizabethan England and could have been found in Holinshed, John Derricke, or any other available tract.[50]

[47] For further details, see Andrew Hadfield, 'Shakespeare, John Derricke and Ireland: *The Comedy of Errors*, III. ii. lines 105–6', *N. & Q.* 44 (1997), 53–4. The *OED* claims that this use of 'bog' is 'a low word, scarcely found in literature, however common in coarse, colloquial language'.

[48] On prophecy in the play, see Howard Dobin, *Merlin's Disciples: Prophecy, Poetry, and Power in Renaissance England* (Stanford: Stanford University Press, 1990), 64–5.

[49] Compare the descriptions in Edmund Spenser, *The Mutabilitie Cantos* (VII. vi. 54–5), ed. Sheldon P. Zitner (London: Nelson, 1968), 116.

[50] The best analysis of contemporary representations of the Irish remains David Beers Quinn, *The Elizabethans and the Irish* (Ithaca, NY: Cornell University Press, 1966). All accounts borrowed extensively from Gerald of Wales; see *The History and Topography of Ireland*, trans. J. J. O'Meara (Harmondsworth: Penguin, 1982, rpt. of 1951).

Not surprisingly, given Shakespeare's prolific output of history plays, references to Ireland and the Irish are most commonly found in these works. Ireland in *Henry VI, Part Two* (*c.*1591) is represented as a recalcitrant kingdom full of rebellious kern (Irish footsoldiers) where Richard of Plantagenet, Duke of York, cuts his fighting teeth. In a soliloquy at the end of III. i, York confesses to the audience that 'Whiles I in Ireland nourish a mighty band, / I will stir up in England some black storm / Shall blow ten thousand souls to heaven, or hell' (III. i. 348–50). This will be achieved through fuelling the rebellion of Jack Cade, whose reputation as a powerful mischief maker derives from his service in Ireland: 'In Ireland I have seen this stubborn Cade / Oppose himself against a troop of kerns, / And fought so long, till that his thighs with darts / Were almost like a sharp-quill'd porpentine' (III. i. 361–4). York returns with 'his army of Irish' planning to usurp the throne: 'From Ireland thus comes York to claim his right, / And pluck the crown from feeble Henry's head' (V. i. 1–2). The dramatic entry could hardly be more loaded and specific. Ireland is not simply a difficult kingdom to control, but the locus from which rebellion spreads, in which lowly rebels like Cade can learn their trade and from where even more dangerous figures like Richard of York can build up a power base. The most serious threat to Henry's rule comes, somewhat ironically, from his Irish viceroy, a prophetic prefiguration of events at the end of Elizabeth's reign.

The equal and opposite case is represented in *Richard II* (*c.*1595). This time the king himself travels to Ireland to sort out 'those rough rug-headed kerns, / Which like venom where no venom else, / But only they have privilege to live' (II. i. 156–8). Richard's expedition, like his namesake's, is successful in military terms, but it leads to his deposition and murder, and places a curse upon the crown which works itself out in a series of bloody civil wars.[51] The expedition can be seen as a deliberate attempt to avoid solving problems at home, signalled by Richard's dramatic and abrupt announcement of his intentions,

[51] See John Wilders, *The Lost Garden: A View of Shakespeare's English and Roman History Plays* (London: Macmillan, 1978), *passim*; Erskine-Hill, *Poetry and the Realm of Politics*, ch. 3.

immediately after he has refused to heed the advice of the dying—now dead—John of Gaunt. When the disgruntled nobles discuss the affairs of the king at the end of the scene, the fear of future financial penury as a result of Richard's foolish overspending is one of their many grievances: 'He hath not money for these Irish wars, / His burthenous taxations notwith-standing' (II. i. 259–60). The scene ends with Northumberland bringing the news that Bolingbroke's army is about to land— probably timed to meet with the king's absence ('Perhaps they had ere this, but that they stay / The first departing of the king for Ireland': II. i. 289–90)—and Willoughby, Ross, and Northumberland hastening to join his forces in order to revive the fortunes of the English people and 'shake off our slavish yoke' (II. i. 291). While Richard III indirectly gained a crown through his father's ruthless use of Ireland's advantages for the usurper, Richard II lost his through his failure to comprehend its dangers for the incumbent monarch.

Furthermore, if the representation of Ireland in *Henry VI, Part Two* appears to predict the role that the country played in the most disturbing intrigue at the English court in the last years of the reign of the Tudors, then *Richard II* actually went one better in that it was a part of the events themselves. Before his suicidal rebellion, Robert Devereux, second Earl of Essex, paid the Lord Chamberlain's company to perform—presum-ably—Shakespeare's *Richard II* as a spur to his followers. The performance took place on 7 February 1601. It was an open act of provocation in numerous ways, especially given that the Privy Council had examined and subsequently imprisoned Dr John Hayward because the dedication to his *History of Henry IV* 'alluded too obviously to the similarity between Essex and Bolinbroke'.[52] Elizabeth had no difficulty reading the script: 'I am Richard II, know ye not that?'[53]

But Shakespeare's involvement with the machinations of the Earl of Essex does not finish here. At the start of Act V of

[52] Robert Lacey, *Robert, Earl of Essex: An Elizabethan Icarus* (London: Weidenfeld and Nicolson, 1971), 283; *The First and Second Parts of John Hayward's The Life and Raigne of King Henrie IIII*, ed. John J. Manning (London: Royal Historical Society, 1991; Camden Soc., 4th ser., vol. 42), introduction, 17–34; Clare, 'Art Made Tongue-Tied by Authority', 62–4; Dutton, *Mastering the Revels*, 119–22.   [53] Neale, *Queen Elizabeth*, 381.

Henry V, the chorus confidently anticipates the Earl's return from his Irish campaign 'Bringing rebellion broached on his sword' (v. i. 32) and makes an explicit comparison between the Earl and the King: 'How many would the peaceful city quit / To welcome him! Much more, and much more cause, / Did they this Harry' (v. i. 33–5), sentiments which resemble those published in contemporary patriotic ballads.[54] The first line contains a splendid irony in that Essex was to bring rebellion on his sword from Ireland, but not in the way the text would appear to imply.[55] It was in Ireland that Essex built up his power base through the creation of numerous knights, a move which makes him rather closer to Richard III than Henry V.[56]

As many critics have argued, *Henry V*, with its wealth of topical allusion and unusual device of the chorus directing the audience's responses, appears to be at least as much concerned with Ireland as with France.[57] Furthermore, the famous scene (III. ii) where the four captains representing the four nations of the British Isles finish their analysis of recent military events with a discussion of the problematic conception of national identity marks the play out as a distinctly British work. John of Gaunt's description of England as 'this scept'red isle' (*Richard II*, II. i. 40) involves the common geographical confusion between England and the island of Britain, an equation reinforced by Richard's own feeling that his expedition to Ireland had been a 'wand'ring with the Antipodes' (III. ii. 49). The now-threatened civil unity of England is contrasted to the alien nature of Ireland (the Antipodes are the people who 'dwell on the opposite side of the earth'). *Richard II*, like the plays which make up the first tetralogy, tells a distinctly English history,

[54] See e.g. 'A new ballade of the tryumphes kept in *Ireland* uppon Saint *Georg's* day last, by the noble Earle of *Essex* and his followers, with their resolution againe there', in Andrew Clark (ed.), *The Shirburn Ballads, 1585–1616* (Oxford: Clarendon Press, 1907), 321–6.

[55] See Annabel Patterson, *Shakespeare and the Popular Voice* (Oxford: Basil Blackwell, 1989), 86–7.

[56] For details see Lacey, *Robert, Earl of Essex*, ch. 24.

[57] See Philip Edwards, *Threshold of a Nation: A Study in English and Irish Drama* (Cambridge: Cambridge University Press, 1979), 78; Jonathan Dollimore and Alan Sinfield, 'History and Ideology: The Instance of *Henry V*', in John Drakakis (ed.), *Alternative Shakespeares* (London: Methuen, 1985), 206–27; Jardine, *Reading Shakespeare Historically*, 12–14.

which represents Ireland as a threatening and sometimes exotic 'other'. Such straightforward antitheses clearly no longer apply in *Henry V* as the resonant dialectically inflected question, 'What ish my nation?' (III. ii. 124) indicates.[58] What is the Irish captain Macmorris asking here? Is he denying the efficacy of his Irishness and affirming a solidarity with the other Britons with whom he is fighting? Or is he anticipating an attack on his national identity, and so preparing to defend the loyalty of the Irish to the English/British crown?[59] The text is enigmatic, confronting the audience with the urgent need to define the boundaries of the nation in question, whether that nation be Britain, Ireland, or England.

If earlier plays had employed Irishness—albeit often no more than tangentially—to affirm a concomitant Englishness, it is fitting that the development of a more complex notion of Britishness should also stem from a consideration of Ireland. Such a change in Shakespeare's conception of political geography and its influence upon the varieties of British identities first appears at the turn of the century in the much-analysed *Henry V*.[60] However, it appears that the text of *Henry V* was to run into problems with the Master of the Revels, Edmund Tilney, probably owing to the Irish content and the consideration of what the notion of 'Britain' might mean.[61] As will become clear, fear of censorship, rather than conscious choice was probably the factor which led to the dearth of references to Ireland in Shakespeare's plays after 1600.

---

[58] One should note that the process had already begun in *I Henry IV* with the representation of Owen Glendower's rebellion. For an analysis of this question see Edwards, *Threshold of a Nation*, 75–7; David J. Baker, ' "Wildehirissheman": Colonialist Representation in Shakespeare's *Henry V*', ELR 22 (1992), 37–61, 43–50; Andrew Murphy, 'Shakespeare's Irish History', *Literature and History*, 3rd ser., 5 (1996), 38–59, at 52–3.

[59] An analogous text would then be Ben Jonson's *Irish Masque at Court* (1613). See David Lindley, 'Embarrassing Ben: The Masques for Frances Howard', in Arthur F. Kinney and Dan S. Collins (eds.), *Renaissance Historicism: Selections from 'English Literary Renaissance'* (Amherst, Mass.: University of Massachusetts Press, 1987), 248–64.

[60] For a recent analysis see Brian Gibbons, 'The Wrong End of the Telescope', in Maquerlot and Willems (eds.), *Travel and Drama in Shakespeare's Time*, 141–59, at 144–51.

[61] On Tilney's role as Master of the Revels, 1579–1610, see Dutton, *Mastering the Revels*, chs. 2–6.

The first quarto of 1600, possibly derived from the acted work, contains a number of significant omissions which appear later in the folio text, some of which may have been the result either of direct censorship or the fear that censorship would occur unless action were taken. The most significant for my argument here include all the choruses (which, as Gary Taylor argues, cannot have been simply owing to problems of casting), the opening scene where the Archbishop of Canterbury and the Bishop of Ely detail the self-interested reasons for the church's support of the war, Henry's bloodcurdling speech before the gates of Harfleur, and the scene which contains the confrontation between Macmorris and Jamy, the Scottish captain.[62] As Janet Clare has pointed out, such references were perilous from the summer of 1599 onwards, when it became clear that Essex's Irish campaign was not going to plan. On 21 July 1599 Francis Cordale wrote to Humphrey Galdelli in Venice that he could 'send no news of the Irish wars, all advertisements thence being prohibited, and such news as comes to Council carefully concealed. I fear our part has had little success, lost many captains and whole companies, and has little hopes of prevailing.'[63] He also added that Essex was known not to be trusted in high places, even though lower down the social scale he commanded affection:

He has little grace at Court. The Queen is quite averted from him, and is wholly directed by Mr. Secretary, who now rules as his father did; though he pretends friendship to the Earl, he is thought at heart his greatest enemy, envying his former greatness with the Queen, and intending his utter overthrow, if Irish affairs take no better effect. Essex dissembles his discontent . . . The common people still favour the Earl, hoping by his means to be freed from their intolerable exactions.[64]

If Cordale's assessment of the situation were accurate—and subsequent events would indeed suggest that he was a sound political judge—and his opinions were held by many who mattered, it is inconceivable that *Henry V* would not have

---

[62] For a list of the omissions see Gary Taylor (ed.), *Henry V* (Oxford: Oxford University Press, 1982), App. F, 312–15. Taylor suggests that the censorship is owing to fears of offending James VI through the representation of Jamy. He does also acknowledge that 'The Irishman [MacMorris] may have seemed rather less funny after Essex's return than he did in spring 1599' (313).

[63] *CSPD 1598–1601*, 251. Cited in Clare, '*Art Made Tongue-Tied by Authority*', 95.   [64] Ibid.

fostered suspicion, especially as it was written by the author of *Richard II*, a play clearly dear to Essex's heart. As Clare astutely comments, many of the rousing patriotic speeches in the play 'would have evoked thoughts of Essex's venture; but when reports of wastage of men and resources, irresolution and an apparently dishonourable truce with Tyrone became widespread, the analogy would have become subversive of actual events'.[65]

After *Henry V*, Shakespeare only refers to Ireland again in two plays. In *Macbeth* (*c*.1605), Donalbain escapes to Ireland (II. iii. 136). In *Henry VIII* (*c*.1612–13), the first gentleman refers to the attainder of the Earl of Kildare which was organized by Wolsey (II. i. 41–2), and Surrey complains to Wolsey that he had him sent to Ireland as Lord Deputy away from the influence of the King and the help of his father-in-law, Buckingham (III. ii. 260–1).[66] Why was this? It would seem highly unlikely that Shakespeare suddenly lost interest in Ireland, especially given his subsequent composition of two British plays, *King Lear* (*c*.1605) and *Cymbeline, King of Britain* (*c*.1610). It would seem equally implausible that events in Ireland, with the culmination of the Nine Years' War and the triumph of Mountjoy's campaign against Hugh O'Neill, failed to interest him in the early 1600s in the same way as they had done in the 1590s.[67] The reasons for Shakespeare's avoidance of *direct* treatment of Irish issues is more likely to be explained by reference to the restrictions which were placed on the stage representation of English history after June 1599. It is most probable that Shakespeare's ostensible silence is directly related to Anglo-Irish relations reflecting a desire not to be connected too closely to the Earl of Essex and his Irish adventures, and, perhaps even more importantly, an understanding that any sustained reference to Ireland in a play was likely to solicit unfavourable attention from the authorities.[68] It is not as if

---

[65] Clare, *'Art Made Tongue-Tied by Authority'*, 73.

[66] These last two comments may come from scenes written by John Fletcher rather than Shakespeare.

[67] A convenient and recent narrative of events is Lennon, *Sixteenth-Century Ireland*, ch. 10.

[68] Clare, *'Art Made Tongue-Tied by Authority'*, 74; Dutton, *Mastering the Revels*, ch. 5; Hadfield, 'Was Spenser's *A View of the Present State of Ireland* censored?'.

any other dramatist of the period writes extensively on Irish affairs.

Such circumstantial evidence, I would suggest, indicates that the ghostly presence of Ireland haunts many of Shakespeare's works, and that some plays can be read as displaced allegories of Irish events. The most sustained, bloody, and costly conflict of the last years of Elizabeth's reign was the Nine Years' War. Essex's army consisted of 16,000 foot and 1,300 horse, and Mountjoy's of 14,000 foot and 1,200 horse.[69] Numerous plays written after *Henry V* and in the last years and immediate aftermath of the Nine Years' War—*Julius Caesar* (*c*.1599), *Hamlet* (*c*.1599–1601), *Troilus and Cressida* (*c*.1602), *Othello* (*c*.1604), *King Lear* (*c*.1605), *Macbeth* (*c*.1606)—are concerned with the problems of civil war and international conflict. It would be odd, given the general and local topical references within so many of Shakespeare's plays (references which many critics have been keen to point out), were none of these to cast at least a glance over the Irish Sea.

Othello, a play which is intimately concerned with the problem of transgression, appears to possess a (ghostly) Irish context. The play's elaborate military settings and display of military knowledge—expanded well beyond Cinthio's Italian story—open it out to readings in terms of England's contemporary military struggles.[70] Othello's command is to defend Cyprus, a Venetian colony, from the Turks, so that Cyprus represents, in Virginia Mason Vaughan's words, 'a liminal zone between Venice's Christian civility and the Ottomite's pagan barbarism ... Cyprus is the frontier, the uttermost edge of Western civilization, simultaneously vulnerable to attack from without and subversion from within.'[71] Vaughan pursues this analysis further, pointing out that 'on a mythic level, the conflict [between Christian Venice and the pagan Ottoman Empire] was Manichean, symbolic of the universal struggle

[69] Lacey, *Robert, Earl of Essex*, 224; Cyril Falls, *Elizabeth's Irish Wars* (London: Methuen, 1950), 262.

[70] For analysis of the play's military discourse, see Virginia Mason Vaughan, *Othello: A Contextual History* (Cambridge: Cambridge University Press, 1994), ch. 2. My reading of *Othello* owes much to Vaughan's perceptive comments, even though she makes no mention of Ireland.

[71] Vaughan, *Othello: A Contextual History*, 22.

between the forces of good and evil'. Vaughan applies this situation to the condition of England: 'Just as England must have felt in 1603 that it was entering a new era, with all the anticipation, excitement, and anxiety of a dynastic transition, Shakespeare's Venice rests on a shaky foundation.'[72] Perhaps this insecurity was the result not simply of the transformation from the Tudors to the Stuarts, but also stemmed from recent events in England's first overseas colony.

The plot of *Othello* revolves around the problematic and fragile nature of individual and national identities. Othello's own personal and public identity is fashioned in terms of Venetian—which, in this case, are also obviously Elizabethan/Jacobean—conceptions of the savage 'other', denying what his masters believe him to be at heart. When summoned before the council to defend himself against Brabantio's charge that he had bewitched and abducted his daughter, Othello explains how he used to answer Brabantio's requests that he tell tales of his eventful life:

> Wherein I spake of most disastrous chances,
> Of moving accidents by flood and field . . .
> And sold to slavery, and my redemption thence,
> And with it all my travel's history;
> Wherein of antres vast, and deserts idle,
> Rough quarries, rocks and hills, whose heads touch heaven,
> It was my hint to speak, such was the process:
> And of the Cannibals, that each other eat;
> The Anthropophagi, and men whose heads
> Do grow beneath their shoulders. . . .
>
> (I. iii. 134–5, 138–45)

Othello represents himself as though he were the most robust of Elizabethan travellers recorded in the pages of Hakluyt's *Principal Navigations*, a strategy which serves simultaneously to efface his exotic—savage—origins, and draw attention to them. When Iago's 'monstrous birth' (I. iii. 402) has finally gone full term and the Moor has become the barbarous savage many in Venice always knew him to be, Othello's suicide illustrates that even now he accepts the cultural values foisted on

---

[72] Vaughan, *Othello: A Contextual History*, 27.

him by his adopted homeland. As with the tales which won him Desdemona, Othello narrates an official version of himself ready for later readers (here, in the state papers or contemporary reports of his obituary):

> set you down this,
> And say besides, that in Aleppo once,
> Where a malignant and a turban'd Turk
> Beat a Venetian, and traduc'd the state,
> I took by the throat the circumcised dog,
> And smote him thus.
>
> (V. ii. 352–7)

The Venetian within Othello asserts its mastery and destroys the Turk, an apparent final victory for the forces of good.

Othello's own Manichean identity is an extreme example of the general fear expressed throughout the play that the boundaries between self and other are not quite as rigid as they might be.[73] During his witty exchange with Desdemona while they are awaiting Othello's arrival, Iago claims that if his misogynistic comments are not true, 'I am a Turk' (II. i. 114). After the drunken brawl, Othello asks rhetorically, 'Are we turn'd Turks, and to ourselves do that / Which heaven has forbid the Ottomites?' (II. iii. 161–2). Othello's anxieties are part of a general uncertainty and lack of confidence in a stable identity highlighted in the liminal space of the colonial scene. It is, after all, Iago, a Venetian, who is more villainous than either Othello, the black general, or Cassio, the Florentine mercenary.[74]

Othello is, in Homi Bhabha's terms, a 'mimic man', desperately attempting to become absorbed into his adopted society, but always exposed by his irredeemably alien characteristics, so that his service to the state is rendered worse than useless at the end of the play: colonial Cyprus is left exposed, and only the providential destruction of the Turkish fleet at the start of Act II prevents the internal divisions among the colonizers from being more disastrous. He is *'almost the same but not quite'*.[75] As Bhabha continues in his analysis of the phenomenon, 'The

---

[73] For some perceptive comments on this problem, see Islam, *Ethics of Travel*, 43–55. [74] See Vaughan, *Othello: A Contextual History*, 45.
[75] Bhabha, *Location of Culture*, 86.

menace of mimicry is its *double* vision which in disclosing the ambivalence of colonial discourse also disrupts its authority.'[76] Brabantio welcomes Othello as a friend who tells stories of exotic lands, but has fearful nightmares about him copulating with his daughter ('This accident is not unlike my dream' [I. i. 142]), presumably reflections of his fear of miscegenation and of the production of subjects who are, like Othello, impure or inauthentic Venetians. However hard he tries, Othello can never be what he attempts to make himself into, and he will aways serve as a reminder to the metropolitan authorities that he is a dangerous figure inhabiting the boundary between their civilization and the barbarism of others.

In this way *Othello* expresses exactly the contemporary fears the English had of Ireland as a colonial space and the Irish as a colonized people. To take the second point first: in his contribution to the second edition of Holinshed's *Chronicles* (1586), John Hooker provides a lengthy and studiously ambivalent description of the character and actions of Sir Cormac MacTeige, sheriff of Cork during the Desmond Rebellion (1579–83):

[T]his Sir Cormac, in dutie and obedience to hir majestie and hir lawes, and for his affection to all Englishmen, surpasseth all his own sept & familie, as also all the Irishrie in that land. For albeit a meere Irish gentleman can hardly digest anie Englishman or English government, & whatsoever his outward appearance be, yet his inward affection is corrupt and naught: being not unlike to Jupiters cat, whome though he had transformed into a beautiful ladie, and made hir a noble princesse; yet when she saw the mouse, she could not forbeare to snatch at him; and as the ape, though he be never so richlie attired in purple, yet he will still be an ape. . . . And if at anie time he were had in suspicion, he would by some kind of service purge & acquite himselfe.[77]

However hard Sir Cormac tries to assimilate himself into English society, he will always remain a scandalous outsider, having to perform acts of loyalty in order to preserve his status.

[76] Ibid. 88.

[77] Sir John Hooker, *The Chronicles of Ireland* in Holinshed's *Chronicles* (1586), cited in Andrew Hadfield and John McVeagh (eds.), *'Strangers to that Land': British Perceptions of Ireland from the Reformation to the Famine* (Gerrards Cross: Colin Smythe, 1994), 44.

Even so, his identity will not remain fixed or stable, and the true nature of his 'Irishness', a hidden inner residue, will one day reappear to tear away the English façade. This is exactly what happens to Othello; not only do those around him create their racist perception of his essentially atavistic nature, but Othello himself believes their version and represents himself as their eyes saw him. Although more loyal and more Venetian/Elizabethan than the Venetians themselves in his self-fashioned identity as a bold traveller, he constantly has to police himself. Eventually, however, he loses control and fulfils the prophetic fears of Brabantio in the first act. Brabantio, having been absent from the middle three acts, makes a ghostly reappearance when Gratiano remarks, 'Poor Desdemona, I am glad thy father's dead' (V. ii. 205), enabling him to miss the grisly conclusion which his dreams had foretold.

A more famous transgressive Irish figure than Sir Cormac was, of course, Hugh O'Neill, who, although brought up in English ways, and encouraged by the government in his claims in Ulster under the mistaken belief that he could easily be manipulated as a loyal Irishman, went on to provide the greatest threat to English control in Ireland in the sixteenth century.[78] O'Neill was employed in May 1593 by the Lord Deputy, William Fitzwilliam, to bring in the rebellious Hugh Maguire; and, fighting alongside Marshal Henry Bagenal, they defeated Maguire at Beleek on 10 October. Steven Ellis has argued that '[h]is strategy . . . was . . . to underline his importance in controlling the north by allowing O'Donnell, Maguire and other O'Neill clans to create disturbances which he could then settle'.[79] Within a year Tyrone had been proclaimed a traitor (23 June), and the Nine Years' War had broken out.

Christopher Highley has suggested that Shakespeare based Owen Glendower in *Henry IV, Part One* on the figure of Hugh O'Neill, clearly a significant bogeyman for the English from the late 1590s onwards, and a traitor as dangerous and reviled as

---

[78] See Hiram Morgan, *Tyrone's Rebellion: The Outbreak of the Nine Years War in Tudor Ireland* (Woodbridge: Boydell and Brewer / Royal Historical Society, 1993), ch. 5. Morgan points out that there is almost certainly no substance to the belief, popularized by Sean O'Faolain's biography, that O'Neill was educated in England (92–3). [79] Ellis, *Tudor Ireland*, 299.

any such Jesuit as Edmund Campion or Robert Southwell.[80] I am not attempting to claim that Othello bears any straightforward resemblance to O'Neill (Othello is, after all, from North Africa, not Turkey or Cyprus). However, in Andrew Murphy's words, 'What O'Neill's career—especially during the period of the Nine Years' War—served to do was both to focus the traditional problematics of applying the colonial paradigm to Ireland and *to intensify the sense of uncertainty about the nature of Irish identity*' [my emphasis].[81] If any one of Shakespeare's plays registers the problematic nature of identity formation and hybridity it is *Othello*: another reason for assuming that it possesses a significant Irish dimension.

English writers traditionally regarded Ireland as a dangerous colonial space, a land where they were likely to lose their identity and 'degenerate' by going native (analogous to Brabantio's dream that his daughter had eloped with a Moor (I. i. 142)). In Edmund Spenser's *A View of the Present State of Ireland* (written *c*.1596, but extremely unlikely to have been known by Shakespeare, as it was not published until 1633), Irenius describes what has happened to many Old English families outside the Pale:

they are nowe growen to be allmoste as lewde as the Irishe I meane of suche Englishe as weare planted aboue towarde the weste. . . . some in Leinster and ulster are degenerate | degenerate and growen to be as verye Patchokes as the wilde Irishe yea and some of them haue quite shaken of theire Englishe names and put on Irishe that they mighte be alltogether Irishe.[82]

Spenser was merely repeating Gerald of Wales's claim, made over four hundred years earlier, that 'this place finds people already accursed or makes them so', a fear of Ireland which was to become a widespread cliché.[83] Cyprus can easily be read as

[80] Christopher Highley, 'Wales, Ireland and *I Henry IV*', RD 21 (1990), 91–114.

[81] Murphy, 'Shakespeare's Irish History', 41–2. Murphy suggests that this is a reason 'for the relative silence of English writers on the question of the war in Ireland' (42). It would seem to me that fear of censorship or punishment is a more probable explanation of such silence.

[82] Spenser, *A View of the Present State of Ireland*, 115. 'Patchoke' is not found elsewhere but appears to mean 'a base or mean fellow? a ragamuffin' (n., 346).

[83] Gerald of Wales, *History and Topography of Ireland*, 109.

Ireland, a place where confidence in civilized identity was, more often than not, shattered rather than confirmed, where the fear of turning into one's worst nightmare often became a reality.

If we are to read Cyprus as analogous to Ireland, then presumably Venice demands to be read as England. Or, to put the comparison into perspective and express the matter less bluntly, we are provided with yet another invitation to weigh up the pros and cons of English political life and the English constitution against Venice. Can Venice deal with problems which appear insurmountable in England and threaten the very foundations of the state? Is Venetian society in *Othello* more just than English society? Does it represent the ideal of civilized European liberty, as William Thomas and Lewis Lewkenor asserted, or display the dangers of that liberty in the form of an excessive licentiousness, tempting but dangerous for Protestant Englishmen, as Roger Ascham argued?[84] In fact, formal justice in Venice appears to be exceptionally well administered, in line with the comments of Lewkenor and Thomas.[85] When Brabantio brings his case before a special council meeting held on Othello and Desdemona's wedding night, to deal with the imminent Turkish threat to Cyprus, both his confidence that the Duke and councillors will 'feel this wrong, as 'twere their own' and his fear that if Othello and Desdemona's marriage is not annulled then Venetian liberty will be overturned, 'Bond-slaves, and pagans, shall our statesmen be', (I. ii. 97–9), are shown to be unfounded.[86]

---

[84] See also Coryat's famous description of the Venetian courtesans, *Coryat's Crudities*, i. 401–8. See also Livesay, *Elizabethan Image of Italy*, 5; McPherson, *Shakespeare, Jonson, and the Myth of Venice*, ch. 2.

[85] The representation of Venice in *Othello* differs significantly from that in the earlier *The Merchant of Venice* (*c.*1596). As Mark Matheson notes, 'There is a notable shift, for instance, to a more explicitly republican discourse [in *Othello*] than he [Shakespeare] had used in *The Merchant of Venice*'; 'Venetian Culture and the Politics of *Othello*', *Sh. Sur.* 48 (1995), 123–33, at 124. On Shakespeare's Venice, see also Gillies, *Shakespeare and the Geography of Difference*, 64–8, 137–40; Jardine, *Reading Shakespeare Historically*, 99; Vaughan, *Othello: Contextual History*, ch. 1; Erskine-Hill, *Poetry and the Realm of Politics*, 127–31; McPherson, *Shakespeare, Jonson, and the Myth of Venice*, ch. 4.

[86] The scene in the council chamber has no counterpart in Cinthio's novella of the Moor of Venice in *Gli Hecatommithi* (1566), one which was not translated into English, although a French translation was published in 1584, which Shakespeare probably used. For details of the relationship between Cinthio and Shakespeare see *Othello*, ed. Norman Sanders (Cambridge: Cambridge University Press, 1984),

The Duke's opening lines to the group who have burst into the council meeting emphasize the democratic nature of Venetian government, where matters of public importance are discussed openly, and equal respect is granted to both the alien Othello and the native Brabantio: 'Valiant Othello, we must straight employ you, / Against the general enemy Ottoman; / [To Brabantio] I did not see you; welcome, gentle signior, / we lack'd your counsel and your help to-night' (I. iii. 48–51). The Venetian council is shown to be able to react quickly to events in order to defend itself. The fact that the Turkish fleet has changed course in order to deceive Venetian observers in Cyprus, and that Marcus Luccios, the first-choice general, is away in Florence, does not significantly reduce the effectiveness of the council's response to the crisis.[87] Othello is included within the upper echelons of the Venetian state and defined against the common enemy, the Turks, by the Duke, a gesture he repeats in his 'round unvarnish'd tale' (l. 90), by identifying with European travellers against the bizarre races of his native Africa.[88] In writing his own traveller's tale he gives the Venetians exactly what they want to hear. Although the Duke promises Brabantio that 'the bloody book of law' will be used against whoever has bewitched his daughter, the actual trial scene vindicates the newlyweds against the bigoted law of the father. The Duke refuses to accept Brabantio's assertions as proof. Both Othello and Desdemona are able to conduct a proper defence of their actions, with the result that a just outcome is swiftly reached

intro., 2–10. As Sanders remarks, 'the changes made by Shakespeare as he refashions the tale', are more striking than the similarities (8). See also Vaughan, *Othello: A Contextual History*, 83–4.

[87] This scene has no counterpart in Cinthio's story.

[88] There has been much recent comment on Othello's racial identity and his attempt to assimilate himself into European society; see e.g. G. K. Hunter, '*Othello* and Colour Prejudice', in *Dramatic Identities and Cultural Tradition* (Liverpool: Liverpool University Press, 1978), 31–59; Karen Newman, ' "And wash the Ethiop white": Femininity and the Monstrous in *Othello*', in Jean E. Howard and Marion O'Connor (eds.), *Shakespeare Reproduced: The Text in History and Ideology* (London: Routledge, 1987), 143–62; Patricia Parker, 'Fantasies of "Race" and "Gender": Africa, *Othello*, and Bringing to Light', in Margo Hendricks and Patricia Parker (eds.), *Women, 'Race', and Writing in the Early Modern Period* (London: Routledge, 1994), 84–100.

before the council return to the problem of the defence of Cyprus.[89]

There are, of course, limits to the solution, which hint at the tragedy to come; Desdemona's love for Othello is based on her perception of his inner self—'I saw Othello's visage in his mind' (l. 252)—which suggests that she may well have fallen 'in love with what she fear'd to look on' (l. 98), as her father asserted. Her lines also expose the problem of Othello's 'self', elaborately constructed to suit the role of a European adventurer, and his access to knowledge. At this stage in the play it seems likely that the couple will eventually have to deal with Brabantio's bitterness, which is expressed at great length and spills over into a feeble stoicism at odds with the resolution of the rest of the council: 'So let the Turk of Cyprus us beguile, / We lose it not so long as we can smile' (ll. 210–11), a reminder of the dangers which need to be faced as well as a foresight of the problem of 'turning Turk' in Cyprus.[90] Moreover, the casual use of the metaphor 'tyranny' (ll. 197, 229) hints that, in the military garrison of Cyprus, Venice's democratic norms will not apply, closing off the possibility of open discussion and effective justice.[91]

The tragedy, although conceived in Venice by Iago, unfolds exclusively in Cyprus, significantly enough after the Turkish fleet has foundered in a storm and the military threat has evaporated. In other words, the destruction of Desdemona and Othello takes place when they are outside the protection of the liberal republic which respects their desires, and are having to establish a life together in a military outpost. It is important to note that, *pace* John Gillies, the play does not represent Venetian women as anything other than faithful and pure. Desdemona may well be slandered as 'that cunning whore of Venice, / That married Othello' (IV. ii. 91–2) by her deluded

[89] For a very different reading of this scene, see Gillies, *Shakespeare and the Geography of Difference*, 138–9.

[90] Although Gratiano reports Brabantio's death in the final scene of the play (V. ii. 205), allegedly the direct result of grief caused by her marriage to Othello.

[91] David McPherson argues that the play is haunted by a sense of impending doom, partly a result of the audience's knowledge that 'The fall of the real, as opposed to the fictional, Cyprus was not a possibility but a *fait accompli*; and the fall of the real Cyprus in a sense overshadows the fall of Othello himself' (*Shakespeare, Jonson, and the Myth of Venice*, 90).

husband, but the truth is clearly the opposite. It is the myth of Venetian women, not its 'reality', which damns her after Iago has persuaded Othello that adultery is accepted behaviour in Venice. Emilia, who in Cinthio's story is aware of his designs from the start but is too fearful to challenge her overbearing husband, is represented as loyal to her spouse, despite her taste for bawdy humour (occasionally shared by her mistress). Indeed, given the notorious reputation of Venice for promiscuity, a discursive construct which is vital to the functioning of the plot—the fact that the only courtesan encountered is Bianca, a woman who clearly lives in Cyprus—acts as an explicit denial of the negative side of the Venetian myth.

Venice in *Othello* is represented as a society which is liberal enough to accommodate citizens from other cultures—a necessary virtue in a city-state, which served as the economic and military bridge between Europe and the East[92]—and strong enough to control its own citizens who wished to undermine its democratic traditions, exactly as Contarini/Lewkenor and William Thomas saw the republic.[93] Cyprus does not possess these advantages, and is continually represented in contrast to the motherland. After the Turkish fleet has been destroyed Othello issues a proclamation ordering revelry, which is also to celebrate his marriage. The resulting 'full liberty' (II. ii. 9) is that of a carnival, not a settled state, a holiday from the rigours of military service rather than the institutional freedom enjoyed in the metropolis. The celebrations lead to the first important action in the tragedy, the drunken brawl which sees Michael Cassio demoted. Initially Othello is capable of dealing with the crisis, imposing his authority on the unruly soldiers and restoring

[92] Lisa Jardine, *Worldly Goods* (London: Macmillan, 1996), 45–9, *passim*; Vaughan, *Othello: A Contextual History*, ch. 1.

[93] Contarini sees the respect for strangers and foreigners as one of Venice's main strengths (*Commonwealth and Gouernment of Venice*, fo. 105); yet the citizens were powerful enough to have a corrupt and tyrannous Duke, Marino Phalerio, beheaded (fo. 82). See also Thomas, *Historie of Italie*, fos. 81–2, 85, 103. Venice's ability to accept different citizens can be contrasted to Elizabeth I's notorious proclamation ordering the expulsion of 'Negroes and blackamoors' from the realm, *c.* January 1601, 3 years before *Othello* was probably first performed (cited in Parker, 'Fantasies of "Race" and "Gender" ', 97). See also Ania Loomba, *Gender, Race, Renaissance Drama* (Manchester: Manchester University Press, 1989), 43; Eldred Jones, *Othello's Countrymen* (London: Oxford University Press, 1965), pl. 5.

order through military command, just as he separated Roderigo and Brabantio with his eloquence in Venice (I. ii. 59–61). However, Iago has already started to spread rumours designed to undermine the general's political authority and to have the governor, Montano, question his competence as a leader of men. Ostensibly speaking in defence of Cassio, Iago undermines both him and his superior:

IAGO. You see this fellow that is gone before,
　　He is a soldier fit to stand by Caesar,
　　And give direction: and do but see his vice,
　　'Tis to his virtue a just equinox,
　　The one as long as th'other: 'tis pity of him,
　　I fear the trust Othello put him in,
　　On some odd time of his infirmity,
　　Will shake this island.
MON.　　　　　　　　But is he often thus?
IAGO. 'Tis evermore the prologue to his sleep . . .
MON.　　　　　　　　　　　　'Twere well
　　The general were put in mind of it;
　　Perhaps he sees it not, or his good nature
　　Praises the virtues that appear in Cassio,
　　And looks not on his evils: is this not true?

(II. iii. 114–28)

Iago's scandal-mongering serves as a pointed—and, I would suggest, quite deliberate—contrast to the institutional checks and balances of the Venetian republic. His tactics can only work in the closed male society of the garrison, where the exclusion of the voices of women is to prove crucial later. Here, Iago succeeds in planting doubts about Othello's competence in the mind of the departing governor, Montano, who then becomes involved in the brawl when he tries to separate Cassio and Roderigo, so that Iago is able to reprove him in front of Othello: 'Lieutenant,—sir,—Montano,—gentlemen,— / Have you forgot all place of sense, and duty?' (ll. 157–8). The extent of Iago's success is indicated by Montano's question, which concludes the passage cited above: Montano, believing that Othello's judgement is not to be trusted, has turned to Iago for advice (again, a contrast to the open counsel of Venice). Rumour has now started to dominate every aspect of life in Cyprus, a situation which paves the way for the introduction of damaging slanders, and specifically the false reputation of Venetian women.

Who, it might well be asked, is Iago, the scheming soldier who works so hard to undermine the pluralistic nature of the Venetian republic, symbolized in the marriage of the mature, middle-aged, and much respected black general, a converted Moor, and the younger white aristocratic woman? Iago is of no certain origin in the play, having been designated simply as 'a Villaine' in the folio text. Whereas there seems little reason to doubt that all the characters originate from Venice apart from Othello, Cassio, and, possibly, Bianca, Iago's place of birth is a matter of significant importance within the play.[94] His name, an invention of Shakespeare's, suggests that he is Spanish rather than Italian.[95] When he is attempting to convince Roderigo to continue with his doomed suit of Desdemona at the end of Act I, he refers to the couple's bond as a 'frail vow' between 'an erring barbarian, and a super-subtle Venetian' (I. iii. 356–7), which indicates that he, like Othello, is an outsider in the service of the Venetian state. If Iago's name is significantly Spanish—and I suggest that the action and structure of *Othello* indicate that it is—then a number of consequences follow, and certain apparently strange details become comprehensible.

While the unnamed ensign in Cinthio's story had a very definite motive in wanting to destroy Desdemona—namely, that he had fallen in love with her and when he realized that her intention was to remain faithful to Othello, he wished to prevent the Moor enjoying her—Iago, notoriously, as generations of critics have pointed out, has no specific motive.[96] The lack of a motive for Iago's actions serves two main functions within the play. First, it focuses attention on him as an unusually vicious villain, versed in the arts of Machiavellian polity. More importantly,

---

[94] The list marks Lodovico and Gratiano as Venetian and Othello as 'the Moore'; the text makes it clear that Brabantio, Roderigo and Desdemona are Venetian and that Cassio is Florentine (III. i. 40–1). For the cast list in the folio, see Shakespeare, *Othello*, ed. Ridley, 2.

[95] See Parker, 'Fantasies of "Race" and "Gender" ', 91; Hunter, '*Othello* and Colour Prejudice', 53.

[96] The argument is too well-known to require substantiating here; see e.g. Vaughan, *Othello: A Contextual History*, 158–9; Shakespeare, *Othello*, ed. Sanders, 24–7, for convenient overviews.

the reader/observer is forced to ask, like Lodovico: why has Iago contrived to perform his devilish plot?

If Iago is Spanish, then his resentment of the racially mixed marriage becomes clearer. The Spanish defeat of the Moors and destruction of their last stronghold in Spain in 1492 was well known; only four years before the (probable) first performance of *Othello*, John Pory had published his translation of and additions to Leo Africanus's *A Geographical Description of Africa* on the recommendation of Richard Hakluyt, a work which documented the Spanish wars against the Moors in Spain and North Africa.[97] Spanish intolerance and global ambition were further symbolized in that year by the expulsion of the Jews and Columbus's first voyage to the Americas.[98] Pory's translation emphasizes the civilized nature of the North African Moors: 'This is the most noble and worthie region of all Africa, the inhabitants whereof are of a browne or tawnie colour, being a ciuill people, and prescribe wholesome lawes and constitutions unto themselues' (p. 123). He often contrasts such peoples to those who live in the more barbarous regions of central Africa such as Numidia (pp. 126–7).[99] As Pory's preface to the reader emphasizes, John Leo (Africanus) himself was a highly educated Moor, possibly born in Granada, who had been converted to Christianity, having been kidnapped by Italian pirates and presented to the Pope. He had travelled extensively in his native continent and had endured a number of dangers in the compilation of his invaluable work: 'I maruell much how euer he should haue escaped so manie thousands of imminent dangers ... For how many desolate cold mountaines, and huge, drie, and barren deserts passed he? How often was he in hazard to haue beene captiued, or to haue had his throte cut by the prouling Arabians, and wilde Mores?' (p. 6)

---

[97] Leo Africanus, *The History and Description of Africa*, trans. John Pory, ed. Robert Brown, 3 vols. (London: Hakluyt Society, 1896), ii. 511, 518, 534, *passim*. Subsequent references to this edition in parentheses in the text. For an analysis of the relationship between Leo Africanus's history and *Othello*, see Parker, 'Fantasies of "Race" and "Gender" '. See also Newman, ' "And wash the Ethiop white" ', 148.   [98] See Greenblatt, *Marvelous Possessions*, 51.

[99] Pory/Africanus is inconsistent on the separation of the races of Africa; at times he indicates that there is a clear distinction which can be made between those of African descent and those of Arabic descent (128, 135); at others, he suggests that all are really the one people descended from the race of Noah's son, Cham (130).

Pory's description of Leo Africanus makes him resemble Othello in many ways. He, too, was an educated adventurer from a sophisticated—but barbarous—culture, keen to assimilate himself into European society (specifically Italian) by serving his adopted homeland well, fashioning his own sense of self against hostile invaders (for Othello, the Turks), and savages. Othello stands as an image of the 'other' whom every tolerant or strategically pragmatic society would want to adopt and have work for them, given his loyalty, his attempt to become accepted (not least by marrying a native woman, an ambivalent desire which can be read as a scandalous violation of a taboo, or, as the Venetian council concur, a legitimate act signifying assimilation), and useful knowledge of how the 'other' operates (a skill he, unlike Leo Africanus, is unable to employ because peace breaks out when the Turkish fleet is destroyed by the elements). Iago, by way of contrast, is a soldier of inferior rank from a significantly intolerant culture; he has no loyalty to anyone but himself and is openly racist, as the opening scene of the play establishes. Iago's taunt to Brabantio, 'you'll have your daughter cover'd with a Barbary horse' (I. i. 110–11)—punning on the term 'barbarian'—might indicate a familiarity with the peoples of Africa consistent with a Spanish origin: Barbary is undoubtedly the region of Africa from which Othello comes.[100] Iago's absorption of deceitful, self-interested tactics, his resort to deception and lying, makes him one of the feared and hated Machiavels of the late Elizabethan and early Jacobean stage, a sign that he has assimilated the opposite side of Italian politics to Othello, values more consistently associated with Naples or Genoa than Venice, so that the two figures confront each other as outsiders.[101]

Central questions *Othello* seems to pose are: what limits should be made to people's liberty? How far can a liberal republic tolerate enemies within? The first act of the play seems to divide the characters up into two distinct groups: on one side

---

[100] Africanus, *History and Description of Africa*, 125–6.
[101] On Machiavelli, see Raab, *English Face of Machiavelli*, ch. 5. On Italian politics, see Thomas, *Historie of Italie*, fos. 114, 121, 170–4, *passim*. Thomas's work points out a significant contrast between the sympathetic treatment of foreigners in Venice and the less happy relationship with the Moors in Naples and Genoa; fos. 118, 176.

are Desdemona and Othello, the Duke and the council, who approve of the racially mixed match; on the other, Iago, Roderigo, and Brabantio, all of whom are shown on stage making racist taunts.[102] There are hints that the marriage between Othello and Desdemona may have its limitations, but nothing to suggest that it is anything other than a union which should be viewed positively and celebrated as a sign of liberty.[103] Desdemona's love for Othello and defence of 'the Moor' (I. iii. 248) is a stark contrast to the attitude of her father, who welcomed Othello into his home before he turned his attentions to his daughter.

The politics of *Othello* are slippery and intricate. I would suggest, however, that it is far more of an overtly anti-Spanish play than one which exhibits an easy racial prejudice based on pigmentation.[104] Whereas Venice is able to accommodate the black outsider and has the institutions powerful enough to resist, if not nullify, indigenous prejudice, Iago, who is never assimilated, works from within to make sure that such harmony can never be achieved. The noble Moor who serves Venice and is respected and trusted by the highest authorities becomes the vicious, raving, violent savage of Act IV, who wants to chop his wife into messes and throw Cassio's nose to the dogs, a transformation which Iago's deception has achieved. The contrast bears a striking resemblance to the representations of the native Americans of the New World in De Bry's *America*; those whom the English have encountered are friendly, independent, and often ready to become civilized; the Spanish, on the other hand, encounter aggressive savages and cannibals (see above, p. 116).[105]

---

[102] See e.g. I. i. 66, 88–9, 126; I. ii. 70–1.

[103] For recent readings of the inherent problems in Othello and Desdemona's marriage, see Jardine, ' "Why should he call her whore?" '; Hugh Grady, *Shakespeare's Universal Wolf: Studies in Early Modern Reification* (Oxford: Clarendon Press, 1996), 127–8, 133–6.

[104] I hope it is clear that I am not denigrating readings of the play based on Othello's race, as if such an issue were not important, merely suggesting that the politics of *Othello* are not necessarily centred solely on this issue, as generations of readers have (not unreasonably) assumed; for discussions, see Jyotsna Singh, 'Othello's Identity, Postcolonial Theory, and Contemporary African Rewritings of *Othello*', in Parker and Hendricks (eds.), *Women, 'Race', and Writing*, 287–99; Newman, ' "And wash the Ethiop white" '; Hunter, '*Othello* and Colour Prejudice'. *Othello* seems to be a more obviously anti-Spanish play than *The Massacre at Paris*.

[105] For further details see Maltby, *Black Legend*, chs. 2, 5.

Venice in *Othello* cannot be read as a straightforward representation of England. Nevertheless, it is plausible to suggest that it functions, yet again, as an ideal to which England might aspire, as well as having obvious parallels to the situation of England in the early 1600s, links which, I would argue, are emphasized by Shakespeare's additions to Cinthio's novella. The play serves as a triple warning to England: first, of the havoc which an uncontrolled colony like Ireland could wreak to the certainties of a (supposedly) established, civilized identity; second, of the need for interaction with Africans to be benevolent, in order to outflank the Spanish and secure loyal state servants;[106] and third, of the problem of tolerating subversives within the state, a key theme of anti-Catholic and anti-Spanish propaganda after the Reformation, one which had particular—but not exclusive—relevance to Ireland.[107] It is a strength of Venice that it is able to employ a successful general such as Othello; as Lewkenor/Contarini pointed out, Venice was notable for its ability to use outsiders in such key roles.[108] Conversely, it is a weakness, one which precipitates the tragedy represented in the play, that the city-state tolerates subversives such as Iago in its midst. Clearly Ireland was a source of both types of citizens in the early 1600s, after the success of Mountjoy's campaign to end the Nine Years' War, and *Othello* can be read as a warning that surface appearances do not always tell the truth ('There's no art / To find the mind's construction in the face', as one of Shakespeare's less effective

---

[106] Parker argues that Iago's name 'evokes not Venice but England's Iberian rivals in the African trade [ie slavery]' ('Fantasies of "Race" and "Gender" ', 90). I would suggest that the play is more concerned with the rather more positive representations of Africans in Leo Africanus's *History and Description of Africa* than the (much earlier) slaving voyages of Sir John Hawkins (as Parker's note implicitly acknowledges). On Hawkins' slaving voyages, see the accounts in Hakluyt, *Principal Navigations*, ix. 445–65; x. 9–74, 226–45, *passim*. See also Calder, *Revolutionary Empire*, 69–71, *passim*.

[107] See Maltby, *Black Legend*, ch. 3; Carol Z. Weiner, 'The Beleaguered Isle: A Study of Elizabethan and Early Jacobean Anti-Catholicism', *P. & P.* 51 (1971), 27–62; Colm Lennon, 'The Counter-Reformation in Ireland, 1542–1641', in Ciaran Brady and Raymond Gillespie (eds.), *Natives and Newcomers: Essays on the Making of Irish Colonial Society, 1534–1641* (Dublin: Irish Academic Press, 1986), 75–92.

[108] Lewkenor, *Commonwealth and Government of Venice*, 130–1; McPherson, *Shakespeare, Jonson, and the Myth of Venice*, 73.

kings put it). The state needs to be both liberal and vigilant in establishing a *via media*.

At the end of the play Iago is taken off to be tortured so that 'the nature of [his] fault be known / To the Venetian state' (V. ii. 337–8), despite his adamant refusal to reveal his motives: 'Demand from me nothing, what you know, you know, / From this time forth I never will speak word' (ll. 304–5). The repetition of this threat in Lodovico's last speech—'to you, lord governor, / Remains the censure of this hellish villain, / The time, the place, the torture: O enforce it!' (ll. 368–70)—emphasizes the importance of physical means of extracting a confession for the Venetian authorities. The resemblance to contemporary English treatment of traitors, many of them Catholic, would surely not have been lost on the audience.[109]

'No sovereignty': Locating Government in The Tempest

Whereas the main action of *Othello* occurs at the edge of—but within—the boundaries of Europe, that of *The Tempest* is clearly set outside the parameters of the commonly accepted civilized world. There are, of course, obvious differences between the plays; one is a tragedy, the other probably best described as a 'romance'; one, despite its much-analysed 'double-time scheme', demonstrates a definite verisimilitude in style and action, the other, although it obeys the unities, is conspicuously fantastic in style, the plot relying on the frequent use of magic; one is set in distinct locations, the other conspicuously avoids easily identifiable places. However, both plays share a crucial mutual concern in dramatizing the relationship between European and colonial politics.[110] *The Tempest* is a

---

[109] See John Bellamy, *The Tudor Law of Treason: An Introduction* (London: Routledge, 1979), 109–21. Bellamy points out that the use of torture became more frequent as the century progressed so that 'When Elizabeth died torture was as firmly established as it ever had been' (120). See also Breight, *Surveillance, Militarism and Drama*, 74–6, *passim*.

[110] Far too much recent discussion of *The Tempest* has tended to assume that the play is either a colonial work, or one concerned with politics closer to home, a spurious dichotomy. See e.g. Paul Brown, ' "This Thing of Darkness I Acknowledge Mine": *The Tempest* and the Discourse of Colonialism', in Jonathan Dollimore and Alan Sinfield (eds.), *Political Shakespeares: New Essays in Cultural Materialism*

Utopian play; like More's humanist prose work, it employs contemporary discoveries and documents to help construct a fictional setting.[111] And, like *Utopia* and many subsequent works dealing with questions of the theory and practice of colonialism, the play demonstrates an acute awareness of the interaction and overlap between domestic and colonial politics.[112]

The play is set everywhere and nowhere.[113] The island where Prospero lives is somewhere off the coast of Africa, probably in the region of Algeria or Tunisia.[114] As Gonzalo makes clear, the Europeans are returning from the marriage of Alonso's daughter, Claribel, to the King of Tunis. It is a dynastic match of symbolic importance, since it links Europe to the Moorish kingdoms of North Africa, especially as, after Ferdinand's supposed death, she has become the heir to the kingdoms of Naples and

(Manchester: Manchester University Press, 1985), 48–71; Deborah Willis, 'Shakespeare's *The Tempest* and the Discourse of Colonialism', *SEL* 29 (1989), 277–89; Alden T. Vaughan and Virginia Mason Vaughan, *Shakespeare's Caliban: A Cultural History* (Cambridge: Cambridge University Press, 1991), ch. 2; Jeffrey Knapp, 'Distraction in *The Tempest*', in *An Empire Nowhere*, 220–42. Barbara Fuchs claims, somewhat overstating her case, perhaps, that 'It is an axiom of contemporary criticism that *The Tempest* is a play about European colonial experience in America' ('Conquering Islands: Contextualizing *The Tempest*', *Sh. Q.* 48 (1997), 45–62).

[111] On Shakespeare's use of the as-yet-unpublished Strachey letter, see William Shakespeare, *The Tempest*, ed. Stephen Orgel (Oxford: Oxford University Press, 1987), 32, 63, 209–19. The original text, 'A true report of the wracke, and redemption of Sir Thomas Gates Knight; upon, and from the Ilands of the Bermudas', was published in Purchas, *Purchas His Pilgrimes*, xix. 5–72.

[112] For a sophisticated analysis of the links, see Hamilton, *Virgil and The Tempest*.

[113] A point perhaps made in the heated exchange between Gonzalo and Sebastian and Antonio, when they argue whether modern Tunis is the ancient Carthage of Dido. The debate ends with Antonio's sarcastic aside, 'What impossible matter will be made easy next?' and Sebastian's response, 'I think he will carry this island home in his pocket, and give it his son for an apple', a recognition of the fictional, Utopian nature of the play's geographical location; William Shakespeare, *The Tempest*, ed. Frank Kermode (London: Methuen, 1964, rpt. of 1950), II. i. 71–89. All subsequent references to this edition in parentheses in the text. For further comment on the lines and Shakespeare's debt to Virgil, see *Tempest*, ed. Orgel, 39–43; Hamilton, *Virgil and The Tempest*, 17–30.

[114] See Richard Wilson, 'Voyage to Tunis: New History and the Old World of *The Tempest*', *ELH* 64 (1997), 333–57; Fuchs, 'Conquering Islands', 54–61. See also Peter Hulme, ' "Hurricanes in the Caribbes": The Constitution of the Discourse of English Colonialism', in Francis Barker *et al.* (eds.), *1642: Literature and Power in the Seventeenth Century* (Colchester: University of Essex, 1981), 55–83.

Milan (II. i. 239–57).[115] However, as John Gillies has pointed out, 'Shakespeare's play is vitally rather than casually implicated in the discourses of America and the Virginia colony' because of its participation within contemporary debates about colonialism which were inevitably centred on the English colonies in the New World.[116] The principal players are the Milanese and Neopolitan nobility. The plot centres around the dispossession of a bookish European prince who neglected to govern his king-dom and so was usurped by his ambitious younger brother. In a sense, the play revolves around an intrigue of dynastic politics which dominates the pages of a work such as Francesco Guicciardini's *History of Italy* (recently reprinted in 1599), espe-cially the portrayal of the ruthless ruler of Milan, Francesco Sforza.[117] Such intrigues also dominate the history and politics of the island, just as they clearly link the Italian kingdoms to Africa. Caliban asserts that 'This island's mine, by Sycorax my mother' (II. ii. 333); yet, according to Prospero and Ariel, 'The foul witch Sycorax' came from Algiers (I. ii. 257–67), a country significantly similar in the Elizabethan imagination to Tunisia, where Alonso has just married off his daughter. Such links complicate a straightforward reading of *The Tempest* as a colo-nial text. If the island has an original native inhabitant, then, rather than the bellicose Caliban it is the submissive Ariel, grate-ful to serve a master less ferocious than the witch who impris-oned him inside a tree for twelve years.[118] Caliban's claims to

[115] On the contemporary perception of Algeria and Tunisia, see Africanus, *History and Description of Africa*, ii. 682–4; iii. 716–25. See also *Tempest*, ed. Orgel, 40.

[116] Gillies, *Shakespeare and the Geography of Difference*, 149. Ariel's descrip-tion of the tempest which wrecked the ship, and which, after all, gave the play its title, as 'From the still-vexed Bermoothes [Bermuda]' (II. ii. 239), emphasizes the island's link to the Americas.

[117] *Historie of Guicciardini*, trans. Fenton, 3, *passim*. See also Thomas, *Hist-orie of Italie*, fos. 113, 137; 188–201. Thomas characterizes Naples as a kingdom of treacherous, inconstant people who are continually subject to tyrannous rule and are always fighting wars (fo. 114), a marked contrast to his representation of Venice and the Venetians.

[118] See Fuchs, 'Conquering Islands', 53. Contrasting readings include Stephen Greenblatt, 'Learning to Curse: Aspects of Linguistic Colonialism in the 16th Century', in Chiapelli (ed.), *First Images of America*, 561–80; Francis Barker and Peter Hulme, 'Nymphs and Reapers Heavily Vanish: The Discursive Con-Texts of *The Tempest*', in John Drakakis (ed.), *Alternative Shakespeares* (London: Methuen, 1985), 191–205; Hulme, *Colonial Encounters*, ch. 3 ('Prospero and Caliban').

the island are of the same order as those of the usurping Prospero, who displaced Caliban because he was a savage not fit to govern, a move which uncomfortably mirrors Prospero's own removal from office in Milan.

If the play is careful to link European, colonial, and exotic locations, it is equally adept at relating questions of European government and politics to problems Europeans encountered when dealing with peoples from other continents, whether as trading partners or inferiors whose lands were to be colonized.[119] Commentary on the exploitation of Caliban by Prospero and the similarity of their relationship to that between English colonizers and natives in America is legion.[120] What is less frequently observed is the proximity of such a relationship (coupled with that of Prospero and Ariel) to the inequalities of European society. The opening scene—dramatizing the event which gives the play its title—demonstrates the breakdown of social hierarchies at moments of extreme crisis. In response to Gonzalo's plea that he be patient, the boatswain responds with a piece of studied ambiguity: 'What care these roarers / for the name of king?' (I. i. 16–17), where 'roarers' can either refer to the large waves which threaten the boat, or, as was common in early seventeenth-century English, rioters.[121] The boatswain's irritable rejoinder to inappropriate considerations of rank and status, and his assumption of command ('To cabin: silence! trouble / us not', ll. 17–18), serves to define the aristocratic passengers against the working sailors (a division which is to be repeated in the second scene when we observe Prospero's treatment of Caliban and Ariel), especially when they unite to consider the likely fate of their potential saviour: 'methinks he / hath no drowning mark upon him; his complexion / is perfect gallows' (ll. 28–30); 'Hang, cur! you whoreson, insolent noise-maker. We are less afraid to be drowned

---

[119] Wilson, 'Voyage to Tunis', 334–6; Fuchs, 'Conquering Islands', 46.

[120] A convenient overview is provided in Vaughan and Vaughan (eds.), *Shakespeare's Caliban*.

[121] 'Roaring boys', as Kermode points out, 'was a slang expression for young men whose pride it was to break the peace' (*Tempest*, ed. Kermode, 5). Thomas Middleton and Thomas Dekker's comedy, *The Roaring Girl* (1611), about a notorious cross-dressing criminal, appeared in the same year that *The Tempest* was probably first performed. See David Norbrook, ' "What care these roarers for the name of King?": Language and Utopia in *The Tempest*', in Hope and McMullan (eds.), *Politics of Tragicomedy*, 21–54, at 21.

than thou art.' (ll. 43–5); 'He'll be hanged yet' (l. 57). The responses are important in a variety of interrelated ways: they remind the audience that treatment of various underclasses within England was not necessarily better than the treatment of colonial subjects by European masters, a point neatly made when Antonio insults the boatswain as an 'insolent noisemaker', as this was one of the contemporary definitions of 'roarer', thus labelling the boatswain as a dangerous, undoubtedly treasonable, opponent of the king after his own definition.[122] Equally importantly, such comments illustrate that, for all their differences over the question and practice of government, those who hold the reins of power will unite to exclude—or punish—those who do not when it suits them, however much they may have to depend on them when necessary. The boatswain clearly belongs to the 'fourth sort of men which do not rule', in Thomas Smith's well-known phrase, a class which consisted of 'day labourers, poore husbandmen, yea marchauntes or retailers which have no free lande, copiholders, and all artificers, as Taylers, Shoomakers, Carpenters, Brickmakers, Bricklayers, Masons, &c' and who 'have no voice nor authoritie in our common wealth, and no account is made of them but onelie to be ruled, not to rule other'.[123] Shakespeare himself had only definitely ceased to be a member of this class in 1596, when his application for a coat of arms on his father's behalf was successful and he started to acquire land in Stratford; Ben Jonson was the stepson of a bricklayer.[124]

---

[122] See *OED* entry b. For a more general discussion of treason in the play which hints at this particular point, see Curt Breight, ' "Treason doth never prosper": *The Tempest* and the Discourse of Treason', *Sh. Q.* 41 (1990), 1–28, at 10, 22.

[123] Sir Thomas Smith, *De Republica Anglorum: A Discourse on the Commonwealth of England* (1583), ed. L. Alston (Shannon: Irish University Press, 1972, rpt. of 1906), 46. The boatswain's remark when reminded by Gonzalo that he has important passengers on his ship that they are 'None that I love more than myself' (l. 20) is apt. The best that Smith recommends is that the lowest class of men 'be not altogether neglected'. For a more wide-ranging discussion of early modern class structures, see Mark Thornton Burnett, *Masters and Servants in English Renaissance Drama and Culture: Authority and Obedience* (Basingstoke: Macmillan, 1997).

[124] On Shakespeare's social status, see Samuel Schoenbaum, *Shakespeare's Lives* (Oxford: Clarendon Press, 1970), 29–36; on Jonson's origins, see David Riggs, *Ben Jonson: A Life* (Cambridge. Mass.: Harvard University Press, 1989), ch. 1. For contemporary views of the acting profession, see Arthur F. Kinney (ed.), *Markets of Bawdrie: The Dramatic Criticism of Stephen Gosson* (Salzburg: Universität Salzburg, 1974); Russell Fraser, *The War against Poetry* (Princeton: Princeton University Press, 1970).

It is significant that Gonzalo is the first to indulge in wishful thinking about the boatswain's fate, not Antonio or Sebastian, who are to emerge in the second act as the most obviously Italianate (that is, Machiavellian) of the shipwrecked party, keen to use the disaster to further their own fortunes at the expense of everyone else.[125] Gonzalo's famous 'Golden Age' speech is undercut by the asides of Sebastian and Antonio, who point out to the audience the obvious contradiction between Gonzalo's desire for sovereignty and his plan to remove all trappings of European civilization so that rank and hierarchy are abolished.[126] Structurally, the speech is rendered ironic by the frame of European—in this case, undoubtedly English—class relations, which Gonzalo, more than anyone else in the play, is keen to reinforce. Not only is he the most vocal aristocrat who condemns the boatswain in the first scene, but in the last he greets the miraculous reappearance of the sailor with the words: 'O look, sir! here is more of us: / I prophesied, if a gallows were on land, / This fellow could not drown' (V. i. 216–18). The lines may not be in deadly earnest, but they are a grim reminder of the fate of traitors and rebels in the Old World, for all the fine political plans of their masters.[127] They also occur immediately after the dynastic alliances of the Italians have been sorted out and old bonds reunited, as Gonzalo himself recognizes:

> Was Milan thrust from Milan, that his issue
> Should become Kings of Naples? O, rejoice
> Beyond a common joy! and set it down
> With gold on lasting pillars: in one voyage
> Did Claribel her husband find at Tunis,
> And Ferdinand, her brother, found a wife
> Where he himself was lost, Prospero his dukedom
> In a poor isle, and all of us ourselves
> When no man was his own.
>
> (V. i. 205–13)

---

[125] Adding further significance to the boatswain's self-interest (see above, n. 113).

[126] For a relevant recent analysis of this speech, see Norbrook, 'Language and Utopia', 27–34. Although critics are generally agreed that Gonzalo's speech is based on Montaigne's 'Of the Cannibals', see Margaret T. Hogden, 'Montaigne and Shakespeare Again', *HLQ* 16 (1952–3), 23–42. For the relevant passage in Montaigne, see *The Essayes of Michel Lord of Montaigne*, i. 220.

[127] See Breight, 'Treason doth never prosper', 22. On the fate of traitors and rebels, see Bellamy, *Tudor Law of Treason*, ch. 5; Beier, *Masterless Men*, ch. 9.

Celebration is the order of the day for the rulers; all can now return to Italy secure in the knowledge that the kingdoms of Naples and Milan have, at last, been united harmoniously through a fortunate match forged by the wonder of the New World. A successful link with a powerful African dynasty has been made, with the marriage of Claribel and the King of Tunisia, and Prospero has returned in triumph as Duke of Milan. The symbolic game of chess which Miranda and Ferdinand are discovered playing has an imperial sub-text:

MIR. Sweet lord, you play me false.
FER.   No, my dearest love,
    I would not for the world.
MIR. Yes, for a score of kingdoms you should wrangle,
    And I would call it fair play.

The lines remind the audience that, although the couple are united by mutual affection, their union is not a simple bond of affection between two ordinary people, but part of the strategic alliances which made and preserved a state's political inter-ests.[128] Ferdinand would have to play Miranda false if circumstances dictated. As it is, their game of chess appears to reflect the fortunate solidarity of their love-match, and they can now look outwards towards imperial ambitions, a consideration further indicated in Miranda's exclamation when she first makes contact with a large number of human beings a few lines later: 'O brave new world, / That has such people in't!' (ll. 183–4).[129] Miranda and Ferdinand bear a striking resemblance—in name if nothing else—to that most successful of imperial couples, Ferdinand and Isabella, sponsors of the first European voyages to the Americas.[130]

There is some cause for the less socially exalted characters, if not to celebrate, then at least to heave a sigh of relief. Nothing

---

[128] For one suggestion of a match which stands behind the action of the play, see Wilson, 'Voyage to Tunis', 338–52.

[129] See Stephen Greenblatt, *Marvelous Possessions*, ch. 3. Miranda's lines undoubtedly connote an American context; even here, however, the normal movement West is inverted so that Miranda looks back from the island of her birth to Europe.

[130] For details see Gianni Granzotto, *Christopher Columbus: The Dream and the Obsession, A Biography*, trans. Stephen Sartarelli (London: Collins, 1988, rpt. of 1986), 73–5, 90–2, *passim*.

happens to Stephano and Trinculo when their hopeless plot fails. Although Caliban fears further torment for his rebellion, Prospero, albeit rather ungraciously, acknowledges him as his own (V. i. 275–6). Nothing happens to the boatswain, and Ariel is finally set free after his service to Prospero (ll. 316–18). However, given the 'Golden Age' speech of Gonzalo which envisages the island as a site for radical, egalitarian social engineering, and the clear suggestion that Prospero feels that his exile on the island has taught him how to govern, with the result that he is now ready to return to the old world of Milan and rule properly, one is entitled to ask what exactly has changed at the end of the play.[131] It is unclear exactly what happens to Caliban, although his claim in his final speech that he will 'be wise hereafter, / And seek for grace' (V. i. 294–5) perhaps signals a conversion to Christianity and a rejection of his previous appeals to the pagan Setebos. He is set free from his bonds and pardoned by Prospero, but Prospero's lines to Alonso about the fate of the conspirators suggest that the status quo has been restored: 'Two of these fellows you / Must know and own; this thing of darkness I / Acknowledge mine' (ll. 274–6). Whether 'own' needs to be glossed as a synonym for 'acknowledge', or can assume the more modern meaning of 'possess', is not crucial here. Either way, Stephano and Trinculo are seen to have the same relationship to the King of Naples as Caliban, described as a 'mis-shapen knave' (l. 268) by his master—a judgement which reinforces rather than qualifies Prospero's ferocious insults earlier in the play—has to the reinstated Duke of Milan.[132] The link neatly confirms suspicions that the treatment of the lower classes in Europe paralleled attitudes towards the savages of more distant continents.[133]

---

[131] See e.g. James Black, 'The Latter End of Prospero's Commonwealth', *Sh. Sur.* 43 (1990), 29–41. Elsewhere, *The Tempest* appears to endorse Prospero's right as a proper ruler: see Edwards, *Threshold of a Nation*, 103–9; Leslie A. Fiedler, *The Stranger in Shakespeare* (London: Granada, 1974), ch. 4.

[132] The actual fate of Caliban is also unclear: does he return to Milan with Prospero, or remain on the island? For opposing views, see A. D. Nuttall, 'Two Unassimilable Men', in Malcolm Bradbury and David Palmer (eds.), *Shakespearian Comedy* (London: Arnold, 1972), 210–40, at 212, 239; Edwards, *Threshold of a Nation*, 109.

[133] See Greenblatt, 'Invisible Bullets'. See also Andrew Hadfield, 'The Naked and the Dead: Elizabethan Perceptions of Ireland', in Maquerlot and Willems (ed.), *Travel and Drama in Shakespeare's Time*, 32–54.

Ariel ends the play as a free spirit, but the liberty provided for the other servant-classes is strictly limited, and one should bear in mind that Ariel is deliberately placed outside the realm of the human. Caliban's last two utterances illustrate that his desire to conform is motivated by fear, not repentance. Prospero's lines suggest to Caliban that he will 'be pinch'd to death' (l. 276), words which recall one of the most common ways of describing torture in Renaissance England.[134] Accordingly, he obeys Prospero's next order and accepts his pardon, commenting, 'I'll be wise hereafter, / And seek for grace. What a thrice-double ass / Was I, to take this drunkard fool for a god, / And worship this dull fool!' (ll. 294–7).

The play has come full circle, and has returned to the problem of the right to exercise authority which was originally posed by the tempest in the opening scene. Caliban acknowledges his error in mistaking Trinculo for a king fit to replace the 'tyrant' that he serves (II. ii. 163), but this leads only on to the further question of how fit Prospero is to rule, especially if every third thought is to be directed towards his grave (V. i. 310–11). Could it not be argued that Antonio and Alonso appear to have managed well enough—certainly no worse than their bookish predecessor, whatever rights he might have on his side (rights which are undeniably undermined by his wresting the island from its previous owner and subsequent behaviour towards Caliban and Ariel)? After all, the alliance with Tunis was exactly the sort of match Italian states were seeking to counteract the threat of the Turks which was such an important factor in *Othello*.[135]

Caliban's words recall the scene in *Henry V* when the king disguises himself as an ordinary Welshman in order to demonstrate to himself and the audience that 'the king is but a man, as I am' (IV. i. 101–2). Here he discovers in the process that what distinguishes the king from 'private men' is nothing more nor less than the assumption of power and its attendant

[134] Breight, 'Treason doth never prosper', 24–7. See also Stephano's complaint, 'I am not Stephano, but a cramp' (l. 286).

[135] Jardine, *Worldly Goods*, 27, 326. Tunis was an important naval base of the Ottoman Empire, which Charles V of Spain won from the Muslim Corsair, Barbarossa, in 1535, an event celebrated in many lavish art works by Charles (387–90).

responsibilities.[136] As numerous New Historicists have pointed out, such power is essentially a matter of role-playing: 'And what have kings that privates have not too, / Save ceremony, save general ceremony?' (ll. 244–5).[137] The suggestion surely is that Prospero's powerful magic art is what enables him to govern, not any innate abilities. Prospero's plot—which is an equal and opposite approach to government than that of Gonzalo, although both lead to the same conclusion—involves no more nor less than a restoration of the status quo. His enemies are humiliated, then pardoned, and he returns as Duke of Milan, having fortuitously enough secured a stable succession. There is no indication that the political life of Milan will change in any way as a result of its ruler's sojourn on the island.[138]

The Tempest, unlike *Othello*, is not a play which provides the audience with any obvious moral and political centre or ideal, a feature, I would argue, of much Renaissance Utopian literature written in the wake of More's fiction.[139] Certainly, it is hard to envisage an alternative political vision in the clumsy counter-plot of Trinculo and Stephano, whose plans to exhibit Caliban as an exotic curiosity are significantly less palatable than Prospero's initial efforts to teach him language, or even Caliban's own desire to people the island with little Calibans fathered on the unwilling Miranda.[140] Each, in its way, apes the established mechanics of upper-class European politics, just as Gonzalo's airy idealism and Prospero's bitter self-interest amount to the same thing, so that the dominant political mode which the play demonstrates is that of marriage alliance and the securement of dynastic succession.

Instead, as in *Utopia*, *The Tempest* poses questions more

---

[136] The implications of this discovery are radical indeed, given Henry's own dubious claim to the throne, and the topicality of the subject in the late 1590s (see above, pp. 33, 44).

[137] Greenblatt, 'Invisible Bullets', 56–65; Leonard Tennenhouse, *Power on Display: The Politics of Shakespeare's Genres* (London: Methuen, 1986), ch. 2.

[138] Although it is symbolically implied via the chess game that Ferdinand and Miranda will opt for imperial expansion in future years (see above, p. 248).

[139] For a related reading, see Knapp, 'Distraction in *The Tempest*'.

[140] On Trinculo and Stephano's plot, see Black, 'Prospero's Commonwealth', 36–7.

than it provides answers.[141] In many ways it can be read as a cynical play, exposing the hollow, absolutist pretentions of Prospero without providing any viable alternative means of government. The circular structure of the plot indicates that the voyage to the Utopian island teaches the characters nothing they did not already know or could not have learned from a European experience if they had only looked hard enough within the boundaries of their own states. All have exported their perceptions and problems to a foreign destination, and the miraculous solution provided within the play does not, in the end, mean that all will change. Politics will continue to be worked out via the marriage alliances of the high and mighty.

The Tempest provides a stark contrast to the opening acts of Othello, and we would do well to remember that in each case Shakespeare is not relying on a known source for the scenes represented. The Venetian state in Othello is shown to be keen to accommodate others within its society and, in order to achieve this noble aim, will stand up to the prejudices of its own citizens. The ship of state represented in the opening scene of The Tempest illustrates that, in a crisis, the reflexes of those that govern—Gonzalo is described in the folio cast list as 'an honest old Councellor'—are to reinforce social boundaries even at the expense of their own natural self-interest. Such divisiveness appears time and again throughout the play, indicating that the ship has brought the politics of the old world along with it, adding a bitter and loaded significance to Miranda's exclamation: 'O brave new world, / That has such people in't!' (V. i. 183–4). Travel brings you right back to where you started. Caliban is loathed by both Prospero and Miranda, frequently tortured, and exploited as a slave. Trinculo and Stephano wish to exploit him as a freakish curiosity, a neat contrast not only to Ferdinand's wonder on meeting Miranda and her sense of awe on encountering Europeans en masse for the first time, but

[141] Boika Sokolova usefully defines The Tempest as an 'interrogative text', but her reading is less than persuasive; Shakespeare's Romances as Interrogative Texts: Their Alienation Strategies and Ideology (Lewiston/Queenston/Lampeter: Edwin Mellen Press, 1992), ch. 7.

also to the Venetian council's treatment of Othello, or Desdemona's reaction to his travellers' tales; while Antonio and Stephano's cunning is based on a selfishness which isolates them as social beings, inscribed within the action of the play by their constant asides. The world of *The Tempest*, in short, contains no means of organizing, shaping, and controlling its citizens' wills, or providing a forum which can legitimately be said to work in the common interest by enfranchising a political public. Politics works simply by autocratic fiat, and the main aim is to preserve the power of a few families, protecting them from the designs of other self-interested parties. In other words, such representations exactly mirror English writers' descriptions of political intrigue in the worst Italian courts.[142] Political dreams such as Gonzalo's are insubstantial and, more importantly, perhaps, hypocritical.

Shakespeare's play, with its deliberately unspecified setting, needs to be read in terms of two interrelated traditions. First, *The Tempest* is indebted to a humanist mode of writing which emphasized the need for counsel, and specifically to More's eponymous work, which deliberately juxtaposed the discovery of the New World with the problem of politics in the old. Second, the play should be read in terms of the wealth of writing from the 1560s to the early 1600s, both fictional and non-fictional, which represented foreign locations in order to reflect on English politics. If the play does have a moral centre, it is surely neither Prospero nor Caliban—although reappropriations of Caliban as a hero by African and Caribbean writers are perfectly legitimate, given the history of the reception of *The Tempest*[143]—but a marginal figure like the boatswain, whose use of his voice leads to thinly veiled death threats, despite his good sense and shrewd awareness of the limits of authority:

[142] See e.g. Moryson, *Shakespeare's Europe*, 138–9, 153, *passim*; Lever, *Tragedy of State*.

[143] On the range and wealth of such rewriting and interpretation see Jonathan Bate, 'Caliban and Ariel Write Back', *Sh. Sur.* 48 (1995), 155–62; Rob Nixon, 'Caribbean and African Appropriations of *The Tempest*', CI 13 (1986–7), 557–78; Thomas Cartelli, 'Prospero in Africa: *The Tempest* as Colonialist Text and Pretext', in Howard and O'Connor (eds.), *Shakespeare Reproduced*, 99–115.

You [Gonzalo] are a counsellor; if you can command these elements to silence, and work the peace of the presence, we will not hand a rope more; use your authority: if you cannot, give thanks you have lived so long, and make yourself ready in your cabin for the mischance of the hour, if so hap. Cheerily, good hearts! Out of our way, I say.

(I. i. 20–6)

If the vessel can be read as the ship of state—or the ship of fools—then these words have a more profound resonance than is at first apparent. The boatswain's sarcasm, directed towards Gonzalo's inappropriate assumption of an authority which he simply does not possess, refers both to his obliviousness of the force of the elements and the refusal of the state to recognize the value of those less exalted citizens on which it nevertheless relies in a crisis (one reason why Gonzalo is evidently such a useless counsellor). The boatswain is clearly not a rebellious underling like Trinculo and Stephano, with grand ambitions of usurpation. However, like them, he is one of those who is 'onelie to be ruled', and, presumably, he represents many more.[144]

'I know the devill': Religion and Colonialism in The Island Princess

A play which is much more directly concerned with England's colonial experience in the reign of James I than *The Tempest* is John Fletcher's *The Island Princess* (1619–22), written about ten years after Shakespeare's play, a complicated and intriguing work which would undoubtedly have merited far more critical attention had it actually been written by Shakespeare.[145]

---

[144] On the growing opposition to the constitutional *status quo*, demands for wider representation, and greater influence for the House of Commons under James I, see Lawrence Stone, *The Causes of the English Revolution, 1529–1642* (London: Routledge, 1972), 91–8, *passim*; Russell, *Crisis of Parliaments*, 266–71; Pocock, *Ancient Constitution*, 255–306; Loach, *Parliament under the Tudors*, 159–60.

[145] Fletcher, who collaborated with Shakespeare at the start of his own career and towards the end of the working life of the older dramatist, did indeed borrow much from *The Tempest* in *The Island Princess* and other plays, notably *The Sea Voyage*, written in collaboration with Philip Massinger (acted 1622). For details see Gordon McMullan, *The Politics of Unease in the Plays of John Fletcher* (Amherst,

Fletcher enjoyed the patronage of Sir Henry Hastings, fifth Earl of Huntington, a Protestant aristocrat of radical leanings who was heavily involved in the enterprises of the Virginia Company at the time when Fletcher wrote the play.[146] Nevertheless, the play appears to be anything but a straightforward endorsement of Hastings' enthusiastic support for colonial ventures. Indeed, it is more of a warning of the dangers which could lie ahead if careful plans are not properly laid.

The Island Princess, unlike The Tempest, has a very definite location. The action is set on the Moluccan island of Tidore, which is occupied by the Portuguese, apart from a brief excursion to Tidore's bitter rival, the island of Ternata. The story centres around the figure of Quisara, princess of Tidore. She is courted by many suitors, but is in love with a Portuguese sailor, Ruy Dias. When the evil governor of Ternata kidnaps her brother, the king of Tidore, Quisara announces that she will marry whoever rescues him, intending the hero to be her lover. However, he fails to rise to the challenge, and the king is rescued by a noble Portuguese, Armusia; and Quisara, eventually overcoming her initial shock, transfers her affections to him. Meanwhile the governor, in order to gain revenge on both the Portuguese and the people of Tidore, disguises himself as a priest and successfully turns the King of Tidore against the Portuguese. When Quisara tries to convert Armusia to her religion—a primitive form of sun- and moon-worship—he resists her persuasions and transforms his love for her into hatred, which serves only to inflame her desire for him. Ruy Dias, whose own animosity towards Armusia had been transformed into respect after he had been comprehensively defeated in a duel, leads a rescue operation. The play ends with the Governor exposed, Armusia and Quisara reunited, and the islanders and Portuguese reconciled.

Mass.: University of Massachusetts Press, 1994), 190–2, 197–9, 232, 236, passim; Anthony Parr (ed.), Three Renaissance Travel Plays (Manchester: Manchester University Press, 1995). Parr points out that The Sea Voyage does indeed borrow from The Tempest, but actually 'overgoes' Shakespeare's play (22). Like The Island Princess, I would argue, The Sea Voyage focuses more clearly on colonial themes than The Tempest. On Fletcher and Shakespeare's collaborative venture, The Two Noble Kinsmen, see Jonathan Hope, The Authorship of Shakespeare's Plays (Cambridge: Cambridge University Press, 1994). McMullan observes the notable lack of recent critical work on The Island Princess (308, n. 56).

[146] McMullan, Politics of Unease, 203–6.

The Island Princess, despite its ostensibly happy ending, is a disturbing play, leaving many questions unanswered. The King of Tidore confesses to Armusia that his noble example has 'halfe perswaded me to be a Christian', but in the very last line indicates that this change in faith has not yet happened: 'the gods give peace at last'.[147] His sister does convert to Christianity, but only because she reads the value of the faith through the character of her lover—'Your faith, and your religion must be like ye, / They that can shew you these, must be pure mirrours; / When the streames flow cleare and faire, what are the fountaines' (ll. 118–20)—lines which suggest that her will follows her erotic desires rather than true conviction, behaviour which is characteristic throughout the play.[148] The inconsistency is important, given the central role of religion in the mechanics of the plot as well as significant allusions and allegorical scenes.

When the Governor seeks to turn Quisara against the Portuguese he uses his bogus identity as a holy man to suggest that religion is the key to future oppression and invasion. Praising the princess's beauty, the Governor urges her to use her physical gift to the advantage of her own people, not the Europeans:

> Use it discreetly,
> For I perceive ye understand me rightly,
> For here the gods regard your helpe, and suddenly;
> The Portugals like sharpe thornes (marke me Lady)
> Sticke in our sides; like razors, wound religion,
> Draw deep, they wound, till the life bloud followes,
> Our gods they spurne at, and their worships scorne,
> A mighty hand they beare upon our government.
> These are the men your miracle must worke on,
> Your heavenly forme, either to roote them out . . .
> Or fairely bring 'em home to our devotions[.]
>
> (IV. ii. 153–65)

---

[147] John Fletcher, *The Island Princess*, ed. George Walton Williams, in *The Dramatic Works in the Beaumont and Fletcher Canon*, ed. Fredson Bowers (Cambridge: Cambridge University Press, 1982), v. 539–669, V. v. 66, 93. All subsequent references to this edition in parentheses in the text.

[148] See Philip J. Finkelpearl, 'John Fletcher as Spenserian Playwright: *The Faithful Shepherdess* and *The Island Princess*', SEL 27 (1987), 285–302, at 290–3.

The Governor's motives may be bad, as his frequent asides remind the audience, but his description of what will happen to native religion is startlingly accurate, and recalls the attitudes expressed throughout the pages of Hakluyt's *Principal Navigations* and the more overly theologically centred collection of Samual Purchas, the first version of which, *Purchas His Pilgrimage, or, Relations of the World and the Religions Observed in All Ages*, appeared in 1613. As a piece of imaginative sympathy with colonized peoples it recalls Thomas Harriot's ventriloquized version of Algonkian voices which were also remarkably astute predictions of what was about to happen to them. The passage takes on a further sinister significance when it is recalled that Quisara is actually white, unlike her fellow islanders, a difference achieved, according to the cynical but good-hearted Pynerio, by her avoidance of the sun (ironically enough, one of the gods she worships) (I. i. 60–5). The Governor suggests that the Portuguese will either embrace the religion of Tidore after Quisara's example—words which inspire her to attempt Armusia's conversion—or, presumably, will be persuaded to leave. Quisara is thus constructed as a go-between, a woman who can form both a link and a bulwark between colonizer and colonized by virtue of her noble rank and her colour.[149] The Portuguese, by implication, want to limit the problem of miscegenation by holding congress only with an honorary white woman.[150] In effect the 'contact zone', observed by the audience as a clash between cultures, is deliberately circumscribed to the familiar by the colonizers.[151]

[149] On the (female) figure of the 'go-between', see Greenblatt, *Marvelous Possessions*, ch. 5. McMullan perceptively links the play to the Pocahontas story; *Politics of Unease*, 222–4. More generally, see Hulme, *Colonial Encounters*, ch. 4; Robert S. Tilton, *Pocahontas: The Evolution of an American Narrative* (Cambridge: Cambridge University Press, 1994).

[150] For further reflection on this problem, see Robert Young's comments on imperial desire in the nineteenth century; *Colonial Desire, passim*.

[151] On the concept of the 'contact zone', see Pratt, *Imperial Eyes*, ch. 1. It should also be pointed out that the inhabitants of Ternata are represented as Moors, a people more usually associated with Africa (see Africanus, *History and Description of Africa*, i. 200–2), complicating the relationship between the peoples in the Moluccan islands represented in the play. The Portuguese make no effort to distinguish between the peoples other than in terms of friends and enemies—as Pynerio's opening speech (I. i. 1–12) makes clear—categories which are by no means fixed within the play.

The Governor's perception of the reality behind the benign surface of Portuguese support for Tidore is borne out repeatedly throughout the play. Pynerio, perhaps the most astute and balanced of all the Portuguese, who disapproves strongly of Ruy Dias's attempt to settle his score with Armusia in a duel, argues that they need to keep a careful watch on the natives because 'They are false and desperate people, when they find / The least occasion open to encouragement, / Cruell, and crafty soules' (I. i. 4–6), indicating the profound contempt the Portuguese have for the people of Tidore. Such hostility surfaces again in the final act after the imprisonment of Armusia, actions which appear to vindicate Portuguese suspicion. On hearing the bad news, Soza, one of Armusia's companions, exclaims, 'Is this the love they beare us / For our late benefit? taken so maliciously, / And clapt up close? is this the thankes they render?' (V. i. 3–5), rhetorical questions which reveal the colonizer's assumption that colonized people should be for ever grateful for the benefits that have been bestowed upon them. Within a few lines, Emanuel and Pynerio have sworn revenge on the 'barbarous slaves' (l. 19) and 'these Barbarians' (l. 24), indicating that the Governor does indeed see matters more clearly than the friendly Tidorians.[152]

Armusia's reactions to the island, and his relationship with Quisara express the familiar dichotomy of the exotic encounter. Armusia's first lines on arriving at Tidore are a common variation on the theme of the earthly paradise:

> We are arriv'd among the blessed Islands,
> Where every wind that rises blowes perfumes,
> And every breath of aire is like an Incence:
> The treasure of the Sun dwels here, each tree
> As if it envied the old Paradice,
> Strives to bring forth immortal fruit; the spices
> Renewing nature . . .
> Nothing we see, but breeds an admiration;
> The bowels of the earth swell with the births
> Of thousand unknowne gems, and thousand riches;

---

[152] For the common European division of native peoples into friendly and hostile groups, see Hulme, *Colonial Encounters*, ch. 2.

> Nothing that bears a life, but brings a treasure;
> The people they shew brave too, civill manner'd,
> Proportioned like the Mastres of great minds,
> The women which I wonder at—
>
> (I. iii. 16–34)[153]

Armusia is interrupted from his reverie of wonder—a word he uses again to describe the court (l. 39)—before he has a chance to elaborate his opinion of the women of Tidore; instead, he immediately falls for Quisara when she appears some seventy lines later, and eventually uses his courtly arts of persuasion to win her from Ruy Dias in Act III. However, when Quisara attempts to convert Armusia to the nature-religion of the islanders under the watchful eye of the scheming Governor of Ternata, he reveals the disgust rather than the wonder of European perceptions of exotic peoples. When Quisara implores Armusia to offer a sacrifice to her gods, he retorts:

> To the Devill, Lady?
> Offer to him I hate? I know the devill;
> To dogs and cats? you make offer to them;
> To every bird that flies, and every worme.
> How terribly I shake! Is this the venture?
> The tryall that you talkt off? where have I bin?
> And how forgot my selfe? how lost my memorie?
> When did I pray or looke up stedfastly?
> Had any goodnesse in my heart to guide me?
> That I should give this vantage to mine enemie,
> The enemie to my peace; forsake my faith?
>
> (IV. v. 39–48)

In representing the religion of the natives as devil worship, and in expressing the fear that cultural traffic will flow the wrong way, Armusia is rehearsing widely held beliefs which were common currency of the discourse of contemporary colonialism. He fears that Europeans will be transformed into barbarians rather than vice versa: an anxiety, ironically enough,

---

[153] Compare e.g. Arber (ed.), *First Three English Books on America*, 156, 343, 374. See also Rennie, *Far-Fetched Facts*, 20–3. Armusia is alluding to the myth of the 'Fortunate Isles'; see Josephine Waters Bennett, 'Britain among the Fortunate Isles', *SP* 53 (1956), 114–40.

manifested in his aggressive assertions to the contrary.[154] Armusia continues in this vein until the hasty resolution in the last few lines of the play, so that his bland final words thanking Ruy Dias for preserving 'my life, my wife and honour' (V. v. 88) do little to offset the audience's impression of his vicious hostility towards the islanders as a counterbalance to his initial seduction by Tidore. Armusia, the ostensible hero of *The Island Princess*, is therefore made to represent the two extreme states of European reaction to the lure of the exotic.

Armusia's stress on the devilish nature of the religion of Tidore, which Pynerio repeats immediately after Armusia has been captured: 'Thinke some abominable names—are they not Devils? / But the devil's a great deale too good for 'em' (V. i. 34–5), has to be set against the action of a crucial scene earlier in the play, one which quite deliberately broadens the contextual significance of the European stress upon religion as a mark of cultural boundaries. Armusia's success in rescuing the King of Tidore is achieved via the use of a barrel of gunpowder, placed in a cellar next to the Governor's store-house, which blows open the prison where the king is incarcerated and enables the Portuguese to escape with him in the ensuing confusion. Whilst this is happening Fletcher includes a scene which represents the ordinary citizens of Ternata commenting on the disaster. Three of them have just helped to put out one of the many fires, and one comments, with appropriately grim humour, 'Lets home and fright our wives, for we looke like Devils' (II. iv. 13–14). It was yet another commonplace of colonial writing that natives were helpless when confronted by superior European technology. This is precisely what has happened here, and it is a feature of the play repeated later when, in the final Act, Ruy Dias leads his forces against the people of Tidore.[155] Armusia's actions appear not to

---

[154] On the first point, see e.g. Arber (ed.), *First Three English Books on America*, 189, 302, 342; Hakluyt, *Principal Navigations*, ix. 386–7; x. 424–5; Pagden, *Fall of Natural Man*, 99–103. On the second, see Hadfield, *Spenser's Irish Experience*, 22, 163–4. Armusia's ravings might usefully be compared to Othello's in *Othello*, IV. On Armusia's behaviour, see McMullan, *Politics of Unease*, 234–5. Finkelpearl, in contrast, considers Armusia unique among Fletcher's 'later, full-length, male characterizations . . . in being utterly flawless' ('Fletcher as Spenserian playwright', 297).

[155] For comment, see McMullan, *Politics of Unease*, 231, 309. See also Harriot, *Brief and True Report*, 28–9.

show him in a favourable light: not only does his underhand and destructive means of rescuing the king—he poses as a merchant in order to secure the gunpowder—undermine his pretensions to honourable behaviour, but Fletcher graphically depicts the innocent victims of his actions as stage devils in a flaming hell, perhaps akin to the devils in miracle plays.[156] The perceptions of the Portuguese have become self-fulfilling prophecies; it is their intervention in the islanders' conflict which is shown to create the devils which loom so large in their representation of the natives.

The Island Princess, then, is a play which, at the very least, voiced concerns about the desirability of colonial expansion, and about whether the motives of the principal European actors were at all admirable.[157] The question which must be posed is whether the Portuguese are meant to stand for the English, or be contrasted with them. Fletcher was relying on a Spanish source, probably consulted via a French translation.[158] However, *The Island Princess*, unlike *The Tempest*, has a very specific location in the Moluccan islands in the Bay of Bengal. These islands were assuming considerable importance for English imperial and trading interests in the second decade of James's reign, reflected in the growing influence of the East India Company, which had received its charter in 1600.[159] There were a number of well-publicized voyages to the East Indies and Japan in this decade, one of which, John Saris's account of his voyage to Japan, had been included in the growing editions of Samuel Purchas's encyclopaedic collection of English voyages published in 1613, 1614, and 1617, and which also contained Saris's observations of Tidor and Ternate.[160]

---

[156] For a reading of Fletcher's (and Francis Beaumont's) attacks on rigid codes of honour and the dangers of tyranny in other plays, see Philip J. Finkelpearl, *Court and Country Politics in the Plays of Beaumont and Fletcher* (Princeton: Princeton University Press, 1990), esp. 204–6. More generally, see McCoy, *Rites of Knighthood*; James, *English Politics and the Concept of Honour*, 72–91.

[157] This is the thrust of McMullan's generally persuasive argument; *Politics of Unease*, 235.

[158] See Edward M. Wilson, 'Did Fletcher Read Spanish?', *PQ* 27 (1948), 187–90.

[159] Calder, *Revolutionary Empire*, 101, 162–3.

[160] See Purchas, *Purchas His Pilgrimes*, iii. 355–519. The material on the Moluccas is contained on 408–42. Purchas's text is taken from Saris's log, published as *The Voyage of Captain John Saris to Japan, 1613*, ed. Sir Ernest M. Satow (London: Hakluyt Society, 1900). See also Peter Flores, *His Voyage to the*

Saris's voyage contains the description of an incident which bears some resemblance to the description of the conflict between the two islands as represented in *The Island Princess*. He writes of his encounter with the Prince of Tidor, who arrives with the heads of a hundred Ternatans, including that of Key Chilly Sadang, son of the king of Ternate. He had been slain when returning from the island of Machian, where he had been kept by the Dutch to prevent him selling cloves to the English. The Tidorians had lain in wait and lured the Ternatans into a trap via the use of 'two small Praws to fish', where they had 'spared not one man of an hundred and sixtie'. At this point Saris adds a confusing and enigmatic detail: 'At their first incounter, a barrell of powder, which the Prince had bought of us at Machian, tooke fire, which was the confusion and losse of them all. With the Prince was slaine one of his younger bretheren, and the King of Geilola.'[161]

It is not clear from Saris's account when this explosion occurred, or on which island, or, indeed, which prince was slain.[162] Nevertheless, given the topical importance of the location of *The Island Princess*, it seems likely that there is some relation between these details of Saris's experience in Tidor and Fletcher's play, the former probably providing the basis for the story of the King of Tidore's kidnap when out rowing (I. i. 1–28) and the explosion which helps to rescue him.[163] This would suggest that Fletcher's eye was on documents of English voyages abroad, that his play was designed as a reflection on contemporary English colonization and trade, and that the Portuguese can be read as English, a dramatic convention which stretched back into the second half of the previous monarch's reign.[164] Such a conclusion is strengthened, albeit in

East Indies in the Globe, 1611–1615, ed. W. H. Moreland (London: Hakluyt Society, 1934), who refers to Tidor (84); *The Voyage of Thomas Best to the East Indies, 1612–14*, ed. Sir William Foster (London: Hakluyt Soc., 1934).

[161] Purchas, *Purchas His Pilgrimes*, iii. 429–30.

[162] Saris's journal contains a slightly differently worded account which does not help sort out the confusion; *Voyage of Captain John Saris*, 55.

[163] McMullan points out that this detail has no counterpart in the Spanish source; *Politics of Unease*, 231.

[164] See e.g. J. R. Mulryne, 'Nationality and Language in Thomas Kyd's *The Spanish Tragedy*'.

an oblique manner, by the fact that the Portuguese were no longer the dominant force in that area, having largely given way to the Dutch and the English, which indicates that the topical relevance of the play is displaced from its ostensible focus.[165]

The Island Princess is therefore a play centrally concerned with the question of the relationship between European and non-European peoples, which is why it can be described as a colonial—or, possibly, an anti-colonial—text in the broadest sense. Like *The Tempest*, its range of reference is wide. Fletcher's drama is vigorously informed by contemporary writing describing the Americas, as well as encounters with other cultures and contemporary political issues. Unlike *The Tempest*, *The Island Princess* does not focus on the 'Utopian' problem of Europeans exporting their political obsessions to the locations in which they find themselves. Instead, Fletcher concentrates much more directly than Shakespeare on the colonial encounter, suggesting that ill-considered projects would lead only to a self-perpetuating cycle whereby European and non-European cultures would view each other with mutual suspicion. The final words of the King of Tidore, that he is 'halfe perswaded to be a Christian' (V. v. 66), imply that all is not irrevocably lost and that there is some hope for more mutual benefit and understanding between different peoples. In the final analysis, the location of *The Island Princess* is undoubtedly significant. The East Indian setting strongly implies that, if fruitful exchanges were to be established between Europe and the rest of the world, it was more likely to occur through trade in commodities such as cloves than through the Manichean fantasies of adventurers like Armusia, whose relationship with Quisara recalls the infamous alliance between Pocahontas (who died in 1617) and John Rolfe.[166]

---

[165] *Voyage of Captain John Saris*, Introduction, pp. xxxii–xlii.

[166] See Hulme, *Colonial Encounters*, ch. 4; Tilton, *Pocahontas*, 7–8; McMullan, *Politics of Unease*, 222–4. For a more general reflection on the question of Manichean representation of the colonized subject, see Abdul R. Janmohamed, 'The Economy of Manichean Allegory: The Function of Racial Difference in Colonialist Literature', in Henry Louis Gates (ed.), *'Race', Writing, and Difference* (Chicago: Chicago University Press, 1986), 78–106.

Perhaps the King's half-conversion is better than European attempts to impose an orthodoxy on non-European peoples. After all, European Christianity had hardly been free of sectarian violence in the preceding century, a stubborn reality all too obvious to numerous English writers.[167]

[167] For one overview see Erskine-Hill, *Poetry and the Realm of Politics*, ch. 1. On Fletcher's own religious views, see McMullan, *Politics of Unease*, 4–7, *passim*.

Afterword

A MAJOR link between writers of prose fiction and dramatists is their uncertain status in society, as has frequently been noted.[1] It is hardly surprising that many such writers chose to analyse, whether carefully or obliquely, the existing social order, generally concluding that beneficial changes could be made which might favour them directly, or, at least, enable them—or their masters—to participate more easily in contemporary political processes. However, it was often difficult to state such complaints openly, and writers often resorted to disguising their messages, either through resorting to historical events or through the use of exotic locations, as this book has argued.

Travel writing, a genre which was every bit as uncertain in status and as problematic in the second half of the sixteenth century and early part of the seventeenth as more obviously literary genres, was also frequently produced by writers of dependent or uncertain status, as the examples of William Thomas, Lewis Lewkenor, and Thomas Coryat demonstrate. Just as writers of works which can be classed as 'literary' represented real or imagined locations in order to further discussion of domestic political issues, so did travel writers use their writings to reflect on the state of the body politic.

In making this point I hope it is clear that I do not wish to suggest that this is the only way in which such works should be read. On the contrary, I have no wish to close off readings which concentrate on early modern English representations of foreign lands and cultures as distinctly 'other'. Rather, as I have argued elsewhere in my retrospectively and somewhat loosely conceived trilogy, I want to demonstrate the multiple purposes

---

[1] Recent commentary is to be found in M. T. Burnett, *Masters and Servants in English Renaissance Drama and Culture: Authority and Obedience* (Basingstoke: Macmillan, 1997) and R. Maslen, *Elizabethan Fictions: Espionage, Counter-Espionage and the Duplicity of Fiction in Early Elizabethan Prose Narratives* (Oxford: Clarendon Press, 1997).

of early modern writing and show how one generic form
cannot escape from the marks of another.[2] Representations
which provided images of other cultures and vital information
about other lands—whether that information be for strategic or
touristic purposes—were also often quite conscious reflections
on English or British politics.

Some subjects lent themselves to such meditations more readily
than others. The very process of colonialism involved a consideration of comparative government. One of the longest sections in
Machiavelli's *The Prince*—a favourite work of those involved in
colonial ventures[3]—considered the establishment of new principalities and dealt with the often violent origins of civil society.
Exactly the same political questions had to be asked when colonial establishments were planned in the Americas, as Chapter 2
argues. Equally, the same might be said at times for many other
writings on the French wars of religion, the struggles of Italian
states against invaders, African society, or East Indian trade.

The overall picture which I hope emerges from this book is
that of the early modern period in England as a time of intense
and vigorous political discussion, even if much of this writing
involved careful disguise and now requires careful decoding. I
want to suggest an alternative political picture of early modern
England to that of some New Historicists, who write as if
power were a monolithic entity which could either be accepted
or confronted, as well as those historians who refuse to accept
that political debates were carried on by anyone other than
politicians. Undoubtedly an 'official ideology' of Tudor and
Stuart England can be reconstructed by cultural and literary
historians. However, any such ideology was continually inter-
rogated, challenged, and undermined by the manifold writings
of the growing literate populace.

---

[2] A. Hadfield, *Literature, Politics and National Identity: Reformation to
Renaissance* (Cambridge: Cambridge University Press, 1996), 19; *Spenser's Irish
Experience: Wilde Fruit and Salvage Soyl* (Oxford: Clarendon Press, 1997), 10–11.

[3] See R. Beacon, *Solon His Follie, or a Politique Discourse touching the
Reformation of common-weales conquered, declined or corrupted* (1594) ed.
Vincent Carey and Clare Carroll (Binghampton, NY: MRTS, 1996), introduction,
pp. xxxvi–viii; Lisa Jardine, 'Encountering Ireland: Gabriel Harvey, Edmund
Spenser, and English Colonial Ventures', in Bradshaw, Hadfield, and Maley (eds.),
Representing Ireland: Literature and the Origins of Conflict, 1534–1660
(Cambridge: Cambridge University Press, 1993), 60–75, at 65.

Bibliography

PRIMARY SOURCES

Place of publication is London unless otherwise stated.

ACOSTA, JOSÉ DE, *Historia Natural y Moral de las Indias* (1590) (Mexico: Fondo de Cultura Economica, 1940).

ACOSTA, FATHER JOSEPH DE, *The Natural and Moral History of the Indies*, trans. Edward Grimstone (1604), ed. Clements R. Markham, 2 vols. (London: Hakluyt Society, 1880).

AFRICANUS, LEO, *The History and Description of Africa*, trans. John Pory (1600), ed. Robert Brown, 3 vols. (London: Hakluyt Society, 1896).

ANON., *Gamelyn*, in Walter Hoyt French and Charles Brockway Hale (eds.), *Middle English Metrical Romances*, 2 vols. (New York: Russell & Russell, 1964), i. 207–35.

—— 'An Homily against Disobedience and Wilful Rebellion', in *Certain Sermons Appointed for the Queen's Majesty* (1574) (Cambridge: Parker Society, 1850), 551–601.

—— 'A new ballade of the tryumphes kept in *Ireland* uppon Saint *Georg's* day last, by the noble Earle of *Essex* and his followers, with their resolution againe there', in Andrew Clark (ed.), *The Shirburn Ballads, 1585–1616* (Oxford: Clarendon Press, 1907), 321–6.

ARBER, EDWARD (ed.), *The First Three English Books on America* (Birmingham: privately printed, 1885).

ALEXANDER, MICHAEL (ed.), *Discovering the New World, Based on the Works of Theodor De Bry* (London: London Editions, 1976).

ASCHAM, ROGER, *The Scholemaster* (1570), ed. Lawrence V. Ryan (Ithaca, NY: Cornell University Press, 1967).

D'AVITY, PIERRE, *The Estates, Empires and Principalities of the World*, trans. Edward Grimstone (1615).

BALDWIN, WILLIAM, *Beware the Cat / The Funerals of Edward VI*, ed. William P. Holden (N. London, Conn.: Connecticut College, 1963).

BALE, JOHN, *The Vocacyon of Johan Bale to the Bishopricke of Ossorie* (1553).

BARCLAY, JOHN, *Argenis* (Paris, 1621).

BARCLAY, JOHN, *Barclay his Argenis or the loves of Poliarchus and Argenis*, trans. Kingsmill Long (1625).

—— *Argenis*, trans. Sir Robert Le Grys (1628).

BEACON, RICHARD, *Solon His Follie, or a Politique Discourse touching the Reformation of common-weales conquered, declined or corrupted* (1594) ed. Vincent Carey and Clare Carroll (Binghampton, NY: MRTS, 1996).

BEHN, APHRA, *Oronooko, The Rover and Other Works*, ed. Janet Todd (Harmondsworth: Penguin, 1992).

BENSON, PAMELA (ed.), *Italian Tales from the Age of Shakespeare* (London: Everyman, 1996).

BEST, THOMAS, *The Voyage of Thomas Best to the East Indies, 1612–14*, ed. Sir William Foster (London: Hakluyt Society, 1934).

BETHUNE, PHILIPPE, *The Counsellor of Estate*, trans. Edward Grimstone (1634).

BRYSKETT, LODOWICK, *A Discourse of Civill Life* (1606), ed. Thomas E. Wright (Northridge, Cal.: San Fernando Valley State College Renaissance Editions, 1970).

BYRCHENSA, RALPH, *A Discourse occasioned upon the late defeat, giuen to the Arch-rebels, Tyrone and Odonnell, by the right Honourable Lord Mountjoy* (1602).

CASAS, BARTOLOMÉ DE LAS, *The Spanish colonie, or briefe chronicle of the acts and gestes of the Spaniardes*, trans. M. M. S. (1583).

—— *A Short Account of the Destruction of the Indies*, trans. Nigel Griffin (Harmondsworth: Penguin, 1992).

CHAPMAN, GEORGE, *The Revenge of Bussy D'Ambois* (c.1610), ed. Maurice Evans (London: Ernest Benn, 1966).

CORYAT, THOMAS, *Coryat's Crudities, Hastily gobled up in five Monthes travells . . .* (1611) (rpt. Glasgow: MacLehose, 1905), 2 vols.

—— *Coryats Crambe, or his colwort twise sodden* (1611).

DALLINGTON, SIR ROBERT, *The View of France* (1604).

—— *The Survey of the Great Dukes State of Tuscany* (1605).

—— *Aphorismes civill and militarie, amplified with authorities* (1613).

DE BRY, THEODOR, *Iani Iacobi Boissardi Emblematum* (Frankfurt, 1593).

—— *America* (Frankfurt, 1594).

DERRICKE, JOHN, *The Image of Irelande* (1581).

DÍAZ, BERNAL, *The Conquest of New Spain*, trans. J. M. Cohen (Harmondsworth: Penguin, 1963).

DONNE, JOHN, *The Complete English Poems*, ed. A. J. Smith (Harmondsworth: Penguin, 1971).

EDEN, RICHARD, *The decades of the newe worlde or west India* (1555), in Edward Arber (ed.), *First Three English Books on America* (Birmingham: privately printed, 1885).

ELTON, GEOFFREY (ed.), *The Tudor Constitution: Documents and Commentary* (Cambridge: Cambridge University Press, 1972).

ELYOT, SIR THOMAS, *The Boke named the Governour* (1531).

FENTON, GEOFFREY, *Certain Tragicall Discourses of Bandello* (1567), 2 vols., ed. Robert Langston Douglas (London: David Nutt, 1898).

—— *A discourse of the Ciuile warres & late troubles in France . . . 1568 and 1569* (1570).

—— *Acts of conference in religion . . . drawen out of French into English* (1571).

—— *A forme of Christian pollicie drawne out of French* (1574).

—— trans., *The Historie of Guicciardini containing the warres of Italie and Other Partes* (1599, rpt. of 1579).

FLETCHER, JOHN, *The Island Princess* (*c.*1620), ed. George Walton Williams, in *The Dramatic Works in the Beaumont and Fletcher Canon*, ed. Fredson Bowers (Cambridge: Cambridge University Press, 1982), v. 539–669.

FLORES, PETER, *His Voyage to the East Indies in the Globe, 1611–1615*, ed. W. H. Moreland (London: Hakluyt Society, 1934).

GATES, SIR THOMAS, 'A true reportory of the wracke, and redemption of Sir Thomas Gates; upon, and from the Ilands of the Bermudas', in Samuel Purchas, *Hakluytus Posthumus or Purchas His Pilgrimes*, 20 vols. (1625) (Glasgow: MacLehose, 1905), xix. 5–72.

GERALD OF WALES, *The History and Topography of Ireland*, trans. J. J. O'Meara (Harmondsworth: Penguin, 1982, rpt. of 1951).

GOODMAN, CHRISTOPHER, *How Superior Powers Ought to be Obeyed* (1558).

GOSSON, STEPHEN, *Markets of Bawdrie: The Dramatic Criticism of Stephen Gosson*, ed. Arthur F. Kinney (Salzburg: Universität Salzburg, 1974).

GRANDSON, K. W. (ed.), *Tudor Verse Satire* (London: Athlone, 1970).

GREENE, ROBERT, *Gwydonius. The Carde of Fancie* (1584), in George Saintsbury (ed.), *Shorter Novels: Elizabethan* (London: Dent, 1966, rpt. of 1929), 157–260.

HADFIELD, ANDREW and JOHN MCVEAGH (eds.), *Strangers to that Land: British Perceptions of Ireland from the Renaissance to the Famine* (Gerrards Cross: Colin Smythe, 1994).

HAKLUYT, RICHARD, 'Discourse of Western Planting', in E. G. R. Taylor (ed.), *The Original Writings and Correspondence of the Two Richard Hakluyts* (London: Hakluyt Society, 1935), 211–326.

HAKLUYT, RICHARD, *The Principal Navigations, Voyages, Traffiques & Discoveries of the English Nation* (1600), 12 vols. (Glasgow: MacLehose, 1903).

—— *The Original Writings and Correspondence of the Two Richard Hakluyts*, ed. E. G. R. Taylor (London: Hakluyt Society, 1935).

HARRIOT, THOMAS, *A Briefe and True Report of the New Found Land of Virginia* (1588), reprinted in D. B. Quinn (ed.), *The Roanoke Voyages: Documents to Illustrate the English voyages to North America under the Patent Granted to Walter Raleigh in 1584*, 2 vols. (London: Hakluyt Society, 1955).

—— *A Briefe and True Report of the New Found Land of Virginia* (1590), ed. Paul Hulton (New York: Dover, 1972).

HAYWARD, JOHN, *The First and Second Parts of John Hayward's The Life and Raigne of King Henrie IIII*, ed. John J. Manning (London: Royal Historical Society, 1991; Camden Soc., 4th series, vol. 42).

HOLINSHED, RAPHAEL, *Chronicles of England, Scotland and Ireland* (1577).

JAMES I, *Basilikon Doron*, in *The Workes* (1616) (Hildesham and New York: Verlag, 1971), 137–92.

—— *The Trew Law of Free Monarchies*, in *The Workes*, 193–210.

JONSON, BEN, *Poems*, ed. Ian Donaldson (Oxford: Oxford University Press, 1975).

LEWKENOR, SIR LEWIS, *A Discourse of the Usage of the English Fugitives by the Spaniard* (1595).

—— *The Estate of the English Fugitives under the king of Spaine and his ministers* (1595).

—— trans., *The Commonwealth and Gouernment of Venice. Written by the Cardinall Gaspar Contareno* (1599).

LODGE, THOMAS, *Rosalynde* (1590), ed. Brian Nellist (Keele: Keele University Press, 1995).

LYLY, JOHN, *The Works of John Lyly*, ed. R. W. Bond, 3 vols. (Oxford: Oxford University Press, 1902).

MACHIAVELLI, NICCOLÒ, *The Prince*, trans. George Bull (Harmondsworth: Penguin, 1961).

MANDEVILLE, SIR JOHN, *The Travels of Sir John Mandeville*, trans. C. W. R. D. Moseley (Harmondsworth: Penguin, 1983).

MARCO POLO, *The Travels*, trans. Ronald Latham (Harmondsworth: Penguin, 1958).

MARLOWE, CHRISTOPHER, *The Complete Plays*, ed. Mark Thornton Burnett (London: Everyman, 1998, forthcoming).

—— *Dido Queen of Carthage and The Massacre at Paris*, ed. H. J. Oliver (London: Methuen, 1968).

—— *The Massacre at Paris*, in *The Complete Works of Christopher*

Marlowe, ed. Fredson Bowers (Cambridge: Cambridge University Press, 1973), 354–417.

—— *Edward II*, ed. Charles R. Forker (Manchester: Manchester University Press, 1994).

—— *Lucan's First Book* in *The Poems*, ed. Millar McLure (London: Methuen, 1968).

MARTYR, PETER D'ANGHERA, *De Orbe Novo: The Eight Decades of Peter Martyr D'Anghera*, trans. Francis Augustus MacNutt, 2 vols. (New York: Burt Franklin, 1970, rpt. of 1912).

A Mirror for Magistrates, ed. Lily B. Campbell (Cambridge: Cambridge University Press, 1938).

MONTAIGNE, MICHEL DE, *The Essayes of Michael Lord of Montaigne*, trans. John Florio (1603), 3 vols. (London: Everyman, 1910).

MORE, THOMAS, *Utopia*, ed. Edward Surtz, S. J., and J. H. Hexter (New Haven: Yale University Press, 1965).

—— *Utopia*, ed. George M. Logan, Robert M. Adams and Clarence H. Miller (Cambridge: Cambridge University Press, 1995).

MORYSON, FYNES, *An Itinerary Containing His Ten Yeeres Travell through the Twelve Dominions of Germany, Bohmerland, Sweitzerland, Netherland, Denmarke, Poland, Italy, Turky, France, England, Scotland & Ireland* (1617), 4 vols. (Glasgow: MacLehose, 1907).

—— *Shakespeare's Europe: Unpublished Chapters of Fynes Moryson's Itinerary*, ed. Charles Hughes (London: Sherratt and Hughes, 1903).

NASHE, THOMAS, *The Unfortunate Traveller* in *The Unfortunate Traveller and Other Works*, ed. J. B. Steane (Harmondsworth: Penguin, 1972), 251–370.

—— *The Works of Thomas Nashe*, ed. R. B. McKerrow, rev. F. P. Wilson, 5 vols. (Oxford: Oxford University Press, 1958).

OVID, *Metamorphoses*, trans. Mary M. Innes (Harmondsworth: Penguin, 1955).

PAINTER, WILLIAM, *The Palace of Pleasure* (1566, 1567, 1575), 3 vols., ed. Joseph Jacobs (Hildesheim: Georg Olms Verlagsbuchhandlung, 1968, rpt. of 1890).

PALMER, THOMAS, *An essay of the meanes how to make our travailes more profitable* (1606).

PAYNE, ROBERT, *A Brife Description of Ireland: Made in this yeere. 1589* (1590), ed. Aquilla Smith (Dublin: Irish Archaeological Society, 1841).

PECKHAM, GEORGE, 'A true report of the late discoveries, and possessions taken in the right of the Crowne of England of the Newfound Lands, By that valiant and worthy Gentleman, Sir Humphrey

Gilbert Knight', in Richard Hakluyt, *The Principal Navigations, Voyages, Traffiques & Discoveries of the English Nation* (1600), 12 vols. (Glasgow: MacLehose, 1903), viii. 89–131.

PERCY, GEORGE, ' "A Trew Relacyon": Virginia from 1609 to 1612', *Tyler's Magazine*, 3 (1922), 259–82.

PETTIE, GEORGE, *The Pettie Palace of Pettie his Pleasure* (1576?).

PLUTARCH, *Life of Julius Caesar* in *Shakespeare's Plutarch*, ed. T. J. B. Spencer (Harmondsworth: Penguin, 1964), 21–101.

PONET, JOHN, *A Shorte Treatise of Politicke Power* (1556).

PURCHAS, SAMUEL, *Hakluytus Posthumus or Purchas His Pilgrimes*, 20 vols. (1625) (Glasgow: MacLehose, 1905).

QUINN, DAVID BEERS, ed., *The Roanoke Voyages, 1584–1590: Documents to Illustrate the English voyages to North America under the Patent Granted to Walter Raleigh in 1584*, 2 vols. (London: Hakluyt Society, 1955).

RALEIGH, SIR WALTER, *The discoverie of the large, rich, and beautifull Empire of Guiana* (1596) in Richard Hakluyt, *The Principal Navigations, Voyages, Traffiques & Discoveries of the English Nation* (1600), 12 vols. (Glasgow: MacLehose, 1903), vii. 338–431.

RICH, BARNABY, *His Farewell to his Militarie Profession* (1581).

SARIS, JOHN, *The Voyage of Captain John Saris to Japan, 1613*, ed. Sir Ernest M. Satow (London: Hakluyt Society, 1900).

—— 'The eighth Voyage set forth by the East-Indian Societie ... under the command of Captain John Saris', in Samuel Purchas, *Hakluytus Posthumus or Purchas His Pilgrimes*, 20 vols. (1625) (Glasgow: MacLehose, 1905), iii. 355–519.

SHAKESPEARE, WILLIAM, *King Henry VI, Part Two* (c.1591), ed. A. S. Cairncross (London: Methuen, 1957).

—— *The Comedy of Errors* (c.1593), ed. R. A. Foakes (London: Methuen, 1962).

—— *King Richard III* (c.1594), ed. Anthony Hammond (London: Methuen, 1981).

—— *King Richard II* (c.1595), ed. Peter Ure (London: Methuen, 1956).

—— *King Henry IV, Part One* (c.1597), ed. A. R. Humphries (London: Methuen, 1960).

—— *The Merry Wives of Windsor* (c.1597), ed. H. J. Oliver (London: Methuen, 1971).

—— *King Henry V* (1598–9), ed. John H. Walter (London: Methuen, 1954).

—— *Henry V*, ed. Gary Taylor (Oxford: Oxford University Press, 1982).

—— *As You Like It* (*c*.1599), ed. Agnes Latham (London: Methuen, 1975).

—— *Julius Caesar* (1599), ed. T. S. Dorsch (London: Methuen, 1955).

—— *Othello* (1603–4), ed. M. R. Ridley (London: Methuen, 1958).

—— *Othello*, ed. Norman Sanders (Cambridge: Cambridge University Press, 1984).

—— *King Lear* (*c*.1605), ed. Kenneth Muir (London: Methuen, 1972).

—— *Macbeth* (*c*.1605–6), ed. Kenneth Muir (London: Methuen, 1951).

—— *Coriolanus* (1607–9), ed. R. B. Parker (Oxford: Oxford University Press, 1994).

—— *Cymbeline, King of Britain* (*c*.1610), ed. J. M. Nosworthy (London: Methuen, 1955).

—— *The Tempest* (1611), ed. Frank Kermode (London: Methuen, 1964, rpt. of 1950).

—— *The Tempest*, ed. Stephen Orgel (Oxford: Oxford University Press, 1987).

—— *Henry VIII* (1612–13), ed. R. A. Foakes (London: Methuen, 1957).

SIDNEY, SIR PHILIP, *An Apology for Poetry*, ed. Geoffrey Shepherd (Manchester: Manchester University Press, 1973, rpt. of 1965).

SMITH, SIR THOMAS, *De Republica Anglorum: A Discourse on the Commonweal of England* (1583), ed. L. Alston (Shannon: Irish University Press, 1972, rpt. of 1906).

SPENSER, EDMUND, *The Faerie Queene*, ed. A. C. Hamilton (London: Longman, 1977).

—— *A View of the Present State of Ireland*, ed. W. L. Renwick (Oxford: Clarendon Press, 1970).

—— *The Mutabilitie Cantos*, ed. Sheldon P. Zitner (London: Nelson, 1968).

—— and GABRIEL HARVEY, *Three Proper, and wittie, familiar Letters* (1580), in *The Poetical Works of Edmund Spenser*, ed. J. C. Smith and E. de Selincourt (London: Oxford University Press, 1912), 609–32.

STARKEY, THOMAS, *A Dialogue between Pole and Lupset*, ed. T. F. Mayer (London: Royal Historical Society, 1989).

—— *A Dialogue between Pole and Lupset*, ed. Katherine Burton (London: Routledge, 1948).

STRACHEY, WILLIAM, *The Historie of Travell into Virginia Britania* (1612), ed. Louis B. Wright and Virginia Freund (London: Hakluyt Society, 1953).

STUBBS, JOHN, *John Stubbs's Gaping Gulf with Letters and Other*

Relevant Documents, ed. Lloyd E. Berry (Charlottesville, Va.: The University of Virginia Press, 1968).

THOMAS, WILLIAM, *Historie of Italie* (1549).

—— *The History of Italy*, ed. George B. Parks (Ithaca, NY: Cornell University Press, 1963), introduction.

—— *Principal Rules of Italian Grammar with Dictionarie for the better understanding of Boccace, Petrarcha, and Dante* (1550).

WARNER, WILLIAM, *Syrinx, or a sevenfold history* (1584, 1597), ed. Wallace A. Bacon (Evanston, Ill.: Northwestern University Press, 1950).

SECONDARY SOURCES

ADAMS, J. Q., 'The Massacre at Paris Leaf', *The Library*, 4th series, 14 (1934), 447–69.

ALBANESE, DENISE, 'Making it New: Humanism, Colonialism, and the Gendered Body in Early Modern Culture', in Valerie Traub, M. Lindsay Kaplan and Dympna Callaghan (eds.), *Feminist Readings of Early Modern Culture* (Cambridge: Cambridge University Press, 1996), 16–43.

ANDERSON, BENEDICT, *Imagined Communities: Reflections on the Origins and Spread of Nationalism* (London: Verso, 1983).

—— 'Exodus', *CI* 20 (1993–4), 314–27.

ANDREWS, K. R., *Elizabethan Privateering during the Spanish War, 1585–1603* (Cambridge: Cambridge University Press, 1964).

—— *Trade, Plunder and Settlement: Maritime Enterprise and the Genesis of the British Empire, 1480–1630* (Cambridge: Cambridge University Press, 1984).

—— N. P. CANNY and P. E. H. HAIR (eds.), *The Westward Enterprise: English Activities in Ireland, the Atlantic and America, 1480–1650* (Liverpool: Liverpool University Press, 1978).

ANGLO, SYDNEY, 'A Machiavellian Solution to the Irish problem: Richard Beacon's *Solon His Follie* (1594)', in Edward Chaney and Peter Mack (eds.), *England and the Continental Renaissance: Essays in Honour of J. B. Trapp* (Woodbridge: Boydell and Brewer, 1990), 153–64.

AXTELL, JAMES, *After Columbus: Essays in the Ethnohistory of Colonial North America* (New York: Oxford University Press, 1988).

AXTON, MARIE, *The Queen's Two Bodies: Drama and the Elizabethan Succession* (London: Royal Historical Society, 1977).

BAKER, DAVID J., ' "Wildehirrissheman": Colonialist Representation in Shakespeare's *Henry V*', *ELR* 22 (1992), 37–61.

BAKER-SMITH, DOMINIC, *More's 'Utopia'* (London: Unwin, 1991).

BALDWIN, T. W., *Shakespeare's Small Latin and Lesse Greek* (Urbana, Ill.: University of Illinois Press, 1944).

BARBOUR, REID, *Deciphering Elizabethan Fiction* (Newark: University of Delaware Press, 1993).

BARISH, JONAS A., 'The Prose Style of John Lyly', *ELH* 23 (1956), 14–35.

BARKER, FRANCIS and PETER HULME, 'Nymphs and Reapers Heavily Vanish: The Discursive Con-Texts of *The Tempest*', in John Drakakis (ed.), *Alternative Shakespeares* (London: Methuen, 1985), 191–205.

BATE, JONATHAN, *Shakespeare and Ovid* (Oxford: Clarendon Press, 1993).

—— 'Caliban and Ariel Write Back', *Sh. Sur.* 48 (1995), 155–62.

—— 'The Elizabethans in Italy', in Jean-Pierre Maquerlot and Michèle Willems (eds.), *Travel and Drama in Shakespeare's Time* (Cambridge: Cambridge University Press, 1996), 55–74.

BATES, CATHERINE, *The Rhetoric of Courtship in Elizabethan Language and Literature* (Cambridge: Cambridge University Press, 1992).

BEIER, A. L., *Masterless Men: The Vagrancy Problem in Tudor England* (London: Methuen, 1985).

BELLAMY, JOHN, *The Tudor Law of Treason: An Introduction* (London: Routledge, 1979).

BELSEY, CATHERINE, *The Subject of Tragedy: Identity and Difference in Renaissance Drama* (London: Methuen, 1985).

BENNET, JOSEPHINE WATERS, *The Evolution of* The Faerie Queene (Chicago: University of Chicago Press, 1942).

—— 'Britain among the Fortunate Isles', *SP* 53 (1956), 114–40.

BERRY, PHILIPPA, *Of Chastity and Power: Elizabethan Literature and the Unmarried Queen* (London: Routledge, 1989).

BEVINGTON, DAVID, *From 'Mankind' to Marlowe* (Cambridge, Mass.: Harvard University Press, 1962).

BHABHA, HOMI K., *The Location of Culture* (London: Routledge, 1994).

BLACK, JAMES, 'The Latter End of Prospero's Commonwealth', *Sh. Sur.* 43 (1990), 29–41.

BOKLUND, GUNNAR, *The Duchess of Malfi: Sources, Themes, Characters* (Cambridge, Mass.: Harvard University Press, 1962).

BONHEIM, HERBERT, 'Robert Greene's *Gwydonius. The Carde of Fancie*', *Anglia*, 96 (1978), 45–64.

BORN, L. K., 'The Perfect Prince: A Study in Thirteenth and Fourteenth-Century Ideals', *Speculum*, 3 (1928), 470–504.

BOUWSMA, WILLIAM J., *Venice and the Defence of Republican Liberty: Renaissance Values in the Age of the Counter-Reformation* (Berkeley and Los Angeles: California University Press, 1968).

BRADSHAW, BRENDAN, 'Sword, Word and Strategy in the Reformation in Ireland', *HJ* 21 (1978), 492–7.

—— ANDREW HADFIELD and WILLY MALEY (eds.), *Representing Ireland: Literature and the Origins of Conflict, 1534–1660* (Cambridge: Cambridge University Press, 1993).

—— and PETER ROBERTS (eds.), *British Consciousness and Identity* (Cambridge: Cambridge University Press, 1998).

BRADY, CIARAN, 'Court, Castle and Country: The Framework of Government in Tudor Ireland', in Ciaran Brady and Raymond Gillespie (eds.), *Natives and Newcomers: The Making of Irish Colonial Society, 1534–1641* (Dublin: Irish Academic Press, 1986), 22–49.

BREIGHT, CURTIS, ' "Treason doth never prosper": *The Tempest* and the Discourse of Treason', *Sh. Q.* 41 (1990), 1–28.

—— *Surveillance, Militarism and Drama in the Elizabethan Era* (Basingstoke: Macmillan, 1996).

BRENNAN, MICHAEL G., *Literary Patronage in the Renaissance: The Pembroke Family* (London: Routledge, 1988).

—— 'The Texts of Peter Martyr's *De orbe novo decades* (1504–1628): A Response to Andrew Hadfield', *Connotations* 6, (1996/7), 227–45.

BRIGGS, JULIA, 'Marlowe's *Massacre at Paris*: A Reconsideration', *RES*, n.s., 34 (1983), 257–78.

BROWN, PAUL, ' "This thing of darkness I acknowledge mine": *The Tempest* and the Discourse of Colonialism', in Jonathan Dollimore and Alan Sinfield (eds.), *Political Shakespeares: New Essays in Cultural Materialism* (Manchester: Manchester University Press, 1985), 48–71.

BUCHER, BERNADETTE, *Icon and Conquest: A Structural Analysis of the Illustrations of the New Found Land of Virginia*, trans. Basia Miller Gulati (Chicago: Chicago University Press, 1981).

BURNETT, MARK THORNTON, *Masters and Servants in English Renaissance Drama and Culture: Authority and Obedience* (Basingstoke: Macmillan, 1997).

—— '*Edward II* and Elizabethan Politics', in Paul Whitfield White (ed.), *Marlowe, History, Sexuality: New Essays on Christopher Marlowe* (New York: AMS Press, 1998, forthcoming), 114–30.

BURROW, COLIN, *Epic Romance: Homer to Milton* (Oxford: Clarendon Press, 1993).

BUSHNELL, REBECCA W., *A Culture of Teaching: Early Modern Humanism in Theory and Practice* (Ithaca, NY: Cornell University Press, 1996).

CAIN, T .H., *Praise in* The Faerie Queene (Nebraska: University of Nebraska Press, 1978).

CALDER, ANGUS, *Revolutionary Empire: The Rise of the English-Speaking Empires from the Fifteenth Century to the 1780s* (London: Collins, 1968).

CAMPBELL, LILY B., 'The Suppressed Edition of *A Mirror for Magistrates*', *Huntington Library Bulletin*, 6 (1934), 1–16.

—— *Shakespeare's Histories: Mirrors of Elizabethan Policy* (San Marino: Huntington Library, 1947).

CANNY, NICHOLAS P., 'The Ideology of English Colonisation: From Ireland to America', *WMQ* 30 (1973), 575–98.

CARLSON, DAVID R., *English Humanist Books: Writers and Patrons, Manuscripts and Print, 1475–1525* (Toronto: University of Toronto Press, 1995).

CARTELLI, THOMAS, 'Prospero in Africa: *The Tempest* as Colonialist Text and Pretext', in Jean E. Howard and Marion O'Connor (eds.), *Shakespeare Reproduced: The Text in History and Ideology* (London: Routledge, 1987), 99–115.

CHADWICK, OWEN, *The Reformation* (Harmondsworth: Penguin, 1985, rpt. of 1964).

CHALKER, JOHN, *The English Georgic: A Study in the Development of a Form* (London: Routledge, 1969).

CHAMBERS, R. W., *Thomas More* (London: Cape, 1935).

CHATERJEE, PARTHA, *The Nation and its Fragments: Colonial and Postcolonial Histories* (Princeton: Princeton University Press, 1993).

CLARE, JANET, *'Art made tongue-tied by authority': Elizabethan and Jacobean Dramatic Censorship* (Manchester: Manchester University Press, 1990).

CLEGG, CYNDIA SUSAN, *Press Censorship in Elizabethan England* (Cambridge: Cambridge University Press, 1997).

COHEN, WALTER, *Drama of a Nation: Public Theater in Renaissance England and Spain* (Ithaca, NY: Cornell University Press, 1985).

COLIE, ROSALIE L., *The Resources of Kind: Genre-Theory in the Renaissance*, ed. Barbara K. Lewalski (Berkeley: University of California Press, 1973).

COLLINSON, PATRICK, *The Elizabethan Puritan Movement* (Oxford: Clarendon Press, 1967).

—— 'A Comment: Concerning the Name "Puritan" ', *JEH* 31 (1980), 483–8.

CRAIG, HARDIN, JR., 'The Geneva Bible as a Political Document', PHR 7 (1938), 40–9.

CRESSY, DAVID, Birth, Marriage and Death: Ritual, Religion, and the Life-Cycle in Tudor and Stuart England (Oxford: Oxford University Press, 1997).

DAVIES, C. S. L., Peace, Print and Protestantism, 1450–1558 (St Albans: Paladin, 1977).

DAVIES, R. TREVOR, The Golden Century of Spain, 1501–1621 (London: Macmillan, 1967, rpt. of 1937).

DAVIS, J. C., Utopia and the Ideal Society: A Study of English Utopian Writing (Cambridge: Cambridge University Press, 1981).

DAVIS, RICHARD BEALE, George Sandys, Poet Adventurer: A Study in Anglo-American Culture in the Seventeenth Century (London: Bodley Head, 1955).

DAVIS, WALTER R., 'Masking in Arden: The Histrionics of Lodge's Rosalynde', SEL 5 (1965), 151–63.

—— Idea and Act in Elizabethan Fiction (Princeton: Princeton University Press, 1969).

DEANE, SEAMUS (ed.), The Field Day Anthology of Irish Writing, 3 vols. (Derry: Field Day Publications, 1991).

DEBUS, ALLEN G., Man and Nature in the Renaissance (Cambridge: Cambridge University Press, 1978).

DENT, ROBERT W., 'Greene's Gwydonius: A Study in Elizabethan Plagiarism', HLQ 24 (1960–1), 151–62.

DICKENS, A. G., 'Wilfrid Holme of Huntington: Yorkshire's First Protestant Poet', Yorkshire Archaeological Journal, 39 (1956–8), 119–35.

—— 'The Elizabethans and Saint Bartholomew', in Alfred Soman (ed.), The Massacre of Saint Bartholomew: Reappraisals and Documents (The Hague: Martinus Nijhoff, 1974), 52–70.

—— The English Reformation (Glasgow: Collins, 1986, rpt. of 1964).

DOBIN, HOWARD, Merlin's Disciples: Prophecy, Poetry, and Power in Renaissance England (Stanford: Stanford University Press, 1990).

DODDS, R. and M. H., The Pilgrimage of Grace, 1536–7, and the Exeter Conspiracy, 1538, 2 vols. (Cambridge: Cambridge University Press, 1915).

DOLLIMORE, JONATHAN, 'Introduction: Shakespeare, Cultural Materialism and the New Historicism', in Jonathan Dollimore and Alan Sinfield (eds.), Political Shakespeares: New Essays in Cultural Materialism (Manchester: Manchester University Press, 1985), 2–17.

—— Radical Tragedy: Religion, Ideology and Power in the Drama of Shakespeare and his Contemporaries (Hemel Hempstead: Harvester, 2nd ed., 1989).

—— and ALAN SINFIELD, 'History and Ideology: The Instance of *Henry V*', in John Drakakis (ed.), *Alternative Shakespeares* (London: Methuen, 1985), 206–27.

DOODY, MARGARET, *The True Story of the Novel* (New Brunswick, NJ: Rutgers University Press, 1996).

DORAN, SUSAN, *Monarchy and Matriarchy: The Courtships of Elizabeth I* (London: Routledge, 1996).

DUNCAN-JONES, KATHERINE, *Sir Philip Sidney: Courtier Poet* (New Haven: Yale University Press, 1991).

DUTTON, RICHARD, *Mastering the Revels: The Regulation and Censorship of English Renaissance Drama* (Basingstoke: Macmillan, 1991).

EDWARDS, PHILIP, *Threshold of a Nation: A Study in English and Irish Drama* (Cambridge: Cambridge University Press, 1979).

—— 'Edward Hayes explains away Sir Humphrey Gilbert', *RS* 6 (1992), 270–86.

EISENSTEIN, ELIZABETH L., *The Printing Press as an Agent of Change* (Cambridge: Cambridge University Press, 1979).

ELLIOTT, J. H., *Europe Divided, 1559–1598* (London: Collins, 1968).

—— *The Old World and the New, 1492–1650* (Cambridge: Cambridge University Press, 1970).

—— 'Renaissance Europe and America: A Blunted Impact?', in Fredi Chiapelli (ed.), *First Images of America: The Impact of the New World on the Old*, 2 vols. (Berkeley: University of California Press, 1976), 11–23.

—— 'The Spanish Conquest and Settlement of America', in Leslie Bethell (ed.), *The Cambridge History of Latin America* (Cambridge: Cambridge University Press, 1984), i. 149–206.

ELLIS, STEPHEN G., *Tudor Ireland: Crown, Community and the Conflict of Cultures, 1470–1603* (Harlow: Longman, 1985).

ELTON, GEOFFREY, *England under the Tudors* (London: Methuen, 1965, rpt. of 1955).

—— *Reform and Reformation: England, 1509–1558* (London: Arnold, 1977).

ENGLAND, SYLVIA LENNIE, *The Massacre of Saint Bartholomew* (London: John Long, 1938).

ERSKINE-HILL, HOWARD, *Poetry and the Realm of Politics: Shakespeare to Dryden* (Oxford: Clarendon Press, 1996).

FALLS, CYRIL, *Elizabeth's Irish Wars* (London: Methuen, 1950).

FEASEY, IRIS EVELINE, 'The Licensing of the *Mirror for Magistrates*', *The Library*, 4th series, 3 (1923), 177–93.

FIEDLER, LESLIE A., *The Stranger in Shakespeare* (London: Granada, 1974).

FINKELPEARL, PHILIP J., 'John Fletcher as Spenserian Playwright: *The Faithful Shepherdess* and *The Island Princess*', *SEL* 27 (1987), 285–302.

—— *Court and Country Politics in the Plays of Beaumont and Fletcher* (Princeton: Princeton University Press, 1990).

FINLEY, M. I., 'Colonies—An Attempt at a Typology', *TRHS*, 5th series, 26 (1976), 167–88.

FIRTH, KATHERINE, *The Apocalyptic Tradition in Reformation Britain, 1530–1645* (Oxford: Oxford University Press, 1979).

FLETCHER, ANTHONY, *Tudor Rebellions* (Harlow: Longman, 1968).

FOUCAULT, MICHEL, 'What is an Author?', in *The Foucault Reader*, ed. Paul Rabinow (Harmondsworth: Penguin, 1984), 101–20.

FOX, ALASTAIR, *Thomas More: History and Providence* (Oxford: Basil Blackwell, 1982).

FRANKLIN, JULIAN H., *Jean Bodin and the Rise of Absolutist Theory* (Cambridge: Cambridge University Press, 1973).

FRASER, RUSSELL, *The War Against Poetry* (Princeton: Princeton University Press, 1970).

FUCHS, BARBARA, 'Conquering Islands: Contextualizing *The Tempest*', *Sh. Q.* 48 (1997), 45–62.

FULLER, MARY C., *Voyages in Print: English Travel to America, 1576–1624* (Cambridge: Cambridge University Press, 1995).

GEERTZ, CLIFFORD, 'Thick Description: Toward an Interpretative Theory of Culture', in *The Interpretation of Cultures: Selected Essays* (New York: Basic Books, 1973), 3–30.

GIBBONS, BRIAN, 'The Wrong End of the Telescope', in Jean-Pierre Maquerlot and Michèle Willems (eds.), *Travel and Drama in Shakespeare's Time* (Cambridge: Cambridge University Press, 1996), 141–59.

GILBERT, FELIX, *Machiavelli and Guicciardini: Politics and History in Sixteenth-Century Florence* (Princeton: Princeton University Press, 1965).

—— 'The Venetian Constitution in Florentine Political Thought', in Nicolai Rubenstein (ed.), *Florentine Studies: Politics and Society in Renaissance Florence* (London: Faber, 1968), 463–500.

GILLIES, JOHN, *Shakespeare and the Geography of Difference* (Cambridge: Cambridge University Press, 1994).

GLENN, JOHN RONALD, 'The Martyrdom of Peter Ramus in Marlowe's *The Massacre at Paris*', *PLL* 9 (1973), 365–79.

GORDON, WALTER M., *Humanist Play and Belief: The Seriocomic Art of Desiderius Erasmus* (Toronto: Toronto University Press, 1990).

GOSLING, WILLIAM GILBERT, *The Life of Sir Humphrey Gilbert, England's First Empire Builder* (London: Constable, 1911).

GOTTFRIED, RUDOLF B., 'Geoffrey Fenton's *Historie of Guicciardini*' (Indiana University Publications; Humanities Series 3, 1940).

GRADY, HUGH, *Shakespeare's Universal Wolf: Studies in Early Modern Reification* (Oxford: Clarendon Press, 1996).

GRANT, EDWARD, *Planets, Stars, and Orbs: The Medieval Cosmos, 1200–1687* (Cambridge: Cambridge University Press, 1994).

GRANZOTTO, GIANNI, *Christopher Columbus: The Dream and the Obsession, A Biography*, trans. Stephen Sartarelli (London: Collins, 1988, rpt. of 1986).

GREENBLATT, STEPHEN J., 'Learning to Curse: Aspects of Linguistic Colonialism in the Sixteenth Century', in Fredi Chiapelli (ed.), *First Images of America: The Impact of the New World on the Old*, 2 vols. (Berkeley: University of California Press, 1976), ii. 561–80.

—— *Renaissance Self-Fashioning: From More to Shakespeare* (Chicago: Chicago University Press, 1980).

—— 'Invisible Bullets', in *Shakespearian Negotiations: The Circulation of Social Energy in Renaissance England* (Oxford: Clarendon Press, 1988), 21–65.

—— *Marvelous Possessions: The Wonder of the New World* (Oxford: Clarendon Press, 1991).

GOLDBERG, JONATHAN, *James I and the Politics of Literature: Jonson, Shakespeare, Donne and their Contemporaries* (Baltimore: Johns Hopkins University Press, 1983).

GRESHAM, STEPHEN, 'William Baldwin: Literary Voice of the Reign of Edward VI', *HLQ* 44 (1980–1), 101–16.

GUY, JOHN, *Tudor England* (Oxford: Oxford University Press, 1988).

—— (ed.), *The Reign of Elizabeth I: Court and Culture in the Last Decade* (Cambridge: Cambridge University Press, 1995).

GWYN, DAVID, 'Richard Eden: Cosmographer and Alchemist', *Sixteenth-Century Journal*, 15 (1984), 13–34.

HABER, JUDITH, *Pastoral and the Poetics of Self-Contradiction: Theocritus to Marvell* (Cambridge: Cambridge University Press, 1995).

HACKETT, HELEN, *Virgin Mother, Maiden Queen: Elizabeth I and the Cult of the Virgin Mary* (Basingstoke: Macmillan, 1995).

—— 'Courtly Writing by Women', in Helen Wilcox (ed.), *Women and Literature in Britain, 1500–1700* (Cambridge: Cambridge University Press, 1996), 169–89.

HADFIELD, ANDREW, 'Writing the New World; More "Invisible Bullets" ', *L. & H.*, 2nd series, 2/2 (Autumn 1991), 3–19.

—— 'Translating the Reformation: John Bale's Irish *Vocacyon*', in Brendan Bradshaw, Andrew Hadfield and Willy Maley (eds.), *Representing Ireland: Literature and the Origins of Conflict,*

1534–1660 (Cambridge: Cambridge University Press, 1993), 43–59.

HADFIELD, ANDREW, 'Briton and Scythian: Tudor Representations of Irish Origins', *IHS* 112 (Nov. 1993), 390–408.

—— *Literature, Politics and National Identity: Reformation to Renaissance* (Cambridge: Cambridge University Press, 1994).

—— 'The Naked and the Dead: Elizabethan Perceptions of Ireland', in Jean-Pierre Maquerlot and Michèle Willems (eds.), *Travel and Drama in Shakespeare's Time* (Cambridge: Cambridge University Press, 1996), 32–54.

—— 'Was Spenser's *A View of the Present State of Ireland* Censored? A Review of the Evidence', *N. & Q.*, n.s. 41 (1994), 459–63.

—— 'Peter Martyr, Richard Eden and the New World: Reading, Experience and Translation', *Connotations*, 5 (1995/6), 1–22.

—— 'Shakespeare, John Derricke and Ireland: *The Comedy of Errors*, III. ii. lines 105–6', *N. & Q.* 44 (1997), 53–4.

—— 'Richard Eden and Peter Martyr: Author's Response', *Connotations*, 6 (1996/7), 227–45.

—— *Spenser's Irish Experience: Wilde Fruit and Salvage Soyl* (Oxford: Clarendon Press, 1997).

—— 'An Allusion to Spenser's Writings: Matthew Lownes and Ralph Byrchensa's *A discourse occasioned on the late defeat given to the Arch-rebels, Tyrone and Odonnell (1602)*', *N. & Q.*, n.s. 44 (1997), 478–80.

—— 'Utopian/Dystopian Fiction', in Paul E. Schellinger (ed.), *Encyclopedia of the Novel* (Chicago: Fitzroy Dearborn, 1998).

—— 'Crossing the Borders: Ireland and the Irish between England and America', in Paul A. S. Harvey (ed.), *Rethinking Cultural Encounter: The Diversity of English Experience, 1550–1700* (Amherst, Mass.: University of Massachusets Press, 1999, forthcoming).

HAIGH, CHRISTOPHER, *Elizabeth I* (Harlow: Longman, 1988).

HALE, D. G., *The Body Politic: A Political Metaphor in Renaissance English Literature* (The Hague: Mouton, 1971).

HAMILTON, A. C. (ed.), *The Spenser Encyclopedia* (London and Toronto: Routledge/Toronto University Press, 1990).

HAMILTON, DONNA B., *Virgil and* The Tempest: *The Politics of Imitation* (Columbus: Ohio State University Press, 1990).

HAMLIN, WILLIAM, 'On Reading Early Accounts of the New World', *Connotations*, 6 (1996/7), 46–50.

HANSEN, MELANIE, 'The Word and the Throne: John Knox's *The First Blast of the Trumpet against the Monstrous Regiment of Women*', in Kate Chedgzoy, Melanie Hansen and Suzanne Trill (eds.),

Voicing Women: Gender and Sexuality in Early Modern Writing (Keele: Keele University Press, 1996), 11–24.

HAUGAARD, W. P., *Elizabeth and the English Reformation* (Cambridge: Cambridge University Press, 1968).

HAYES-MCCOY, G. A., 'The Royal Supremacy and Ecclesiastical Revolution, 1534–47', in T. W. Moody, F. X. Martin and F. J. Byrne (eds.), *A New History of Ireland, iii. Early Modern Ireland, 1534–1691* (Oxford: Clarendon Press, 1976), 39–68.

HEALY, THOMAS, *Christopher Marlowe* (London: Northcote House, 1994).

HECHTER, MICHAEL, *Internal Colonialism: The Celtic Fringe in British National Development, 1536–1966* (Berkeley: University of California, 1975).

HELGERSON, RICHARD, *The Elizabethan Prodigals* (Berkeley: University of California Press, 1976).

—— *Forms of Nationhood: The Elizabethan Writing of England* (Chicago: University of Chicago Press, 1992).

HENDRICKS, MARGO and PATRICIA PARKER (eds.), *Women, 'Race', and Writing in the Early Modern Period* (London: Routledge, 1994).

HEXTER, J. H., *More's Utopia: The Biography of an Idea* (New Haven: Yale University Press, 1952).

HIBBERT, CHRISTOPHER, *The Grand Tour* (London: Weidenfeld and Nicolson, 1969).

HIGHLEY, CHRISTOPHER, 'Wales, Ireland and *I Henry IV*', RD 21 (1990), 91–114.

HOGDEN, MARGARET T., 'Montaigne and Shakespeare Again', *HLQ* 16 (1952–3), 23–42.

—— *Early Anthropology in the Sixteenth and Seventeenth Centuries* (Philadelphia: Philadelphia University Press, 1964).

HÖLTGEN, KARL JOSEPH, 'Sir Robert Dallington (1561–1637): Author, Traveller, and Pioneer of Taste', *HLQ* 47 (1984), 147–77.

HOPE, JONATHAN, *The Authorship of Shakespeare's Plays* (Cambridge: Cambridge University Press, 1994).

HOWARD, CLARE, *English Travellers of the Renaissance* (London: John Lane, 1914).

HULME, PETER, ' "Huricanes in the Caribbes": The Constitution of the Discourse of English Colonialism', in Francis Barker *et al.* (eds.), *1642: Literature and Power in the Seventeenth Century* (Colchester: University of Essex, 1981), 55–83.

—— *Colonial Encounters: Europe and the Native Caribbean, 1492–1797* (London: Methuen, 1986).

—— 'Making No Bones: A Response to Myra Jehlen', *CI* 20 (1993–4), 179–86.

HULTON, PAUL, 'Jacques Le Moyne De Morgues: A Biographical Sketch', in Paul Hulton (ed.), *The Works of Jacques Le Moyne De Morgues: A Huguenot Artist in France, Florida and England*, 2 vols. (London: British Museum, 1977), i. 3–12.

—— (ed.), *The Works of Jacques Le Moyne De Morgues: A Huguenot Artist in France, Florida and England*, 2 vols. (London: British Museum, 1977).

—— 'Images of the New World: Jacques Le Moyne de Morgues and John White', in K. R. Andrews, N. P. Canny and P. E. H. Hair (eds.), *The Westward Enterprise: English Activities in Ireland, the Atlantic and America, 1480–1650* (Liverpool: Liverpool University Press, 1978), 195–214.

—— (ed.), *America 1585: The Complete Drawings of John White* (London: British Museum, 1984).

—— and DAVID BEERS QUINN (eds.), *The American Drawings of John White, 1577–1590*, 2 vols. (London: British Museum, 1964).

HUNTER, G. K., *John Lyly: The Humanist as Courtier* (London: Routledge, 1962).

—— *Dramatic Identities and Cultural Tradition* (Liverpool: Liverpool University Press, 1978).

HUTSON, LORNA, *Thomas Nashe in Context* (Oxford: Clarendon Press, 1989).

—— 'Fortunate Travellers: Reading for the Plot in Sixteenth-Century England', *Representations*, 41 (1993), 83–103.

—— *The Usurer's Daughter: Male Friendship and Fictions of Women in Sixteenth-Century England* (London: Routledge, 1994).

ISLAM, SYED MANZURUL, *The Ethics of Travel: From Marco Polo to Kafka* (Manchester: Manchester University Press, 1996).

JANMOHAMED, ABDUL R., 'The Economy of Manichean Allegory: The Function of Racial Difference in Colonialist Literature', in Henry Louis Gates, Jr. (ed.), *'Race', Writing, and Difference* (Chicago: Chicago University Press, 1986), 78–106.

JAMES, MERVYN E., *English Politics and the Concept of Honour, 1485–1642, P. & P.*, supplement, 3 (1978).

JARDINE, LISA, 'Encountering Ireland: Gabriel Harvey, Edmund Spenser, and English Colonial Ventures', in Brendan Bradshaw, Andrew Hadfield, and Willy Maley (eds.), *Representing Ireland: Literature and the Origins of Conflict, 1534–1660* (Cambridge: Cambridge University Press, 1993), 60–75.

—— *Reading Shakespeare Historically* (London: Routledge, 1996).

—— *Worldly Goods* (London: Macmillan, 1996).

JEHLEN, MYRA, 'History Before the Fact: Or, Captain John Smith's Unfinished Symphony', *CI* 19 (1992–3), 677–86.

—— 'Response to Peter Hulme', *CI* 20 (1993–4), 187–91.

JOHNSON, R. S., *More's Utopia: Ideal and Illusion* (New Haven: Yale University Press, 1969).

JONES, ELDRED, *Othello's Countrymen: The African in English Renaissance Drama* (London: Oxford University Press, 1965).

JORDAN, CONSTANCE, 'Womens' Rule in Sixteenth-Century British Political Thought', *RQ* 40 (1987), 421–51.

JORDAN, JOHN CLARK, *Robert Greene* (New York: Columbia University Press, 1915).

JORDAN, W. K., *Edward VI: The Young King* (Cambridge, Mass.: Harvard University Press, 1971).

JOWITT, CLAIRE, ' "Monsters and Straunge Births": The Politics of Richard Eden. A Response to Andrew Hadfield', *Connotations*, 6 (1996/7), 51–65.

KAMPS, IVO, *Historiography and Ideology in Stuart Drama* (Cambridge: Cambridge University Press, 1996).

KANTOROWICZ, ERNST H., *The King's Two Bodies: A Study in Medieval Political Theology* (London: Royal Historical Society, 1977).

KAULA, DAVID, 'The Low Style in Nashe's *The Unfortunate Traveller*', *SEL* 6 (1966), 43–57.

KEARNEY, HUGH, 'The Making of an English Empire', in Hugh Kearney (ed.), *The British Isles: a History of Four Nations* (Cambridge: Cambridge University Press, 1989), ch. 7.

KING, JOHN N., *English Reformation Literature: The Tudor Origins of the Protestant Tradition* (Princeton: Princeton University Press, 1982).

—— *Tudor Royal Iconography: Literature and Art in an Age of Religion* (Princeton: Princeton University Press, 1989).

—— *Spenser's Poetry and the Reformation Tradition* (Princeton: Princeton University Press, 1990).

KING, WALTER N., 'John Lyly and Elizabethan Rhetoric', *SP* 52 (1955), 149–61.

KINGDON, ROBERT M., *Myths about the St. Bartholomew's Day Massacres, 1572–1576* (Cambridge, Mass.: Harvard University Press, 1988).

KINGHORN, A. M., *The Chorus of History: Literary-Historical Relations in Renaissance Britain, 1485–1558* (London: Blandford, 1971).

KINNEY, ARTHUR F., *Humanist Poetics: Thought, Rhetoric, and Fiction in Sixteenth-Century England* (Amherst, Mass.: Massachusets University Press, 1986).

KIPLING, GORDON, *The Triumph of Honour: Burgundian Origins of the Elizabethan Renaissance* (Leiden: Sir Thomas Browne Institute, 1977).

KIPLING, GORDON, 'Henry VII and the Origins of Tudor Patronage', in Guy Fitch Lytle and Stephen Orgel (eds.), *Patronage in the English Renaissance* (Princeton: Princeton University Press, 1981), 117–64.

KIRKPATRICK, ROBIN, *English and Italian Literature from Dante to Shakespeare: A Study of Sources, Analogy, and Divergence* (Harlow: Longman, 1995).

KNAPP, GEOFFREY, *An Empire Nowhere: England, America, and Literature from* Utopia *to* The Tempest (Berkeley: University of California Press, 1992).

KOCHER, PAUL H., 'François Hotman and Marlowe's *The Massacre at Paris*', *PMLA* 56 (1941), 349–68.

—— 'Contemporary Pamphlet Backgrounds for Marlowe's *The Massacre at Paris*', *MLQ* 8 (1947), 151–73, 309–18.

KUPPERMAN, KAREN ORDHAL, *Settling with the Indians: The Meeting of English and Indian Cultures in America, 1580–1640* (Totowa, NJ: Rowman and Allanheld, 1980).

—— *Roanoke: The Abandoned Colony* (Totowa, New Jersey: Rowman and Allanheld, 1984).

KURIYAMA, CONSTANCE BROWN, 'Marlowe's Nemesis: The Identity of Richard Baines', in Kenneth Friedenreich, Roma Gill, and Constance B. Kuriyama (eds.), *'A Poet and a filthy Play-maker': New Essays on Christopher Marlowe* (New York: AMS Press, 1988), 343–60.

LACEY, ROBERT, *Robert, Earl of Essex: An Elizabethan Icarus* (London: Weidenfeld and Nicolson, 1971).

LASLETT, PETER, *The World we have Lost* (London: Methuen, 2nd ed., 1971).

LEERSSEN, JOESEPH TH., *Mere Irish and Fíor-Ghael: Studies in the Idea of Irish Nationality, its Development and Literary Expression Prior to the Nineteenth Century* (Amsterdam: Benjamins, 1986).

LEGGATT, ALEXANDER, *English Drama: Shakespeare to the Restoration, 1590–1660* (Harlow: Longman, 1988).

LENNON, COLM, 'The Counter-Reformation in Ireland, 1542–1641', in Ciaran Brady and Raymond Gillespie, (eds.), *Natives and Newcomers: Essays on the Making of Irish Colonial Society, 1534–1641* (Dublin: Irish Academic Press, 1986), 75–92.

—— *Sixteenth-Century Ireland: The Incomplete Conquest* (Dublin: Gill and Macmillan, 1995).

LEVER, J. W., *The Tragedy of State* (London: Methuen, 1971).

LEVITAS, RUTH, *The Concept of Utopia* (Hemel Hempstead: Philip Allan, 1990).

LEVY, F. J., 'Hayward, Daniel, and the Beginnings of Politic History in England', *HLQ* 50 (1987), 1–34.

LINDLEY, DAVID, 'Embarrassing Ben: The Masques for Frances Howard', in Arthur F. Kinney and Dan S. Collins (eds.), *Renaissance Historicism: Selections from 'English Literary Renaissance'* (Amherst: University of Massachusets Press, 1987), 248–64.

LINTOTT, ANDREW, 'The Crisis of the Republic: Sources and Source-Problems', in J. A. Crook, Andrew Lintott, and Elizabeth Rawson (eds.), *The Cambridge Ancient History*, 12 vols., *The Last Age of the Roman Republic, 146–43 BC* (Cambridge: Cambridge University Press, 2nd edition, 1994), ix. 1–15.

LIVESAY, J. L., *Stefano Guazzo and the English Renaissance, 1575–1675* (Chapel Hill, NC: University of North Carolina Press, 1961).

—— *The Elizabethan Image of Italy* (Ithaca, NY: Cornell University Press, 1964).

LOACH, JENNIFER, *Parliament Under the Tudors* (Oxford: Clarendon Press, 1991).

LOADES, DAVID, *Two Tudor Conspiracies* (Cambridge: Cambridge University Press, 1965).

—— 'The Theory and Practice of Censorship in Sixteenth-Century England', *TRHS*, 5th series, 24 (1974), 141–57.

—— *Mary Tudor: A Life* (Oxford: Basil Blackwell, 1989).

LOOMBA, ANIA, *Gender, Race, Renaissance Drama* (Manchester: Manchester University Press, 1989).

LOVE, HAROLD, 'Scribal Publication in Seventeenth-Century England', *TCBS* 9 (1987), 130–54.

LUCAS, CAROLINE, *Writing for Women: The Example of the Woman Reader in Elizabethan Romance* (Milton Keynes: Open University Press, 1989).

MCCABE, RICHARD A., 'Elizabethan Satire and the Bishops' Ban of 1599', *YES* 11 (1981), 188–93.

—— *Incest, Drama and Nature's Law, 1550–1700* (Cambridge: Cambridge University Press, 1993).

MCCARTHY-MORROGH, MICHAEL, *The Munster Plantation: English Migration to Southern Ireland, 1583–1641* (Oxford: Clarendon Press, 1986).

MCCOY, RICHARD C., *The Rites of Knighthood: The Literature and Politics of Elizabethan Chivalry* (Berkeley: University of California Press, 1989).

MCLANE, PAUL E., *Spenser's* Shepheardes Calender*: A Study in Elizabethan Allegory* (Notre Dame, Ind.: Notre Dame University Press, 1961).

MCMULLAN, GORDON, *The Politics of Unease in the Plays of John*

Fletcher (Amherst: The University of Massachusetts Press, 1994).
—— and JONATHAN HOPE (eds.), *The Politics of Tragicomedy: Shakespeare and After* (London: Routledge, 1992).
MCPHERSON, DAVID, 'Lewkenor's Venice and its Sources', *RQ* 41 (1988), 459–66.
—— *Shakespeare, Jonson, and the Myth of Venice* (Newark, Del.: University of Delaware Press, 1990).
MALEY, WILLY, *A Spenser Chronology* (Basingstoke: Macmillan, 1994).
MALTBY, WILLIAM S., *The Black Legend in England: The Development of Anti-Spanish Sentiment, 1558–1660* (Durham, NC: Duke University Press, 1971).
MAQUERLOT, JEAN-PIERRE and MICHÈLE WILLEMS (eds.), *Travel and Drama in Shakespeare's Time* (Cambridge: Cambridge University Press, 1996).
MARCU, E. D., *Sixteenth-Century Nationalism* (New York: Abaris, 1976).
MARX, KARL, *Economic and Philosophical Manuscripts* in *Early Writings*, trans. Rodney Livingstone and Gregor Benton (Harmondsworth: Penguin, 1975), 279–400.
MASLEN, ROBERT, *Elizabethan Fictions: Espionage, Counter-Espionage and the Duplicity of Fiction in Early Elizabethan Prose Narratives* (Oxford: Clarendon Press, 1997).
MATHESON, MARK, 'Venetian Culture and the Politics of *Othello*', *Sh. Sur.* 48 (1995), 123–33.
MATHEW, DAVID, *James I* (London: Eyre & Spottiswoode, 1967).
MATTINGLY, GARRETT, *Renaissance Diplomacy* (Harmondsworth: Penguin, 1965, rpt. of 1955).
MAYER, THOMAS F., *Thomas Starkey and the Commonweal: Humanist Politics and Religion in the Reign of Henry VIII* (Cambridge: Cambridge University Press, 1989).
MEMMI, ALBERT, *The Colonizer and the Colonized*, trans. Howard Greenfield (New York: Orion, 1965).
MILLER, E. H., 'The Relationship of Robert Greene and Thomas Nashe (1588–92)', *PQ* 33 (1954), 353–67.
MILLS, SARAH, *Discourses of Difference: An Analysis of Women's Travel Writing and Colonialism* (London: Routledge, 1991).
MILTON, GILES, *The Riddle and the Knight: In Search of Sir John Mandeville* (Bridgend: Allison & Busby, 1996).
MONTROSE, LOUIS ADRIAN, 'Of Gentlemen and Shepherds: The Politics of Elizabethan Pastoral Form', *ELH* 50 (1983), 415–59.
MOODY, T. W., F. X. MARTIN and F. J. BYRNE (eds.), *A New History of Ireland, iii. Early Modern Ireland, 1534–1691* (Oxford: Clarendon Press, 1976).

MORGAN, HIRAM, *Tyrone's Rebellion: The Outbreak of the Nine Years War in Tudor Ireland* (Woodbridge: Boydell and Brewer/Royal Historical Society, 1993).

MORISON, SAMUEL ELIOT, *The European Discovery of America: The Northern Voyages, AD 500–1600* (New York: Oxford University Press, 1971).

—— *The European Discovery of America: The Southern Voyages, AD 1492–1616* (New York: Oxford University Press, 1974).

MORRILL, JOHN, *The Nature of the English Revolution* (Harlow: Longman, 1993).

MORTON, A. L., *The English Utopia* (London: Lawrence and Wishart, 1952).

MULRYNE, J. R., 'Nationality and Language in Thomas Kyd's *The Spanish Tragedy*', in Jean-Pierre Maquerlot and Michèle Willems (eds.), *Travel and Drama in Shakespeare's Time* (Cambridge: Cambridge University Press, 1996), 87–105.

—— and MARGARET SHEWRING (eds.), *Theatre and Government under the Early Stuarts* (Cambridge: Cambridge University Press, 1993).

MURPHY, ANDREW, 'Shakespeare's Irish History', *L. & H.* 3rd series 5.i (Spring 1996), 38–59.

NEALE, J. E., *Queen Elizabeth* (London: Cape, 1934).

NEWMAN, KAREN, ' "And wash the Ethiop white": Femininity and the Monstrous in *Othello*', in Jean E. Howard and Marion O'Connor (eds.), *Shakespeare Reproduced: The Text in History and Ideology* (London: Routledge, 1987), 143–62.

NICHOLL, CHARLES, *The Reckoning* (London: Picador, 1993, rpt. of 1992).

NIXON, ROB, 'Caribbean and African Appropriations of *The Tempest*', *CI* 13 (1986–7), 557–78.

NORBROOK, DAVID, ' "What care these roarers for the name of king?": Language and Utopia in *The Tempest*', in Gordon McMullan and Jonathan Hope (eds.), *The Politics of Tragicomedy: Shakespeare and After* (London: Routledge, 1992), 21–54.

NOSWORTHY, J. M., 'The Marlowe Manuscript', *The Library*, 4th series, 26 (1946), 158–71.

NUTTALL, A. D., 'Two Unassimilable Men', in Malcolm Bradbury and David Palmer (eds.), *Shakespearian Comedy* (London: Arnold, 1972), 210–40.

O'DAY, ROSEMARY, *The Longman Companion to the Tudor Age* (Harlow: Longman, 1995).

ONG, WALTER J., *Ramus, Method and the Decay of Dialogue: From the Art of Discourse to the Art of Reason* (Cambridge, Mass.: Harvard University Press, 1958).

ORGEL, STEPHEN, *The Illusion of Power: Political Theater in the English Renaissance* (Berkeley: University of California Press, 1975).

PAGDEN, ANTHONY, *The Fall of Natural Man: The American Indian and the Origins of Comparative Ethnology* (Cambridge: Cambridge University Press, 1982).

—— 'The Savage Critic: Some European Images of the Primitive', *YES* 13 (1983), 32–45.

—— *European Encounters with the New World* (New Haven: Yale University Press, 1993).

PARADISE, N. BURTON, *Thomas Lodge: The History of an Elizabethan* (New Haven: Yale University Press, 1931).

PARKER, ANDREW, MARY RUSSO, DORIS SOMMER and PATRICIA YAEGER (eds.), *Nationalisms and Sexualities* (London: Routledge, 1992).

PARKER, GEOFFREY, 'The Emergence of Modern Finance in Europe, 1500–1730', in Carlo M. Cipolla (ed.), *The Fontana Economic History of Europe: The Sixteenth and Seventeenth Centuries* (Glasgow: Collins, 1974), 527–89.

PARKER, JOHN, *Books to Build an Empire: A Bibliography of English Overseas Interests to 1630* (Amsterdam: New Israel, 1965).

—— 'Religion and the Virginia Colony', in K. R. Andrews, N. P. Canny, and P. E. H. Hair (eds.), *The Westward Enterprise: English Activities in Ireland, the Atlantic and America, 1480–1650* (Liverpool: Liverpool University Press, 1978), 245–70.

PARKER, PATRICIA, 'Fantasies of "Race" and "Gender": Africa, *Othello*, and bringing to light', in Margo Hendricks and Patricia Parker (eds.), *Women, 'Race', and Writing in the Early Modern Period* (London: Routledge, 1994), 84–100.

PASK, KEVIN, *The Emergence of the English Author* (Cambridge: Cambridge University Press, 1996).

PATTERSON, ANNABEL, *Censorship and Interpretation: The Conditions of Writing in Early Modern England* (Madison, Wis.: University of Wisconsin Press, 1984).

—— *Shakespeare and the Popular Voice* (Oxford: Basil Blackwell, 1989).

—— *Reading Holinshed's Chronicles* (Chicago: University of Chicago Press, 1994).

PELTONEN, MARKKU, *Classical Humanism and Republicanism in English Political Thought, 1570–1640* (Cambridge: Cambridge University Press, 1995).

PEPPER, JON V., 'Harriot's Earlier Work on Mathematical Navigation:

Theory and Practice', in John Shirley (ed.), *Thomas Harriot: Renaissance Scientist* (Oxford: Clarendon Press, 1974), 54–90.

PHILLIPS, JAMES E., 'George Buchanan and the Sidney Circle', *HLQ* 12 (1948–9), 23–55.

POCOCK, J. G. A., *The Machiavellian Moment: Florentine Political Thought and the Atlantic Tradition* (Princeton: Princeton University Press, 1975).

—— *The Ancient Constitution and the Feudal Law: A Study of English Historical Thought in the Seventeenth Century* (Cambridge: Cambridge University Press, rev. ed., 1987).

POTTER, DAVID, 'Marlowe's *Massacre at Paris* and the Reputation of Henri III of France', in Daryll Grantley and Peter Roberts (eds.), *Christopher Marlowe and English Renaissance Culture* (Aldershot: Scolar Press, 1996), 70–95.

POUND, JOHN, *Poverty and Vagrancy in Tudor England* (Harlow: Longman, 1971).

PRATT, MARY LOUISE, *Imperial Eyes: Travel Writing and Transculturation* (London: Routledge, 1992).

PRAZ, MARIO, *The Flaming Heart* (Gloucester, Mass.: Peter Smith, 1966, rpt. of 1958).

PRESCOTT, ANNE LAKE, 'Burbon', in *The Spenser Encyclopedia*, ed. A. C. Hamilton (London and Toronto: Routledge/Toronto University Press, 1990).

PRUVOST, RENÉ, *Robert Greene et ses Romans (1558–1592): Contribution a l'Histoire de la Renaissance en Angleterre* (Paris: Faculté des Lettres d'Algier, 1938).

PURDIE, SUSAN, *Comedy: The Mastery of Discourse* (London: Harvester, 1993).

QUINN, D. B., *Raleigh and the British Empire* (London: Hodder and Stoughton, 1947).

—— *The Elizabethans and the Irish* (Ithaca, NY: Cornell University Press, 1966).

—— 'Thomas Harriot and the New World', in John Shirley (ed.), *Thomas Harriot: Renaissance Scientist* (Oxford: Clarendon Press, 1974), 36–53.

—— (ed.), *The Hakluyt Handbook*, 2 vols. (London: Hakluyt Society, 1974).

—— and JOHN SHIRLEY, 'A Contemporary List of Hariot References', *RQ* 22 (1969), 9–26.

RAAB, FELIX, *The English Face of Machiavelli: A Changing Interpretation, 1500–1700* (London: Routledge, 1977).

RAMBUSS, RICHARD, *Spenser's Secret Career* (Cambridge: Cambridge University Press, 1993).

RAMBUSS, RICHARD, 'Spenser's Lives, Spenser's Careers', in Judith H. Anderson, Donald Cheney, and David A. Richardson (eds.), *Spenser's Life and the Subject of Biography* (Amherst, Mass.: University of Massachusetts Press, 1996), 1–17.

RAMSEY, LEE C., *Chivalric Romances: Popular Literature in Medieval England* (Bloomington, Ind.: Indiana University Press, 1983).

READ, DAVID, 'Colonialism and Coherence: The Case of Captain John Smith's *Generall Historie of Virginia*', *MP* 91 (1994), 428–48.

RELIHAN, CONSTANCE C., *Fashioning Authority: The Development of Elizabethan Novelistic Discourse* (Kent, Oh.: Ohio State University Press, 1994).

RENNIE, NEIL, *Far-Fetched Facts: The Literature of Travel and the Idea of the South Seas* (Oxford: Clarendon Press, 1995).

RIGGS, DAVID, *Ben Jonson: A Life* (Cambridge, Mass.: Harvard University Press, 1989).

RINGLER, WILLIAM A., JR., 'The Immediate Source of Euphuism', *PMLA* 53 (1938), 678–86.

—— 'Beware the Cat and the Beginnings of English Fiction', *Novel*, 12 (1979), 113–26.

ROBERTS, JOSEPHINE, 'An Unpublished Literary Quarrel Concerning the Suppression of Mary Wroth's *Urania*', *N. & Q.*, n.s. 24 (1977), 532–5.

—— 'Mary Wroth', in M. Thomas Hester (ed.), *Seventeenth-Century British Nondramatic Poets* (Detroit and London: Gale Research, 1992), 296–309.

ROBERTSON, GEORGE *et al.* (eds.), *Travellers' Tales: Narratives of Home and Displacement* (London: Routledge, 1994).

ROSEN, EDWARD, 'Harriot's Science, The Intellectual Background', in John Shirley (ed.), *Thomas Harriot: Renaissance Scientist* (Oxford: Clarendon Press, 1974), 1–15.

ROWSE, A. L., *Sir Richard Grenville of the Revenge* (London: Cape, 1937).

RUSSELL, CONRAD, *The Crisis of Parliaments: English History, 1509–1660* (Oxford: Oxford University Press, 1971).

—— 'The British Problem and the English Civil War', *History*, 73 (1988), 395–415.

SALMON, J. H. M., 'Stoicism and Roman Empire: Seneca and Tacitus in Jacobean England', *JHI* 50 (1989), 199–225.

SALZMAN, PAUL, 'Contemporary References in Mary Wroth's *Urania*', *RES* 24 (1978), 178–81.

—— *English Prose Fiction, 1558–1700: A Critical History* (Oxford: Clarendon Press, 1985).

SANDERS, WILBUR, *The Dramatist and the Received Idea* (Cambridge: Cambridge University Press, 1968).

SANDLER, FLORENCE, 'The Faerie Queene: An Elizabethan Apocalypse', in C. A. Patrides and Joseph Wittreich (eds.), *The Apocalypse in English Renaissance Thought and Literature: Patterns, Antecedents and Repercussions* (Manchester: Manchester University Press, 1984), 148–74.

SCHOENBAUM, SAMUEL, *Shakespeare's Lives* (Oxford: Clarendon Press, 1970).

SELLS, A. LYTTON, *The Paradise of Travellers: The Italian Influence on Englishmen in the Seventeenth Century* (London: George Allen and Unwin, 1964).

SHAMMAS, CAROL, 'English Commercial Development and American Colonization', in K. R. Andrews, N. P. Canny, and P. E. H. Hair (eds.), *The Westward Enterprise: English Activities in Ireland, the Atlantic and America, 1480–1650* (Liverpool: Liverpool University Press, 1978), 151–74.

SHARPE, JIM, 'Social Strain and Social Dislocation, 1585–1603', in John Guy (ed.), *The Reign of Elizabeth I: Court and Culture in the Last Decade* (Cambridge: Cambridge University Press, 1995), 192–211.

SHEEHAN, A. J., 'The Overthrow of the Plantation of Munster in October 1598', *The Irish Sword*, 15 (1982–3), 11–22.

SHEEHAN, BERNARD W., *Savagism and Civility: Indians and Englishmen in Colonial Virginia* (Cambridge: Cambridge University Press, 1980).

SHIRLEY, JOHN (ed.), *Thomas Harriot: Renaissance Scientist* (Oxford: Clarendon Press, 1974).

—— 'Sir Walter Raleigh and Thomas Harriot', in John Shirley (ed.), *Thomas Harriot: Renaissance Scientist* (Oxford: Clarendon Press, 1974), 16–35.

SILKE, J. J., *Ireland and Europe, 1559–1607* (Dundalk: Dundalgan, 1966).

SINFIELD, ALAN, *Faultlines: Cultural Materialism and the Politics of Dissident Reading* (Oxford: Clarendon Press, 1992).

SINGH, JYOTSNA, 'Othello's Identity, Postcolonial Theory, and Contemporary African Rewritings of *Othello*', in Margo Hendricks and Patricia Parker (eds.), *Women, 'Race', and Writing in the Early Modern Period* (London: Routledge, 1994), 287–99.

SKINNER, QUENTIN, *The Foundations of Modern Political Thought*, 2 vols. (Cambridge: Cambridge University Press, 1978).

SMITH, ALAN G. R., 'Constitutional Ideas and Developments in

England, 1603–1625', in Alan G. R. Smith (ed.), *The Reign of James VI and I* (London: Macmillan, 1973), pp. 160–76.

SOKOL, B. J., 'The Problem of Assessing Thomas Harriot's *A briefe and true report* of his Discoveries in North America', *Annals of Science*, 51 (1994), 1–16.

SOKOLOVA, BOIKA, *Shakespeare's Romances as Interrogative Texts: Their Alienation Strategies and Ideology* (Lewiston/Queenston/Lampeter: Edwin Mellen Press, 1992).

STEINBERG, THEODORE L., 'The Anatomy of *Euphues*', *SEL* 17 (1977), 27–38.

STERN, VIRGINIA F., *Gabriel Harvey: His Life, Marginalia and Library* (Oxford: Clarendon Press, 1979).

STONE, LAWRENCE, *The Causes of the English Revolution, 1529–1642* (London: Routledge, 1972).

STOYE, JOHN W., *English Travellers Abroad, 1604–1667* (New Haven: Yale University Press, rev. ed., 1989).

STRACHAN, MICHAEL, *The Life and Adventures of Thomas Coryate* (London: Oxford University Press, 1962).

STRONG, ROY, *Henry, Prince of Wales and England's Lost Renaissance* (London: Thames and Hudson, 1986).

SWART, J., 'Lyly and Pettie', *ES* 23 (1941), 9–18.

TENNENHOUSE, LEONARD, *Power on Display: The Politics of Shakespeare's Genres* (London: Methuen, 1986).

THOMAS, VIVIEN and WILLIAM TYDEMAN (eds.), *Christopher Marlowe: The Plays and Their Sources* (London: Routledge, 1994).

TILTON, ROBERT S., *Pocahontas: The Evolution of an American Narrative* (Cambridge: Cambridge University Press, 1994).

TODOROV, TZVETAN, *The Conquest of America: The Question of the Other*, trans. Richard Howard (New York: Harper/Collins, 1984).

—— *Genres in Discourse*, trans. Catherine Porter (Cambridge: Cambridge University Press, 1990).

TUCK, RICHARD, *Philosophy and Government, 1572–1651* (Cambridge: Cambridge University Press, 1993).

VAUGHAN, VIRGINIA MASON, *Othello: A Contextual History* (Cambridge: Cambridge University Press, 1994).

—— and ALDEN T. VAUGHAN, *Shakespeare's Caliban: A Cultural History* (Cambridge: Cambridge University Press, 1991).

VEESER, H. ARAM (ed.), *The New Historicism* (London: Routledge, 1989).

WALKER, GREG, *Plays of Persuasion: Drama and Politics at the Court of Henry VIII* (Cambridge: Cambridge University Press, 1991).

—— *Persuasive Fictions: Faction, Faith and Political Culture in the Reign of Henry VIII* (Aldershot: Scolar Press, 1996).

WALZER, MICHAEL, *The Revolution of the Saints: A Study in the Origins of Radical Politics* (Cambridge, Mass.: Harvard University Press, 1965).

WEIL, JUDITH, 'Mirrors for Foolish Princes', in *Christopher Marlowe: Merlin's Prophet* (Cambridge: Cambridge University Press, 1977).

WEIMANN, ROBERT, *Authority and Representation in Early Modern Discourse* (Baltimore: Johns Hopkins University Press, 1996).

WEINER, CAROL Z., 'The Beleaguered Isle: A Study of Elizabethan and Early Jacobean anti-Catholicism', *P. & P.* 51 (1971), 27–62.

WERNHMAN, R. B., *After the Armada: Elizabethan England and the Struggle for Western Europe, 1588–1595* (Oxford: Clarendon Press, 1984).

WHIGHAM, FRANK, *Seizures of the Will in Early Modern English Drama* (Cambridge: Cambridge University Press, 1995).

WHITE, HAYDEN, 'The Noble Savage: Theme as Fetish', in Fredi Chiapelli (ed.), *First Images of America: The Impact of the New World on the Old*, 2 vols. (Berkeley: University of California Press, 1976), i. 121–35.

WHITWORTH, CHARLES, '*Rosalynde*: *As You Like It* and as Lodge Wrote It', *ES* 58 (1977), 114–17.

WILDERS, JOHN, *The Lost Garden: A View of Shakespeare's English and Roman History Plays* (Basingstoke: Macmillan, 1978).

WILLIAMS, NEVILLE, *Henry VIII and his Court* (London: Cardinal, 1973).

—— *The Life and Times of Elizabeth I* (London: Weidenfeld and Nicolson, 1972).

WILLIAMS, PENRY, *The Tudor Regime* (Oxford: Clarendon Press, 1979).

WILLIS, DEBORAH, 'Shakespeare's *The Tempest* and the Discourse of Colonialism', *SEL* 29 (1989), 277–89.

WILSON, CHARLES, *Queen Elizabeth and the Revolt of the Netherlands* (London: Macmillan, 1970).

WILSON, EDWARD M., 'Did Fletcher Read Spanish?', *PQ* 27 (1948), 187–90.

WILSON, JOHN DOVER, 'Euphues and the Prodigal Son', *The Library*, n.s., 10 (1909), 337–61.

WILSON, RICHARD, 'Voyage to Tunis: New History and the Old World of *The Tempest*', *ELH* 64 (1997), 333–57.

WOLFF, SAMUEL LEE, 'A Source of *Euphues: The Anatomy of Wit*', *MP* 7 (1910), 577–85.

WOODS, FRANCES, *Did Marco Polo go to China?* (London: Secker and Warburg, 1995).

WORMALD, JENNY, 'Ecclesiastical Vitriol: The Kirk, the Puritans and the Future King of England', in John Guy, *The Reign of Elizabeth I: Court and Culture in the Last Decade* (Cambridge: Cambridge University Press, 1995), 171–91.

WOUDHUYSEN, H. R., 'Letters, Spenser's and Harvey's', in A. C. Hamilton (ed.), *The Spenser Encyclopedia* (London and Toronto: Routledge/Toronto University Press, 1990), 434–5.

—— *Sir Philip Sidney and the Circulation of Manuscripts, 1558–1640* (Oxford: Clarendon Press, 1996).

WRIGHT, ANTHONY, 'Republican Tradition and the Maintenance of "National" Religious Traditions in Venice', *RS* 10 (1996), 405–16.

WRIGHT, LOUIS B., *Middle-Class Culture in Elizabethan England* (Chapel Hill, NC: University of North Carolina Press, 1935).

YOUNG, ROBERT, *Colonial Desire: Hybridity in Theory, Culture and Race* (London: Routledge, 1995).

ZEEVELD, W. GORDON, *Foundations of Tudor Polity* (Cambridge, Mass.: Harvard University Press, 1981).

Index